An Introduction to the *Zhou yi* (Book of Changes)

Written in Chinese by Liu Dajun
Translated into English by Zhang Wenzhi

CHIRON PUBLICATIONS • ASHEVILLE, NORTH CAROLINA

© 2019 by Chiron Publications. All rights reserved. No part of this publication may be reproduced, stored in a retrieval system, or transmitted, in any form by any means, electronic, mechanical, photocopying, recording, or otherwise, without the prior written permission of the publisher, Chiron Publications, P.O. Box 19690, Asheville, N.C. 28815-1690.

www.ChironPublications.com

Interior and cover design by Danijela Mijailovic
Printed primarily in the United States of America.

ISBN 978-1-63051-687-1 paperback
ISBN 978-1-63051-688-8 hardcover
ISBN 978-1-63051-689-5 electronic
ISBN 978-1-63051-690-1 limited edition paperback

Library of Congress Cataloging-in-Publication Data Pending

The program of translation of the book is sponsored
by the Chinese Fund for the Humanities and Social Sciences
An achievement of the Center for Zhouyi & Ancient Chinese Philosophy
of Shandong University—one of the key research institutes of
humanities & social science in China.
The translation of the book was primarily proof-checked
by Lawrence Scott Davis

Contents

Part I

The Original Contents of the *Zhou yi gailun* 周易概论 (Introduction to the *Book of Changes*) — 7

Preface — 9

1. Extensive Explanations of the *Zhou yi* 周易 — 11
2. The "Great Commentaries on the *Zhou yi*" — 23
3. Imagery of the *Changes* — 57
4. Hexagram Changes — 83
5. Divination by Milfoil Stalks — 107
6. Divinatory Cases in the *Zuo zhuan* 左传 and the *Guo yu* 国语 — 121
7. Are the Prognostications Determined Only by the Changing Line(s)? — 147
8. A Brief Introduction to the Studies of the *Changes* in the Past Dynasties (I) — 157
9. A Brief Introduction to the Studies of the *Changes* in the Past Dynasties (II) — 211

Part II

Some Prefaces and Speeches Related to the Scholarship on the *Changes* — 265

10. A Preface to the *Najia shifa* 纳甲筮法 (Three-Coin Method of Divination) — 267

11. A Postscript to the *Najia shifa* 纳甲筮法 (Three-Coin Method of Divination)	271
12. Opening Speech at the International Conference on Confucianism and *Changes* Studies	277
13. Preface to Mr. Liu Junzhu's *Yi jing and Contemporary Life* (《易经》与现代生活)	285
14. Characteristics of the *Yi* Studies in the 20th Century: A Preface to the *Collected Quintessential Articles of the Yi Studies of the Past Century and Decade* (1900-2009)	291
Endnotes	319
List of Proper Nouns	349
Glossary	365

PART I

The Original Contents of the *Zhou yi gailun* 周易概论 (Introduction to the *Book of Changes*)

Preface

The *Zhou yi* 周易, usually rendered as the *Book of Changes*, the *Classic of Changes*, or the *Zhou Changes*, and so on, is a cryptic, archaic book. Several hundred types of exegetical books about it have been written from the Han dynasty (206 B.C.E.-220 C.E.) through contemporary times, and yet the *Zhou yi* still presents many enigmas. Liu Dajun 刘大钧 has been studying the *Zhou yi* for many years and completed this *Zhou yi gai lun* 周易概论 (An Introduction to the Book of Changes) based upon his comprehensive insights, setting forth his unique perspectives on many puzzles related to the *Zhou yi*. Liu Dajun avers that, in studying the *Zhou yi*, we should not only highlight the verbal exegesis but also take image-numerology[1] into account: "Today our interpretations of the text come mainly from verbal exegesis, but at the same time, we should also give consideration to the imagery which can still be seen from the basic text." Based on concrete evidence, he asserts: "The authors of the *Zhou yi* certainly had used the inverted images in the imagery of the *Changes*." These views are really incisive. The book also examines many divinatory stories and points out that "The fortune or misfortune of the hexagram or line statements in question is not of great significance to the

---

[1] Translator's note: Image-numerology is a terminology in the hermeneutics of the *Yi jing*, which insists that each word of the hexagram and line statements in the *Yi jing* is derived from some image and/or number of a trigram, hexagram, or line. It had given rise to a hermeneutic school of the *Yi jing*; and the other school in contrast to it is the school of meanings-and-principles, which contends that the hexagram and line statements of the *Yi jing* aim to reveal philosophical connotations free from images and numbers.

consultant, since the interpreters of the hexagrams can always find their own reasons," which is particularly on the mark in demonstrating the superstitious quality of divination. So far as the origin of the *Yi zhuan* 易传 ("Commentaries on the *Changes*," or the "Ten Wings") is concerned, Liu agrees by and large with my conclusions in "On the Dating and Philosophical Ideas of the *Yi zhuan*" (*Lun Yidazhuan de zhuzuo niandai yu zhexue sixiang* 论易大传的著作年代与哲学思想) and adds important supplements, proving with sufficient evidence that the *Wenyan* 文言 ("Commentary on Words of the Text") came into being earlier than the *Xici* 系辞 ("Commentary on the Appended Phrases"), the *Tuan* 彖 ("Commentary on the Judgments") appeared earlier than the *Wenyan*, and the *Da xiang* 大象 ("Commentary on the Great Images") was completed earlier than the *Tuan*. This part of his argument is indeed tenable. It is only his conclusion that the *Shuogua* 说卦 ("Explaining the Trigrams") came into being earlier than the *Xici* that apparently needs further discussion, given that the composite terms like *daode* 道德 (literally, way and virtue) and *xingming* 性命 (literally, nature and fate) in the *Shuogua* are not available in *Mencius* 孟子 and *Zhuang zi neipian* 庄子内篇 ("Internal Chapters" of *Zhuang zi*), but frequently appear in *Zhuang zi waipian* 庄子外篇 ("External Chapters" of *Zhuang zi*) and *Xun zi* 荀子, and therefore ought to be the terms prevailing in the late Warring States period (475-221 B.C.E.). So, at least the first two paragraphs of the *Shuogua* ought to appear later than the "Internal Chapters" of *Zhuang zi* but are contemporary with its "External Chapters," which could not have existed earlier than most of the material of the *Xici*. These issues can be further investigated, but I am very pleased to see this new achievement in *Zhou yi* studies.

Zhang Dainian 张岱年 at Peking University
August 1983

1.
Extensive Explanations of the *Zhou yi* 周易

I

The term *Zhou yi* 周易 was recorded for the first time in the *Zuo zhuan* 左传 (Zuo's Commentary on the *Spring and Autumn Annals*). For example, the chapter of the "Twenty-second Year of Duke Zhuang" (672 B.C.E.) (*Zhuang gong ershier nian* 庄公二十二年) records: "Some official historian of the Zhou (1046-256 B.C.E.) paid a visit to Marquis Chen陈 with the *Zhou yi*."[i] Similarly, in the "Ninth Year of Duke Xiang" (567 B.C.E.) (*Xiang gong jiu nian* 襄公九年), "(Mu 穆) jiang 姜 said: 'No. As it says in the *Zhou yi*…'"[ii], and in the "Seventh Year of Duke Zhao" (535 B.C.E.) (*Zhao gong qi nian* 昭公七年), "Kong Chengzi 孔成子 [a minister of the State of Wei 卫] divined by milfoil stalks and the *Zhou yi*."[iii] All these records can be taken as evidence that, in the Spring and Autumn period (770-476 B.C.E.) or earlier, the book name of *Zhou yi* came into being.

Why was this book called *Zhou yi*? Ancient scholars had many discussions about it. As early as the Han (206 B.C.E.-220 C.E.) and Tang (618-907) dynasties, there were two interpretations of the term *Zhou* 周.

According to the "Grand Official Diviners" (*taibu* 太卜) chapter of the *Zhou li* 周礼 (Zhou Rituals), grand official diviners "master three systems of changes: The first one is called *Lianshan* 连山 (literally, Linked

Mountains), the second *Guicang* 归藏 (Return to the Hidden), and the third *Zhou yi*. Each of them includes eight cardinal trigrams and sixty-four hexagrams."[iv] As the Eastern Han (25-220) scholar Zheng Xuan 郑玄 (127-200) explained in his *Yi zan* 易赞 (Praising the *Changes*), "[The *Changes* of] the Xia 夏 (c. 2100-c. 1600 B.C.E.) is called the *Lianshan*, (that of) the Yin 殷 (c.1600-1046 B.C.E.) the *Guicang*, and (that of) the Zhou (1046-256 B.C.E.) the *Zhou yi*."[v] "[The image of the first hexagram in] *Lianshan* is like the constantly appearing clouds from the mountains; *Guicang* means that the myriad things will return to it; *Zhou yi* means the Dao (Way) of changes is circular, universal and all-inclusive."[vi]

Therefore, in Zheng Xuan's opinion, the character *Zhou* 周 connotes circularity, universality, and all-inclusiveness. This exegesis is consistent with the state that "change and action in the world never stand still but keep flowing all through the six positions"[vii] (*bian dong buju, zhouliu liuxu* 变动不居, 周流六虚) mentioned in the *Xici* 系辞 ("Commentary on the Appended Phrases," also rendered as the "Great Treatise"), and conforms to what the "Interpreting *Laozi*" (*Jielao* 解老) chapter of the *Hanfeizi* 韩非子 (Master Hanfei [c. 280-233 B.C.E.]) described: "The sages observe its [here referring to the Dao of Heaven] mystery and vacuity, and make use of its function of circular motions."[viii] Thus, this interpretation obtained further affirmation in the Tang (618-907) scholar Lu Deming's 陆德明 (c. 550-630) *Jingdian shiwen* 经典释文 (Exegetical Texts of the Classics): "*Zhou* 周 as the name of a dynasty also means coming from all around, universality and completeness. Now that it is named as the book, it takes meanings of circularity and all-inclusiveness."[ix]

Yet another famous Tang scholar, Kong Yingda 孔颖达 (574-648), objected to this exegesis in the preface to his *Zhou yi zhengyi* 周易正义 (Correct Meaning of the *Zhou Changes*): "In spite of this exegesis of his, Zheng Xuan did not cite any evidence. [...] According to *Shipu* 世谱 (Genealogy of Past Dynasties) and a good number of other books, Sheng Nong 神农 (c. late Neolithic Age, the inventor of Chinese agriculture, medicine, and pharmacy) is also called Lianshan shi 连山氏 (Lord Lianshan) and sometimes Lieshan shi 列山氏 (Lord Lieshan); Huangdi 黄帝 [the Yellow Emperor, a Neolithic figure viewed as an immortal] is also referred to as Guicang shi 归藏氏 [Lord Guicang]. Therefore, either Lianshan or Guicang refers to the name of a dynasty (or ruling period), and accordingly 'Zhou' in the *Zhou yi* derives from the place name of

Qiyang 岐阳 [present-day in a county of Shaanxi 陕西 Province], which was mentioned as the place of origin of the Zhou dynasty in the *Maoshi* 毛诗 (Mao edition of the *Classic of Poetry*)."ˣ

Thus, Kong Yingda interpreted the "Zhou" in the *Zhou yi* as the name of a dynasty, i.e., the Zhou dynasty (1046-256 B.C.E.). This viewpoint is very influential, and even today there are still some people who believe the *Zhou yi*, the *Classic of Changes*, was written in the Zhou dynasty. This is another possible interpretation.

Now, let's turn to the meanings of the *yi* 易 in the *Zhou yi* 周易.

According to the chapter of *Qian kun zaodu* 乾坤凿度 (Opening Up the Regularities of the [Hexagrams] Qian [☰] and Kun [☷]) of the *Yi wei* 易纬 (Apocrypha of the *Changes*), "The *yi* 易 contains four implications, (all of which are) based on the linking of *ri* 日 (sun) and *yue* 月 (moon)." According to Zheng Xuan's interpretation, "The *yi* 易 is (constructed by) the sun 日 and the moon 月."ˣⁱ As the *Shuowen jiezi* 说文解字 (Explanation of Simple and Composite Characters) notes, "It is said in some secret books that the sun 日 and the moon 月 constitute the *yi* 易 and symbolize *yin* 阴 and *yang* 阳."ˣⁱⁱ It also states in the chapter of *Qiankun shewei* 乾坤设位 (Establishment of the Positions with Qian [☰] and Kun [☷]) of the *Zhouyi cantongqi* 周易参同契 (Token for the Agreement of the Three According to the *Zhou Changes*): "The sun 日 and the moon 月 make up the *yi* 易, matching one another with their respective hardness and softness" (*riyue wei yi, gangrou xiangdang* 日月为易, 刚柔相当). *Jingdian shiwen* 经典释文 (Exegetical Texts of the Classics) asserts: "The *yi* 易 is the name of a Classic. According to Yu Fan's 虞翻 (164-233) annotations to the *Zhou yi cantongqi* 周易参同契 (Token for the Agreement of the Three According to the *Zhou Changes*), '(The *yi* 易 is graphically) constituted by the sun 日 in the upper and the moon 月 in the lower position.'"ˣⁱⁱⁱ

Is the Han (206 B.C.E.-220 C.E.) scholars' explanation that "the sun 日 and the moon 月 constitute the *yi* 易" correct or not? Let us look at how it is interpreted in the *Xici* 系辞 (Commentary on the Appended Phrases) written in the Warring States period (475-221 B.C.E.): "What the *yi* discourses about are images, and the term image means 'the making of semblances.'"ˣⁱᵛ "In Heaven this [process] creates images, and on Earth it creates physical forms."[xv] "Of images that are suspended above and emit brightness, none are greater than the sun and the moon."[xvi] "(He [Bao Xi 包牺, a.k.a. Fu Xi 伏羲, c. mid- or late Neolithic Age, the domesticator of animals and progenitor of Chinese civilization]) looked upward and observed the images in heaven...."[xvii] It is evident that the authors of the *Xici* contend that the *yi* 易 is derived from images, and the greatest images in the heavens are the sun and the moon. Therefore, the Han scholars' exegesis on the character *yi* 易 is tenable and can be accepted.

According to the Tang 唐 (618-907) scholar Jia Gongyan's 贾公彦 annotations to the "Grand Official Diviners" (*dabu* 大卜) chapter of the *Zhou li* 周礼 (Zhou Rituals), Gen [☷], in which the trigram Gen [☶] symbolizes a mountain, is put in the first place of the 64 hexagrams in the *Lianshan* 连山, hence its name of linked mountains[xviii] as in Zheng Xuan's exegesis mentioned above; Kun [☷], in which the trigram Kun [☷] symbolizes earth[xix], is put in the first place of the 64 hexagrams in the *Guicang* 归藏, hence its meaning that the myriad things are nourished by earth and at last return into earth, also as previously mentioned in Zheng Xuan's interpretations of it; Qian [☰], in which the trigram Qian [☰] symbolizes heaven, is the first hexagram in the *Zhou yi* 周易 in which the character *yi* 易 is constituted by *ri* 日 (the sun) and *yue* 月 (the moon), and signifies that the sun and the moon illuminate all things surrounding the round (or what is cyclic, circular, all-inclusive, the meaning of *zhou* 周) heaven, and hence the above-mentioned exegesis by Zheng Xuan of the name. Jia Gongyan 贾公彦 also points out that, because either the *Lianshan* or *Guicang* in the *Zhou li* 周礼 (Zhou Rituals) does not refer to the name of a place, the character Zhou 周 in the *Zhou yi* 周易 ought not to refer to the name of a place, either. Since, in the *Zhou yi*, hexagram Qian [☰] is put in the first place of the 64 hexagrams, what it stresses is heaven that gives rise to the cycle of the four seasons.[xx] In this way, Jia Gongyan 贾公彦 refuted Kong Yingda's 孔颖达 assertion that the *zhou* 周 in the *Zhou yi* 周易 refers to the place of origin of the Zhou dynasty. Therefore, according to these accounts, Lu Deming's interpretation in his *Jingdian shiwen* 经典释文 (Exegetical Texts of the Classics) that *zhou* 周 in the *Zhou yi* 周易 connotes circularity, universality, and all-inclusiveness is pertinent.

II

Zhuang zi's 庄子 (369-286 B.C.E.) remark that "the *yi* (Changes) is that which discourses upon *yin* 阴 and *yang* 阳" (*Yi yi dao yin yang* 易以道阴阳) hits the mark. Though there is not any word like *yin* 阴[xxi] or *yang* 阳 mentioned in the basic text of the *Zhou yi*, the *yin* [- -] and/or *yang* [—] lines in it constitute the eight trigrams of Qian 乾 [☰], Kan 坎 [☵], Gen 艮 [☶], Zhen 震 [☳], Xun 巽 [☴], Li 离 [☲], Kun 坤 [☷], and Dui 兑 [☱], the pairing of any two of which finally gives rise to the 64 hexagrams manifesting the changes of *yin* and *yang*. The basic text of the *Zhou yi* only comprises 64 judgments attached to the 64 hexagrams and 384 line statements to the 384 lines respectively—in addition to a statement attached to *yong jiu* 用九 [literally, "the Using of Nine"] in the hexagram Qian 乾 [☰, The Creative, the first hexagram in the received version of the *Zhou yi*, hereafter 1] and a statement attached to *yong liu* 用六 [literally, "the Using of Six"] in the hexagram Kun 坤 [☷, The Receptive, 2].

When did the doubling of the eight trigrams to the 64 hexagrams happen? Scholars of the past did not arrive at a unanimous viewpoint, as Wang Bi 王弼 (226-249) credited it to Fu Xi 伏羲 (c. mid- or late Neolithic Age, the domesticator of animals and progenitor of Chinese civilization), Zheng Xuan 郑玄 (127-200) identified Sheng Nong 神农 (c. late Neolithic Age, the inventor of Chinese agriculture, medicine, and pharmacy as the inventor, and some claim it was Da yu 大禹 (Yu the Great, a legendary sage ruler prior to the Xia 夏 [c. 2100-c. 1600 B.C.E.] dynasty), whereas Sima Qian 司马迁 (145-90 B.C.E.), Ban Gu 班固 (32-92), Yang Xiong 扬雄 (53 B.C.E.-18 C.E.), and Wang Chong 王充 (27-c.97) insisted that it was King Wen 文王 (1152-1056 B.C.E.) who invented the 64 hexagrams.

In my opinion, what is mentioned in the "Great Plan" (*Hongfan* 洪范) chapter of the *Shangshu* 尚书 (Classic of History)—"Then, they select and establish official tortoise-shell and milfoil-stalk diviners and order them to divine,"[xxii] which demonstrates that the trigrams had been doubled into the hexagrams in or before the Zhou dynasty—is credible. As is stated in the "Grand Official Diviners" (*dabu* 大卜) of the *Zhou li* 周

礼 (*Zhou Rituals*), "Each of the three systems of *Changes* consists of eight cardinal trigrams and sixty-four hexagrams."[xxiii] Though we are not sure whether the other two kinds of *Changes*, i.e., *Lianshan* 连山 and *Guicang* 归藏, are really divinatory books of the Xia 夏 (c. 2100-c. 1600 B.C.E.) and Shang 商 (c. 1600-1046 B.C.E.) dynasties respectively, the 64 hexagrams might have come into being a very long time before. Additionally, it is cited in the *Xici* 系辞 (Commentary on the Appended Phrases) that Fu Xi 伏羲 "tied cords together and made various kinds of snare nets for catching animals and fish. He probably got the idea for this practice from the Li,"[xxiv] where the "Li" 离 must refer to the hexagram Li ䷝ rather than the trigram Li ☲ in that the latter cannot remind us of the image of snare nets. Therefore, according to the *Xici*, the doubling of the trigrams to the 64 hexagrams had been accomplished in the times of Fu Xi [c. mid- or late Neolithic Age, the domesticator of animals and progenitor of Chinese civilization]. It also states in the "Summary" (*Yao lue* 要略) chapter of the *Huainanzi* 淮南子 [written by the intellectuals surrounding Liu An 刘安 (179-122 B.C.E.), then the king of the state of Huainan] that "Fu Xi 伏羲 made it the 64 changes,"[xxv] which means it was Fu Xi who doubled the eight trigrams to the 64 hexagrams. Fu Xi is a legendary figure, and, accordingly, the pairing of the trigrams by Fu Xi is also a legend. But by these accounts, we can see that the hexagrams ought to have been completed a very long time ago, at least before the Western Zhou dynasty (1046-771 B.C.E.).

  The course from the *yin* [- -] and *yang* [—] lines to the formation of the eight trigrams, to the 64 hexagrams, and finally to the composition of the whole book of the *Zhou yi*, might have lasted over a very long period; especially the judgments attached to the hexagrams and the line statements must have been collected, redacted, and supplemented by many people until the text finally took the form we can see today, around the turn of the Shang 商 (c. 1600-1046 B.C.E.) and Zhou 周 (1046-256 B.C.E.) dynasties. To put it another way, the whole book of the *Zhou yi* is most likely to have been composed by many predecessors in several generations rather than by one single person.

III

In the pre-Qin (before 221 B.C.E.) period, the *Zhou yi* was referred to as *er pian* 二篇 (literally, "two chapters"). For example, it says in the "Commentary on the Appended Phrases" (*Xici* 系辞) that "the stalks in the two chapters number 11,520."[xxvi] It also states in the "Biography of Shu Xi" (*Shu Xi zhuah* 束皙传) of the *Jin shu* 晋书 (History of the Jin Dynasty [265-420]) that the manuscript version of the *Changes* (excavated from the tomb of King Xiang of Wei [r. 381-296 B.C.E.]) possesses "two chapters of the *Yi jing* 易经 (Classic of Changes), which is commensurate with the 'upper and lower scriptures' (*shangxia jing* 上下经) of today's *Zhou yi*."[xxvii] Even until the Han dynasty (206 B.C.E.-220 C.E.), it was also referred to as "chapters"—as in the "Treatise on Art and Literature" (*Yiwen zhi* 艺文志) of the *Han shu* 汉书 (History of the Western Han Dynasty [206 B.C.E.-9 C.E.]), where it says that "King Wen juxtaposed the trigrams to make the hexagrams of the *Changes* and composed the upper and lower chapters,"[xxviii] and in "Opening Up the Regularities of the [Hexagram] Qian" (*Qian zao du* 乾凿度) chapter of the *Yi wei* 易纬 (Apocrypha of the *Changes*), which states: "Therefore there are thirty hexagrams in the upper chapter which symbolize *yang* [in regard to the odd number of three, ten times of which is equal to thirty], whereas the Dao (Way) of *yin* correspond to an even number and thus there are thirty-four hexagrams in the lower chapter which takes *yin* as its principle."[xxix]

Kong Yingda 孔颖达 (574-648) asserted in *Zhou yi zhengyi Juanshou* 周易正义卷首 (the "Prologue" to the *Correct Meaning of the Zhou yi*): "Zi Xia's 子夏 [one of Confucius's 72 sagacious disciples] Commentary, though it is divided into two chapters, does not use the word *jing* 经 (scripture)," "whereas in Meng Xi's 孟喜 (fl. c. 50 B.C.E.) version of the *Changes* of the Former Han (206 B.C.E.-9 C.E.) it was referred to as the upper and lower scriptures, attesting to the fact that before Meng Xi the word *jing* 经 (scripture) had been used as the title."[xxx] Additionally, it is stated in the "Biographies of Confucian Scholars" (*Ru lin zhuan* 儒林传) of the *Han shu* 汉书 (History of the Western Han Dynasty [206 B.C.E.-9 C.E.]) that "Fei Zhi 费直 interprets the upper and lower scriptures merely by the ten texts of Commentaries such as *Tuan* 彖 (Commentary on the

Judgments), *Xiang* 象 (Commentary on the Images), *Xici* 系辞 (Commentary on the Appended Phrases) and so on."[xxxi] According to the "Biography of Xun Shuang" (*Xun Shuang zhuan* 荀爽传) of the *Houhan shu* 后汉书 (History of the Eastern Han Dynasty [25-220]), "King Wen composed the *Changes*, of which the upper scripture begins with hexagrams Qian 乾 [☰, The Creative, 1] and Kun 坤 [☷, The Receptive, 2], while the lower starts from hexagrams Xian 咸 [☶, Influence, 31] and Heng 恒 [☳, Perseverance, 32]."[xxxii] In his annotations to the "Orderly Sequence of the Hexagrams" (*Xugua* 序卦), Hang Kangbo 韩康伯 asserted: "Former Confucians arranged hexagrams Qian 乾 [☰, The Creative, Heaven, 1] to Li 离 [☲, Fire, Cohesion, 30] as the upper scripture so as to signify the Dao (Way) of heaven; and Xian 咸 [☶, Reciprocity, Influence, 31] to Weiji 未济 [☲, Ferrying Incomplete, 64] as the lower scripture, in order to symbolize human affairs."[xxxiii]

By the above-mentioned records, we can see that, after Meng Xi 孟喜 (fl. c. 50 B.C.E.), people began to use the upper and lower scriptures, and thus Kong Yingda's 孔颖达 (574-648) viewpoint proves to be tenable. The concrete time of this appellation ought to be established as during the period ranging from Tian He 田何 (fl. c. 200 B.C.E.) to Meng Xi 孟喜 (fl. c. 50 B.C.E.).

There are in total 64 hexagrams in the two parts of the *Zhou yi*, in which all *yang* (—) lines are called "Nine" and all *yin* (- -) lines "Six." The *yang* (—) line from the bottom to the top in a hexagram is named "Nine the Initial," "Nine the Second," "Nine the Third," "Nine the Fourth," "Nine the Fifth," or "Nine the Top" respectively, and accordingly, the *yin* (- -) line from the bottom to the top in a hexagram is called "Six the Initial," "Six the Second," "Six the Third," "Six the Fourth," "Six the Fifth," or "Six the Top" respectively. Additionally, the hexagram Qian [☰, The Creative, Heaven, 1] boasts an extra statement called *yong jiu* 用九 (the Using of Nine) and the hexagram Kun [☷, The Receptive, 2] an extra statement called *yong liu* 用六 (the Using of Six), signifying alternations of *yin* and *yang* lines.

In fact, in the beginning there was not any reference to "Nine" and "Six" in the *Zhou yi*. Even in the Spring and Autumn period (770-476 B.C.E.), according to the records in the *Zuo zhuan* 左传 (Zuo's Commentary on the *Spring and Autumn Annals*) and the *Guo yu* 国语 (Sayings of the States), when people were divining or arguing over the *Zhou yi* through analyzing lines, they never employed the words "Nine" or "Six" to mark the *yang* or *yin* lines. It was in the "Ten Wings" (*Shiyi* 十翼) credited to later generations that the "Nine" and "Six" frequently came into view. For example, the "Commentary on the Images" (*Xiang* 象) in the hexagram Kun [☷, The Receptive, 2] says: "Actions associated with 'Six the Second' are straight and thus square."xxxiv "The 'Using of Six' signifies that greatness and final success are achieved through the practice of perpetual constancy."xxxv And the "Commentary on the Words of the Text" (*Wenyan* 文言) also says: "Here the fundamentality of Qian is expressed in the *yong jiu* 用九 (Using of Nine), signifying the entire world well governed."xxxvi Thus it can be seen that the "Nine" and "Six" ought to have come into existence with the composition of the "Commentary on the Images "and the "Commentary on the Words of the Text" or earlier.

In the beginning, the contents of the *Zhou yi* are merely composed by these two chapters, i.e. the 64 hexagrams, their judgments, and their line statements, in addition to the statements attached to the "Using of Nine" in the hexagram Qian [☰, The Creative, Heaven, 1] and the "Using of Six" in the hexagram Kun [☷, The Receptive, 2]. From the Western Han (206 B.C.E.-9 C.E.) on, the *Zhou yi* came to be the *Yi jing* 易经 (Classic of Changes), and the "Ten Wings," commenting upon the basic text, were also included in the Classic, as it states in the "Treatise on Art and Literature" (*Yiwen zhi* 艺文志) of the *Han shu* 汉书 (History of the Western Han Dynasty [206 B.C.E.-9 C.E.]), "*Yi jing* contains twelve chapters, the exegesis of which is divided into three schools of Shi Chou 施雠 (fl. c. 50 B.C.E.), Meng Xi 孟喜 (fl. c. 50 B.C.E.) and Liangqiu He 梁丘贺 (fl. c. 60 B.C.E.)."xxxvii According to Yan Shigu's 颜师古 (581-645) annotations, here the "twelve chapters" refers to the "Two Chapters" and the "Ten Wings,"xxxviii by which it can be seen that, at that time, the basic text of the *Changes* and the *Commentaries* [i.e., the "Ten Wings"] were not incorporated into one entity. It was the Eastern Han scholar Zheng Xuan 郑玄 (127-200) who combined the *Commentaries* with the basic text, as it states in the "Biography of Duke Gaoguixiang" (*Gaoguixiang gong zhuan* 高贵乡公传) of the *Sanguo zhi* 三国志 (History of the Three Kingdoms [220-280]): "The emperor continued to ask: 'Confucius composed the "Commentaries on the Judgments" (*Tuan*

彖) and "Commentary on the Images" (*Xiang* 象) and Zheng Xuan gave annotations. Though they are not at the same level, the meanings of the *Classic* they elaborated are consistent. Now the *Tuan* and *Xiang* are not linked with the basic text but the annotations are affiliated to it. Why?' The Erudite of the *Changes* Chunyu Jun 淳于俊 (fl. 256) answered: 'The reason Zheng Xuan combined the *Tuan* and *Xiang* into the *Classic* was to let learners get a shortcut. The emperor said: 'As Zheng Xuan's combination can really facilitate studies, why didn't Confucius combine them together to give learners an easier way?'..."[xxxvix]

According to these questions and answers, it is evident that Zheng Xuan 郑玄 (127-200) combined the *Tuan* and *Xiang* into the Classic. In spite of this, the *Tuan* and *Xiang* were still independent chapters even though they, together with the basic text, were compiled in one book, unlike the format of the received version of the *Zhou yi* in which the commentaries on the judgments and images are separated, and affiliated to the 64 hexagrams and 384 lines, respectively. It was not until the Wei 魏 (220-265) and Jin 晋 (265-420) periods that Wang Bi 王弼 (226-249) separated the commentaries on the judgments and images, and affiliated them with the 64 hexagrams and 384 lines, and further disconnected the "Commentary on the Words of the Text" (*Wenyan* 文言) to the hexagrams Qian [☰, The Creative, Heaven, 1] and Kun [☷, The Receptive, 2] respectively. This is the pattern we see today in the received version of the *Changes*.

By the Song dynasty (960-1279), Shao Yong 邵雍 (1011-1077) restored the appearance of the ancient *Changes*.[xl] Zhu Xi 朱熹 (1130-1200) also abandoned Wang Bi's 王弼 (226-249), but used Lü Zhuqian's 吕祖谦 (1137-1181) edition in composing his *Zhou yi benyi* 周易本义 (Original Meaning of the *Zhou Changes*) according to the number of "twelve chapters" in the "Art and Literature Treatise" (*Yiwen zhi* 艺文志) of the *Han shu* 汉书 (History of the Western Han Dynasty [206 B.C.E.-9 C.E.]), which refers to the "upper and lower scriptures as well as the Ten Wings"[xli] as having been annotated by Yan Shigu 颜师古 (581-645), the basic text occupying two *juan* 卷 (literally, scrolls, i.e., chapters) and the "Ten Wings" ten *juan* 卷.

Zhu Xi, on the one hand, restored the form of ancient ways in interpreting the *Changes* and, on the other, adopted innovations to the contents of the *Changes* insofar as he included the *he tu* 河图 (Yellow River Chart) and *luo shu* 洛书 (Luo River Diagram) in the beginning of his *Zhou yi benyi* 周易本义 (hereafter "*Benyi* 本义") in order to highlight the two diagrams. Many Ming 明 (1368-1644) and Qing 清 (1616-1912) Confucians then followed him, and thus the later generations considered them to be very important components of the *Zhou yi*.

Because *Cheng shi yi zhuan* 程氏易传(Cheng Yi's 程颐 [1033-1107] Commentary on the *Changes*) employed Wang Bi's version, but Zhu Xi's *Ben yi* used Lü Zhuqian's edition of the *Changes* for the arrangement of the basic text and the Ten Wings, later on when the Song 宋 (960-1279) scholar Dong Kai 董楷 (fl. 1265-74) was writing his *Zhou yi zhuan yi fu lu* 周易传义附录 (Appended Discussions to [Cheng Yi's] Commentary and [Zhu Xi's] Original Meaning of the *Zhou Changes*), he separated the *Benyi* into Cheng Yi's *Yi zhuan*. During the Yongle 永乐 (1403-24) period of the Ming dynasty (1368-1644), the emperor ordered scholars to compile the *Wujing daquan* 五经大全 (Great Comprehensive [Compilation of] the Five Classics), while the *Zhou yi daquan* 周易大全 (Great Comprehensive [Compilation of] the *Zhou Changes*), which was widely disseminated, adopted Dong's edition and followed his mistakes. So, the format of the *Benyi* we see today originated from Dong's segmentation and affiliation.

Most of the Ming 明 (1368-1644) and Qing 清 (1616-1912) Confucians advocated this edition, except for an occasional scholar such as the Ming Confucian He Kai 何楷 (1594-1645) who, in writing his *Gu Zhou yi dinggu* 古周易订诂 (Rectification and Phonetic and Semantic Exegesis of the Ancient *Zhou Changes*), still separated the basic text and Commentaries to show his idea of returning to the ancients. By the Qing dynasty (1616-1912), Emperor Kangxi 康熙 (r. 1662-1722) commissioned Li Guangdi 李光地 (1642-1718) to edit the *Zhou yi zhezhong* 周易折中 (A Balanced Compendium on the *Zhou Changes*), which separated the Commentaries from the basic text and further corrected the disorder caused in the *Zhou yi daquan* edition.

Therefore, the received version of the *Zhou yi* is actually divided into two parts: one is the basic text composed of the upper and lower chapters, and the other is the Ten Wings, i.e., the 10 chapters of the *Zhou yi dazhuan* 周易大传 (Great Commentaries on the *Zhou Changes*).

2.
The "Great Commentaries on the *Zhou yi*"

I

The *Zhou yi dazhuan* 周易大传 (Great Commentaries on the *Zhou Changes*) was called *Shiyi* 十翼 (Ten Wings) in ancient times.

The name of the "Ten Wings" was first seen in the "Opening Up the Regularities of the [Hexagrams] Qian [☰] and Kun [☷]" (*Qian kun zao du* 乾坤凿度) chapter of the *Yi wei* 易纬 (Apocrypha of the *Changes*) in the documents extant: "Confucius ... began to study the *Changes* when he was fifty years old. It is evident that he composed the Ten Wings."[xlii] The "Great Commentaries" include 10 chapters of "Commentary on the Judgments" (*Tuan zhuan* 彖传, I and II), "Commentary on the Images" (*Xiang zhuan* 象传, I and II), "Commentary on the Appended Phrases" (*Xici zhuan* 系辞传, I and II), "Commentary on the Words of the Text" (*Wenyan zhuan* 文言传), "Discussion of the Trigrams" (*Shuogua zhuan* 说卦传), "Orderly Sequence of the Hexagrams" (*Xugua zhuan* 序卦传), and "Hexagrams in Irregular Order" (*Zagua* 杂卦). They came to be authoritative writings by which the ancient predecessors extensively explained the hexagram names, judgments, and line statements.

Before the Qin 秦 dynasty (221-206 B.C.E.), the works explicating the hexagram and line statements of the *Zhou yi* had been referred to as

Yi zhuan 易传 (Commentaries on the *Changes*). As Yan Chu 颜斶 discussed in the "King Xuan of Qi Interviews Yan Chu" (*Qi Xuanwang jian Yan Chu* 齐宣王见颜斶) chapter of the *Zhanguo ce* 战国策 (Strategies of the Warring States):

> It is why the *Yi zhuan* says: "If those who occupy high official positions have no substantial contributions but like the fame, they are certain to be arrogant and excessive in action and thus harm will follow them. Therefore, those who love dignitary positions but have no substantial contributions will fade out, those who cherish happiness but have no virtues will be constrained, and those who accept rewards but have no merits will receive humiliation and tremendous catastrophe." hence the saying that "boasted merits will not endure and empty wishes will not arrive."[xliii]

These words are not available in the Ten Wings, suggesting that there were different versions of "Commentaries on the *Changes*" prevailing at that time.

The earliest extant document that contains the term *Yi dazhuan* 易大传 (Great Commentaries on the *Changes*) can be traced back to the Western Han dynasty (206 B.C.E.-9 C.E.). Both the "Author's Postscript" (*Taishigong zixu* 太史公自序) of the *Shiji* 史记 (Historical Records) and the "Biography of Sima Qian [145-90 B.C.E.]" (*Sima Qian zhuan* 司马迁传) of the *Han shu* 汉书 (History of the Western Han Dynasty [206 B.C.E.-9 C.E.]) cite a sentence from the *Yi dazhuan* that "All in the world ultimately comes to the same end, though the roads to it are different, so there is an ultimate congruence in thought, though there might be hundreds of ways to deliberate about it,"[xliv] which can be seen in the received "Commentary on the Appended Phrases" (*Xici zhuan* 系辞传), one of the Ten Wings. But the "Outskirts Sacrifice Treatise" (*Jiaosi zhi* 郊祀志) of the *Han shu* 汉书 (History of the Western Han Dynasty [206 B.C.E.-9 C.E.]) quoted a sentence from the alleged *Yi dazhuan* 易大传, "Those who blaspheme gods will bring disaster to their descendants for three generations"[xlv] (*Wushen zhe yang ji san shi* 诬神者殃及三世), which is not available in the Ten Wings. Therefore, the contents of the *Yi dazhuan*

The "Great Commentaries on the *Zhou yi*"

might refer extensively to all of the commentaries explicating the *Changes* rather than be rigidly confined to the Ten Wings. There are many sayings purportedly drawn from the *Book of Changes* that cannot be seen in the Ten Wings, either.

At least the following citations can attest to this point: 1) The "Profound Percepts" (*Miucheng xun* 缪称训) Chapter of the *Huainan zi* 淮南子 [written by the intellectuals surrounding Liu An 刘安 (179-122 B.C.E.), then king of the State of Huainan] states: "So the *Changes* says: 'Bo 剥 [☷☶, Peeling, 23] (means the things) ought not to be completely peeled apart, this is why it is followed by Fu 复 [☷☳, Return, 24]."[xlvi] 2) The "Biography of Sima Qian [145-90 B.C.E.]" (司马迁传) chapter of the *Han shu* 汉书 (History of the Western Han Dynasty [206 B.C.E.-9 C.E.]) states: "As the *Changes* says, 'If at the beginning you are off by a hair, in the end you will miss it by miles (*cha yi haoli, miu yi qianli* 差以毫鳌,谬以千里).'"[xlvii] 3) Similarly, in the "Biography of Dongfang Shuo" (*Dongfang Shuo zhuan* 东方朔传) of the *Han shu* 汉书 (History of the Western Han Dynasty [206 B.C.E.-9 C.E.]), we read: "As the *Changes* says, 'If the foundations are correctly established, the myriad things and events will be orderly regulated; If at the beginning you are off by a hair, in the end you will miss it by miles.'"[xlviii] 4) The *Shuowen jiezi* 说文解字 (Explanation of Simple and Composite Characters) explains the character *xiang* 相 in this way: "It means 'examining and looking.' It is made up of *mu* 目 (literally, eyes) and *mu* 木 (wood, tree). As the *Changes* says, 'Nothing on the earth is more observable than trees.'"[xlix] 5) As the "Reverence and Prudence" chapter (*Jingshen pian* 敬慎篇) of the *Shuoyuan* 说苑 (Garden of Sayings) states, "The *Changes* says: 'There is one Dao (Way) by which a whole world under heaven can be defended in its larger sense, a state can be guarded in its intermediate sense; and a person can be protected in its smaller sense. This is nothing but (the Way revealed in hexagram) Qian 谦 [☷☶, Modesty, 15].'"[l] The chapter of "Reverence for Dao (Way)" (*Zundao pian* 遵道篇) of the *Yantie lun* 盐铁论 (Discussions over Salt and Iron) [written in 81 B.C.E.] tells us: "The literati cited from the *Changes*: 'Even if a petty man holds a dignitary position, he will surely be ruined, in that without fulfillment of duty and constancy of virtues no one can end well, hence the case of first climbing up to the heaven but then entering into the earth (the top line statement of hexagram Mingyi 明夷 [☷☲, Suppression of the Light, 36]).'"[li]"[lii]

None of these citations are available in the Ten Wings. Suffice it to say that there were indeed different versions of commentaries on the *Changes* prevalent at that time which used to be cited by scholars. These commentaries including the Ten Wings might have been called *Yi dazhuan* 易大传, *Yi zhuan* 易传 or *Yi yue*《易》曰 (literally, the *Changes* says) by the Western Han people, unlike the way in which today's name of the "Great Commentaries on the *Changes*" (*Yi dazhuan* 易大传) merely refers to the Ten Wings. But people have hitherto formed the habit of saying that the "*Yi dazhuan*易大传" only refers to the Ten Wings, so in this book we still call the Ten Wings the *Zhou yi dazhuan* 周易大传 ("Great Commentaries on the *Zhou Changes*").

II

So far as the dating of the "Great Commentaries on the *Changes*" (*Yi dazhuan* 易大传) is concerned, modern scholars have not yet arrived at a unanimous point of view. As Guo Moruo 郭沫若 (1892-1978) asserted in his "Dating of the *Zhou Changes*" (*Zhou yi zhi zhizuo shidai* 周易之制作时代), "I believe the chapters of 'Discussion of the Trigrams' (*Shuogua* 说卦), 'Orderly Sequence of the Hexagrams' (*Xugua* 序卦) and 'Hexagrams in Irregular Order' (*Zagua* 杂卦) would have been written before the Qin dynasty (221-206 B.C.E.). But it was impossible for the 'Commentary on the Judgments' (*Tuan* 彖), 'Commentary on the Images' (*Xiang* 象), 'Commentary on the Appended Phrases' (*Xici* 系辞), and 'Commentary on the Words of the Text' (*Wenyan* 文言) chapters to come out before the Qin dynasty. The latter three commentaries might have been written by the disciples of Xun zi 荀子 (c. 313-238 B.C.E.) during the Qin period."[liii]

Li Jingchi 李镜池 (1902-75) avers in his *Zhou yi tanyuan* 周易探源 (An Investigation into the Origins of the *Zhou Changes*): "The 'Commentary on the Judgments' and the 'Commentary on the Images' should have been composed around the turn of the Qin (221-206 B.C.E.) and Western Han (206 B.C.E.-9 C.E.) dynasties; the dating of the 'Commentary on the Appended Phrases' and the 'Commentary on the Words of the Text' should be after Sima Qian 司马迁 (145-90 B.C.E.) and approximately between the reigns of emperors Zhao 昭帝 (r. 87-74 B.C.E.) and Xuan 宣帝 (r. 74-49 B.C.E.); the 'Discussion of the Trigrams,' the 'Orderly Sequence of the Hexagrams' and the 'Hexagrams in Irregular Order' should be [understood as having been] completed after the reign of Emperor Xuan."[liv] He further pointed out that the "Commentary on the Judgments" and the "Commentary on the Great Images" (*Da xiang* 大象) should have been written in the Qin (221-206 B.C.E.) dynasty, and the "Commentary on the Small Images" (*Xiaoxiang* 小象) around the turn of the Qin and Western Han (206 B.C.E.-9 C.E.) periods[lv]; the "Commentary on the Appended Phrases" and the "Commentary on the Words of the Text" were but compilations of the orally transmitted remarks on the *Changes* by the teachers from Tian He 田何 (fl. c. 200 B.C.E., the progenitor of the teaching of the *Changes* after the foundation of the Han dynasty [206 B.C.E.-220 C.E.]) to Tian Wangsun 田王孙 (an Erudite of the *Classic of Changes* during the reign of Emperor Xuan [r. 74-49 B.C.E.]), and the other three chapters should have been completed approximately between emperors Xuan 宣帝 (r. 74-49 B.C.E.) and Yuan 元帝 (r. 48-33 B.C.E.)[lvi].

But most scholars hold that the "Great Commentaries on the *Changes*" took form in the Warring States period (475-221 B.C.E.).

Recently, Zhang Dainian 张岱年 (1909-2004) in his "On the Dating and Philosophical Ideas of the 'Great Commentaries on the *Changes*'" (*Lun Yi dazhuan de zhuzuo niandai yu zhexue sixiang* 论易大传的著作年代与哲学思想) pointed out that Guo Moruo 郭沫若 and Li Jingchi 李镜池 were doubtful about (the antiquity and authenticity of) the ancient works. Based upon textual research, Zhang contends that "the 'Great Commentaries on the *Changes*' should have been completed at the time after Lao zi 老子 (c. 571-471 B.C.E.) but before Zhuang zi 庄子 (369-286 B.C.E.)," and "the basic part of the 'Commentary on the Appended Phrases' can be traced back to the mid-Warring States period (475-221 B.C.E.), after Lao zi 老子 but before Zhuang zi 庄子 and Hui zi 惠子 (i.e., Hui Shi 惠施 [390-318 B.C.E.]); the 'Commentary on the Judgments' should have been composed before the era of Xun zi 荀子 (c. 313-238 B.C.E.). For the 'Commentary on the Words of the Text' and 'Commentary on the Images,' we do not have direct material, but the former is similar to the 'Commentary on the Appended Phrases' and the latter to the

'Commentary on the Judgments,' so they should be compositions of the mid- and late-Warring States period. Judging from the contents of the 'Commentary on the Images,' we can see that it might have come into being later than the 'Commentary on the Judgments.' All in all, the basic part of the 'Great Commentaries on the *Changes*' are writings of the mid to late Warring States period."[lvii]

For the dating of the "Great Commentaries on the *Changes*," at first, I agree with Zhang Dainian's view that it should be dated to the era after Lao zi, but before Hui zi and Zhuang zi. The first person in the pre-Qin period who set forth the relationship between *dao* 道 (Way) and *qi* 器 (utensils) was *Lao zi*, as stated in the chapter of "Virtues" (*de pian* 德篇) of the Mawangdui 马王堆 silk manuscript of *Lao zi*, "Dao (Way) produces it, virtues show its accumulation, things show its form, and *qi* (utensils) show its accomplishment," while the "Commentary on the Appended Phrases" states: "What is prior to physical form pertains to the Dao, and what is subsequent to physical form pertains to *qi* 器 (the phenomenal world)."[lviii] It can be seen that the sentence in the "Commentary on the Appended Phrases" ought to be an extension and elaboration upon the relationship between the terms of Dao and *qi* 器 raised by *Lao zi*, which gives us evidence that it must have come into being later than the time of Lao zi (c. 571-471 B.C.E.).

Zhang Dainian employed a proposition ascribed to Hui Shi 惠施 (390-318 B.C.E.) from the "Under Heaven" (*Tian xia* 天下) chapter of the *Zhuang zi* 庄子—that "both heaven and earth are inferior, mountain and lake are on the same level"[lix]—in order to attest to the fact the "Commentary on the Appended Phrases" (*Xici* 系辞) must have come into existence before Hui Shi, in that this proposition was just a negative expression of the phrase, "Heaven is high and noble and Earth is low and humble"[lx] in the very beginning of the "Commentary on the Appended Phrases," and "in general a negative proposition appeared later than the positive one."[lxi] I agree with this point.

Additionally, we find evidence in *Zhuang zi* that can support this opinion. As it says in the "Dao [Way] of Heaven" (*Tian yun* 天道) chapter, "Nobility and humbleness, the prior and the posterior manifest the quality of motions of heaven and earth, and thus the sages draw upon these to take images."[lxii] "Highness of Heaven and lowness of Earth reveals the positions of the spirits."^lxiii "Since there are orders of superiority and inferiority for the spirits of heaven and earth, how much more so ought human society also to have them!"^lxiv These arguments, especially that "thus the sages draw upon these to take images,"^lxv are surely inspired by the "Commentary on the Appended Phrases" (*Xici* 系辞). As for the proposition of Hui Shi noted above, it is not only a negative proposition in question from the "Commentary on the Appended Phrases," but also a negative proposition concerning "Heaven [symbolized by trigram Qian ☰] and Earth [☷] establishing positions, [and] Mountain [☶] and Lake [☱] reciprocally circulating vital force"^lxvi in the "Discussion of the Trigrams" (*Shuogua* 说卦). Accordingly, the "Discussion of the Trigrams" could have come into existence before Hui Shi 惠施 (390-318 B.C.E.) and Zhuang zi 庄子 (369-286 B.C.E.). Moreover, it states in the "Dao (Way) of Heaven" (*Tian dao* 天道) chapter: "Quiescence and *yin* 阴 [symbolized by trigram Kun ☷] share the same quality, movement resonates with the wave of the *yang* 阳 force [symbolized by trigram Qian ☰]... thus its movement is (revealed by) heaven and quiescence (by) earth."^lxvii "The illumination of the sun and the moon gives rise to the cyclical motions of the four seasons like regular alternations of day and night, and thus 'clouds scud and rain falls' (*yunxing yushi* 云行雨施)[1]."^lxviii And in the chapter of "Footloose" (*Zaiyou* 在宥), one reads: "I help you reach the most illuminating realm and the origin of the *yang* energy [i.e., pure *yang* symbolized by trigram Qian ☰]."^lxix Only those who had read the "Discussion of the Trigrams" and the "Commentary on the Words of the Text" could have offered these remarks. As it says in the "Old Fisherman" (*Yufu* 渔父) chapter, "Things of the same kind follow each other, and things with the same tonality resonate together. This is an inherent principle."^lxx This statement was surely inspired by the utterance that "Things with the same tonality resonate together; things with the same material force seek out one another"^lxxi from the "Commentary on the Words of the Text" (*Wenyan* 文言). We can also read in the "Autumn Water" (*Qiu shui* 秋水) chapter:

---

[1] A term from the "Commentary on the Judgments" regarding the hexagram Qian [䷀, The Creative, 1]). Please see Richard John Lynn, *The Classic of Changes: A New Translation of the I Ching as Interpreted by Wang Bi*. New York: Columbia University Press, 1994, 130.

"The year cannot be urged to stay, and the time cannot be stopped. Rise and decline, waxing and waning form a cycle, and ending will be succeeded with a new beginning."[lxxii] Similarly, the "Commentaries on the Judgments" for hexagrams *Feng* 丰 [䷶, Abundance, 55], *Bo* 剥 [䷖, Peeling, 23], and *Sun* 损 [䷨, Diminution, 41] state respectively: "When the sun is at midday, it begins to set, and when the moon is at its full, it begins to wane. Everything in Heaven and Earth always waxes and wanes at the proper moment."[lxxiii] "The noble man holds in esteem how things ebb and flow, wax and wane, for this is the course of Heaven."[lxxiv] "Diminution and increase or waxing and waning take place in tandem with their proper times."[lxxv] It is evident that the former remarks were inspired by the latter three.

It is therefore credible that the "Commentary on the Judgments" (*Tuan* 彖), the "Discussion of the Trigrams" (*Shuogua* 说卦), the "Commentary on the Words of the Text" (*Wenyan* 文言), and the "Commentary on the Appended Phrases" (*Xici* 系辞) date to before Zhuang zi 庄子 (369-286 B.C.E.). In spite of this, the dating of the "Commentary on the Appended Phrases" could not be much earlier than the era of Hui zi (i.e., Hui Shi 惠施 [390-318 B.C.E.]) and Zhuang zi, as it states in this text, "The *Changes* make evident both that which has already happened and scrutinizes what is yet to come, thus subtlety comes to light, revealing what is hidden. The hexagrams are elucidated in such a way that they suit their names. These elucidations, in their differentiation of things and rectification of language, form decisive phrases. Thus they are perfect and complete"[lxxvi]—which was obviously branded with the features of the School of Logicians (*Ming jia* 名家) initiated by Hui zi. Therefore, in my opinion, the dating of the "Commentary on the Appended Phrases" ought to be a little earlier than or at the era of Hui zi and Zhuang zi.

Xun zi 荀子 (c. 313-238 B.C.E.) must have been conversant with the "Commentary on the Judgments" (*Tuan* 彖), as he states in the "Great Strategies" (*Da lüe* 大略) chapter of the *Xun zi* that "In the hexagram Xian 咸 [䷞, Influence or Reciprocity, 31] of the *Changes*, we can see husband [symbolized by the lower trigram ☶] and wife [symbolized by the upper trigram ☱]. The Dao (Way) for the relationship between husband and wife has to be rectified, for it is the root for dealing with relationships between monarch and subject, between father and son. Reciprocity is a matter of stimulation. What is high takes its place below the low; the male takes a place below the female; and the soft and yielding is above, and the hard and strong is below."[lxxvii] This progression evidently drew upon and directly copied some words from the "Commentary on the Judgments" for hexagram Xian 咸 [☱☶, Reciprocity, 31]: "Reciprocity is a matter of stimulation. Here the soft and yielding [Dui (☱, Joy), here representing the Youngest Daughter] is above, and the hard and strong [Gen (☶, Restraint), representing the Youngest Son] is below. The two kinds of material force [qi 气] stimulate and respond and so join together. The one is self-restricting, and the other joyous. The male takes a place below the female, and this is how 'one achieves prevalence,' how 'it is fitting to practice constancy,' and how 'to marry a woman means good fortune.'"[lxxviii]

At the same time, he was deeply influenced by the "Commentary on the Appended Phrases" (Xici 系辞) and further elaborated some ideas upon it. As it says in the "Commentary on the Appended Phrases," "Therefore the noble man, when secure, does not forget danger; when enjoying continuance, does not forget ruin; when maintaining order, does not forget disorder. This is the way his person is kept secure and his state remains protected."[lxxix] Upon this statement, Xun zi states in the "Zhongni" (仲尼, i.e. Confucius) chapter: "The wise man, in dealing with affairs, when at peak will consider humbleness, when secure will consider danger, and when enjoying continuance will consider ruin."[lxxx] It also reads in the commentary: "The Yellow Emperor, Yao, and Shun let their robes hang loosely down, yet the world was well governed. They probably got the idea for this from the hexagrams Qian [☰] and Kun [☷]."[lxxxi] Similarly, Xun zi stated in the "Kings and Monarchs" (Wang ba 王霸) chapter: "… Though he let his robes hang loosely down, and without leaving his seat, all people under heaven wished to obtain him as their emperor."[lxxxii] We can read in the commentary: "As all in the world ultimately comes to the same end, though the roads to it are different, so there is an ultimate congruence in thought, though there might be hundreds of ways to deliberate about it."[lxxxiii] Xun zi used another way to express the same idea in the chapter of "Enriching the State" (Fu guo 富国): "People may have the same pursuit but adopt different approaches; people may share the same desire but have different levels of wisdom."[lxxxiv] It states in the commentary: "If one's virtue be meager but position noble, or knowledge little but plans grandiose, or powers few but responsibilities heavy, then it is rare indeed that such a one will not be outstripped. The *Changes* say: 'The Caldron breaks its legs and overturns all its pottage, so its form is drenched, which means misfortune.' This speaks of someone who is unequal to his responsibilities."[lxxxv] Xun zi had similar remarks in the "Effects of Confucians" (*Ru xiao* 儒效) chapter: "So, if one is incompetent but his undertakings large—comparable to a person who has meager power but bears heavy responsibilities—there will be no other end except fracture of his bones."[lxxxvi] Here the "fracture of bones" was evidently derived from "the Caldron breaks its legs." Therefore, by his manner of writing, it is evident that Xun zi extended some ideas conceived in the "Commentary on the Appended Phrases" (*Xici* 系辞).

After the dating of the "Commentary on the Appended Phrases" (*Xici* 系辞) is ascertained, we should focus on that of the other main chapters, including the "Discussion of the Trigrams" (*Shuogua* 说卦), the "Commentary on the Words of the Text" (*Wenyan* 文言), and the "Commentary on the Judgments" (*Tuan* 彖), as well as the "Commentary on the Images" (*Xiang* 象). If we can further ascertain the dating of these chapters in contrast to that of the "Commentary on the Appended Phrases," the date of composition of the entire *Yi dazhuan* 易大传 (Great Commentaries on the *Changes*) will be clarified in general.

For the chronological order of the dating of the main chapters in the "Great Commentaries on the *Changes*," I am sure that the "Commentary on the Words of the Text" (*Wenyan* 文言) must have appeared earlier than the "Commentary on the Appended Phrases" (*Xici* 系辞), considering the passage reading, "'A dragon that overreaches should have cause for regret.' The Master said: 'One might be noble yet lack the position, might be lofty yet lack the subjects, and might have worthy men in subordinate positions who yet will not assist him. If such a one acts with all this being so, he will have cause for regret'"[lxxxvii] — phrases in the latter were fully cited from the former.

Many statements in the *Xun zi* 荀子 were also drawn from the "Commentary on the Words of the Text." For example, Xun zi wrote in the "Encouraging Study" (*Quan xue* 劝学) and "Great Strategies" (*Da lüe* 大略) chapters respectively: "Dry wood is easy to burn, as fire goes toward where it is dry; lowland is easy to be wet, as water flows to where it is wet. Grasses tend to grow in clumps, and wild animals like roaming in packs, as things with regular tendencies divide up according to groups."[lxxxviii] "If we apply fire to a bunch of wood, the fire will begin from where the wood is drier; if we pour water in a flat ground, it will flow to the lower land. It is quite obvious that each thing follows its own kind."[lxxxix] These words are evidently drawn from the following remarks in the "Commentary on the Words of the Text" (*Wenyan* 文言): "Things with the same tonality resonate together; things with the same material force seek out one another. Water flows to where it is wet; fire goes toward where it is dry. Clouds follow the dragon; wind follows the tiger. The sage bestirs himself, and all creatures look to him. What is rooted in Heaven draws close to what is above; what is rooted in Earth draws close to what is below. Thus each thing follows its own kind."[xc] Additionally, Xun zi also addressed in the "Meticulousness" (*Bugou* 不苟) chapter that "(one's) ordinary speech must be trustworthy and ordinary conduct must be prudent,"[xci] which was derived from the remark that "He is trustworthy in ordinary speech and prudent in ordinary conduct" in the "Commentary on the Words of the Text"[xcii] that pertained to the second line of the hexagram Qian 乾 [☰, The Creative, Heaven, 1]. Therefore, as with the "Commentary on the Appended Phrases" (*Xici* 系辞) and the "Commentary on the Judgments" (*Tuan* 彖), the "Commentary on the Words of the Text" also largely influenced Xun zi, and, accordingly, the main chapters of the *Yi dazhuan* proved to have been prevalent in the era of Xun zi 荀子 (c. 313-238 B.C.E.).

Regarding the "Commentary on the Words of the Text" (*Wenyan* 文言), I suspect it originally comprised not only the two chapters pertaining to hexagrams Qian 乾 [☰ The Creative, Heaven, 1] and Kun 坤 [☷ The Receptive, Earth, 2], but 64 chapters [corresponding to the 64 hexagrams] which could be the class notes from the masters of the scripture. Later generations, in redacting these chapters, took only the two initial chapters as representatives, probably because the entire chapters were too long. My evidence lies in the citations in the "Commentary on the Appended Phrases," where the style of the Master's remarks on the 18 lines in 16 hexagrams was extremely congruent with that of the "Commentary on the Words of the Text." And particularly the commentary on the top line statement (i.e., "A dragon that overreaches should have cause for regret.") of the hexagram Qian 乾 in the *Xici* was the same as that in the *Wenyan* 文言. It therefore can be seen that the author(s) of the "Commentary on the Appended Phrases" (*Xici* 系辞) had seen the entire 64 chapters, but that he (or they) only excerpted remarks on the 18 lines' statements in the 16 hexagrams. Later, only the remarks on the Qian and Kun were preserved, hence the identical remarks on the top line statement of hexagram Qian 乾 in the two commentaries.

The dating of the "Commentary on the Judgments" (*Tuan* 彖) was certainly earlier than the "Commentary on the Words of the Text" (*Wenyan* 文言). This can easily be made clear if we compare both commentaries affiliated to the first hexagram Qian 乾. We read in the former:

> How great is the fundamental nature of Qian! The myriad things are provided their beginnings by it, and, as such, it controls Heaven. It allows clouds to scud and rain to fall and things in all their different categories to flow into forms. Manifestly bright from beginning to end, the positions of the six lines form, each at its proper moment. When it is the moment for it, ride one of the six dragons to drive through the sky...[xciii]

In contrast, it says in the latter:

> How great Qian is! It is strong, dynamic, central, correct, and it is absolutely pure in its being unadulterated and unsullied. The six lines emanate their power and exhaustively explore all innate tendencies. In accord with the moment, ride the six dragons to drive through the sky. Then clouds will move, and rain will fall, and all under heaven will be at peace....[xciv]

It is very clear that the language used in the former is concise and natural. It was the author of the latter who shifted some words of the former and adopted them into his own discourse. So, it is obvious that the former came into existence earlier than the latter.

The "Commentary on the Images" is divided into two parts—the "Commentary on the Great Images" (*Da xiang* 大象) [interpreting the judgments of the hexagrams] and the "Commentary on the Small

Images" (*Xiaoxiang* 小象) [interpreting the 384 lines statements]. Regarding the dating of the "Commentary on the Images," I agree with Li Jingchi's 李镜池 (1902-75) point of view as expressed in his *Zhou yi tanyuan* 周易探源 (An Investigation into the Origins of the *Zhou Changes*): The former predated the latter.

Here I can assure you that the "Commentary on the Great Images" (*Da xiang* 大象) was composed earlier than the "Commentary on the Judgments" (*Tuan* 彖). Let us at first take a look at the *Da xiang* 大象 for hexagram Ding 鼎 [䷱, The Caldron, 50]: "Above Wood [symbolized by ☴], there is Fire [☲]: this constitutes the image of the Caldron. In the same way, the noble man rectifies positions and solidifies his mandate."[xcv] By contrast, we read in the "Commentary on the Judgments": "The Caldron is an image. It is by taking Wood [☴] and putting it in Fire [☲] that one cooks food. The sage cooks in order to sacrifice to the Supreme Deity and…."[xcvi] Obviously, the latter was an extension based upon the former.

As the *Da xiang* 大象 for hexagram Bo 剥 [䷖, Peeling, 23] indicates, "The Mountain [☶] is attached to the Earth [☷]: this constitutes the image of Bo [Peeling]. In the same way, those above make their dwellings secure by treating those below with generosity,"[xcvii] whereas it states in the "Commentary on the Judgments" (*Tuan* 彖): "Bo means '*bo*' [peeling], for here the soft and weak [i.e., yin (--) line(s)] are making the hard and strong [yang (—) line(s)] change. 'It would not be fitting should one set out to do something,' for the petty man [symbolized by yin (--) line(s)] is in the ascendant. One should try to restrain things in such a way that one remains compliant with circumstances, for this is inspired by observing the image. The noble man holds in esteem how things ebb and flow, wax and wane, for this is the course of Heaven."[xcviii] Here, what does "observing the image" refer to? It certainly refers to the image of "the Mountain being attached to the Earth" noted in the *Da xiang* 大象, in which the trigram Kun 坤 [☷] symbolizes the earth and compliance, and Gen 艮 [☶] the mountain and restraint, hence the related address in the "Commentary on the Judgments."

This case can be particularly seen in hexagram Kun 坤 [䷁, The Receptive, 2], as the "Commentary on the Great Images" (*Da xiang* 大象) tells us that "Here is the basic disposition of Earth: this constitutes the image of Kun. In the same manner, the nobleman with his generous virtue carries everything,"[xcix] inspired by which the "Commentary on the Judgments" reorganized some key words and developed them into marvelous remarks, such as "… It is the generosity of Kun that lets it carry everything, the integrative force of its virtue that accounts for its limitlessness…"[c] The latter was apparently drawn from the former.

Additionally, this is also the case in hexagram Xun 巽 [☴, Compliance, 57], as it states in the *Da xiang* 大象, "Wind [☴] follows wind: this constitutes the image of Compliance. In the same way, the noble man reiterates commands and has endeavors carried out,"[ci] whereas the "Commentary on the Judgments" almost copied these words in this way: "The separated Xun [☴, Compliance] trigrams express how commands are reiterated. If the hard and strong can practice Compliance while adhering to centrality and rectitude with effort, his will shall be realized."[cii]

Moreover, this situation is also evident in hexagrams Jin 晋 [䷢, Advance, 35] and Mingyi 明夷 [䷣, Suppression of the Light, 36]. As the *Da xiang* 大象 for hexagram Jin states, "Brightness [☲] appears above the Earth [☷]: this constitutes the image of Advance. In the same way, the noble man illuminates himself with bright virtue," whereas the "Commentary on the Judgments" copied some words and extended its significance in this way: "Jin 晋 [advance] means *jin* 进 [making progress, moving forward]. Here brightness appears above the Earth. It is obedience [☷] that allows one to adhere to this great brightness [☲]…."[ciii] For hexagram Mingyi, as its *Da xiang* 大象 explains, "The light [☲] has gone into the earth [☷]: this constitutes the image of Suppression of the Light. In the same way, the noble man approaches the mass of common folk. It is by keeping it dark that brilliance is achieved,"[civ] which was directly copied and extended in the "Commentary on the Judgments" in the following way: "When the light [☲] has gone into the earth [☷], there is Suppression of the Light. Inside all cultivation and light and outside all yielding and obedience, so should one be when beset with great adversity, as was King Wen."[cv]

Therefore, it has been clearly demonstrated in the literary remarks that the "Commentary on the Great Images" (*Da xiang* 大象) predated the "Commentary on the Judgments" (*Tuan* 彖).

Finally, let us determine the dating of the "Discussion of the Trigrams" (*Shuogua* 说卦). In my opinion, in the main chapters of the *Yi dazhuan* 易大传 (i.e., the Ten Wings), the "Discussion of the Trigrams" surely predated the "Commentary on the Appended Phrases" (*Xici* 系辞), and its main contents, concerning the symbolic associations of the eight trigrams, must have been compiled before the composition of the "Commentary on the Great Images" (*Da xiang* 大象) and the "Commentary on the Judgments" (*Tuan* 彖).

It is evident that the "Discussion of the Trigrams" predated the "Commentary on the Appended Phrases" (*Xici* 系辞), as we can read in the former:

> In the distant past, the way the sages made the *Changes* is as follows: It was to be used as a means to stay in accord with principles of nature and fate. It was for this reason that they determined what the Dao (Way) of Heaven was, which they defined in terms of *yin* and *yang*, what the Dao of Earth was, which they defined in terms of hard and soft, and what the Dao of Man was, which they defined in terms of benevolence and righteousness. They brought these three powers together and doubled them; this is why the *Changes* forms its hexagrams out of six lines. They provided *yin* allotments and *yang* allotments, so their functions alternate between soft and hard; this is why the *Changes* forms its patterns out of six positions.[cvi]

Yet in the latter, it claims:

> As a book, the *Changes* is something which is broad and great, complete in every way. There is the Dao (Way) of Heaven in it, the Dao of Man in it, and the Dao of Earth in it. It brings these three powers together and then doubles them. This is the reason for there being six lines. What these six embody is nothing other than the Dao of the three powers.[cvii]

By comparing these two paragraphs, it becomes clear that the latter paragraph was composed after the author of the latter had read the former, and not the reverse.

The "Discussion of the Trigrams" is a treatise specially recounting the attributes and identifications of the eight trigrams, whereas the "Commentary on the Great Images" (*Da xiang* 大象), the "Commentary on the Judgments" (*Tuan* 彖), and the "Commentary on the Words of the Text" (*Wenyan* 文言) apply to the 64 hexagrams, and the "Commentary on the Appended Phrases" (*Xici* 系辞) analyzes and discusses the theoretical system of the *Changes*. Generally speaking, recounting came prior to theoretical analysis and discussions. In respect to this matter, the "Discussion of the Trigrams" commentary could have appeared earlier.

By scrutinizing the "Commentary on the Judgments" (*Tuan* 彖), we can find that its explications were based upon and extended from the basic symbolic associations of the constituent trigrams in a hexagram. For instance, the commentary for hexagram Meng 蒙 [☷, Juvenile Ignorance, 4] states: "Meng [Juvenile Ignorance] consists of a dangerous place [☵] below a mountain [☶]. In danger and brought to a halt: this is Meng. 'Meng brings about prevalence': Meng operates through prevalence and is a matter of timeliness and the Mean. 'It is not I who seek the Ignorant Juvenile but the Ignorant Juvenile who seeks me': their intentions resonate. 'An initial rendering of the yarrow stalks should be answered': this he can do because of his virility and the position of the mean. 'But a second and a third would result in blasphemy. If there were such blasphemy, I should not answer him.' The one who would bring about this blasphemy is the Ignorant Juvenile. To take Juvenile Ignorance and cultivate rectitude in it is the meritorious task of the sage."[cviii] It is well known that according to the "Discussion of the Trigrams" (*Shuogua* 说卦), Kan [☵] symbolizes water and dangerous places, and Gen [☶] mountain and halt. Therefore, it is evident that the terms of "dangerous place" and "mountain" in the Tuan (Commentary on the Judgments) regarding hexagram Meng [☷, Juvenile Ignorance, 4] were based on the "Discussion of the Trigrams" (*Shuogua* 说卦).

To take another example, as it states in hexagram Xu 需 [☰, Waiting, 5], "Xu means 'waiting,' as danger [☵] lies in front. Hard and strong, one does not founder here—the meaning of which is, one will not find himself dire straits. 'As there is sincerity in waiting, so prevalence shall be gloriously manifest, and constancy result in good fortune': here one abides in the place of Heaven and does so with rectitude and within the Mean. 'It is fitting to cross the great river': this means that if one were to set forth, he would gain meritorious achievement."[cix] The constituent trigrams of the hexagram *Xu* [☵/☰] are *Qian* [☰] in the inner position, which in the "Discussion of the Trigrams" signifies hard and strong, and *Kan* [☵] in the outer position, which represents danger in front, hence the saying of "danger [☵] lies in front. Hard and strong, one does not founder here, the meaning of which is, one will not find himself dire straits," which was followed by citations of the hexagram's judgment with particular further elaboration.

In this case, at least two questions ensue. First, if the "Discussion of the Trigrams" was composed later than the "Commentary on the Judgments," what should the masters transmitting the scripture of *Changes* have based their ideas upon to explicate the constituent trigrams in a hexagram? Second, for the eight hexagrams of Qian [☰], Kun [☷], Zhen [☳], Kan [☵], Gen [☶], Xun [☴], Li [☲], and Dui [☱], each of which is composed of two identical trigrams, the images of the two constituent trigrams had never been mentioned as an introduction to initiate further elaborations on the hexagram statements in the "Commentary on the Judgments." What could account for this irregular phenomenon after all? There is only one reason for it: Since the "Discussion of the Trigrams" commentary had specially explicated the symbolic associations of the eight trigrams—and thus the attributes and identifications of the trigrams—the same two of which form one of the above-mentioned hexagrams, as elaborated upon in detail in the "Discussion of the Trigrams," it was unnecessary to mention them again in the "Commentary on the Judgments" for these eight hexagrams. In this sense, the former would predate the latter.

Similarly, the "Discussion of the Trigrams" could not appear later than the "Commentary on the Great Images" (*Da xiang* 大象); otherwise, how can we account for the sayings related to the trigram images like "the Mountain [☶] is attached to the Earth [☷]" for hexagram Bo 剝 [☷/☶, Peeling, 23], "Heaven [☰] located within the Mountain [☶]" for hexagram Daxu 大畜 [☰/☶, Great Domestication, 26], and so on in the latter?

Therefore, the part about the complex symbolic associations of the eight trigrams in the "Discussion of the Trigrams" on all accounts could not have appeared after the "Commentary on the Judgments" and the

"Commentary on the Great Images." Additionally, according to the "Biography of Shu Xi" (Shu Xi zhuan 束皙传) in the *Jin shu* 晋书 (History of the Jin Dynasty [265-420]), among the dozens of carts of manuscripts (bamboo slips) found in the tomb of King Xiang of Wei 魏襄王 (r. 318-296 B.C.E.), there was a chapter called the "Scripture of the *Changes* under the Trigrams" (*Guaxia yijing* 卦下易经) which was "similar to the 'Discussion of the Trigrams' except [in] some differences."[cx] This demonstrates that there had been this kind of treatise explicating the images of the eight trigrams before that time, which therefore could further attest to our above-mentioned conclusions. However, we should not claim, based on this understanding, that the "Discussion of the Trigrams" in the era of King Xiang of Wei had not as of yet come into being, since at that time the circulation of books was very difficult and the books in his tomb might only have included his favorites or sacrificial books for him, the range of which would have been extremely limited—and none of the received versions of the Ten Wings was included in these manuscripts, either.

Nevertheless, based on the styles and terms used in the "Discussion of the Trigrams," the "Commentary on the Judgments," and the "Commentary on the Great Images," they could not have antedated the "Commentary on the Appended Phrases" by very much. In these commentaries the terms like *xingming* 性命 (nature and fate), *daode* 道德 (way and virtue), and *ren yu yi* 仁与义 (benevolence and righteousness),[cxi] and those like *zhi dushu* 制数度 (establishing limits), 德行 (moral conduct),[cxii] *yufang* 豫防 (taking steps beforehand to prevent the threat),[cxiii] *ganying* 感应 (stimulus and response),[cxiv] and *dushi* 笃实 (the sincere and substantial),[cxv] were all marked with the stamp of the Warring States period (475-221 B.C.E.). Therefore, although these three commentaries predated the "Commentary on the Appended Phrases" (*Xici* 系辞), they could not have come prior to the early Warring States period.

It is my view that the main parts of the "Great Commentaries on the *Changes*" (*Yi dazhuan* 易大传, i.e., the Ten Wings) were composed from the early to the mid-Warring States period.

III

As for the permutation patterns of the 64 hexagrams, the Tang scholar Kong Yingda 孔颖达 (574-648) tells us that, regarding the annotations to the "Orderly Sequence of the Hexagrams" (*Xugua* 序卦) in his *Zhou yi zhengyi* 周易正义 (Correct Meaning of the *Zhou Changes*), there are two distinguishing features. The first one is that the 64 hexagrams were arranged in terms of sequentially numbered, paired groupings, each pair consisting of two hexagrams. The other one is that each pair was based on one of two structural principles—"inversion" (*fu* 覆) or "conversion" (*bian* 变)[cxvi]. The first principle—"inversion"—refers to when one of the two hexagrams in each pair seems to have been turned upside down to create the other (e.g., Zhun [䷂, 3] and Meng [䷃, 4]; Xu [䷄, 5] and Song [䷅, 6]). The second principle—"conversion"—means that all lines in one hexagram of the pair become their opposites in the other (e.g., Qian [䷀, 1] and Kun [䷁, 2]; Yi [䷚, 27] and Da guo [䷛, 28]).

At first glance, Kong's conclusion seems tenable. But if we think it over more carefully, we can locate its flaws. For instance, should the relationship between hexagrams Tai [䷊, 11] and Pi [䷋, 12] in a pair be attributed to the principle of "inversion" or "conversion"? Kong's distinction is not precise enough, as some pairs of hexagrams are congruent with both his "inversion" and "conversion" principles. Besides Tai and Pi, the relationship between Jiji [䷾, 63] and Weiji [䷿, 64] also illustrates to this ambiguity.

By exposing this flaw in Kong's assertion, which may seem to be digressing from the subject, my purpose is to point out that the author of the "Orderly Sequence of the Hexagrams" must not have taken the above-mentioned principles into account, but instead attempted to disclose an interconnected chain formed by the 64 hexagrams according to the implications of the hexagrams' names—each hexagram being an indispensable link. Of course, this endeavor could only lead him into a forced analogy, which even brought harm to some modern scholars who took painstaking efforts to extrapolate subtle meanings from this. Zhang Taiyan's 章太炎 (1869-1936) *Yi lun* 易论 (Discussion on the *Changes*) exemplifies this exertion. Obviously influenced by the "Orderly Sequence of the Hexagrams," Zhang tried hard to adopt the sequence of the 64 hexagrams as a way to interpret the track of social evolution. His hypothesis was only applicable to several hexagrams from the beginning but could not entirely be threaded through all hexagrams.

As a matter of fact, the discovery of the Mawangdui 马王堆 silk manuscript version of the *Changes* demonstrates that, even until the Western Han (206 B.C.E.-9 C.E.) dynasty, there were still different versions of the *Zhou yi* characterized by disparate permutations of the hexagrams prevailing at that time. As Gao Heng 高亨 (1900-86) asserted in the first chapter of his *Zhou yi dazhuan jinzhu* 周易大传今注 (Modern Annotations to the *Great Commentaries on the Zhou Changes*), "There must have been some different permutations of the sixty-four hexagrams in ancient times."[cxvii] It was in order to promote and elevate the position of the received version of the *Zhou yi* and distinguish it from other versions with different permutations of the time that the masters of the received version composed the "Orderly Sequence of the Hexagrams" so as to account for the permutation and lift its prestige. Therefore, the composition of this chapter might be dated later than the "Discussion of the Trigrams," the "Commentary on the Images," the "Commentary on the Judgments," the "Commentary on the Appended Phrases," and the "Commentary on the Words of the Text." It probably came into existence in the Qin (221-206 B.C.E.) or even in the Western Han (206 B.C.E.-9 C.E.) dynasty.

As for the "Hexagrams in Irregular Order" (*Zagua* 杂卦), which revealed the characteristics of each hexagram in a very concise and unique way, we cannot determine its date of composition because the given literary documents are insufficient. Since it had its own system, I estimate that its dating would not be very late.

In regard to the sequence and dating of the chapters of the "Great Commentaries on the *Zhou yi*," because they were too ancient, Han scholars credited them to Confucius. It was not until the Song dynasty (960-1279) that some scholars began to doubt their authorship. However, it is difficult to find evidence that is convincing enough to determine it. Even today, it is still a subject of intense scholarly debate. In reading the Ten Wings, I do find some traces in the lines and attempt to set forth my own opinion on it. It is my hope that if there are deficiencies in my inference and points of view, they may be pointed out so that they can be corrected.

IV

Now let us talk about the attribution of ideas in the "Commentaries on the *Changes*."

The Qing scholar Cui Shu 崔述 (1740-1816) pointed out in the *juan* three (卷三) of the "Textual Research on Confucius's Life Story" (*Zhusi kao xin lu* 洙泗考信录) chapter in the *Cui Dongbi yishu* 崔东壁遗书 (Posthumous Papers of Cui Dongbi [i.e., Cui Shu]) that the "Commentary on the Images" (*Xiang zhuan* 象传) had cited Zeng zi's 曾子 (505-435 B.C.E.) (as a renowned disciple of Confucius, he was credited with the *Da xue* 大学—Great Learning—one of the *Four Books*) saying: "According to the *Analects of Confucius* (14:26), Zeng zi told us that 'the noble man is mindful of how he should not go beyond his position,' which was adopted in the 'Commentary on the Images.'"[cxviii][cxix] This discovery merits our attention.

If we take a look at the "Commentary on the Judgments" (*Tuan* 彖), the "Commentary on the Images" (*Xiang* 象), and the "Commentary on the Words of the Text" (*Wenyan* 文言), especially in the "Commentary on the Great Images (*Da xiang* 大象)" we can find that some remarks evidently amplified Zeng zi's idea, such as the following: "The noble man is beset with fear and so cultivates and reflects upon himself."[cxx] "'Return before going far' provides the way one should cultivate his person."[cxxi] "'This one returns with simple honesty, so there will be no regret,' for the mean is used as the standard for self-scrutiny."[cxxii] "The noble man shifts to the good when he sees it and corrects his errors when he has them."[cxxiii] "The noble man reflects upon himself and cultivates virtue."[cxxiv] "The noble man consistently practices virtuous conduct and constantly engages in moral transformation."[cxxv] "The noble man is prudent with his language and practices restraint in his use of food and drink."[cxxvi] "The noble man prudently distinguishes among things and situates them in their correct places."[cxxvii] How consistent these remarks are with the idea of self-examination articulated by Zeng zi in the *Analects of Confucius*!

In addition, the *Analects of Confucius* (8:5) also cited Zeng zi's remarks: "In the past, my friend ... seemed to know nothing though he was a learned man. His knowledge is broad and substantial [*shi* 实] but seemed void [*xu* 虛].'' The "Commentary on the Images" for hexagram Xian [☱☶, Reciprocity, 31] gave us remarks with the similar idea: "The noble man receives others with self-effacement [*xu* 虛, literally, void]."[cxxviii] When Zeng zi was voicing his opinions, he used to say, "I have heard from the Master [i.e. Confucius] that..." (e.g., his remarks in the *Analects of Confucius* [19: 17]). The commentary for hexagram Daxu [☶☰, Great Domestication, 26] also praises the noble man in this way: "The noble man acquires much knowledge of things said and done in the past and so domesticates and garners his own virtue."[cxxix]

This congruence can naturally inspire us to correlate the Ten Wings with the Si-Meng (i.e., Zi si 子思 [483-402 B.C.E., with whom the composition of the *Zhong yong* 中庸 (Doctrine of the Mean) was credited, the grandson of Confucius and a renowned disciple of Zeng zi] and Mencius [372-289 B.C.E.]) Confucian school (*Si-Meng xuepai* 思孟学派).

Hou Wailu 侯外廬 (1903-87), in volume one of his *Zhongguo sixiangshi* 中国思想通史 (A General History of Chinese Thought), analyzed from methodological perspectives the inseparability between the "Commentaries on the *Changes*" and the spirit of the Si-Meng school, "in that the methods of allowing 'subtlety come to light and revealing what is hidden,'[cxxx] 'delving into mysteries and searching out what is hidden,' and 'hooking things up from depths and extending a reach to the distances'[cxxxi] (advocated by the Ten Wings) were not in alignment with Xun zi's 荀子 (c. 313-238 B.C.E.) disposition but similar to the methods taken by the Si-Meng school criticized by Xunzi."[cxxxii]

This conclusion is pertinent. Although the term "five-agent" (*wuxing* 五行, here referring to the five virtues of benevolence, righteousness, propriety, wisdom, and trustworthiness), which was denounced by Xun zi as a term applied by the Si-Meng school, was not in the Ten Wings, there were indeed many remarks related to ancient legends, which were condemned by Xun zi in his "Criticizing the Twelve Masters" (*Fei shier zi* 非十二子) as "forging the so-called theory of five-agents according to ancient legends,"[cxxxiii] such as: "After Lord Bao Xi Bao Xi包牺 (a.k.a. Fu Xi 伏羲 [c. mid- or late Neolithic Age, the domesticator of animals and progenitor of Chinese civilization]) perished, Lord Shen Nong 神农 (c. late Neolithic Age, the inventor of Chinese agriculture, medicine, and pharmacy) applied himself to things. He hewed wood and made a plowshare [symbolized by ☳] and bent wood and made a plow handle [☴]. The benefit of plowing and hoeing he taught to the world. He probably got the idea for this from the hexagram Yi 益 [䷩, Increase, 42]. He had midday [symbolized by ☲] become market time, had the people of the world gather [☷], had the goods [☵, ☶] of the world brought together, had these exchanged, had them then retire to their homes, and enabled each one to get what he should. He probably got the idea for this from the hexagram Shihe [䷔, Bite Together]." Also: "After Lord Shen Nong perished, the Lord Yellow Emperor, Lord Yao 尧 [c. 2300-c. 2200 B.C.E., a legendary sage ruler in ancient China], and Lord Shun 舜 [c. 2250-c. 2150 B.C.E., a legendary sage ruler in ancient Chinese who succeeded to the throne after Lord Yao尧] applied themselves to things, they allowed things to undergo the free flow of change and so spared the common folk from weariness and sloth. With their numinous powers they transformed things and had the common folk adapt to them. As for [the Dao of] change, when one process of it reaches its limit, a change from one state to another occurs. As such, change achieves free flow, and with this free flow, it lasts forever. This is why 'Heaven will help him as a matter of course; this is good fortune, and nothing will be to his disadvantages.' The Yellow Emperor, Yao, and Shun let their upper outer garments [which covers clothes under it and can be symbolized by ☰] and lower undergarments [☷] hang loosely down, yet the world was well governed. They probably got the idea for this from the trigrams Qian [☰] and Kun [☷]."[cxxxiv]

Moreover, the "Commentary on the Appended Phrases" (*Xici* 系辞) states: "The *Changes* is without consciousness and is without deliberate action. Being utterly still it does not initiate movement, but when stimulated it is commensurate with all the causes for everything that happens in the world. As such, it has to be the most numinous thing in the world, for what else could possibly be up to this! It is by means of the *Changes* that the sages plumb the utmost profundity and dig into the very incipience of things. It is profundity alone that thus allows one to penetrate the aspirations of all the people in the world; it is a grasp of incipience alone that thus allows one to accomplish the great affairs of the world; and it is the numinous alone that thus allows one to make quick progress without hurrying and reach goals without forcing one's way."[cxxxv] These remarks were undoubtedly "particularly eccentric, incommensurate with decorum, and too profound to be explicated," which characterized the Si-Meng school in the eyes of Xun zi.

Our assertion that the "Commentary on the Words of the Text" (*Wenyan* 文言), the "Commentary on the Judgments" (*Tuan* 彖), and the "Commentary on the Images" (*Xiang* 象) would likely have been redacted and embellished by the Si-Meng school—and the "Commentary on the Appended Phrases" also contains elements identified with the school—is mainly based on the following evidence.

It is well known that there were many places referring to *zhong* 中 ("centrality," also rendered "the Mean," "middle," "mid," "center," and so on) in these commentaries. Here are some examples. In the "Commentary on the Words of the Text" for hexagram Qian [☰, The Creative, 1], we can read: "One who has a dragon's virtue and has achieved rectitude and centrality";[cxxxvi] "Nine in the third place signifies a double strength but one that is non-mean";[cxxxvii] "[The originality of Qian is] strong, dynamic, central, and correct."[cxxxviii] In the commentary for hexagram Kun [☷, The Receptive, 2], we can find "The noble man, garbed in yellow and maintaining the Mean. ... Excellence abides within [literally, in the center of] him."[cxxxix]

There were more mentions of *zhong* 中 in the "Commentary on the Judgments" and the "Commentary on the Images." The number of the terms related to "*zhong* 中" in the two commentaries amounts to 29, such as "*zhong zheng* 中正" (centrality and rectitude), "*zheng zhong* 正中" (rectitude and centrality), "*de zhong* 得中" (gaining centrality), "*shi zhong* 时中" (timely centrality), and so on, which are distributed in 36 hexagrams in the former commentary and 43 lines among 38 hexagrams in the latter.

Further scrutiny can enable us to find that all of these hexagram judgments and line statements correlating with *zhong* 中 were pronounced auspicious. Here are several examples. The second line statement in hexagram Qian [☰, The Creative, 1], that "a dragon appears in the fields, it is fitting to see the great man,"[cxl] is a propitious line. The "Commentary on the Words of the Text" accounted for it in this way: "This refers to one who has a dragon's virtue and has achieved *zheng zhong* 正中 (rectitude and centrality)."[cxli] The fifth line statement in hexagram Kun [☷, The Receptive, 2], that "a yellow lower garment means fundamental good fortune,"[cxlii] is also a propitious line, hence the "Commentary on the Words of the Text" and the "Commentary on the Images" told us that the subject of the line had attained to the realm of the Mean.[cxliii] The judgment of hexagram Song 讼 [☲, Contention, 6] is that "In Contention, there should be sincerity. Exercise prudence in handling obstruction. To halt halfway means good fortune. To persist to the end means misfortune. It is fitting to cross the great river."[cxliv] The "Commentary on the Judgments" indicates that it is "the hard line [i.e., the yang line in the second place] which arrives and takes up a middle position" that brings good fortune in the halfway halt, and it is one's "adherence to the Mean and his rectitude" that leads the "fitting to see the great man."[cxlv] Therefore, in the eyes of the authors of these commentaries, all auspicious pronouncements are closely related to "zhong 中".

Actually, however, the idea of valuing the "zhong 中" was not initiated by the authors of these commentaries but inherited from the basic text of the Zhou yi. Except for the above-mentioned judgment for hexagram Song, the following hexagram or line statements also mention the term "zhong 中":

> The second line statement in hexagram Shi 师 [☷, The Army, 7]: "Here in Shi, one practices the Mean, so he has good fortune and so suffers no blame. His sovereign confers a threefold commendation on him."[cxlvi]
>
> The second line statement in hexagram Tai 泰 [☷, Peace, 11]: "One here embraces the uncouth, makes use of those who wade rivers, and does not leave out those who are far away, thus cliques disappear, and he succeeds in being worthy of the practice of centrality [the Mean]."[cxlvii]
>
> The fourth line statement in hexagram Fu 复 [☷, Return, 24]: "It is by traveling a middle course that this one alone returns."[cxlviii]
>
> The third and fourth line statements in hexagram Yi 益 [☴, Increase, 42]: "This one brings about Increase, but if he were to use it to save a bad situation, he should be without blame. He has sincerity, and to report to the duke that he treads the

path of the Mean he uses a *gui* [jade table]"; "If one treads the path of the Mean and so reports to the duke, he shall have his way. It is fitting to rely on such behavior to seek support to move the capital of the state."[cxlix]

The fifth line statement in hexagram Guai 夬 [☱, Resolution, 43]: "The pokeweed is dispatched with perfect Resolution. If this one treads the middle path, he shall be without blame."[cl]

The judgment, and the second and fourth line statements in hexagram Feng 丰 [☲, Abundance, 55]: "Abundance means prevalence, which the true king extends to the utmost. Stay free from worry, and you shall be fit to be a sun at midday [*rizhong* 日中, literally, the sun at the middle position, i.e., its zenith. The same below]"; "This one has his Abundance screened off, so the polar constellation could be seen at midday. If he were to set forth, he would reap doubt and enmity, but if he were to have sincerity and develop accordingly, he should have good fortune"; "This one has his Abundance screened off, so the polar constellation could be seen at midday. He meets a master who is his equal, which means good fortune."[cli]

This idea of the Zhou people was also recounted in the "Complying with the Dao (Way) in Military Affaires" (*Wushun* 武顺) chapter of the *Yi zhoushu* 逸周书 (Lost Book of Zhou), in that "The Dao (Way) of heaven values left and thus the sun and the moon move towards the west; The Dao of earth values right, and thus waters flow to the east; the Dao of man values centrality, and thus ears and eyes are commanded by heart-mind." It also says in the "Thirteenth Year of Duke Cheng" (*Chenggong shisan nian* 成公十三年) (578 B.C.E.) chapter of the *Zuo zhuan* 左传 (Zuo's Commentary on the *Spring and Autumn Annals*): "Liu zi 刘子 (the founding monarch of the State of Liu) says: 'I heard that people were born through receiving the centrality of heaven and earth.'"[clii] Since Liu zi said he "heard," the wording implies there had been this kind of saying before him. The "Fifth Year of Duke Zhao" (*Zhaogong wu nian* 昭公五年) (537 B.C.E.) chapter also mentions that "the sun rises to its middle."

The Zhou people's idea of valuing *zhong* 中 was further affirmed and eulogized by Confucius in the *Analects*. Then, both Zi si and Meng zi held the "Dao (Way) of the Mean" (*zhongdao* 中道) in esteem. In the *Zhong yong* 中庸 (Doctrine of the Mean), the "Mean" was elevated to great importance: "The Mean is the root of the world; harmony is the thorough way under heaven. Once the Mean and harmony are attained, the heaven and earth will be positioned and the myriad things be nourished." (1:4 and 1:5)

As a link in the long chain of this idea, the thought of valuing *zhong* 中 in the Ten Wings can naturally be attributed to the Si-Meng school.

Nonetheless, the terms *zhong* 中 and *zheng* 正 (rectitude) initially might have been the terminologies used in ancient astronomical observation. For example, in hexagram Feng [☰, Abundance, 55], both the judgment and the second and third line statements referred to *rizhong* 日中 ("midday" or "the sun at zenith"). The "Calendrical Book" (*lishu* 历书) chapter of the *Shiji* 史记 (Historical Records) cited from the *Zuo zhuan*: "When ancient kings rectify the time (*zhengshi* 正时, to make calendar), they search for an appropriate day when the sun and the moon have no complementary variations as the beginning [e.g. a Jiazi 甲子 day when the winter solstice just meets its midnight], correct (*zheng* 正) the time of a month to make the *Qi* 气 (material force) in the middle [i.e., not overstepping to the next month], and finally sum the epact into an intercalary month." As Wei Zhao 韦昭 (204-273) annotated, "If the *Qi* conforms with the middle (*zhong* 中) of a month when the moon will be full, the hour, day, dawn and dusk can be rectified (*zheng* 正)." "If the middle Qi (*zhongqi* 中气) appears on the last day of a lunar month, the next month will be an intercalary month; if it appears on the day when the moon is full, it gets its rectitude and middle (*zhengzhong* 正中)."[cliii]

In the "Commentary on the Judgments" and the "Commentary on the Images," the connotations of the "*zhong* 中" vary in different hexagrams. On one hand, the commentaries adopted some materials or terms oriented to astronomical observation by which ancient predecessors interpreted the basic text of the *Zhou yi*, such as in the "Commentary on the Judgments": "The noble man holds in esteem how things ebb and flow, wax and wane, for this is the course of Heaven"[cliv] for hexagram Bo [☰, Peeling, 23]; "This is a particular time when Diminution for the hard and strong [symbolized by *yang* (—) lines(s)] and increase for the soft and weak [symbolized by *yin* (- -) line(s)] takes place. Diminution and increase or waxing and waning take place in tandem with their proper times"[clv] for hexagram Sun 损 [☱☶, Diminution, 41]; "'The Dao that he goes out and comes back on is such that he returns after seven days,' for this is the course of Heaven"[clvi] for hexagram Fu [☷☳, Return, 24]; and "the hard and the soft intersperse among each other and so form a pattern from there, and this is the pattern of Heaven [literally, astronomy]"[clvii] for hexagram Bi 贲 [☶☲, Elegance, 22]; etc. As it says in the commentary for hexagrams Xu [☵☰, Waiting, 5] and Gou 姤 [☰☴, Encounter, 44], "here one abides in the place of Heaven and does so with rectitude and within the Mean (*zhengzhong* 正中)."[clviii] and "when the hard and strong meets the central and the correct (*zhongzheng* 中正), this worldwide process achieves effect under heaven."[clix] Here, the terms *zhengzhong* 正中 and *zhongzheng* 中正 had not lost their initially astronomical implications. On the other hand, in spite of the fact that the "*zhong* 中" in the two commentaries, especially in the "Commentary on the Images," also refers to the position of a line in a hexagram (for a more detailed discussion, see the chapter on "Imagery of the *Changes*"), it was mainly associated with man's moral cultivation. Here are several examples:

> The "Commentary on the Judgments" for hexagram Meng [☶☵, Juvenile Ignorance, 4] indicates: "'Meng brings about prevalence': Meng operates through prevalence and is a matter of timeliness and the Mean [*shizhong* 时中];"[clx] for hexagram Song [☰☵, Contention, 6], it announces: "'It is fitting to see the great man': what one esteems is his adherence to *the Mean and his rectitude* [*zhongzheng* 中正]";[clxi] for hexagram Tongren 同人 [☰☲, Fellowship, 13], it states: "Exercising strength through the practice of civility and enlightenment, they [the second *yin* (--) line and the fifth *yang* (—) line] each respond to the other with their adherence to *the Mean and their uprightness* [*zhongzheng* 中正]: such is the rectitude of the noble man."[clxii]
>
> The "Commentary on the Words of the Text" for hexagram Qian [☰☰, The Creative, 1] states: "It [i.e., Qian] is strong, dynamic, *central, correct* [*zhongzheng* 中正], and it is absolutely pure in its being unadulterated and unsullied."[clxiii]

The "Commentary on the Images" for the second line statement in hexagram Gu 蛊 [䷑, Ills to be Cured, 18] says: "That 'One straightens out misdeeds caused by the mother' indicates that one manages to practice *the Dao of the Mean* [*zhongdao* 中道]."clxiv

The terms "*shizhong* 时中," "*zhongzheng* 中正," and "*zhongdao* 中道" mentioned were also available in the *Zhong yong* 中庸 (Doctrine of the Mean) [which was credited to Zi si 子思 grandson of Confucius]:

> The reason why the noble man is said to be congruent with the Doctrine of the Mean is that his conducts are always in alignment with the Mean [*shizhong* 时中]. (2:2)
> He whose mind is purified and whose conducts conform with the Mean and rectitude [*zhongzheng* 中正] is sufficient to be venerated by others. (31:1)
> Those who are congenitally sincere can follow the Dao of heaven without any effort, can obtain the subtlety of the Dao without thinking, and can naturally be consistent with the Dao of the Mean [*zhongdao* 中道]. These figures are sages. (20:8)

The fact that both the *Doctrine of the Mean* and the commentaries on the judgments and the images highly value "*zhong* 中" demonstrates that they would have originated from the same school.

Careful analysis will help us to find that the "Dao of the Mean" advocated by the Si-Meng school resides concretely in "sincerity" (*cheng* 诚). Guo Moruo 郭沫若 (1892-1978) in the "Critique of the Eight Confucian Schools" (*Rujia ba pai de pipan* 儒家八派的批判) chapter of his *Shi pipan shu* 十批判书 (A Book of Ten Critical Chapters) pointed out that the Si-Meng Confucian school "matched benevolence, righteousness, propriety and wisdom with the 'Dao of Heaven,' which was actually embodied by 'sincerity,' as they upheld that 'Sincerity is the Dao of heaven, pursuing sincerity is the Dao of man, no one who has attained to utmost sincerity fails to move others, and no one who is insincere can be able to move others.' In the *Doctrine of the Mean*, these remarks are expressed in this way: 'Sincerity is the Dao of heaven, attaining to sincerity is the Dao of man, those who are inherently sincere can follow the Dao of heaven without any effort, can obtain the subtlety of the Dao without thinking, and can naturally be in alignment with the Dao of the Mean [zhongdao 中道]. These figures are sages.' (20:8)"[clxv] At the same time, Guo told us that "sincerity refers to the Dao of the Mean [zhongdao 中道]." It therefore can be seen that the "sincerity" esteemed by the Si-Meng school not only embodies the Dao of heaven, but also associates with the Dao of the Mean in the Dao of man.

Bearing this in mind, let us contrast this "sincerity" with the "sincerity" in the "Commentary on the Words of the Text." In this commentary, we can read: "... This refers to one who has a dragon's virtue and has achieved rectitude [zheng 正] and centrality [zhong 中, the Mean]. He is trustworthy in ordinary speech and prudent in ordinary conduct. He wards off depravity and preserves his sincerity. He does good things in the world but does not boast of them. His virtue spreads wide and works transformations. When the *Changes* says, 'when there appears a dragon in the fields, it is fitting to see the great man,' it refers to the virtue of a true sovereign."[clxvi] "The noble man fosters his virtue and cultivates his task. He fosters his virtue by being loyal and trustworthy; he keeps his task in hand by cultivating his words and establishing his sincerity."[clxvii]

Since these remarks concerning "sincerity" aim to explain hexagram Qian [☰, The Creative, 1], which symbolizes heaven, it is evident that "sincerity" here was associated with the Dao of Heaven. Also, "sincerity" here refers to the "virtue of rectitude and centrality" and "being trustworthy in ordinary speech and being prudent in ordinary conduct," these connections seeming to have been composed by the same author who wrote in the *Doctrine of the Mean* about "practicing virtue in ordinary conduct and being prudent in ordinary speech" (13:2). Obviously, the "Commentary on the Words of the Text" also insists on preserving "sincerity" through abiding by the "Dao of the Mean." It therefore can be seen that the "Commentary on the Words of the Text" and the Si-Meng school share the same understandings on "sincerity."

Additionally, the *Doctrine of the Mean* raised the following issue. "There are generally nine strategies for one to regulate a state or the world: cultivating his moral character; venerating the sagacious; loving family members; respecting major ministers; showing consideration for ordinary officials; regarding commoners as his own children; attracting craftsmen; amiably accommodating people from afar; and placating vassals." (20:5) In reading the Ten Wings, we can find that almost all of these items for statecraft are available in the commentaries on the judgments and the images.

The *Doctrine of the Mean* also exposed inclinations for withdrawal from society time and again, such that "The noble man abides by the Mean, and will not regret even if he is unknown to the public over the course of his life. Only the sages are able to attain to this realm."(11) Similarly, in the "Commentary on the Words of the Text," one reads: "… This refers to one who has a dragon's virtue yet remains hidden. He neither changes to suit the world nor seeks fulfillment in fame. He hides from the world but does not regret it, and though this fails to win approval, he is not sad. When he takes delight in the world, he is active in it, and when he finds it distresses him, he turns his back on it. He who is resolute in his unwillingness to be uprooted, this is a submerged dragon."[clxviii] The "Commentary on the Images" for hexagram Daguo 大过 [☰, Major Superiority, 28] also expressed this type of idea: "Though the noble man may stand alone, he does so without fear, and, if he has to withdraw from the world, he remains free from resentment."[clxix]

As Zeng zi 曾子 (505-435 B.C.E.) was the progenitor of the Si-Meng school, the author of the *Doctrine of the Mean* also signaled a disinterest in politics: "The noble man when in a superior position does not bully and oppress his subordinates, when in an inferior position does not fawn up to his superiors. He rectifies his own conduct without excessive demands on others." (14) In the "Commentary on the Appended Phrases," we can read similar remarks, such as: "The noble man is not fawning toward what is above and is not contemptuous of what is below."[clxx]

The affinities between the *Doctrine of the Mean* and the Ten Wings can also be seen in the following remarks. In the former, we have "The noble man learns extensively, inquires thoroughly, ponders prudently, discriminates clearly, and practices devotedly," (20) while we can read in the "Commentary on the Words of the Text" that "The noble man accumulates knowledge by studying and becomes discriminating by posing questions. It is magnanimity that governs his repose, and it is benevolence that guides his action."[clxxi] In the former, we see that "The wise men lesser than the sages tend to devote themselves to a specific virtue (literally, a turn), by which they can also attain to sincerity. Once one has arrived at sincerity, there will be manifestations, manifestations will gradually lead to notability, notability will lead to carrying forward, carrying forward will make others move, making others move will give rise to transformation, transformation will help the myriad things to be nourished. Only those who are of utmost sincerity can nourish the myriad things," (23) whereas in the "Commentary on the Appended Phrases" we can read that the sage "follows every twist and turn of the myriad things and so deals with them without omission"[clxxii] and "The meanings are far-reaching, and the phrasing elegant. The language twists and turns but hits the mark."[clxxiii]

Significantly, one reads in the "Commentary on the Words of the Text" that "The great man is someone whose virtue is consonant with *Heaven* and *Earth*, his brightness with *the sun* and *the moon*, his consistency with the *four seasons*, and his prognostications of the auspicious and inauspicious with the workings of gods and spirits."[clxxiv] In the "Commentary on the Appended Phrases," we read that "In capaciousness and greatness, change corresponds to *Heaven* and *Earth*; in the way change achieves complete fulfillment, change corresponds to the *four seasons*; in terms of the concepts of *yin* and *yang*, change corresponds to *the sun* and *the moon*; and in the efficacy of its ease and simplicity, change corresponds to perfect virtue,"[clxxv] and "Of things that serve as models for images, none are greater than *Heaven* and *Earth*. Of things involving the free flow of change, none is greater than the *four seasons*. Of images that are suspended above and emit brightness, none are greater than *the sun* and *the moon*."[clxxvi] While in the *Doctrine of the Mean*, we can see: "Zhongni's 仲尼 [courtesy name of Confucius] Dao originated from emperors Yao and Shun, modeled upon and promoted the systems formulated by King Wen (*Wen wang* 文王) (1152-1056 B.C.E.) and King Wu (*Wu wang* 武王) (c.1087-1043 B.C.E.). It adapted to the orderly changes of time above and adjusted to the conditions of land below. His virtue is just like *Heaven* and *Earth*, by which all the myriad things are covered and carried. His virtue is also comparable to the alternation of the *four seasons* and illumination of *the sun* and *the moon* in turn." (30)

Obviously, the terms "Heaven," "Earth," "four seasons," "the sun," and "the moon" were unanimously juxtaposed in turn in all of the three texts. The important question is whether this juxtaposition could expose some contents of the Si-Meng school that were criticized by Xun zi 荀子 (c. 313-238 B.C.E.) as "forging the so-called theory of five-agent according to ancient legends."[clxxvii]

In the "Critique of the Eight Confucian Schools" (*Rujia ba pai de pipan* 儒家八派的批判) chapter of his *Shi pipan shu* 十批判书 (A Book of Ten Critical Chapters), Guo Moruo 郭沫若 (1892-1978) cited the "Monthly Ordinances" (*Yue ling* 月令) chapter of the *Liji* 礼记 (Record of Ritual), noting that "*Heaven* takes charge of *yang* and the sun and stars affiliated to it; *Earth* represents *yin* and its orifices open in rivers and mountains; the five agents are spread into the *four seasons*, the harmony of which leads to the emergence of *the moon* (at proper time),"[clxxviii] and attributed this chapter to the Si-Meng school. This paragraph also juxtaposed "Heaven," "Earth," "four seasons" and "the moon." One thing we should not neglect is the "spreading [of] the five agents into the four seasons." Noting that the "Commentary on the Words of the Text," the "Commentary on the Appended Phrases," and the *Doctrine of the Mean* also referred to the "four seasons" with the same orderly sequence as in the "Monthly Ordinances," do the references in question in the former three texts contain the element "spreading the five agents into the four seasons"? Merely because all books of this kind were circulating at that time, the authors of the three texts considered it unnecessary for it to be clearly pointed out.

In conclusion, it is clear that the three commentaries related to the judgments, the images, and the words of the texts in the Ten Wings were redacted and embellished by the Si-Meng school, and that the "Commentary on the Appended Phrases" also contains elements attributed to the school.

3.
Imagery of the *Changes*

From the Spring and Autumn period (770-476 B.C.E.) through the era of Republican China (1912-49) on the mainland, all Chinese scholars had to draw upon images to interpret the basic text of the *Zhou yi*. Even Wang Bi 王弼 (226-249), who was renowned for his position on "sweeping away images" (*shaoxiang* 扫象) in the "Clarifying the Images" (*Mingxiang* 明象) chapter of his *Zhou yi lüeli* 周易略例 (General Remarks on the *Zhou yi*), still admitted that "one can ponder the images and so observe what the ideas are"; "the ideas are yielded up completely by the images, and the images are made explicit by the words."[clxxix] Superficially, Wang Bi seemed not to accept image-numerology, but when he was annotating the basic text of the *Zhou yi*, he placed emphasis on *yin* and *yang* and discriminated line positions, which demonstrated that he was well versed in the Han (206 B.C.E.-25 C.E.) scholars' image-numerological tradition. For example, the fifth line statement of hexagram Tongren 同人 [☰, Fellowship, 13], "For the Fellowship here there is first howling and wailing, but afterward there is laughter, for with the victory of the great army, they manage to meet,"[clxxx] he explained in this way: "Since the fifth line abides in the Mean and is located in this noble position, it is sure to achieve victory in battle. Thus the text says: 'Afterward there is laughter.'"[clxxxi] Additionally, he still applied images to his exegesis. For instance, the "Commentary on the Images" for hexagram Dayou 大有 [☰, Great Holdings, 14] indicates that "Fire on top of Heaven constitutes the image of *Dayou* (Great Holdings). In the same way, the virtuous man suppresses evil and promulgates good, for he obeys the will of Heaven and so brings out the beauty inherent in life." Wang Bi interpreted it such that "*Dayou* (Great Holdings) is an *image* of inclusiveness, thus it deals with the suppression of evil and the promulgation of goodness."[clxxxii] Taken apart from its images, can we ever interpret the *Changes* solely via literary exegesis?

Bearing this question in mind, we can further investigate whether the hexagram and line statements of the *Zhou yi* were derived from the images or had nothing to do with them.

With a thorough reading of the 384 line statements, we discover that when a hexagram is used to symbolize some specific thing, its bottom line statement is always associated with the bottom or rear part of the thing. Here are some examples: 1) The bottom line statement in hexagram Qian [☰, The Creative, 1]: "A submerged [*under water*] dragon does not act";[clxxxiii] 2) in hexagram Kun [☷, The Receptive, 2]: "The frost one treads [i.e., the image of *ground*] on reaches its ultimate stage as solid ice";[clxxxiv] 3) in hexagram Lü 履 [☰, Treading, 10]: "If one treads [image of *ground*] with simplicity, to set forth will bring no blame";[clxxxv] 4) in hexagram Tai [☰, Peace, 11]: "When one pulls up the rush plant [from the root], it pulls up others of the same kind together with it, so if one goes forth and acts, there will be good fortune";[clxxxvi] 5) in hexagram Shihe 噬嗑 [☰, Bite Together, 21]: "Made to wear whole foot shackles, his *toes* are destroyed, but he will be without blame";[clxxxvii] 6) in hexagram Bi [☰, Elegance, 22]: "He furnishes his *toes* with Elegance, discards carriage, and goes on foot";[clxxxviii] 7) in hexagram Bo [☷, Peeling, 23]: "The bedstead has suffered Peeling from the *base*; so does constancy meet with destruction. This means misfortune";[clxxxix] 8) in hexagram Daguo [☰, Major Superiority, 28]: "Use white rushes for a mat [on the *ground*], and one will be without blame";[cxc] 9) in hexagram Kan 坎 [☵, The Constant Sink Hole, 29]: "one falls into the abyss at the bottom, and this means misfortune";[cxci] 10) in hexagram Li [☲, Cohesion, 30]: "This one treads [image of *ground*] with reverence and care. As he takes it seriously, there will be no blame";[cxcii] 11) in hexagram Xian [☰, Reciprocity, 31]: "Reciprocity is in the *big toe*";[cxciii] 12) in hexagram Dun 遯 [☰, Withdrawal, 33]: "There is danger here at the *tail* of Withdrawal, so do not use this as an opportunity to go forth";[cxciv] 13) in hexagram Dazhuang 大壮 [☳, Great Strength, 34]: "Here strength resides in the *toes*, so to go forth and act would mean misfortune, in this one should be confident";[cxcv] 14) in hexagram Guai [☰, Resolution, 43]: "This one put his strength into his advancing *toes*, went forth but was not victorious, and so incurs blame";[cxcvi] 15) in hexagram Kun 困 [☱, Impasse, 47]: "This one suffers Impasse in the buttocks here on the *root* of the tree, so he enters a secluded *valley* and does not appear for three years";[cxcvii] 16) in hexagram Jing 井 [☵, The Well, 48]: "As the Well here is fouled with mud [an image of the *bottom* of the well], one should not partake of it. At such an old Well there are no birds";[cxcviii] 17) in hexagram Ding 鼎 [☲, The Cauldron, 50]: "The Caldron has its *toes* turned upward here, for it is fitting that any obstruction be expelled. One acquires a concubine for the sake of her son, so there is no blame";[cxcix] 18) in hexagram Gen 艮 [☶, Restraint, 52]: "Restraint takes place with the *toes*, so there is no blame, and it is fitting that such a one practices perpetual constancy";[cc] 19) in hexagram Jiji [☵, Ferrying Complete, 63]: "This one drags his *wheels* and wets his *tail*, so there is no blame";[cci] 20) in hexagram Weiji 未济 [☲, Ferrying Incomplete, 64]: "This one gets his *tail* wet, which means humiliation."[ccii] The italicized terms in the line statements mentioned above are reminiscent of the image of the lower or rear part of a thing or man[1].

On the other hand, when symbolizing a thing, the top line statement of a hexagram is always associated with the top or upper part of the thing. Examples include: 1) the top line statement in hexagram Qian [☰, The Creative, 1]: "A dragon that *overreaches* should have cause for regret";[cciii] 2) in hexagram Bi 比 [☵, Closeness, 8]: "One who joins in Closeness here lacked the means to follow a *head*, so he will have misfortune";[cciv] 3) in hexagram *Dayou* [☲, Great Holdings, 14]: "*Heaven* will help him as a matter of course; this is good fortune, and nothing will fail to be fitting";[ccv] 4) in hexagram Shihe [☲, Bite Together, 21]: "Made to bear a cangue, his *ears* are destroyed, and this means misfortune";[ccvi] 5) in hexagram

---

[1] All the italics are from the author and translator. So it is with those in similar cases in the following paragraphs.

Daxu [☰, Great Domestication, 26]: "What is the Highway of *Heaven* but prevalence";[ccvii] 6) in hexagram Daguo [☰, Major Superiority, 28]: "If one tries to ford across here, he will submerge his *head*, and there will be misfortune, no other one should be blamed";[ccviii] 7) in hexagram Xian [☰, Reciprocity, 31]: "Reciprocity is in the *jowls*, *cheeks*, and *tongue*";[ccix] 8) in hexagram Jin [☰, Advance, 35]: "This one has advanced to the *top* [literally, *horn*], so now all he can do is attack the city. Although there will be danger, [as he has recognized it and will be cautious to prevent its occurrence,] he shall have good fortune and so will have no blame, there will be a distress if he keeps still";[ccx] 9) in hexagram Jie 解 [☰, Release, 40]: "The duke uses this opportunity to shoot at a hawk located *atop a high wall*, so he gets it, and nothing fails to be fitting";[ccxi] 10) in hexagram Gou [☰, Encounter, 44]: "Here one encounters the *horns*, and, though there will be distress, it does not incur blame";[ccxii] 11) in hexagram Ding [☰, The Cauldron, 50]: "The Cauldron has jade *lifters*, which means great good fortune and that nothing will fail to be fitting";[ccxiii] 12) in hexagram Lü 旅 [☰, The Wanderer, 56]: "The birds get its *nest* burnt. The Wanderer first laughs and then later howls and wails. He loses his ox in a time of ease, which means misfortune";[ccxiv] 13) in hexagram Zhongfu 中孚 [☰, Inner Trust, 61]: "This one's high flying sound climbs up to *Heaven*, but he should have misfortune even though he tries to practice constancy";[ccxv] 14) in hexagram Jiji [☰, Ferrying Complete, 63]: "This one gets his *head* wet, which means danger";[ccxvi] 15) in hexagram Weiji 未济 [☰, Ferrying Incomplete, 64]: "This one has confidence and so engages in drinking wine, about which there is no blame, but he might get his *head* wet, for this one with his confidence could do violence to what is right."[ccxvii] It is evident that all of the italic words in these line statements remind us of the image with focus on the top or upper part of a thing or man.

I contend that this phenomenon occurring in the basic text is not a coincidence.

Let us further examine how the images change from the bottom to the top lines when a hexagram symbolizes an object or a body. For example, we can view the spatial order in line statements from the bottom to the top in hexagram Xian [☰, Reciprocity, 31], which takes a nearby human body as the object:

Line 1 [at the bottom]: Reciprocity is in the big toe.
Line 2: Reciprocity is in the calf of the leg.
Line 3: Reciprocity is in the thigh.
Line 4: You pace back and forth in consternation, and friends follow your thoughts [i.e., reciprocity is in the heart-mind].
Line 5: Reciprocity is in the upper back.
Line 6 [at the top]: Reciprocity is in the jowls, cheeks, and tongue.

We can also see this feature in the line statements in hexagram Qian [☰, The Creative, 1], which adopts a far-off dragon as its object:

Line 1: A dragon is submerged.
Line 2: A dragon can be seen in a field.
Line 4: A dragon jumps in the depths.
Line 5: A dragon flies in the skies.
Line 6: A dragon is in loftiness.

It is evident that the position of the dragon, from the bottom line to the top line, goes upward. Hexagrams Bo [☷, Peeling, 23] and Gen [☶, Restraint, 52] are also characterized by this kind of correspondence.

Based on these features, the "Commentary on the Appended Phrases" (*Xici* 系辞) concludes: "The *Changes* as such consist of *images*";[ccxviii] "The judgments address the *images*";[ccxix] "The sages established *images* in order to express their ideas exhaustively. They established the hexagrams in order to treat exhaustively the true innate tendency of things and their counter tendencies to spuriousness";[ccxx] "When the eight trigrams formed ranks, the [basic] *images* were present there within them."[ccxxi] And the commentary particularly points out: "The sages set down the hexagrams, observed the *images*, and appended phrases to the lines."[ccxxii]

We believe these remarks are reasonable. At the same time, the author of the commentary mentions twice that "the sages had the means to perceive the mysteries of the world and, drawing comparisons to them with analogous things, made images out of those things that seemed appropriate."[ccxxiii] The authors of the *Zhou yi* might have appended the hexagram and line statements just after they had observed the images. These judgments and statements might have been derived as a simulacrum of things, or from the tendencies of things, so that when we read the basic text of the *Zhou yi,* we can frequently find that the pronouncements may shift suddenly from "auspicious" to "inauspicious." For this reason, some hexagram judgments and line statements are so confusing that it is really difficult to discern a logical fit. Since the methods of how the sages applied these analogical correlations in detail have been lost, though a great number of later-generation scholars have engaged in many discussions about the imagery of the *Zhou yi*, most of their arguments have lapsed into far-fetched analogies. Therefore, today when we interpret the basic text of the *Zhou yi*, the correlation between the images and the hexagram and line statements asserted by ancient scholars should neither be utterly discarded nor be totally adopted. If we totally adopt their image-numerological approaches and search for the long-lost meaning of images, providing ourselves with justification by dividing the images to accommodate the basic text, we will inevitably be trapped in a dilemma already experienced by ancient scholars. On the other hand, when interpreting the basic text, if we thoroughly disapprove of the correlation between the images and the hexagram and line statements, and deny the traditional image-numerological hermeneutics, we are also not adopting an attitude that faces up to the facts of the matter, either.

My view is that the hexagram and line statements were originally derived from the composers' "observing the images," but the methods of how they took these images were forgotten long ago. Therefore, when explicating the basic text, we should primarily depend on literary exegesis while also taking references from some images obviously available in the text. In the meantime, we should also know the outline of the imagery employed by the scholars from the Spring and Autumn period on to the Han dynasty.

There are many ways to comprehend the images.

According to Huang Zongxi's 黃宗羲 (1610-95) *Yixue xiangshu lun* 易学象数论 (Discussion of Image-numerology in the *Changes* Scholarship), the images can be divided into seven kinds: 1) eight-trigram images; 2) six-line images; 3) directional images; 4) pictographic images; 5) line-position images; 6) overlapping (*huti* 互体, also rendered "nuclear") images; and 7) inverted images.[ccxxiv]

1) Eight-trigram images (*bagua zhi xiang* 八卦之象). The eight-trigram images refer to the symbolic associations of the eight trigrams illustrated in the "Discussion of the Trigrams"[ccxxv] redacted by scholars of the Warring States period (475-221 B.C.E.). Though the "Discussion of the Trigrams" has been dated back to the Warring States period, its origin must have been rather earlier than the date of its composition. As early as the Spring and Autumn times (770-476 B.C.E.), scholars had been very conversant with these images by which to analyze the *Zhou yi*. Here are some examples. In *Zuo zhuan* 左传 (Zuo's Commentary on the *Spring and Autumn Annals*), the chapter of "Twenty Second Year of Duke Zhuang" (672 B.C.E.) (*Zhuanggong ershier nian* 庄公二十二年) records: "Marquis Chen had the history recorder of Zhou consult the milfoil divination regarding the future of his son who had been just born, [and after he had obtained hexagram Guan [☷☴] transforming into hexagram Pi [☷☰],] the recorder said: 'Kun [☷] means earth, Xun [☴] wind, and Qian [☰] heaven.'"[ccxxvi] In the "Fifth Year of Duke Zhao" (537 B.C.E.) (*Zhaogong wu nian* 昭公五年), we read: "Zhuangshu 庄叔 had consulted the *Zhou yi* by means of milfoil stalks [and he encountered hexagram Jin [☷☲] changing into hexagram Qian [☶☲],] [...] [the diviner] said: 'Li [☲] means fire and Gen [☶] mountain."[ccxxvii] Also, as it is recorded in the *Guo yu* 国语 (Sayings of the States): "[When he encountered hexagram Zhun [☵☳] turning into hexagram Yu [☳☷],] Sikong Jizi 司空季子 (657-570 B.C.E.) explained: 'Zhen [☳] means chariot, Kan [☵] water, and Kun [☷] earth."[ccxxviii]

According to these records in the *Zuo zhuan* and the *Guo yu*, the images of the eight trigrams correspond rather closely to those illustrated in the "Discussion of the Trigrams," which demonstrates that, in the Spring and Autumn period or earlier, these images had been applied to the explanations of the *Zhou yi*, and the images of the eight trigrams in the "Discussion of the Trigrams" were no more than a product of later generations' scholars' redaction and summarization. Through the Han dynasty, some scholars further added many "lost images" (*yixiang* 逸象), which further amplified the contents of the "Discussion of the Trigrams" related to images. We will not, however, illustrate these "lost images" in detail here.

2) Six-line images (*liuhua zhi xiang* 六画之象). The six-line images refer to the 64 hexagrams, each of which resulted from the doubling of two trigrams. The six-line image includes the inner and outer, or lower and upper, trigrams. According to the records of the *Zuo zhuan* and the *Guo yu*, people of the Spring and Autumn era (770-476 B.C.E.) called the inner trigram "*zhen* 贞" (lit, constancy) and the upper one "*hui* 悔" (remorse). This type of image is formed with the six lines from the bottom to the top in a hexagram. According to the "Commentary on the Appended Phrases" and the "Discussion of the Trigrams," the six lines were divided into "three powers" of Heaven, Earth, and Man. As it states in the former commentary, "As a book, the *Changes* is something which is broad and great, complete in every way. There is the Dao of Heaven in it, the Dao of Man in it, and the Dao of Earth in it. It brings these three powers together and then doubles them. This is the reason for there being six lines. What these six embody is nothing other than the Dao of the three powers."[ccxxix] In the latter discussion, we can read: "In the distant past, the way the sages made the *Changes* is as follows: It was to be used as a means to stay in accord with principles of nature and fate. It was for this reason that they determined what the Dao of Heaven was, which they defined in terms of *yin* and *yang*, what the Dao of Earth was, which they defined in terms of hard and soft, and what the Dao of Man was, which they defined in terms of benevolence and righteousness. They brought these three powers together and doubled them; this is why in the *Changes* hexagrams are formed out of six lines. They provided *yin* allotments and *yang* allotments, so their functions alternate between soft and hard; this is why the *Changes* forms its patterns out of six positions."[ccxxx]

Based on these materials, the Han scholars divided the six lines into three parts: The fifth and the top lines correspond to Heaven; the third and fourth lines to Man; the bottom and the second lines to Earth. Additionally, the various positions were assigned with *yin* or *yang* attributes: The bottom, the third, and the fifth lines belong to *yang* positions, while the other three lines are attributed to *yin* positions. If a *yang* line (—) occupies a *yang* position, or a yin line (- -) occupies a *yin* position, it is said to be "gaining a correct position" (*dezheng* 得正) or "matching its position" (*dewei* 得位), indicating auspiciousness. If a *yin* line (--) occupies a *yang* position, or a *yang* line (—) occupies a *yin* position, it is considered to be in an "incorrect position" (*buzheng* 不正) or "losing a correct position" (*shiwei* 失位), indicating inauspiciousness. This concept might derive from the Han scholars' far-fetched analogy, as in the 64 hexagrams, only in hexagram Jiji [䷾, Ferrying Complete, 63] do all lines gain their correct positions, which ought to result in unparalleled auspiciousness; but its judgment pronounces that "things might end in inauspiciousness."[ccxxxi] Therefore, in the eyes of the authors of the *Zhou yi*, the world is ever-changing and transforming, as it says in the "Commentary on the Appended Phrases": "when one process (of the Dao [Way] of change) reaches its limit, a change from one state to another occurs, [and] as such, change achieves free flow,"[ccxxxii] and "as a manifestation of the Dao the *Changes* involves frequent shifts. Change and action never stand fixed but keep flowing all through the six positions."[ccxxxiii] Thus, there is not any fixed "gaining a position" in the world at all.

In addition to the above-mentioned divisions and assignations, the Han scholars, when explicating the basic text of the *Zhou yi*, also held that there existed relationships called "yielding" (*cheng* 承), "mounting" (*cheng* 乘), "adjacent" (*bi* 比), "response" (*ying* 应), "basing" (*ju* 据), and "middle" (*zhong* 中) between the lines in a hexagram. In imperial times, the scholars interpreting the text could not help but apply these relationships to their analyses of the images in each hexagram.

The concept of "yielding" (*cheng* 承) means that, in a hexagram, if under a *yang* line (—) is a *yin* line (--), the latter is taken to be yielding to the former. For example, in hexagram Kan [䷜], the fourth line is a *yin* line and the fifth line is a *yang* line and, according to ancient scholars, the relationship between them is interpreted as the fourth line yielding to the fifth. Similarly, in this same hexagram, the bottom line also yields to the second line. For another example, reference hexagram Jing [䷯], where the bottom line yields to the second line and the fourth line to the fifth.

We can take a piece of Yu Fan's 虞翻 (162-233) annotations to see how an ancient scholar interpreted the *Changes* in view of this sort of relationship. For the second line statement of hexagram Sui 随 [䷐, Following, 17], that "this one ties itself to the little child and loses the mature man,"[ccxxxiv] Yu Fan explained: "It [i.e., the second line] yields to the fourth line but the third line is in the way, so this one lost the mature man."[ccxxxv] He means that, in this hexagram, the second line is a *yin* line that yields to the fourth line, which is a *yang* line and symbolizes a mature man. But the third line is in the way between the second line and the fourth line, and thus the one symbolized by the second line loses the mature man. For another example, for the fifth line statement of hexagram Gu 蠱 [☶☴, Ills to be Cured, 18] that "One who here straightens out Ills to be Cured caused by the father thereby gains a fine reputation,"[ccxxxvi] the *Zhou yi jijie* 周易集解 (Collected Explanations of the *Zhou yi*) cited Xun Shuang's 荀爽 (128-190) annotations: "It [the fifth line] yields to the top *yang* line which symbolizes solidity and steadfastness. To do work with this spirit is a way to gain a fine reputation."[ccxxxvii]

According to ancient scholars' analysis of the images, if there is a *yin* line under several *yang* lines in a hexagram, the *yin* line will be referred to as yielding to all the *yang* lines above it. In hexagram Gou [☰☴], for instance, the bottom *yin* line yields to the other five *yang* lines. Similarly, if several *yin* lines are under a *yang* line in a hexagram, it will mean that all these *yin* lines yield to the *yang* line. For example, for the bottom line statement of hexagram Qian [☷☶, Modesty, 15] that "the noble man is modest and modest [i.e., has utmost modesty],"[ccxxxviii] Xun Shuang accounted for the relationship in this way: "The bottom signifies 'modest,' [and the fact] that the two *yin* lines yield to the third *yang* line also reflects 'modest,' hence [leads to] the 'modest and modest.' The two *yin* lines [i.e., the bottom and the second lines] and the third *yang* line constitute one entity [i.e., trigram Gen ☶], hence the reference of 'noble man.'"[ccxxxix]

In some cases, the relationship between two *yin* lines or two *yang* lines was also called "yielding." For example, for the fourth line statement of hexagram Lü [☰☱, Treading, 10] that "One treads on the tiger's tail, he is carefully cautious, so that in the end he will have good fortune," Wang Bi 王弼 (226-249) explained: "This line is right next to the most noble line [fifth *yang*]. As a *yang* line [the fourth] that yields to another *yang* line [the fifth], it is located at a place that inspires much caution, hence the statement."[ccxl]

Thus, the scholars from the Han dynasty onward applied the term "yielding" in this way to their interpretations of the *Changes*. These analyses might not conform to the original intent of the *Zhou yi*, however; and, moreover, they advance many far-fetched claims.

The concept of "mounting" (*cheng* 乘) means that, in a hexagram, if a *yin* line is immediately above a *yang* line, it is said that the *yin* line is mounting upon the *yang* line. For instance, in hexagram Bi [☷☵], the top *yin* line mounts upon the fifth *yang* line. Similarly, in hexagram Tai [☷☰], the fourth *yin* line mounts upon the third *yang* line. Now let us take a look at how the ancient scholars analyze the basic text with this rule. For the second line statement in hexagram Zhun 屯 [☵☳, Birth Throes, 3] that "... the one rides on [literally, mounts upon] a horse which is yoked ...,"[ccxli] Yu Fan 虞翻 (162-233) explained: "... Zhen [☳] symbolizes horse and foot, the second line mounts upon the bottom line, hence the words of 'mounting upon a horse,' ..."[ccxlii] and he accounted for the top line statement of this hexagram in the same way.

In a hexagram, if several *yin* lines are above a *yang* line, these *yin* lines are referred to as mounting upon the *yang* line. For example, for the fifth line statement of hexagram Qian [☷☶, Modesty, 15] that "This one is not wealthy on account of [his sharing his wealth with] his neighbors [...],"[ccxliii] Xun Shuang 荀爽 (128-190) thought that here the word "neighbors" refers to the fourth and the top lines; all the three lines from the fourth to the top mount upon the *yang* line (the third line) and are not solid, symbolizing "not wealthy," as generally expressed in the fifth line, which is in the middle position (of the upper trigram).[ccxliv]

Sometimes a *yin* line directly above a *yin* line is also called "mounting," as Yu Fan (162-233) ascribed the fourth line statement "riding on a horse which is yoked" in hexagram Zhun [☵☳, Birth Throes] to its "mounting upon the third [*yin*] line."[ccxlv]

The concept of "adjacent" (*bi* 比) refers to the relationship between two neighboring lines. Yu Fan used to apply this concept to his annotations. For example, the fourth line statement of hexagram Bi [☵☷, Closeness, 8] that "Here one joins in Closeness in the outer. Constancy results in good fortune," Yu Fan explained in the following way. "It [i.e., the fourth line] is in the outer trigram, hence the term 'outer'; it gains its position and is adjacent to the sage [symbolized by the fifth line], hence the good fortune resulted from constancy."[ccxlvi] For the "Small Image Commentary" on the second line of hexagram Kan [☵☵, The

Constant Sink Hole, 29] noting that "'This one may pursue his aim and will gain small achievements,' as he has not yet found his way out from inside," Xun Shuang (128-190) explains: "It [the second line] is in the midst [of the lower trigram] and adjacent to the bottom line."[ccxlvii] Wang Bi explained the fourth line statement of hexagram Jie [☳, Release, 40]—"Release your big toe, for a friend will come and then place trust in you"—like this: "It [the fourth *yang* line] loses its correct position [which ought to be a *yin* line in this position] and is adjacent to the third *yin* line, which is thus attached to it [the fourth line], becomes its big toe."[ccxlviii] There are many examples of this sort in Wang Bi's commentaries on the *Changes*.

So far as "response" (*ying* 应) is concerned, as the "Qianzaodu" 乾凿度 (Opening Up the Regularities of the [Hexagram] Qian) chapter of the *Yi wei* 易纬 (Apocrypha of the *Changes*) states, "The three lines of the lower trigram in a hexagram symbolize earth and those of the upper trigram heaven." "If the bottom line moves, the fourth line will respond; if the second line moves, the fifth line will respond; if the third line moves, the top line will respond."[ccxlix] In other words, in the eyes of the Han scholars, in a hexagram there exist relationships called "responses" between the bottom and the fourth lines, between the second and the fifth lines, and between the third and the top lines. For instance, in hexagram Pi [☷], the bottom line responds to the fourth line, the second to the fifth, and the third to the top.

Now I can demonstrate how the Han scholars employed this concept for their analysis of the *Changes*. For the bottom line statement of hexagram Lin 临 [☷, Overseeing, 19] that "This one approaches [to the others] with an attitude of influence, and constancy means good fortune,"[ccl] Yu Fan explained: "[As a *yang* line, the bottom line] gains a correct position and responds to the fourth line, hence constancy will result in good fortune."[ccli] The second line statement of hexagram Da you [☰, Great Holdings, 14] indicates: "As there is a great wagon to carry things, one should set forth, for there will be no blame."[cclii] Yu Fan accounted for it in this way: "The second *yang* line loses its position; if it transforms into its opposite [i.e., a *yin* line], it will gain a correct position and respond to the fifth line, hence there will be no blame when one sets forth."[ccliii] For the judgment of hexagram Kui 睽 [☱, Contrariety, 38] that "In small matters there is good fortune," Zheng Xuan 郑玄 (127-200)

interpreted: "The second line and the fifth respond to each other, but the sovereign [symbolized by the fifth line where there ought to be a *yang* line] is a *yin* line while the subordinate [symbolized by the second line which ought to a *yin* line] is a *yang* line, thus good fortune can only occur in small matters."[ccliv]

Another concept is "basing" (*ju* 据). In a hexagram, if a *yang* line is immediately above a *yin* line, the *yang* line will be described as being "based upon" the *yin* line. For example, in the case of hexagram Weiji [☲], the second line is referred to as based upon the bottom line. In interpreting the second line statement of hexagram Meng [☶, Juvenile Ignorance, 4], Yu Fan noted that the second line "responds to the fifth line and bases itself upon the bottom line."[cclv] In accounting for the top line statement of hexagram Shihe [☲, Bite Together, 21], Xun Shuang told us that the top line "bases itself upon the fifth line and responds to the third line."[cclvi]

In the application of "basing" to the analysis of the images, there is another case to be attended to, as well. In a hexagram, if there is only one *yang* line and this *yang* line is in the upper trigram, this *yang* line can also be described as basing itself upon the other five *yin* lines. For example, in interpreting the fourth line statement of hexagram Yu 豫 [☷, Contentment, 16] that "All others follow this one and obtain contentment in great measure," Yu Fan noted: "[The fourth line] bases itself upon and obtains the other five *yin* lines, and [the inner trigram] Kun [☷] symbolizes multitude and compliance, hence the remarks of the statement."[cclvii]

The so-called "middle" (*zhong* 中) was also referred to as "residing in the middle" (*juzhong* 居中), "gaining the middle" (*dezhong* 得中), and "being located at the middle" (*chuzhong* 处中) by the scholars from the Han period onward. It generally refers to the second line and the fifth line in a hexagram (with some exceptions), as the former is in the "middle" of the inner trigram and the latter in the "middle" of the outer. For instance, in hexagram Xu [☵], both the second and the fifth lines are called "gaining the middle" or "being located at the middle." For the second line statement of hexagram Lin [☷, Overseeing, 19] that "This one approaches [the others] with an attitude of influence, which means good fortune such that nothing fails to be fitting," Yu Fan explained the relationship in the following way: "[The second line] gains the middle and thus can obtain more reputations, hence the remarks of the statement."[cclviii] In interpreting the fifth line statement of hexagram Guan 观 [☷☴, Viewing, 20] that "Here one's Viewing is of his own activity and nature, the noble man shall be without blame,"[cclix] Yu Fan ascribed the noble man's being without blame to the line's "gaining the Dao and being located at the middle."[cclx]

We will inevitably encounter concepts of "yielding," "mounting," "adjacent," "response," "basing," and "middle" when we read the commentaries on the *Changes* beginning in the Han dynasty.

3) Directional images (*fangwei zhi xiang* 方位之象). "Directional images" refer to the eight directions symbolized by the eight trigrams. Namely, Qian [☰] corresponds to the northwest, Kan [☵] to the north, Gen [☶] to the northeast, Zhen [☳] to the east, Xun [☴] to the southeast, Li [☲] to the south, Kun [☷] to the southwest, and Dui [☱] to the west. These images were accounted for in the "Discussion of the Trigrams": "The myriad things come forth in Zhen; Zhen [☳] corresponds to the east. They are set in order in Xun; Xun [☴] corresponds to the southeast. … Li [☲] here means brightness. That the myriad things are made visible to one another here signifies that this is the trigram of the south. [...] Qian [☰] here is the trigram of the northwest. … Gen [☶] is the trigram of the northeast."[cclxi]

By the Song dynasty (960-1279), the "directional images" were also divided into the "prior to heaven (*xiantian* 先天) directions" and "posterior to heaven (*houtian* 后天) directions." The directions mentioned above were pegged to the latter. According to the Song scholars' views, in the former, Qian [☰] corresponds to the south and Kun [☷] to the north; Li [☲] to the east and Kan [☵] to the west; Zhen [☳] to the northeast and Xun [☴] to the southwest; Gen [☶] to the northwest and Dui [☱] to the southeast. The provenance of the "prior to heaven directions" will be taken up in other chapters of this book and will not here be introduced in detail.

4) Pictographic images (*xiangxing zhi xiang* 像形之象). What is a pictographic image? Let us take hexagram Ding [☲☴, The Cauldron, 50] as an example. The name of this hexagram might be derived from its structure, which is a simulacrum of a cauldron. We can see that the bottom line is like the feet; the second, third, and fourth lines the belly; the fifth line the ears; and the top line the lifters (or cap) of a cauldron.

The names of other hexagrams such as Yi 颐 [☲☳, Nourishment, 27], Shihe [☲☳, Bite Together, 21], and Jie [☲☳, Control, 60] might also be derived from pictographic images, respectively.

5) Line-position images (*yaowei zhi xiang* 爻位之象). For the line-position images, according to the "Qianzaodu" 乾凿度 (Opening Up the Regularities of the [Hexagram] Qian) chapter of the *Yi wei* 易纬 (Apocrypha of the *Changes*), in a hexagram, the bottom line represents gentlemen beginning their official careers (*yuanshi* 元士), the second line grand masters (*dafu* 大夫), the third line the three dukes (*sangong* 三公), the fourth line feudal lords (*zhuhou* 诸侯), the fifth line the Son of Heaven (*tianzi* 天子), and the top line the ancestral temple (*zongmiao* 宗庙). Thus, in the six lines of a hexagram, the most important one is the fifth line. Zheng Xuan 郑玄 (127-200) and Yu Fan 虞翻 (164-233) used to apply this idea to their explanations of the *Changes*. This set of correlations, however, was mostly employed in the divinations and was not of specific significance to the exegesis of the basic text of the *Zhou yi*.

6) Overlapping images, or nuclear trigrams (*huti zhi xiang* 互体之象). Nuclear trigrams or hexagrams were frequently applied to the explanations of the *Changes* and occupied a relatively significant position in the Han scholars' works on the *Changes*. I will discuss this idea in some detail.

In a hexagram, besides the primary upper and lower trigrams, the second, the third, and the fourth line can form a new trigram, and so it is with the third, the fourth, and the fifth line. These trigrams—resulting from the reconstitution from the second to the fourth, or from the third to the fifth, lines in a hexagram—were called overlapping trigrams or overlapping images. For example, in hexagram Kan [☲☳], aside from the two identical primary trigrams of Kan [☵], line 2, line 3, and line 4 can constitute a new trigram called Zhen [☳]; and similarly, line 3, line 4, and line 5 can form a new trigram referred to as Gen [☶]. In this way, trigrams Zhen [☳] and Gen [☶] are formed through the overlapping of the intermediary lines of the hexagram. In the same way, in hexagram Meng [☲☳], in addition to the two primary trigrams of Kan [☵] and Gen [☶], the second, the third, and the fourth lines can form the trigram Zhen [☳], and the third, the fourth, and the fifth lines the trigram Kun [☷]. In this way, up to four trigrams are included in a hexagram.

As mentioned above, ancient scholars contended that all of the hexagram and line statements of the *Zhou yi* were grounded upon the images, and although some statements did not come from the primary trigrams, they might be found in the overlapping images. For example, the second line statement of hexagram Zhun [☳☵, Birth Throes, 3] states, "… the maid practices constancy at her chastity and refuses to be engaged. Only after ten years will she accept the engagement."[cclxii] In this hexagram, the inner trigram Zhen [☳], according to the "Discussion of the Trigrams," symbolizes the eldest son, and the outer trigram Kan [☵] the middle son, [neither of which has connections with the term "maid" in the statement,] while the second, the third, and the fourth lines can form trigram Kun [☷], which symbolizes female, hence the term "maid" in the statement. Take another example, as stated in the second line statement of hexagram Yu [☷☳, Contentment, 16], "Harder than rock, he does not let the day run its course. Constancy means good fortune."[cclxiii] In this hexagram, neither of the primary trigrams of Kun [☷] and Zhen [☳] has the image of "rock" mentioned in the statement, yet the trigram Gen [☶] as derived from the overlapping of the second, the third, and the fourth lines has the image of "rock." Similarly, the term "ear" appearing in the top line statement of hexagram Shihe [☲☳, Bite Together, 21] that "Made to bear a cangue, his ears are covered, this means misfortune" was also derived from the image of Kan [☵] as it resulted from the overlapping of line 3, line 4, and line 5.

Scholars from the Han dynasty onward in this way employed the overlapping images to search for the derivation of some terms in the hexagram and line statements. This kind of analysis also contains some far-fetched elements and is not always cogent.

Although the term "overlapping images" (*huxiang* 互象) was first seen in the legacy of Jing Fang 京房 (77-37 B.C.E.), this concept was also transmitted by the Eastern Han (25-220) and Jin (265-420) scholars. Its origin must have occurred long before, in that it could be attributed to the ancient divinatory tradition, traced back to before Tian He 田何 (fl. c. 200 B.C.E.), who was a progenitor in transmitting the *Changes* from the foundation of the Western Han dynasty (206 B.C.E.-9 C.E.). As recorded in the "Twenty-second Year of Duke Zhuang" (672 B.C.E.) chapter of the *Zuo zhuan* 左传 (Zuo's Commentary on the *Spring and Autumn Annals*), "Marquis Chen had the recorder of Zhou consult the milfoils about the boy. On encountering hexagram Guan [☷☴, Viewing, 20] transforming into Pi [☷☰, Obstruction, 12], the recorder said: 'It is called "Viewing the culture and customs [literally, lights], so it is fitting that this one be guest to the king [...], Kun [☷] means earth, Xun [☴] wind, and Qian [☰] heaven. Wind [☴] [the upper trigram of the original hexagram] turns into heaven [☰] [the upper trigram of the derivative hexagram] above earth [☷], it is Mountain."'[cclxiv] According to Du Yu's 杜预 (222-285) annotation, the last word, "mountain," refers to the trigram Gen [☶] formed by the second, the third, and the fourth lines of the transformed hexagram Pi [☷☰]. Du Yu's annotation is pertinent, as without the trigram Gen [☶] formed by overlapping the lines, how can we account for the term "mountain" in the statement? (See also the detailed analysis in Chapter 6, "Divinatory Cases in the *Zuo zhuan* 左传 and the *Guo yu* 国语.")

In the meantime, in the "Commentary on the Appended Phrases" we can read that "as for complicated matters, the calculation of the virtues and the determination of the rights and wrongs involved could not be complete without the middle lines [i.e., the lines from the second to the fifth]"; and "the second and the fourth lines involve the same kind of merit but differ as to positions, [...] the third and the fifth lines involve the same kind of merit but differ as to positions."[cclxv] In the "Discussion of the Trigrams" we read, "they provided *yin* allotments and *yang* allotments, and used *yin* and *yang* time and again."[cclxvi] These remarks likely refer to the "overlapping images." If not, how can it "not be complete without the middle lines" and how can the second and the fourth lines, or the third and the fifth lines, "involve the same kind of merit"? The term "time and again" is particularly reminiscent of this idea. Granted, these remarks may not be taken as sufficient to prove the argument that "overlapping images" had been mentioned in the two commentaries, yet it can be affirmed that, as early as the Spring and Autumn period, scholars had applied "overlapping images" to their analysis of the hexagrams.

The Eastern Han scholars also had a concept of "consecutive overlapping" (*lianhu* 连互) defined by taking the two primary trigrams and the two overlapping trigrams together in order to derive more hexagrams through consecutive overlapping. This method is divided into two kinds:

five-line consecutive overlapping (*wuhua lianhu* 五画连互) and four-line consecutive overlapping (*sihua lianhu* 四画连互).

A "five-line consecutive overlapping" refers to taking, in a hexagram, the lines from the bottom to the fifth to form a new hexagram and taking those from the second to the top to constitute another new hexagram. Take hexagram Da xu [䷙], for example: In this hexagram, the bottom, the second, and the third lines are the primary constituent trigram Qian [☰], and the third, the fourth, and the fifth lines constitute trigram Zhen [☳]—in this way, the third line is used twice, by which a new hexagram called Da zhuang [䷡] can be obtained. Similarly, by overlapping the second, the third, and the fourth lines of hexagram Da xu, we can get trigram Dui [☱], and from the fourth to the top line is the primary constituent trigram Gen [☶]; in this way, the fourth line is employed twice, and the two trigrams can form another new hexagram called Sun [䷨]. The feature of the "five-line consecutive overlapping" method is that five consecutively arranged lines in a hexagram could form two new hexagrams, where the middle line (i.e., line 3 or line 4) of the original hexagram will be used twice.

"Four-line consecutive overlapping" signifies that, within a hexagram, from line 1 to line 4, from line 2 to line 5, and from line 3 to line 6 can form a new hexagram. Take hexagram Da xu [䷙] for example. In this hexagram, the bottom line through the fourth line form a tetragram in which line 1 to line 3 is trigram Qian [☰], and line 2 to line 4 can form trigram Dui [☱]. In this way, line 2 and line 3 are used twice and a new hexagram called Guai [䷪] can be derived from the formation. Similarly, by overlapping the lines from the second to the fifth, we can get another tetragram from which hexagram Guimei [䷵] can be derived; by overlapping the lines from the third to the top, we can also get another tetragram from which hexagram Yi [䷚] can be obtained.

The characteristic of the four-line consecutive overlapping is that a hexagram can result in three tetragrams, and the three tetragrams can themselves give rise to three new hexagrams respectively through twice using the middle lines of each tetragram. Namely, line 2 and line 3 will be employed twice in order to derive a hexagram from the tetragram formed by the lines from the bottom to the fourth; line 3 and line 4 will be used twice in the tetragram constituted from line 2 to line 5; line 4 and line 5 will be applied twice in the tetragram formed from line 4 to line 6.

Five-line consecutive overlapping can beget only two new hexagrams through the overlapping of the lines from the bottom to the fifth and the overlapping of those from the second to the top. Four-line consecutive overlapping can give rise to only three new hexagrams through the overlapping of lines from the bottom to the fourth, from the second to the fifth, and from the third to the top, respectively. In short, "[simple] overlapping" can generate two new trigrams, "five-line consecutive overlapping" two new hexagrams, and "four-line consecutive overlapping" three new hexagrams. In this way, "[simple] overlapping" and "consecutive overlapping" can overall produce two new trigrams and five new hexagrams.

To help beginners understand these interpretive methods, examples in the following tabulation will illustrate the relationships.

Trigrams (hexagrams) Resulting from Overlapping / Lines to be Overlapping	Original hexagram Qian	Zhun	Meng	Xu	Song
line 2, line 3, and line 5	Qian	Kun	Zhen	Dui	Li
line 3, line 4, and line 5	Qian	Gen	Kun	Li	Xun
line 2 to line 5	Qian	Bo	Fu	Kui	Jiaren
line 1 to line 4	Qian	Fu	Jie	Guai	Weiji
line 3 to line 6	Qian	Jian	Bo	Jiji	Gou
line 1 to line 5	Qian	Yi	Shi	Da you	Huan
line 2 to line 6	Qian	Bi	Yi	Jie	Tongren

Many renowned scholars of the Eastern Han, such as Zheng Xuan 郑玄 (127-200) and Yu Fan 虞翻 (164-233), tended to approach the *Changes* via the use of both simple and consecutive overlapping images. For example, according to the "Ziyi" 缁衣 chapter of *Li ji zhengyi* 礼记正义 (Correct Meaning of the *Record of Ritual*), for the third line statement of hexagram Heng 恒 [☰, Perseverance, 32] that reads "This one does not persevere in maintaining his virtue, so he might have to bear the shame of it, for constancy would be debased,"[cclxvii] Zheng Xuan explained the text as follows: "The overlapping [of line 2, line 3, and line 4] is Qian [☰] which has the virtue of virility [perseverance], but its body [main part] is in Xun [☴] which [by the "Discussion of the Trigrams"] signifies advancing and retreating [i.e., hesitating, not persevering]. And additionally, Dui [☱] derived from the overlapping [of line 3, line 4 and line 5] means deterioration [defects], hence the 'shame.'"[cclxviii]

The following is another example. Interpreting the judgment of hexagram Yi [☰, Nourishment, 27], which says "... Observe his nourishing and how he seeks to fill his own mouth,"[cclxix] Zheng Xuan explained: "From line 2 to line 5, there are two [trigrams of] Kun [☷] that carries and nourishes the myriad things and man's foods are entirely included."[cclxx] Here Zheng Xuan means that, in hexagram Yi, through overlapping, line 2, line 3, and line 4 can form a trigram of Kun [☷]; and line 3, line 4, and line 5 can derive another Kun [☷]. Thus, there will be two trigrams of Kun derived from the overlapping in the hexagram. There are many cases of such overlappings described in Zheng Xuan's commentaries on the *Yi*.

It says in the bottom line statement of hexagram Mingyi [☰, Suppression of the Light, 36], "... When he sets off to a place, the host there reproaches him." The *Jiujia yi* 九家易 (The Nine Schools' *Changes*) accounts for the term "reproaching" in this way: "Line 4 and line 5 are in the body of [the trigram] Zhen [☳] which symbolizes the sound of thunder [hinting the voice of reproach]."[cclxxi] This explication means that line 3, line 4, and line 5 of the hexagram can form trigram Zhen [☳], which connotes the sound of thunder (and inasmuch as the bottom line and the fourth line resonate with each other, the term "reproach" is in the bottom line statement). Similarly, the *Jiujia yi* 九家易 ascribes the term "horse" in the second line statement of hexagram Mingyi that "... he is saved by a horse's strength and as a result has good fortune" as being explained through the following: "Line 3 is [the middle line of] Kan [☵] which is horse [according to the "Discussion of the Trigrams"]."[cclxxii] The foregoing shows that trigram Kan [☵] can be derived from the overlapping of line 2, line 3, and line 4.

Yu Fan also used to apply "overlapping" to his explanations of the *Changes*. For the first line statement of hexagram Bi [䷕, Elegance, 22], that "He furnishes his toes with Elegance, discards carriage, and goes on foot," Yu Fan interpreted: "Its response is in the Zhen [☳], which symbolizes foot, hence the term 'toes' [which belong to a foot]."[cclxxiii] This note means that, in this hexagram, the response line of the bottom line is line 4 which, together with line 3 and line 5, constitute trigram Zhen [☳], and according to the "Discussion of the Trigrams," Zhen [☳] is foot; this is why the statement refers to "toes." It says in the third line statement of hexagram Xian [䷞, Reciprocity, 31]: "Reciprocity is in the thigh..." In Yu Fan's opinion, "Xun [☴] is thigh; it refers to line 2."[cclxxiv] This means that Xun [☴] symbolizes thigh, but in hexagram Xian [䷞], the primary constituent trigrams are Dui [☱] in the outer and Gen [☶] in the inner place without trigram Xun [☴]—it is only through overlapping line 2, line 3, and line 4 that we can get trigram Xun [☴], which starts from line 2, hence Yu Fan's interpretation.

From these examples, we can understand how Eastern Han Confucians applied simple and consecutive overlapping images in their interpretations of the basic text.

For the judgment of hexagram Da xu [䷙, Great Domestication, 26] that "... Not eating at home means good fortune. ...," Zheng Xuan noted: "From line 3 to line 6, there is the image of Yi [䷚, which is likened to mouth and means eating]. As it is located at the outer position, it signifies 'not eating at home means good fortune' and nourishing sagacious men."[cclxxv] Here, the image of hexagram Yi [䷚] was derived from the four-line consecutive overlapping from the third to the top lines of Da xu [䷙]. As is stated in the commentaries on hexagram Yi [䷚, Nourishment, 27]: "'Yi [Nourishment] is such that constancy here means good fortune,' for when Nourishment is correct, there will be good fortune. 'Observing his nourishing' means 'observe the nourishing [of others] that he does'" (the "Commentary on the Judgment"); "Yi means nourishment" (the "Orderly Sequence of the Hexagrams); "Yi means 'the nurturing of correctness'" (the "Hexagrams in Irregular Order").[cclxxvi] Since ancient scholars thought Yi had the image of "nourishment," Zheng Xuan derived the image of hexagram Yi [☲] from Da xu [☲] through the four-line overlapping in order to account for the statement that "not eating at home means good fortune."

In another example, the "Commentary on the Judgment" of hexagram Meng [☲, Juvenile Ignorance, 4] notes: "To adopt [the connotations of] Juvenile Ignorance and cultivate [literally, nourish] rectitude in it is the meritorious task of the sage."[cclxxvii] Yu Fan annotated it like this: "There is the image of hexagram Yi [☲], hence the word 'nourish.'"[cclxxviii] He meant that, through a five-line consecutive overlapping from the second to the top lines of hexagram Meng [☲], we can get the image of hexagram Yi [☲]. As is mentioned above, Yi had the image of "nourishment," and Yu Fan thus obtained hexagram Yi through five-line consecutive overlapping in hexagram Meng in order to account for the "Commentary on the Judgment" of the latter.

For other cases, we can see that the hexagram Guimei 归妹 [☲, Marrying Maid, 54] derived from hexagram Tai [☲, Peace, 11] through a four-line consecutive overlapping from the second to the fifth lines can purportedly account for the fifth line statement of the latter that "The sovereign Yi had his younger sister married (Diyi guimei 帝乙归妹)";[cclxxix] the hexagram Zhongfu 中孚 [☲, Inner Trust, 61] derived from hexagram Dui [☲, Joy, 58] through a five-line consecutive overlapping from the bottom to the fifth lines can allegedly account for the fifth line statement of the latter that "This one puts his trust (fu 孚) in one who embodies deterioration";[cclxxx] and the hexagram Guai [☲, Resolution, 43] resulted from hexagram Da zhuang [☲, Great Strength, 34] through a five-line overlapping from the bottom to the fifth lines can purportedly enable us to account for the similarity between the bottom line statements of the both—which in the former is that "This one put his strength into his advancing toes,"[cclxxxi] while its counterpart in the latter is that "This one put his strength into his toes";[cclxxxii] and so forth. In short, the Eastern Han scholars used both simple overlapping and consecutive overlapping images in order to account for the provenance of some hexagram and line statements. Since the approach of "consecutive overlapping" was employed by some great scholars of the Eastern Han, the approach had originated before that time. During that period, only Wang Bi (226-249) did not advocate this approach and, in fact, discarded it in his commentaries on the *Changes*.

7) Inverted images (*fandui zhi xiang* 反对之象). At last, let us talk about the "inverted images."

"Inverted image" means that, if we invert a hexagram—i.e., turn the hexagram upside down—we can get a new hexagram; in this way, the latter hexagram is called the "inverted image" of the former, and vice versa. For example, if we invert hexagram Pi [☷☰], we can get hexagram Tai [☰☷], and then hexagram Tai is called the "inverted image" of hexagram Pi.

In all the 64 hexagrams, except the eight hexagrams of Qian [☰], Kun [☷], Kan [☵], Li [☲], Da guo [䷛], Yi [䷚], Xiao guo [䷽], and Zhongfu [䷼]—the inverted image of each of these eight being identical to the original—the hexagrams are actually made up of 28 pairs of mutually inverted hexagrams. This relationship of inversion reveals a fundamental principle for the arrangement of the 64 hexagrams.

We can see that, according to the order of the 64 hexagrams, the first hexagram Qian [☰] and the second hexagram Kun's [☷] inverted images, as mentioned above, are the same as the original ones; hexagram 3 is Zhun [䷂] and hexagram 4 is Meng [䷃], and it is evident that the inversion of the former exactly created the latter. So it is with hexagrams 5 and 6, 7 and 8, 9 and 10, and so on. It was by the principle of inversion, and that of conversion, that the author of the *Zhou yi* ordered the 64 hexagrams.

In examining these inverted hexagrams, we discover a phenomenon existing between the two mutually inverted images: the auspiciousness or inauspiciousness in the bottom line statement of one hexagram is mostly identical to that in the top line of the other. Here are some examples: The bottom line statement of hexagram Zhun [䷂, Birth Throes, 3] indicates that "One should tarry here. It is fitting to stand still with integrity. It is fitting to establish a chief,"[cclxxxiii] while the top line statement of its inverted image, hexagram Meng [䷃, Juvenile Ignorance, 4], says, "Strike at Juvenile Ignorance, but it is not fitting to be invaders; it is fitting to guard against invaders."[cclxxxiv] The bottom line statement of hexagram Tai [☰☷, Peace, 11] indicates that "When one pulls up the rush plant, it pulls up others of the same kind together with it, so if one goes forth and acts, there will be good fortune,"[cclxxxv] while in its inverted image, hexagram Pi 否 [☷☰, Obstruction, 12], the top line statement remarks that "Here one overturns obstruction. Before there was obstruction, but afterward happiness."[cclxxxvi] The bottom line statement of hexagram Xiao xu 小畜 [☰☴, Lesser Domestication, 9] states that "In returning, one follows the appropriate Dao [path], so how could there be any blame involved? This means good fortune,"[cclxxxvii] while in its inverted image, hexagram Lü [☱☰, Treading, 10], the top line statement tells us that "One should look where he has trodden and examine the omens involved. Here the cycle starts back, so it means fundamental good fortune."[cclxxxviii] And so forth.

The most fascinating point is that some line statements were directly copied to the relevant inverted image. Here are some cases: The fifth line statement of hexagram Sun 损 [☶☱, Diminution, 41] reads, "Of tens of coteries of tortoises, there are none that act in opposition, so this means fundamental good fortune,"[cclxxxix] while in its inverted image as reflected in the second line of hexagram Yi [☴☳, Increase, 42], the statement was almost directly copied as such: "Of tens of coteries of tortoises, there are none that can act in opposition. The practice of perpetual constancy here will mean good fortune."[ccxc] The third line statement of hexagram Jiji [☵☲, Ferrying Complete, 63] tells us that "When Exalted Ancestor attacked the Demon Territory, it took him three years to conquer it. The petty man must be not used here,"[ccxci] and by contrast, in its counterpart in the inverted image, the fourth line statement in hexagram Weiji [☲☵, Ferrying Incomplete, 64] indicates in a similar way that "Constancy results in good fortune, and thus regret vanishes. As a burst of thunder, this one attacks the Demon Territory, for which after three years he is rewarded with a large state."[ccxcii] Moreover, the bottom line statement of the formerly mentioned "wets his tail" and the top line statement of the latter "wets his head"; the top line statement of the former indicates that "The one gets his head wet, which means danger," and the bottom line statement of the latter, "The one gets his tail wet, which means humiliation."

A careful comparison of the statements between a pair of the two mutually inverted hexagrams in the 56 hexagrams reveals in large part this kind of response between "auspiciousness" and "inauspiciousness," between "head" and "tail".

Ancient scholars applied the inverted image to seeking out the provenance of some hexagram and line statements. For example, the judgment of hexagram Lin [☷☱, Overseeing, 19] indicates that "Lin [Overseeing] is such that in its prevalence it is fundamental, and in its constancy it is fitting, but by the eighth lunar month there will be misfortune,"[ccxciii] which, some scholars averred, derived from its inverted image, hexagram Guan [☴☷, Viewing, 20], which corresponds to the [lunar] eighth month in the 12 waxing and waning months associated with the 12 hexagrams [i.e., the hexagrams of Fu ☷☳, Lin ☷☱, Tai ☷☰, Da zhuang ☳☰, Guai ☱☰, Qian ☰☰, Gou ☰☴, Dun ☰☶, Pi ☰☷, Guan ☴☷, Bo ☶☷, and Kun ☷☷ corresponding to the 11th, 12th, 1st, 2nd, 3rd, 4th, 5th, 6th, 7th, 8th, 9th and 10th lunar months respectively].

No matter whether this point of view is tenable or not, we are sure that the author of the basic text of the *Zhou yi* employed the "inverted images," in that the order of the 64 hexagrams was based upon this idea.

Through the brief discussion on the seven kinds of the images of the *Changes*, it is evident that "image" played an extremely important role in the ancient scholars' approaches to the *Zhou yi*. For over two millennia, from the Spring and Autumn period (770-476 B.C.E.) to the end of the Qing (1616-1912), the application of the images to the interpretation of the *Changes* was always the mainstream in the age-old history of the *Yi* studies. It is for this reason that the imagery of the *Changes* ought to be reexamined and reevaluated by modern scholars. Today, when discussing and studying the basic text of the *Zhou yi*, we should not completely discard our predecessors' imagery of the *Changes* as it was formed in the past, over two millennia.

Here, we had just given preliminarily discussion to the correlations between the images and the hexagram and line statements of the *Zhou yi*, and briefly introduced several image-based approaches to the basic text that were taken by ancient scholars. Our purpose with this section is to let this introduction to the images and their relationships arouse more valuable viewpoints, and more concerns and attention to these issues, through which we wish more scholars to participate in discussing these topics together.

4.
Hexagram Changes

As the "Discussion of the Trigrams" (*Shuogua* 说卦) claims, "(The sages) observed the changes between *yin* and *yang* and so established the trigrams (and hexagrams)."[ccxciv] Scholars of all periods aver that there usually exists a relationship between two hexagrams in the 64 hexagrams when one hexagram changes into another. Such relationships are called "hexagram changes" (*guabian* 卦变).

As early as the Spring and Autumn period (770-476 B.C.E.), according to the divinatory example recorded in the "22nd Year of Duke Zhuang" (672 B.C.E.) chapter of the *Zuo zhuan* 左传 (Zuo's Commentaries on the *Spring and Autumn Annals*), the "overlapping trigrams" (*huti* 互体) method was employed, (the details of which can be seen in Chapter 6). In the meantime, there are a great number of references to hexagram changes in the "Commentary on the Judgments" (*Tuan* 彖), the "Discussion of the Trigrams" (*Shuogua* 说卦), and the "Commentary on the Appended Phrases" (*Xici* 系辞), which basically took form from the early to the mid-Warring States period (475-221 B.C.E.).

As remarked in the "Commentary on the Appended Phrases," "The sages set down the hexagrams, observed the images, and appended statements to the hexagrams and lines in order to clarify whether they signify good fortune or misfortune. The displacement of the hard [i.e., *yang* —] and soft [i.e., *yin* – –] lines will give rise to change and transformation."[ccxcv] "Change and transformation involve images of advance and withdrawal."[ccxcvi] "In acting, its (idea of) change is regarded as the supreme guide."[ccxcvii] "(This is why) closing the gate is called [the manifestation of the attributes of] Kun 坤 [☷, The Receptive, 2], and opening the gate is called [the manifestation of the attributes of] Qian 乾 [☰, The Creative, 1]. One such closing and one such opening are referred to as a *change*, and the inexhaustibility of their alternation is called their free flow."[ccxcviii] "That which transforms things and regulates them is called '*change*.' Extending this to practical action is called free flow."[ccxcix] "When the hard and the soft [i.e., the strong and the weak, the *yang* and *yin* lines] displace each other, *change* is present there within them."[ccc] "As a book, the *Changes* is something that cannot be kept at a distance. As a manifestation of the Dao [Way], the *Changes* involves frequent shifts. Change and action never stand still but keep flowing all through the six vacancies. Rising and falling without any consistency, the hard and the soft lines change one into another, something for which it is impossible to make definitive laws, since they are doing nothing but keeping pace with *change*."[ccci]

The "Commentary on the Judgments" further concretely illustrates its hexagram changes theory in each hexagram. The commentary regarding the following hexagrams can evidently bespeak the relationship between hexagrams: "Zhun 屯 [䷂, Birth Throes, 3] signifies the difficulty of giving birth when the hard and the soft begin to interact";[cccii] "Diminution for those below and increase for those above, so the Dao [Way] of Sun 損 [䷨, Diminution, 41] moves upward";[ccciii] "Yi 益 [䷩, Increase, 42] is such that it means diminution for those above and Increase for those below, so the delight of the common folk is without bounds. That which proceeds downward from above to what is below [referring to the *yang* line of the lower trigram Zhen ☳] is indeed a Dao that is both great and glorious";[ccciv] "'Qian 謙 [䷞, Modesty, 15] is such that it provides prevalence': The Dao of Heaven [symbolized by the *yang* line of the lower trigram Gen ☶] provides succor to all below and shines forth its radiance; the Dao of Earth [symbolized by the upper trigram Kun ☷] consists of humility and so works in an upward direction";[cccv] "Gu 蠱 [䷑, Ills to Be Cured, 18] results from the hard going upward and the soft [moving] downward";[cccvi] "Bo 剝 [䷖, Peeling, 23] means '*bo*' (peeling), for here the soft and weak [i.e., the *yin* lines] are making the hard and strong [yang lines] change (into its opposite lines)";cccvii "'Fu 复 [☷☳, Return, 24] brings about prevalence,' for the hard [yang line] has returned and moves in compliance with the proper order of things";cccviii "Wuwang 无妄 [☰☳, No Errancy, 25] is such that what is hard and strong [the Zhen (Quake) 震 trigram ☳] comes from outside and becomes the ruler inside. Being dynamic and strong, what is hard and strong [i.e., the fifth line] attains centrality [the Mean] and resonance";cccix "Xian 咸 [☱☶, Reciprocity, 31] is a matter of stimulation. Here what is soft and yielding [Dui (Joy), here representing the Youngest Daughter] moves to the upper position, and what is hard and strong [Gen (Restraint), representing the Youngest Son] moves to the lower position. The two kinds of material force [qi] intercourse, and so join together"cccx (here the two kinds of qi obviously refer to yin and yang qi, which evidently demonstrates that the author of the "Commentary on the Judgments" had used the interaction of the two forces of yin and yang to interpret hexagram changes); "Perseverance [☳☴, 32] means 'long lasting.' Here what is hard and strong [the Zhen (Quake) 震 trigram ☳] moves to the upper position and what is soft and yielding [the Xun (Compliance) 巽 trigram ☴] moves to the lower position";cccxi "The movement of fire is such that it goes up, whereas the movement of water is such that it goes down"cccxii (regarding hexagram Kui 睽 [☲☱, Contrariety, 38]); "The soft and weak [the Xun (Compliance) trigram ☴] climb at their proper time. Obedience [symbolized by the upper trigram ☷] is practiced with compliance [symbolized by the lower trigram] and what is hard and strong [i.e., the second line] locates in the middle and has its response"cccxiii (regarding hexagram Sheng 升 [☷☴, Ascending, 46]); "That prevalence is had in Dispersion 涣 [☴☵, 59] is because what is hard and strong [i.e., the yang line in the lower Kan 坎 trigram ☵] comes in, yet is not hard-pressed and because what is soft and weak [i.e., the yin line in the upper Xun trigram ☴] obtains its position outside, yet cooperates with the one above"cccxiv (regarding hexagram Huan [☴☵, 59]); and "Coming to it, the soft [i.e., the yin line in the lower Li 离 trigram ☲] provides the hard with pattern, and this is why there is 'prevalence.' Separating itself out, the hard [i.e., the yang line in the upper Gen 艮 trigram ☶] rises to the top, and in doing so provides the soft with pattern"cccxv (regarding hexagram Bi [☶☲, Adornment, 22]). And so on.

These remarks reflect the scholars' notions from the Warring States period (475-221 B.C.E.) regarding the changes of the hexagrams. But these accounts were too concise. The extant documents systematically explicating hexagram changes can be traced back to the Eastern Han scholars Xun Shuang's 荀爽 (128-190) and Yu Fan's 虞翻 (164-233) commentaries, and therefore later scholars tended to view them as the progenitors of hexagram changes theory.

Though the complete compilation of Xun Shuang's works is not available to us, some features of his theory can also be found in the extant materials.

Some scholars have pointed out that, according to Xun's theory of hexagram changes, hexagrams Qian 乾 [☰] and Kun 坤 [☷] [i.e., the parents] beget the six children hexagrams of Zhen 震 [☳, representing the Eldest Son], Kan 坎 [☵, the Middle Son], Gen 艮 [☶, the Youngest Son], Xun 巽 [☴, the Eldest Daughter], Li 离 [☲, the Middle Daughter], and Dui 兑 [☱, the Youngest Daughter], and then the six children hexagrams produce the other 56 hexagrams. For instance, the "Commentary on the Judgments" in regard to hexagram Zhun 屯 [☵, Birth Throes, 3] indicates: "Zhun [Birth Throes] means the difficulty of giving birth when the hard and the soft begin to interact."[cccxvi] According to Xun Shuang's sub commentary on this sentence, "This is based on hexagram Kan 坎 [☵], with the latter's bottom *yin* line ascending to the second line position and the second *yang* line descending to the bottom line position, hence 'the hard and the soft begin to interact.'"[cccxvii] This means that hexagram Zhun [☵] is transformed from hexagram Kan [☵] when the bottom *yin* line and the second *yang* line of the latter exchange their positions. In this way, Xun Shuan accounted for the sentence that "the hard and the soft begin to interact" in the "Commentary on the Judgments."

Additionally, Xun Shuang interpreted hexagram Meng 蒙 [☵, Juvenile Ignorance, 4] as such: "This hexagram is based on hexagram Gen 艮 [☶]. The second line (of the latter) ascends to the third line position and the third line (of the latter) descends to the second line position, [and] then both the hard [i.e., the second line of the former] and the soft [i.e., the fifth line of the former] can obtain centrality and will result in prevalence."[cccxviii] This explication means that hexagram Meng [☵] will be transformed from hexagram Gen [☶] when the second and third lines of the latter exchange their positions, hence the "Commentary on the Judgments" regarding hexagram Meng 蒙: "'Meng brings about prevalence:' Meng operates through prevalence and is a matter of timeliness and Centrality."[cccxix]

Therefore, in Xun Shuang's view, hexagram Zhun [☵] is changed from hexagram Kan [☵, the Middle Son], and hexagram Meng [☶] is derived from hexagram Gen [☶, the Youngest Son]. Thus, it seems that the six children hexagrams can really produce 56 other hexagrams. But when interpreting hexagram Jie [☳, Release, 40], he accounts for change by noting that "Qian [☰] moves to Kun [☷] and obtains the multitude" and accounts for the "Commentary on the Judgments" regarding hexagram Jie in this way: "Qian [☰] and Kun [☷] communicate and exchange, which then forms Jie [☳]."[cccxx] According to these remarks, hexagram Jie is not derived from the six children hexagrams, but from hexagrams Qian and Kun.

Yet, in hexagram Lü 旅 [☲, The Wanderer, 56], Xun Shuang presents his annotations as follows: "It means the *yin* line ascends to the fifth line position and interacts with the *yang* energy."[cccxxi] This interpretation signifies that hexagram Lü results from a *yin* line's moving upward and residing in the fifth line. That said, it can be seen that in this hexagram the bottom and second lines had already been *yin* lines, whereas only the third and fourth lines are *yang* lines, and the third line is in the lower position; therefore, only through the exchange of the positions of the third line and the fifth can one see where "the *yin* line ascends to the fifth line position" occurs. The exchange of the third line and the fifth line of hexagram Lü [☲] will result in hexagram Pi 否 [☷]. Thus, Xun here means that the former comes from the latter [which does not belong to the six children hexagrams].

Now we draw more of his interpretations from the *Zhou yi jijie* 周易集解 (Collected Explanations of the *Zhou Changes*) [compiled by the Tang scholar Li Dingzuo 李鼎祚] as a basis, so as to find Xun's hermeneutic approach to the *Changes*. For hexagram Song 讼 [☰, Contention, 6], he extended his interpretations like this: "The *yang* line comes and resides in the second line position in order to show its sincerity to the bottom line, hence the hexagram statement, 'In Contention, there should be sincerity.'"[cccxxii] This explication means that, in this hexagram, he accounts for the term "sincerity" (*fu* 孚) via the *yang* line's coming and residing in the second line position. We can see that only the bottom and the third lines in the hexagram are *yin* lines, with the other four lines being *yang* lines. Since Xun Shuang says "the *yang* line comes and resides in the second line position," according to the meanings of "going" and "coming" in hexagram changes, here "coming" apparently refers to the exchanging of positions between the third *yin* line and the second *yang* line. If we exchange the third *yin* line and the second *yang* line of hexagram Song [☰] back again, we can get hexagram Dun 遯 [☰]. In other words, Xun means that the former is changed from the latter.

When interpreting hexagram Jin 晋 [☰, Advance, 35], Xun Shuang tells us: "The *yin* line advances to the fifth line position, the ruling position."[cccxxiii] In this hexagram, as the bottom, the second, and the third lines are all *yin* lines, "advance" must here refer to the exchange of positions of the fourth and the fifth lines. If we exchange the positions of the fourth line and the fifth line of hexagram Jin [☰] back again, we can obtain hexagram Guan 观 [☰]. This is to say, from Xun's perspective, hexagram Jin [☰] is changed from hexagram Guan [☰].

In interpreting hexagram Sun 损 [☰, Diminution, 41], he makes his point in this way: "The third line of trigram Qian 乾 [☰] moves to and resides in the top line position in order to show sincerity to the two *yin* lines."[cccxxiv] This means that the third line of the inner trigram Qian [☰] exchanges positions with the top line. Which hexagram's exchange of the third *yang* line and top *yin* line can give birth to hexagram Sun [☰]? Of course, it ought to be hexagram Tai [☰].

By the above-mentioned excerpts, we can see that in Xun Shuang's view, hexagram Lü [☰] is transformed from hexagram Pi [☰], Song [☰] from Dun [☰], Jin [☰] from Guan [☰], and Sun [☰] from Tai [☰]. Obviously, these hexagrams are transformed from the "twelve sovereign hexagrams" (see below).

These examples are sufficient to demonstrate the irregularity of Xun Shuang's hexagram changes theory, and so the point of view is untenable that he insists the six children hexagrams give birth to the other 56 hexagrams.

Though another Eastern Han scholar Yu Fan's 虞翻 (164-233) hexagram changes theory is similar to Xun Shuang's, the former's theory is more perfect. Scholars of later times hold that the purport of Yu Fan's hexagram changes theory is that hexagrams Qian [☰] and Kun [☷] give birth to the other 10 sovereign hexagrams—Fu [䷗], Lin [䷒], Tai [䷊], Da zhuang [䷡], Guai [䷪], Gou [䷫], Dun [䷠], Pi [䷋], Guan [䷓], and Bo [䷖]—which produce the other 52 hexagrams. These 10 hexagrams, together with hexagrams Qian and Kun, form the 12 sovereign hexagrams.

Yet, according to Yu Fan's annotations related to hexagram changes as compiled in *Zhou yi jijie* 周易集解 (Collected Explanations of the *Zhou Changes*), it can be seen that the other 52 hexagrams are not transformed only from the 10 sovereign hexagrams.

For instance, when analyzing the one-*yang*-line hexagram Bi [䷇, Closeness, 8], he says: "The second line of hexagram Shi [䷆, The Army, 7] moves upward to the fifth line and gets its position so that the other *yin* lines submit to and assist it."[cccxxv] This is to say, in Yu Fan's opinion, that hexagram Bi [䷇] is transformed from hexagram Shi [䷆] with the exchange of the positions of the second line and the fifth one of the latter, rather than from the sovereign hexagram Fu [䷗].

In annotating hexagram Yi [䷚, Nourishment, 27], Yu contends: "The fourth line of hexagram Jin [䷢] moves to the bottom line position, and thus it become laterally linked [*pangtong* 旁通, which will be discussed later] with hexagram Da guo [䷛]."[cccxxvi] By his view, the two-*yang*-line hexagram Yi [䷚] is derived from hexagram Jin [䷢] with the exchange of positions of the fourth *yang* line and the bottom *yin* line of the latter, and these become laterally linked with hexagram Da guo [䷛] rather than coming from the two-*yang*-line sovereign hexagram Lin [䷒].

In interpreting the two-*yin*-line hexagram Zhongfu [䷼, Inner Trust, 61], he states: "The fourth line of hexagram Song [䷅] moves downward to the bottom line."[cccxxvii] This statement means that the former is derived from the latter through the exchange of the positions of the fourth *yang* line and the bottom *yin* line of the latter. He goes on: "In hexagram Song [䷅], the second line is in [the overlapped trigram] Li [☲, constituted by the 2nd, the 3rd, and the 4th lines of the hexagram] which symbolizes 'crane,' yet it is still in the shadow of the lower trigram Kan [☵] [i.e., the middle *yang* line is trapped or shaded by the two *yin* lines] and thus has the meaning of 'a calling crane is in the shadows' [the second line statement of hexagram Zhongfu (☲, Inner Trust, 61)]."[cccxxviii] What he means is that the second *yang* line in hexagram Song [☲] together with the third line and the fourth line can form trigram Li [☲] through overlapping. According to the "Discussion of the Trigrams" (*Shuogua* 说卦), Li [☲] represents a flying bird, hence the term "crane." The second line is also in the middle of the inner trigram Kan [☵], which implies shadows, hence the second line's statement of "A calling crane is in the shadows" in hexagram Zhongfu [☲, Inner Trust, 61]. According to these explanations, we can see that Yu Fan firmly believes that hexagram Zhongfu [☲] comes from Song [☲] but not from Dun [☲], one of the 10 sovereign hexagrams.

Meanwhile, in analyzing hexagram Xiao guo [☲, Minor Superiority, 62], Yu Fan argues: "The top line of hexagram Jin [☲] moves to the third line position." In his opinion, hexagram Xiao guo [☲] is generated through the exchange of the positions of the top *yang* line and the third *yin* line of hexagram Jin [☲]. To verify his argument, Yu Fan further elaborates: "As there is the image of 'flying bird,' we can know that this hexagram comes from Jin [☲]."[cccxxix] He means that the image of "flying bird" in the hexagram statement of Xiao guo [☲] is based on the image of trigram Li [☲] in hexagram Jin [☲], and thus Xiao guo [☲] is transformed from Jin [☲] rather than from Lin [☲], one of the 10 sovereign hexagrams.

There are also many additional excerpts of this kind from Yu Fan in *Zhou yi jijie* 周易集解 (Collected Explanations of the *Zhou Changes*), which will not be illustrated one by one here due to limited space.

When referring to hexagram changes, Yu Fan also frequently follows Xun Shuang's approach. Here are two examples: He insists that hexagram Zhun [☲, Birth Throes, 3] is transformed from hexagram Kan [☵] when the latter's "second line moves to the bottom line position"[cccxxx] and that hexagram Meng [☲, Juvenile Ignorance, 4] is derived from hexagram Gen [☲] when the latter's "third line shifts to the second line position."[cccxxxi] These glosses are in alignment with Xun Shuang's interpretations.

In summarizing their predecessors' theories about hexagram changes, Song (960-1279) scholars further discussed this issue. For

Hexagram Changes

example, Zhu Xi 朱熹 (1130-1200) borrowed Li Zhicai's 李之才 "Table of Hexagram Changes" (*guabian tu* 卦变图) in his *Zhou yi benyi* 周易本义 (Original Meaning of the *Zhou Changes*).[cccxxxii] The table is as follows:

There are six one-*yang*-line hexagrams, all affiliated with hexagram Fu 复 [䷗], and six one-*yin*-line hexagrams, all affiliated with hexagram Gou 姤 [䷫], respectively:

䷗   ䷖   ䷆   ䷏   ䷇   ䷖

Fu 复 Shi 师 Qian 谦 Yu 豫 Bi 比 Bo 剥

䷫   ䷍   ䷉   ䷈   ䷌   ䷪

Gou 姤 Tongren 同人 Lü 履 Xiao xu 小畜 Da you 大有 Guai 夬

There are 15 two-*yang*-line hexagrams, all affiliated with hexagram Lin 临 [䷒], and 15 two-*yin*-line hexagrams, all affiliated with hexagram Dun 遯 [䷠], respectively:

䷒   ䷣   ䷨   ䷂   ䷚

Lin 临 Mingyi 明夷 Zhen 震 Zhun 屯 Yi 颐

䷭   ䷧   ䷜   ䷃

Sheng 升 Jie 解 Kan 坎 Meng 蒙

䷽   ䷦   ䷳

Xiao guo 小过 Jian 蹇 Gen 艮

䷬   ䷢

Cui 萃 Jin 晋

䷓

Guan 观

䷠   ䷅   ䷸   ䷱   ䷛

Dun 遯 Song 讼 Xun 巽 Ding 鼎 Da guo 大过

䷘   ䷤   ䷝   ䷰

Wuwang 无妄 Jiaren 家人 Li 离 Ge 革

Zhongfu 中孚　Kui 睽　Dui 兑

Da xu 大畜　Xu 需

Da zhuang 大壮

There are 20 three-*yang*-line hexagrams, all affiliated with hexagram Tai 泰 [䷊], and 20 three-*yin*-line hexagrams, all affiliated with hexagram Pi 否 [䷋], respectively:

Tai 泰　Guimei 归妹　Jie 节　Sun 损

Fang 丰　Jiji 既济　Bi 贲

Sui 随　Shihe 噬嗑

Yi 益

Heng 恒　Jing 井　Gu 蛊

Kun 困　Weiji 未济

Huan 涣

Xian 咸　Lü 旅

Jian 渐

Pi 否

Hexagram Changes

☷ ☶ ☵ ☴
Pi 否 Jian 渐 Lü 旅 Xian 咸

☵ ☵ ☱
Huan 涣 Weiji 未济 Kun 困

☶ ☴
Gu 蛊 Jing 井

☳
Heng 恒

☴ ☲ ☱
Yi 益 Shihe 噬嗑 Sui 随

☶ ☵
Bi 贲 Jiji 既济

☳
Feng 丰

☶ ☵
Sun 损 Jie 节

☱
Guimei 归妹

☷
Tai 泰

There are 15 four-*yin*-line hexagrams and 15 four-*yang*-line hexagrams, all affiliated with Da zhuang [☳] and Guan [☶], respectively:

☰ ☵ ☶
Da zhuang 大壮 Xu 需 Da xu 大畜

☱ ☲
Dui 兑 Kui 睽

☴
Zhongfu 中孚

93

☲ ☲
Ge 革 Li 离

☲
Jiaren 家人

☲
Wuwang 无妄

☲ ☲
Da guo 大过 Ding 鼎

☴
Xun 巽

☵
Song 讼

☶
Dun 遯

☷ ☷ ☷
Guan 观 Jin 晋 Cui 萃

☶ ☶
Gen 艮 Jian 蹇

☷
Xiao guo 小过

☵ ☵
Meng 蒙 Kan 坎

☳
Jie 解

☷
Sheng 升

☶ ☵
Yi 颐 Zhun 屯

☳ ☷
Zhen 震 Mingyi 明夷

☷
Lin 临

There are six five-*yang*-line hexagrams and six five-*yin*-line hexagrams which are all affiliated with hexagram Guai [☰] and hexagram Bo [☷], respectively:

☰ ☰
Guai 夬 Da you 大有

☰
Xiao xu 小畜

☰
Lü 履

☰
Tongren 同人

☰
Gou 姤

☷ ☷
Bo 剥 Bi 比

☷
Yu 豫

☷
Qian 谦

☷
Shi 师

☷
Fu 复

95

From an overall view of the table, we can find that the hexagrams under the section of the one-*yang*-line and one-*yin*-line portion are the same as those under the section of five-*yang*-line and five-*yin*-line portion but are arranged in opposite sequence. So it is, too, with the relationship between the portion of the two-*yang*-line and two-*yin*-line hexagrams, and the portion of the four-*yang*-line and the four-*yin*-line hexagrams. There are 20 three-*yang*-line hexagrams all affiliated with hexagram Tai 泰 [☷]—the sequence of which begins with Tai [☷] and ends with Pi [☷]—and 20 three-*yin*-line hexagrams derived from hexagram Pi 否 [☷]—the sequence of which begins with Pi [☷] and ends with Tai [☷], illustrating a sequence opposite to the former.

In this way, the 10 sovereign hexagrams change into 62 hexagrams—together with hexagrams Qian [☰] and Kun [☷], there are overall 64 hexagrams.

Yet, even in his *Zhou yi benyi* 周易本义 (Original Meaning of the Zhou Changes), Zhu Xi had not always analyzed the hexagram changes by this regularity.

In the 30 hexagrams of the Upper Scripture of the *Changes*, there are nine hexagrams overall that are interpreted by Zhu Xi from the angle of hexagram changes, among which, however, only hexagram Song [☷, Contention, 6] accords with the "Table of Hexagram Changes."

For instance, in interpreting hexagram Sui [☷, Following, 17], the *Original Meaning of the Zhou Changes* notes: "From the angle of hexagram changes, hexagram Sui [☷] results from the exchange of positions of the bottom line and the second line of hexagram Kun [☷], or from the exchange of positions of the fifth line and the top line of hexagram Shihe [☷], or from the hexagram Weiji [☷] which combines the changes of the above-mentioned two hexagrams, signifying the hard coming to follow the soft."[cccxxxiii] This interpretation is evidently inconsistent with the "Table of Hexagram Changes," which shows that Sui [☷] comes from hexagram Tai [☷] or Pi [☷].

In the 34 hexagrams in the Lower Scripture of the *Changes*, overall, there are 10 hexagrams glossed by Zhu Xi from the angle of hexagram changes, among which only the interpretation of hexagram Jin [☷] is in alignment with the "Table of Hexagram Changes."

Particularly through the above-mentioned discussions, we can see that the Han (206 B.C.E.-220 C.E.) and Song (960-1279) scholars' hexagram changes theory is not rigorous enough and contains many contradictions, and thus cannot correctly reflect the changes and relationships between the hexagrams.

In spite of this fact, however, we should not absolutely deny such relationships between hexagrams.

First, the "Discussion of the Trigrams" (*Shuogua zhuan* 说卦传), the "Commentary on the Appended Phrases" (*Xici zhuan* 系辞传), and the "Commentary on the Judgments" (*Tuanzhuan* 彖传) refer to hexagram changes in many places. Certainly, the original features of the basic text of the *Changes* might have differed from the way these commentaries interpret it; yet, it should not be the case that these interpretations have nothing to do with the original features. Therefore, the discourse about hexagram changes in the "Commentaries on the *Changes*" (*Yi zhuan* 易传) must have some foundations. Yet, the scholars from the Spring and Autumn period on to those of the Warring States times (770-221 B.C.E.) might not have considered hexagram changes in such a strict way as illustrated in the table of hexagram changes, as the "Commentary on the Appended Phrases" indicates that "change and action never stand still but keep flowing all through the six vacancies. Rising and falling without any consistency, the hard and the soft lines change one into the other, something for which it is impossible to make definitive laws, since they are doing nothing but keeping pace with change."[cccxxxiv]

Second, in scrutinizing the hexagram judgments and line statements of the *Zhou yi*, we can find that, in a hexagram's judgment and line statements, the name of another hexagram often appears.

For example, in the bottom line statement of hexagram Xiao xu 小畜 [☰, Lesser Domestication, 9] that "in returning (*fu* 复), one follows the appropriate Dao [path], so how could be there be any blame involved? This means good fortune," and the second line statement that "drawn along, one returns (*fu* 复), and this means good fortune,"[cccxxxv] the name of hexagram Fu 复 [☷, Return, 24] is employed.

This case is by no means solitary. We can further find in the fifth line statement of hexagram Lü 履 [☰, Treading, 10] that "Tread resolutely (*guai* 夬) here, and practice constancy in the face of trouble,"[cccxxxvi] the name of hexagram Guai 夬 [☰, Resolution, 43] is used; in the bottom line statement of hexagram Li 离 [☲, Cohesion, 30] that "This one treads (lü 履) with reverence and care. As he takes it seriously, there will be no blame,"[cccxxxvii] the name of hexagram Lü 履 [☱, Treading, 10] appears; in the fifth line statement of hexagram Dui 兑 [☱, Joy, 58] that "this one puts his trust in one who embodies deterioration (bo 剥, literally, peeling), which means danger,"[cccxxxviii] the name of hexagram Bo 剥 [☶, Peeling, 23] is applied; in the bottom line statement of hexagram Lin 临 [☷, Approaching, 19] that "this one approaches with stimulation (xian 咸) and constancy which here means good fortune" and the second line statement that "this one approaches with stimulation (xian 咸), which means good fortune such that nothing fails to be fitting,"[cccxxxix] the name of hexagram Xian 咸 [☱, Stimulation, 31] is employed; in the fourth line statement of hexagram Meng 蒙 [☶, Juvenile Ignorance, 4] that "Being confronted with impasse (kun 困) on account of Juvenile Ignorance, one becomes base,"[cccxl] the name of hexagram Kun 困 [☱, Impasse, 47] appears; in the fifth line statement of hexagram Sun 损 [☶, Diminution, 41] that "there are those who increase (yi 益) this one. Of tens of coteries of tortoises, there are none that can act in opposition, so this means fundamental good fortune"[cccxli] and in the top line statement that "this one suffers no Diminution but enjoys increase (yi 益) without blame,"[cccxlii] the term of hexagram Yi 益 [☴, Increase, 42] can be found; in the second line statement of hexagram Gen 艮 [☶, Restraint, 52] that "restraint takes place with the calves, which means that this one does not raise up his followers (sui 随). His heart feels discontent,"[cccxliii] there appears the term of hexagram Sui 随 [☱, Following, 17]; in the bottom line statement of hexagram Xu 需 [☵, Waiting, 5] that "when waiting in the countryside, it is fitting to practice perseverance (heng 恒), for then there will be no blame,"[cccxliv] the term of hexagram Heng 恒 [☳, Perseverance, 32] is recalled; and in the fourth line statement of hexagram Weiji 未济 [☲, Ferrying Incomplete, 64] that "constancy results in good fortune, and thus regret vanishes. As a burst of thunder (or quake, zhen 震), this one attacks the Demon Territory, for which after three years he is rewarded with a large state,"[cccxlv] the term of hexagram Zhen 震 [☳, Quake, 51] can be found.

Should the above-mentioned examples be considered coincidences? Or do these line statements which contain the name of another hexagram expose the outlook of the *Zhou yi*'s author on the changes or relationships between the 64 hexagrams? It seems that the latter possibility should not be completely ignored.

Additionally, in the judgment of hexagram Tai [☷☰, Peace, 11] the remarks that "the petty depart, and the great arrive"[cccxlvi] are indeed included there, but when its inner three *yang* lines become the outer trigram and its outer three *yin* lines become the inner trigram—i.e., when it transforms into hexagram Pi [☰☷, Obstruction, 12]—as a result, the judgment becomes "the great depart, and the petty arrive."[cccxlvii] It is evident that the shifts of "great" and "petty" are related to the changes of the *yin* and *yang* lines.

Therefore, the preceding scholars' theory of hexagram changes ought not to be rashly denied. In establishing the hexagrams, how the inventors of the *Zhou yi* "observed the changes between *yin* and *yang*" and how they dealt with the "exchanges of *yin* and *yang*" cannot be found, on account of its antiquity. The matter thus requires our careful study and examination on the basis of preceding explorations.

From the Han (206 B.C.E.-220 C.E.) through Qing (1636-1912) dynasties, "hexagram changes" in some subcommentaries on the *Changes* generally occupied a significant position, and scholars have constantly worked to account for some hexagram and line statements via particular hexagram-change methods. Now we introduce several hexagram-change techniques that are often used in the Han scholars' annotations to the *Changes*.

1) *Pangtong* 旁通 (literally, lateral linkage)

The term *pangtong* might originate from the saying in the "Commentary on the Words of the Text" (*Wenyan* 文言) regarding hexagram Qian that "the six lines emanate their power and all innate tendencies are laterally linked."[cccxlviii]

Yu Fan 虞翻 (164-233) employed this method in interpreting the hexagrams in a detailed way. In his annotations to the *Changes*, he often notes that hexagrams Bi [☷☵, 8] and Da you [☲☰, 14] are laterally linked; hexagrams Xiao xu [☴☰, 9] and Yu [☳☷, 16] are laterally linked; hexagrams Lü [☰☱, 10] and Qian [☶☷, 15] are laterally linked, and so it is with hexagrams Tongren [☰☲, 13] and Shi [☷☵, 7], and so on. A great number of this kind of examples can be found in Yu's annotations to the *Changes* as cited by the *Zhou yi jijie* 周易集解 (Collected Explanations of the *Zhou Changes*) compiled by Li Dingzuo 李鼎祚.

The above-mentioned examples clearly illustrate that what so-called lateral linkage refers to is the relationship between a pair of hexagrams in which the second hexagram is produced by changing each line of the first from *yin* to *yang* or *yang* to *yin*. For instance, hexagrams Qian [☰, 1] and Kun [☷, 2] are laterally linked hexagrams as the lines of the former are all *yang* lines while those of the latter are all *yin* lines. So it is with the above-mentioned pairs of hexagrams.

Some precursors use lateral linkage to interpret the basic text of the *Zhou Changes* in order to seek associations between particular hexagram and line statements. For example, they ascribe the term "army" appearing in the fifth line statement of hexagram Tongren [☰, Fellowship, 13] (that "With the victory of the great army, they manage to meet"[cccxlix]) to its lateral linkage with hexagram Shi [☷, Army, 7].

They also account the same character Yi 夷 (literally, equality) being shared by the fourth line statement of hexagram Feng [☰, Abundance, 55] and the fourth line statement of hexagram Huan [☰, Dispersion, 59] for the lateral linkage between these two hexagrams. So it is with the relationship between hexagrams Zhun [☰, Birth Throes, 3] and Ding [☰, The Cauldron, 50], and therefore the fifth line statement of the former and the third line statement of the latter share the same term of *gao* 膏 (literally, fat).

Many interpretations of this kind are available in past scholars' annotations to the *Changes*. They took advantage of this technique to account for the relationship between laterally linked hexagrams.

Undoubtedly, this kind of interpretation might not avoid forced associations and might not be completely in alignment with the original purport of the basic text of the *Zhou yi*.

2) *shangxia xiang yi* 上下象易 (exchange of positions of the upper and lower trigrams)

The "Commentary on the Appended Phrases" (*Xici* 系辞) tells us: "In remote antiquity, people knotted cords to keep things in order. The sages of later ages had these exchanged for written tallies, and by means of these all the various officials were kept in order, and the myriad folk were supervised. They probably got the idea for this from the hexagram Guai [☰, Resolution, 43]."ᶜᶜᶜˡ

Yu Fan annotated these remarks in this way: "(It derives from) the exchange of positions of the upper and lower trigrams of hexagram Lü [☰, Treading, 10]."ᶜᶜᶜˡⁱ This comment means that hexagram Guai [☰] resulted from the exchange of positions of the upper and lower trigrams of hexagram Lü [☰]. This annotation might be the origin of this hermeneutic technique, which signifies that a hexagram is transformed from the exchange of positions between the upper and lower trigrams of another hexagram. Here are some examples of this relationship between two hexagrams: Heng [☰, Perseverance, 32] and Yi [☰, Increase, 42]; Xian [☰, Reciprocity, 31] and Sun [☰, Diminution, 41]; and Zhun [☰, Birth Throes, 3] and Jie [☰, Release, 40]. Ancient scholars used this method to seek the relationship between two hexagrams.

3) *wanglai* 往来 (going and coming)

As the "Commentary on the Appended Phrases" says that "the inexhaustibility of going and coming is called their free flow,"ᶜᶜᶜˡⁱⁱ this seems to be the origin for the reference of "going and coming" when talking about hexagram changes.

"Going and coming" means that the exchange of positions of two lines of a hexagram will lead to another hexagram.

Let us use hexagram Zhun [☰] as an example. The exchange of positions of the bottom line and the second line of the hexagram (i.e., the bottom line goes to the second line's position while the second line comes to the bottom line's position) will give rise to hexagram Kan [☰], whereas the exchanging of positions for line 2 and line 3, or that of line 3 and line 4, will not lead to another hexagram. But if line 4 and line 5 exchange positions, the hexagram will transform into hexagram Zhen [☰]; if the fifth line and top line exchange positions, it will change into hexagram Yi [☰]; and if the top line and bottom line exchange positions, it will become hexagram Guan [☰]. Here is another example: In hexagram Meng [☰], the exchange of positions between line 1 and line 2 will result in hexagram Yi [☰]; the displacement of line 2 and line 3 will give birth to hexagram Gen [☰]; the exchange of positions of line 3 and line 4, or that of line 4 and line 5, will make no change in the hexagram;

the exchange of positions of the fifth and top lines will lead to hexagram Kan [☵]; and the displacement of the top line and the bottom line will make it change into hexagram Lin [☷].

This technique is referred to as *zhi* 之 (literally, moving to) by Han (206 B.C.E.-220 C.E.) scholars. Here are some specific examples. For hexagram Dun [☰], if "line 3 moves to line 2" (i.e., if these two lines exchange positions), it will transform into hexagram Song [☰]; for hexagram Da zhuang [☰], if its "fourth line moves to the fifth line position," it will change into hexagram Xu [☰]; for hexagram Dun [☰], if its "top line moves to bottom line position," it will turn into hexagram Ge [☰].

Yu Fan is well versed in explaining hexagram changes through the "going and coming" of lines. In interpreting hexagram Zhun [☵, Birth Throes, 3], he states: "Line 2 of hexagram Kan [☵] moves to the bottom line position."[ccclIII] This means that hexagram Zhun [☵] is derived from the exchange of positions of line 1 and line 2 of hexagram Kan [☵]. When annotating hexagram Ding [☲, The Cauldron, 50], he points out: "The top line of hexagram Da zhuang [☰] moves to the bottom line position."[cccliv] He means that the former is derived from the exchange of positions of the top and bottom lines of the latter.

There are many cases of this kind in the Han scholars' annotations to the *Changes*. They frequently apply this technique to elucidating the relationship between two hexagrams, but a careful study of the legacy of their annotations leaves us no fixed rules for this kind of hexagram changes.

4) *xiao xi* 消息 (waning and waxing)

In a hexagram, the increase of the number of *yin* lines [and the according decrease of the number of *yang* lines] is called *xiao* 消 (waning), whereas the increase of the number of *yang* lines [and the according decrease of the number of *yin* lines] is referred to as *xi* 息 (waxing). So, this term actually refers to the waxing and waning of *yin* and *yang* energy in a hexagram, as is indicated in the chapter "Opening Up the Regularities of the [Hexagram] Qian" (*Qian zao du* 乾凿度) of the *Yi wei* 易纬 (Apocrypha of the *Changes*): "Based on *yin-yang*, the sages established waning and waxing, and positioned Qian [symbolizing heaven and pure *yang*] and Kun [symbolizing earth and pure *yin*] so as to govern heaven and earth [i.e., the world under heaven]."[ccclv]

The hermeneutic approach of waning and waxing was reportedly transmitted by the Western Han scholar Meng Xi 孟喜 (fl. c. 50 B.C.E.) while Yu Fan 虞翻 (164-233) often employs it to account for hexagram changes. For example, when he interprets hexagram Fu [☷☳, Return, 24], he presents his point in this way: "*Yang* waxes from hexagram Kun [☷☷, The Receptive, 2] and it is laterally linked [*pangtong* 旁通] with hexagram Gou [☰☴, Encounter, 44]."[ccclvi] This comment signifies that hexagram Fu [☷☳] is derived from the waxing or emergence of a *yang* line in the bottom line position of hexagram Kun [☷☷]. Additionally, because the *yin* and *yang* lines of hexagram Fu [☷☳] are opposite to those of hexagram Gou [☰☴], the former is laterally linked with the latter. Based on the same principle, he traces hexagram Gou [☰☴, Encounter, 44] back in this way: "This is a waning hexagram, laterally linked with hexagram Fu [☷☳, Return, 24]."[ccclvii]

Here is another example. When interpreting hexagram Lin [☷☱, Overseeing, 19], he tells us: "*Yang* waxes to the second line and the hexagram is laterally linked with hexagram Dun [☰☶, Withdraw, 33]."[ccclviii] This means that the bottom and second lines of this hexagram have been transformed into *yang* lines and its laterally linked hexagram is Dun [☰☶].

There are overall 12 waning and waxing hexagrams, i.e., the previously mentioned 12 sovereign hexagrams. Additionally, ancient scholars associated the 12 waning and waxing hexagrams with 12 lunar months: Hexagram Fu [☷☳] corresponds to *zi* 子 [the 1st of the 12 earthly branches, hereafter B1] and rules the 11th lunar month; hexagram Lin [☷☱] corresponds to *chou* 丑 [B2] and governs the 12th lunar month; similarly, Tai [☷☰] is correlated with *yin* 寅 [B3] and the first lunar month, Da zhuang [☳☰] with *mao* 卯 [B4] and the second lunar month, Guai [☱☰] with *chen* 辰 [B5] and the third lunar month, Qian [☰☰] with *si* 巳 [B6] and the fourth lunar month, Gou [☰☴] with *wu* 午 [B7] and the fifth lunar month, Dun [☰☶] with *wei* 未 [B8] and the sixth lunar month, Pi [☰☷] with *shen* 申 [B9] and the seventh lunar month, Guan [☴☷] with *you* 酉 [B10] and the eighth lunar month, Bo [☶☷] with *xu* 戌 [B11] and the ninth lunar month, and Kun [☷☷] with *hai* 亥 [B12] and the 10th lunar month. And hexagrams Tai [☷☰], Da zhuang [☳☰], and Guai [☱☰] are accordingly mated with spring; Qian [☰☰], Gou [☰☴], and Dun [☰☶] with summer; Pi [☰☷], Guan [☴☷], and Bo [☶☷] with autumn; and Kun [☷☷], Fu [☷☳], and

Figure 4.1. Twelve Waning and Waxing Hexagrams[1]

Lin [☷☱] with winter. Thus, the 12 waning and waxing hexagrams cyclically transform in the four seasons. [These associations can be collectively observed in Figure 4.1.]

Some scholars have also attributed the approaches of "overlapping hexagrams" and "inverted hexagrams," as introduced earlier, to hexagram changes.

Of course, the above-mentioned several approaches related to hexagram changes are neither complete nor systematic and can be used only as references.

It should be noted that though the "Commentary on the Judgments" (Tuan 彖) is extremely concise, from the commentary regarding hexagram Xian [☱☶, Reciprocity, 31] that "the soft and yielding [Dui (☱, Joy), here representing the Youngest Daughter] is above, and the hard and strong [Gen (☶, Restraint), representing the Youngest Son] is below. The two kinds of material force [qi] intercourse and so join together,"[ccclix] and in other remarks such as "'A submerged dragon does not act' as the yang force is underneath"[ccclx] in hexagram Qian [☰, The Creative, 1], "'A

---

[1] As is often the case with traditional Chinese charts and diagrams representing geographical space, the north is located at the bottom of the figure.

submerged dragon does not act' in that the *yang* force is hidden in the depths,"[ccclxi] and "as *yin* provokes the suspicions of *yang*"[ccclxii] in the "Commentary on the Words of the Text" (*Wenyan* 文言), it can be seen that the exegetes of the *Changes* in the Warring States period (475-221 B.C.E.) did believe the changes and transformations of the hexagrams can signify the interaction, changes, and transformations of *yin* and *yang* forces. Therefore, it is not difficult for us to understand the words in the chapter "Opening Up the Regularities of the [Hexagram] Qian" (*Qian zao du* 乾凿度) of the *Yi wei* 易纬 (Apocrypha of the *Changes*) that "changes refer to the changes of the material force [*qi*]."[ccclxiii]

In addition to Zhuang zi's 庄子 (369-286 B.C.E.) remark that "the *Yi* (Changes) is that which discourses upon *yin* 阴 and *yang* 阳" and, in the ancient *Changes* discovered in the tomb of King Xiang of Wei 魏襄王 (r. 318-296 B.C.E.) "there is a separate chapter called 'Discussions of *yin* and *yang*' (*yin yang shuo* 阴阳说)" in the "Postscript" to the *Zuo zhuan jijie* 左传集解 (Collected Interpretations of *Zuo's Commentary on the Spring and Autumn Annals*) by Du Yu 杜预 (222-285)[ccclxiv], we are sure that although the characters of *yin* 阴 and *yang* 阳 did not appear in the basic text of the *Zhou yi*, the hexagram changes theory based on the "interaction between the two forces (of *yin* and *yang*)" might not be groundless. Whether the changes and relationships between the hexagrams are based on this principle needs further exploration.

5.
Divination by Milfoil Stalks

Tradition has it that the *Changes* is composed of three elements: images, numbers, and principles.

"Numbers" actually refer to divinatory numbers, in that the *Zhou Changes* is, after all, a book of divination. Thus, an overall study of the *Zhou yi* ought to include not only the exegesis of the classical text, but also analysis of divinatory numbers. The Song scholar Zhu Xi 朱熹 (1130-1200) recognized this point and particularly discussed milfoil-stalk divination in his *Yixue qimeng* 易学启蒙 (Introduction to the Study of the *Changes*), in which he put forth his own new perspectives on this issue.

How did divination take form? To answer this question, we have to discuss its origins and go from there.

The earliest concrete record about divination can be seen in the chapter of "*Hongfan* 洪范" (literally, Great Plan) of the *Shang shu* 尚书 (Classic of History), in that, "then, they select and establish official tortoise-shell (*bu* 卜) and milfoil-stalk (*shi* 筮) diviners and order them to divine," "if you have doubts, [...] [please] seek advice from tortoise-shell and/or milfoil-stalk divinations," and "[under this circumstance] you should follow [the suggestions manifested by] tortoise-shell and/or milfoil-stalk divinations," and so on.

Therefore, it is evident that in the Shang (c. 1600-1046 B.C.E.) and Zhou (1046-256 B.C.E.) dynasties, there had been professional "diviners." But *bu* 卜 (tortoise-shell divination) differs from *shi* 筮 (milfoil-stalk divination). The former refers to plastromancy, which involves the reading of cracks made by the application of heat to the prepared plastrons of tortoises, as stated in *Shuowen jiezi* 说文解字 (Explanation of Simple and Composite Characters): "*Bu* 卜 means scorching the plastrons of tortoises and taking images from cracks."[ccclxv] After the Tang dynasty (618-907), how to obtain and how to read cracks on the plastrons was unavailable in records. Here, what we see introduced is *shi*筮 or *zhan shi* 占筮 (milfoil-stalk divination), which depends on the manipulation of milfoil stalks to form hexagram(s) and predict the future through analyzing the images and the hexagram(s) and/or line statements, as noted in *Shuowen* 说文: "*Shi* 筮 refers to the milfoil-stalk divination applied to the hexagrams of the *Changes*."[ccclxvi] Thanks to the "Commentary on the Appended Phrases" (*Xici* 系辞), the divinatory technique by milfoil stalks is preserved. *Xici* was the earliest and most authoritative document to record the milfoil-stalk divinatory method. Now, let us take a look at the words concerning this mantic art in the "Commentary on the Appended Phrases."

> The number of great expansion (*day an* 大衍) is fifty [milfoil talks]. Of these we use forty-nine. We divide these into two groups, thereby representing the two. [Between our fingers,] we dangle one single stalk, thereby representing the three [i.e., the three powers, or Heaven, Earth, and Man]. We count off the stalks by fours, thereby representing the four seasons. We return the odd ones to a place between the fingers, thereby representing an intercalary month. Within five years, there is a second intercalary month, so we place a second lot of stalks between the fingers; after that we dangle another single stalk [and continue the process].[ccclxvii] 大衍之数五十，其用四十有九。分而为二以象两，挂一以象三，揲之以四以象四时，归奇于扐以象闰，五岁再闰，故再扐而后挂。

Heaven is one, and Earth is two; Heaven is three, and Earth is four; Heaven is five, and Earth is six; Heaven is seven, and Earth is eight; Heaven is nine, and Earth is 10. Heaven's numbers are five, and Earth's numbers are five. The five positions get along with each other, and each has its matches. Heaven's numbers come to 25, and Earth's numbers come to 30. The total sum of Heaven's and Earth's numbers is 55, which indicates how change and transformation are brought about and how gods and spirits are activated.[ccclxviii] 天一地二, 天三地四, 天五地六, 天七地八, 天九地十。天数五, 地数五, 五位相得而各有合。天数二十有五, 地数三十。凡天地之数五十有五。此所以成变化而行鬼神也。

Thus, the stalks needed to form *Qian* [☰, The Creative, 1] number 216, and the stalks needed to form *Kun* [☷, The Receptive, 2] 144. In all, these number 360 and correspond roughly to the days of a year's cycle. The stalks in the two parts [of the *Changes*] number 11,520 and correspond [roughly] to the number of the 10,000 [i.e., "myriad"] things. Therefore, it takes four operations to form a change, and it takes 18 changes to form a hexagram. With the eight trigrams, we have the small completion.[ccclxix] 乾之策, 二百一十有六。坤之策, 百四十有四。凡三百有六十, 当期之日。二篇之策, 万有一千五百二十, 当万物之数也。是故四营而成易, 十有八变而成卦。八卦而小成。

The above-cited words are the earliest and most complete record about milfoil-stalk divination in extant literature. Now, we attempt to interpret this record as follows:

That "the number of great expansion is fifty [milfoil talks], of which we use forty-nine" means that the total number of the stalks used in the manipulation is 50, whereas in actual calculation we use just 49. Why did the ancients apply 50 stalks to the manipulation? From the Han (206 B.C.E.-220 C.E.) dynasty to contemporary times, scholars have not yet reached a consensus. According to the "Treatise on Pitch Pipes and Calendar" (*lüli zhi* 律历志) of the *Han shu* 汉书 (History of the Western Han Dynasty),

> Thereby the original beginning has one single image [corresponding to the number of one], Spring and Autumn [corresponding to the number of] two, Three-*tong* [cycles of years] calendar [corresponding to the number of] three, four

seasons [corresponding to the number of] four. The sum [of the numbers] is ten and forms five bodies. Five times ten is equal to the number of great expansion, in which the Dao [Way] occupies one and the other forty-nine stalks are for use. 是故元始有象一也，春秋二也，三统三也，四时四也，合而为十，成五体。以五乘十，大衍之数也，而道据其一，其余四十九，所当用也。ccclxx

It means: 50 = (1 + 2 + 3 + 4) × 5.

Jing Fang 京房 (77-37 B.C.E.) holds that "fifty means ten days [signified by the ten heavenly stems], twelve months [expressed by the twelve earthly branches], and twenty-eight constellational lodges. The numbers add up to fifty. The one which will not be used refers to the generating *qi* [material force] which will substantiate things, hence using the forty-nine [stalks]."ccclxxi Jing Fang's view is congruent with the assertions expressed in the chapter "Opening Up the Regularities of the [Hexagram] Qian" (*Qian zao du* 乾凿度) of the *Yi wei* 易纬 (Apocrypha of the *Changes*), i.e., 50 = 10 (days) + 12 (months) + 28 (constellational lodges).

Regarding this issue, the *Zhou yi zhengyi* 周易正义 (Correct Meaning of the *Zhou Changes*) compiled by the Tang scholar Kong Yingda 孔颖达 (574-648) also cited Ma Rong's 马融 (79-166) point of view: "*Taiji* 太极 [literally, Supreme Ultimate] in the *Changes* refers to the Pole Star. The Supreme Ultimate produces two modes, which produce the sun and the moon; the sun and the moon produce the four seasons, which produce the five agents; the five agents produce the 12 months that further generate the 24 seasonal points. The Pole Star stays motionless whereas the other 49 elements rotate and function."ccclxxii In his opinion: 50 = 1 (Supreme Ultimate) + 2 (two modes) + 2 (the sun and the moon) + 4 (four seasons) + 5 (five agents) + 12 (twelve months) + 24 (24 seasonal points).

Zhou yi zhengyi 周易正义 (Correct Meaning of the *Zhou Changes*) also quoted Xun Shuang's 荀爽 (128-190) assumption: "Each hexagram has six lines and six times eight is equal to forty-eight, together with the 'two using' in hexagrams Qian [☰, The Creative, 1] and Kun [☷, The Receptive, 2], the whole number adds up to fifty. Since the bottom line statement of the former says 'A submerged dragon does not act,'ccclxxiii the other forty-nine is for use."[ccclxxiv] This signifies that: 50 = 6 (six lines) × 8 (eight trigrams) + 2 (*yongjiu* 用九 [the Using of Nine] in hexagram Qian [☰, The Creative, 1] and *yongliu* 用六 [the Using of Six] in hexagram Kun [☷, The Receptive, 2]).

Additionally, the Three Kingdoms period (220-280) scholar Yao Xin's 姚信 argument is also included in the *Zhou yi zhengyi*: "The total sum of Heaven's and Earth's numbers is fifty-five while the number of six refers to the six lines (of each hexagram) and thus should be deducted from it, hence the remainder forty-nine is employed."[ccclxxv]

The Tang scholar Cui Jing's 崔憬 view is available in Li Dingzuo's 李鼎祚 *Zhou yi jijie* 周易集解 (Collected Explanations of the *Zhou Changes*) as follows: "Gen [☶] is the youngest *yang* [male], the number of which is 3; Kan [☵] is the middle *yang*, the number of which is 5; Zhen [☳] is the eldest *yang*, the number of which is 7; Qian [☰] is the senior *yang*, the number of which is 9; Dui [☱] is the youngest *yin* [female], the number of which is 2; Li [☲] is the middle *yin*, the number of which is 10; Xun [☴] is the eldest *yin*, the number of which is 8; Kun [☷] is the senior *yin*, the number of which is 6. The sum of the numbers of the eight trigrams is fifty [i.e., 3 + 5 + 7 + 9 + 2 + 10 + 8 + 6 = 50]."[ccclxxvi]

When interpreting these phrases in his *Zhou yi benyi* 周易本义 (Original Meaning of the *Zhou Changes*), Zhu Xi 朱熹 (1130-1200) tells us: "The number of fifty of the great expansion might be the product of the heavenly five multiplying earthly ten in the central palace of the *he tu* 河图 [Yellow River Chart, see Chapter 9] whereas in actual divination, only forty-nine (stalks) are used, which is perhaps generated from the naturalness of principle and tendency, and ought not to be dwindled or strengthened by man's power."[ccclxxvii]

The above-mentioned represent the variety of considerations accounting for the origin of the number of "fifty of great expansion," among which we think Zhu Xi's view is comparatively pertinent in that the Han (206 B.C.E.-220 C.E.) scholars regard "five" as the ultimate of the producing numbers [i.e., odd numbers] and "ten" as the ultimate of the completion numbers [i.e., even numbers].

The Han scholars' idea must have had its foundations, and thus the number of 50 in the great expansion might be derived from "five" multiplying "ten."

As for the reason that one stalk should be taken out of the 50 in actual manipulation, by the above-mentioned interpretations from the beginning to the end, there has been no clear answer left to us by the ancients. As Zhu Xi found that the predecessors' explanations are all far-fetched, he straightforwardly claims that this is "generated from the naturalness of principle and tendency, and ought not to be dwindled or strengthened by man's power." This conclusion makes the matter more ambiguous. So, we may leave this question open.

As for the meaning of the statement that "we divide these into two groups" on to the end of the paragraph, basing my on view on Kong Yingda's subcommentary in his *Zhou yi zhengyi* 周易正义 (Correct Meaning of the *Zhou Changes*), and on Zhu Xi's explanation in his famous four-character verse of "Clarifying Milfoil-stalk Divination" (*ming shi* 明筮), together with other Song scholars such as Shao Yong's 邵雍 (1011-77) and Lu Xiangshan's 陆象山 (1139-93) interpretations, I attempt to explain this paragraph as follows:

The remaining 49 milfoil stalks are divided into two at random with two hands. The part in the left hand symbolizes Heaven and that in the right hand Earth, which signifies "representing the two" (*yi xiang liang* 以象两). Then the person takes a single stalk from the stalks in the right hand and places it between the small finger and the fourth finger of the left hand so as to represent Man. Together with the stalks in the left hand and right hand symbolizing Heaven and Earth respectively, the three powers of "Heaven, Earth, and Man" appear. This gestures to "dangling one single stalk to represent the three" (*guayi yi xiang san* 挂一以象三). Having completed this process, the diviner now counts off the milfoil stalks by fours, at first using the right hand to count off the stalks in the left hand by fours and then using the left hand to count off those in the right hand by fours, which symbolizes the four seasons and is referred to as "counting off the stalks by fours, thereby representing the four seasons" (*she zhi yi si yi xiang sishi* 揲之以四以象四时).

After the counting off of the stalks by fours, there must be a remainder in each hand, which should be one, or two, or three, or four stalks. "The odd ones" refer to this remainder. The remainder from the left hand will be placed between the fourth and the middle finger of the left hand and that from the right hand will be placed between the middle and the index finger of the left hand, which symbolizes an intercalary month made up of odd days—this being the so-called "returning [of] the odd ones to a place between the fingers, thereby representing an intercalary month" (*gui ji yu le yi xiang run* 归奇于扐以象闰). Because between two intercalary months there are about 32 months, which is within five years, hence comes the reference that "within five years, there is a second intercalary month" (*wu sui zai run* 五岁再闰).

After counting off by fours, the remainders of both hands have certain regularities: If the remainder in the left hand is one stalk, the remainder in the right hand must be three; if the left one is two, the right one must be two; if the left one is three, the right one must be one; if the left one is four, the right one must be four, too. Then, the number of the stalks placed among the fingers (together with the one between the small finger and the fourth finger which represent "Man") of the left hand is either five or nine. In other words, after this manipulation and after deduction of the stalks between the fingers of the left hand, the total sum of the stalks in both hands will be either 44 or forty.

The above-mentioned manipulation is called by the ancients the "first change." Then the person combines the stalks of both hands [either 40 or 44 stalks] and divides them into two at random, as in the first time of manipulation, and then removes one stalk from the stalks in the right hand and places it between the small finger and the fourth finger of the left hand, counts off the stalks in the left hand by the right hand, and counts off the stalks in the right hand by the left hand; the following process is identical to the first manipulation. After the second manipulation has been finished, if the remainder in the left hand is one stalk, the remainder in the right hand must be two; if the left holds two, the right must hold one; if the left holds three, the right must hold four; if the left holds four, the right must hold three. After this manipulation, the number of the stalks between the fingers (together with the stalk placed between the small and fourth finger) of the left hand is either four or eight. Now the total sum of the stalks in both hands, after removing the four or eight, will be either 40, 36, or 32. The second manipulation by now has been completed, which is referred to as the "second change." Then the diviner combines the stalks in both hands [either 40, 36, or 32] together, divides them into two, takes one from the right hand and places it between the small and fourth finger of the left hand, counting off the stalks of both hands by four and dealing with the remainders in the same way as in the past two "changes." Now, if the remainder in the left hand is one stalk, the remainder in the right hand must be two; if the left hand holds two, the right must hold one; if the left holds three, the right must have four; and if the left holds four, the right must hold three. And the sum of the remaining stalks between the fingers (together with the one originally taken from the right hand and placed between the small finger and the fourth finger) of the left hand will be either four or eight. The third change has been accomplished by now. After three changes, the total number of the stalks of both hands, after removing the four or eight, will be either 36, 32, 28, or 24.

Then the number is divided by four (representing four images), and one line can be established: 36 ÷ 4 = 9 [this is called the number of "old yang" (*laoyang* 老阳) and marked as "—"]; 32 ÷ 4 = 8 [this is called the number of "young yin" (*shaoyin* 少阴) and marked as "- -"]; 28 ÷ 4 = 7 [this is called the number of "young yang" (*shaoyang* 少阳) and marked as "—"]; 24 ÷ 4 = 6 [this is called the number of "old yin" (*laoyin* 老阴) and marked as "- -"].

In the original hexagram, both the numbers of "old yang" (*laoyang* 老阳) and "young yang" (*shaoyang* 少阳) are represented as "—" and both the numbers of "old yin" (*laoyin* 老阴) and "young yin" (*shaoyin* 少阴) are symbolized as "- -", whereas in the derivative hexagram, the "old yang" (*laoyang* 老阳) line [i.e., —] will transform into a yin [- -] line and the "old yin" (*laoyin* 老阴) line [i.e., - -] will transform into a yang [—] line. But the "young yang" (*shaoyang* 少阳) and "young yin" (*shaoyin* 少阴) in the original hexagram will stay the same in the derivative hexagram. This is described as "the old will change (into its opposite) while the young will not change," which is an important criterion in divination. Divination of the *Zhou Changes* is based on "change," and thus a yang line is marked with "nine"—the number of "old yang"—and a yin line with "six"—the number of "old yin"—in the *Book of Changes*.

The passage [in the "Commentary on the Appended Phrases"] from "Heaven is one" to "Earth is ten" comes in regard to the numbers of Heaven and Earth. By this sentence, it can be seen that ancient people regard yang numbers as odd, or heavenly, numbers and yin numbers as even, or earthly, numbers. Thus, the numbers of one, three, five, seven, and nine are referred to as "Heaven" while those of two, four, six, eight, and ten are attributed to "Earth."

These sentences from "Heaven is one" to "Earth is ten" were not originally located here, but under the remark, "When the Master said, 'In the *Changes*, there are four things that pertain to the Dao of the sages,' this is what he meant,"[ccclxxviii] in the "Commentary on the Appended Phrases." But according to a paragraph cited from the *Changes* by the "Treatise on Pitch Pipes and Calendar" (*lüli zhi* 律历志) of the *Han shu* 汉书 (History of the Western Han Dynasty) (by Ban Gu 班固 [32-92]), these sentences are put before the sentence reading: "Heaven's numbers are five, and Earth's numbers are five. ..."[ccclxxix] In this regard, some scholars contend this ought to be the original arrangement of the sentences in the *Changes* seen by Ban Gu and claim that there are indeed some mistakes in the sequences of the sentences in the received version of the "Commentary on the Appended Phrases."

But there have also been some scholars who have had different views and pointed out that the "Treatise on Pitch Pipes and Calendar" (*lüli zhi* 律历志) of *Han shu* 汉书 (History of the Western Han Dynasty) was actually based on the *Santong li* 三统历 (literally, Three-concord Calendar) written by Liu Xin 刘歆 (50 B.C.E.-23 C.E.). But, when Liu Xin was castigated by his contemporary Gongsun Lu 公孙禄 for his "perversion of the Five Classics,"[ccclxxx] did he mean that in the "Three-concord Calendar" the above sentences were ordered in the above-mentioned way as a perversion? Therefore, we should not completely believe Ban Gu's 班固 (32-92) version of these sentences. Though here we discuss these numbers by Ban's version, we also have to point out this discrepancy.

"Heaven's numbers are five" refers to the five odd numbers of one, three, five, seven, and nine, and similarly "Earth's numbers are five" designates the five even numbers of two, four, six, eight, and 10. The "five positions" in "the five positions get along with each other and each has its own match" reference the five odd numbers of one, three, five, seven, and nine, as well as the five even numbers of two, four, six, eight, and 10. As for their "getting along with each other" and their "matches," most scholars from the Han (206 B.C.E.-220 C.E.) to the Song (960-1279) dynasties insisted that one matches six, two matches seven, three matches eight, four matches nine, and five matches 10. The Han scholars also viewed the five numbers of one, two, three, four, and five as the "producing numbers" (*shengshu* 生数), and the other five numbers of six, seven, eight, nine, and 10 as the "completion numbers" (*chengshu* 成数), in that "six" is completed by one added to five, seven is completed by two added to five, and so on. Thus, "five" is the ultimate of the "producing numbers" while "ten" is the ultimate of the "completion numbers." Some scholars even hold that the "matches" refer to the matches between producing numbers and completion numbers. Nowadays, some scholars add the odd numbers of one, three, five, seven, and nine, and get the number of 25, and accumulate the even numbers of two, four, six, eight, and 10, and attain the number of 30, and thus the total sum of the heavenly and earthly numbers is 55. This understanding is also persuasive, yet it cannot embody the spirit of "getting along with each other of the five positions."

As was mentioned above, if the number of the stalks in both hands after three changes is 36, an old *yang* line [—] will be obtained. Hexagram Qian has six *yang* lines, thus the number of stalks for the hexagram is 216 [i.e., 36 × 6 = 216]. Similarly, if there are 24 stalks in both hands after three changes, we will get an old *yin* line [- -]. Hexagram Kun [☷] contains six *yin* lines, and thus the number of the stalks for hexagram Kun is 144 [i.e., 24 × 6 = 144]. The sum of the numbers of the two hexagrams is 360 [i.e., 216 + 144 = 360], thus roughly corresponding to the days of a yearly cycle.

In the *Zhou Changes*, there are overall 64 hexagrams composed of 384 lines, which include 192 *yang* [—] lines and 192 *yin* [- -] lines. The numbers of stalks for the entire 64 hexagrams, i.e., 384 lines, ought to be: 36 × 192 + 24 × 192 = 11,520. If we calculate the stalks by the young *yang* and young *yin*, the result will be the same: 32 × 192 + 28 × 192 = 11,520. Ancient Chinese people made use of this number to represent the changes of the 10,000 (i.e., the myriad) things.

"It takes four operations to form a change" means that the formation of one line needs four operations, as Lu Ji 陆绩 (187-219), an eminent scholar and general in the Eastern Han dynasty (25-220), pointed out: "'Dividing (the 49 stalks) into two in order to represent the two [i.e., Heaven and Earth]' is the first operation; 'dangling one single stalk [between the fingers] in order to represent the three [i.e., the three powers of Heaven, Earth, and Man]' is the second operation; 'counting off the stalks by fours in order to represent the four seasons' is the third operation; 'returning the odd ones to a place between the fingers so as to present an intercalary month' is the fourth operation."ccclxxxi

"Four operations" can lead to a change, and three changes can result in a line. Since a hexagram contains six lines, "it takes eighteen changes to form a hexagram."ccclxxxii A hexagram is made up of two trigrams, and after nine changes we can get the inner trigrams, thus "with the trigram, we have the small completion."ccclxxxiii

This is the process of the milfoil-stalk divination mentioned in the "Commentary on the Appended Phrases."

Some ancient scholars contended that the sayings of "dividing into two," "dangling one," "counting off the stalks by fours," and "returning the odd ones to places between the fingers" must have their origin from and might have been passed down from the Zhou people, while the representations of two [Heaven and Earth], three [Heaven, Earth, and Man], the four seasons, and the intercalary month might have resulted from the redactor's expansion of the "Commentary on the Appended Phrases." So far as the numbers of seven, eight, nine, or six being produced from three changes, and the assertion that "nine" and "six" represent the tendency of change while "seven" and "eight" signify unchanging, are concerned, we cannot find any solid evidence in the "Commentary on the Appended Phrases," nor can we find any foundation for them in the divinatory cases recorded in the *Zuozhuan* 左传 (Zuo's Commentaries on the *Spring and Autumn Annals*) and the *Guo yu* 国语 (Sayings of the States), which do, however, contain several hexagrams related to the divinatory number of "eight." We will talk about this issue further in Chapter 6.

The above-mentioned method to get a number for young *yin*, young *yang*, old *yin*, or old *yang* after three changes by counting off the stalks was used by the Han (206 B.C.E.-220 C.E.) and Tang (618-907) scholars, and by some people during the Song (960-1279). This method is called *guoshe fa* 过揲法 (counting-off-stalk method). But the renowned Song Confucian Zhu Xi 朱熹 (1130-1200) did not approve of it and invented another method called *guale fa* 挂扐法 (dangling-and-clamping-stalk method) in order to obtain numbers related to young *yin*, young *yang*, old *yin*, or old *yang*.

This *guale fa* method correlates the number of the odd stalks (together with the single dangled stalk representing Man) between the fingers of the left hand with young *yin*, young *yang*, old *yin*, or old *yang*. By the above-mentioned manipulations, we can see that, after the first change has been accomplished, the total number of the stalks clamped between the fingers of the left hand (i.e., the so-called number of the stalks dangled and clamped) will be either five or nine; after the second or the third change has been completed, there will in total be four or eight stalks between the fingers of the left hand. Therefore, through the three changes, the number of the stalks dangled and clamped each time will be one of the following cases:

    5, which includes one "four" and thus is figured as an "odd number;"
    4, which includes one "four" and is also viewed as an "odd number;"
    8, which consists of two "fours" and thus is viewed as an "even number;"
    9, which consists of two "fours" and is also reckoned as an "even number."

So, here Zhu Xi used the number of groups of four [symbolizing four seasons] in the stalks placed between the fingers of the left hand to determine an odd or even number. For instance, according his method, if each of the three changes results in an "odd number" (i.e., a number containing one "four"), an old *yang* line will be obtained; if each of the three changes produces an "even number" (i.e., a number consisting of two "fours"), an old *yin* line will be encountered; if through the three changes we get one "odd number" and two "even numbers," a young *yang* line will be marked; if through the three changes there is one "even number" and there are two "odd numbers," a young *yin* line will be produced.

In fact, no matter whether we use *guoshe fa* 过揲法 (counting-off-stalk method) or employ *guale fa* 挂扐法 (dangling-and-clamping-stalk method), the results are the same. In other words, if we get an old *yang* line by the former, we can also get an old *yang* line by the latter. For instance, if we employ the *guoshe fa* 过揲法 (counting-off-stalk method) and after three changes the number of the stalks in both hands is 36, we can get the number of 9 [i.e., 36 ÷ 4 = 9], which is the number corresponding to "old *yang*"; if we make use of Zhu Xi's *guale fa* 挂扐法, after the first changes, the number of the stalks between the fingers of the left hand is five, which includes one "four" and is thus an "odd number"; after the second change, there will be four stalks between the fingers of the left hand and the result is an "odd number"; and, the third change will be four stalks and also result in an "odd number." Since each time of the three changes produces an "odd number," an "old *yang*" line is achieved. The total number of the stalks between the fingers of the left hand in the three changes is 13 [the first time is five, the second four, and the third four, the sum of them being 13]. Forty-nine minus 13 is equal to 36, the number of the remainder of the stalks after three changes which produce an old *yang* line. So it is with an old *yin*, young *yin*, or young *yang* line.

Though the result from both methods is identical, according to the process described in the "Commentary on the Appended Phrases," the "counting-off-stalk" method is more pertinent, and thus it is inappropriate for Zhu Xi to disparage this method in Chapter 3 of his *Yixue qimeng* 易学启蒙 (Introduction to the Study of the *Changes*) in this way: "The number of the stalks between the fingers of the left hand is the origin of the number by which to determine a line, whereas the stalks in both hands after counting off by fours are the product by which to derive a line. But they differ in importance. Those who want to abandon the former and merely use the latter are actually attending to trifles yet neglecting essentials, getting rid of simplicity yet adopting complexity. They do not know they ought not deal with it in this way. It is really a mistake!"[ccclxxxiv] His assertion that "the number of the stalks between the fingers of the left hand is the origin of the number by which to determine a line" is obviously not congruent with the accounts related to divination in the "Commentary on the Appended Phrases," in that, as is mentioned above, all numbers of the stalks for Qian [☰] and Kun [☷], and the 10,000 things, are from the stalks of both hands after certain changes in the manipulation, whereas the stalks between the fingers of the left hand merely function for an intercalary month. Zhu Xi did not recognize this distinction, and his overemphasis on the *guale fa* 挂扐法 (dangling-and-clamping-stalk method) and inconsistency with the "Commentary on the Appended Phrases" thus occasioned criticism from later scholars.

Through the above-mentioned discussion, we can see the process for milfoil-stalk divination. But another question ensues immediately: After we have obtained a hexagram, how can we prognosticate fortune or misfortune by the hexagram(s) or line(s)? The answer to this question was not clearly explicated by the scholars from the Han (206 B.C.E.-220 C.E.) to the Tang (618-907) dynasties, and it was not until the Song dynasty (960-1279) that this question was clarified by Zhu Xi in Chapter 4 of his *Yixue qimeng* 易学启蒙 (Introduction to the Study of the *Changes*):

> In the case that the hexagram we get does not have any changing lines, we prognosticate on the basis of the original hexagram's judgment, taking the inner trigram as *zhen* 贞 [the question, or present situation] and the outer trigram as *hui* 悔 [the prognostication]. When only one line changes, we take the statement of the original hexagram's changing line as the prognostication. When two lines change, we take the statements of the two changing lines of the original hexagram as the prognostication, but we take the uppermost line as ruler. When three lines change, the prognostication is the judgment of the original hexagram and the resulting hexagram, and we use the original hexagram as *zhen* and the resulting hexagram as *hui*. When four lines change, we use the two unchanging lines in the resulting hexagram as the prognostication, but we take the lower line as the ruler. When five lines change, we use the unchanging line of the resulting hexagram as the prognostication. When all six lines change, in the cases of Qian and Kun, the prognostications of "both using" [i.e., the "Using of Nine" and the "Using of Six"] are consulted, yet for other hexagrams, the prognostication is the judgment of the resulting hexagram.[ccclxxxv]

This is the so-called *bianzhan* 变占 (literally, prognostication by changing line(s)) method invented by Zhu Xi. Any hexagram obtained in divination will not go beyond one of the following cases: 1) without any changing line; 2) with one changing line; 3) with two changing lines; 4) with three changing lines; 5) with four changing lines; 6) with five changing lines; 7) with all changing lines. An eighth case will not appear.

Taking Zhu Xi's perspective on the prognostication as reference and through analyzing some of the divinatory cases given account in the *Zuo zhuan* 左传 (Zuo's Commentaries on the *Spring and Autumn Annals*) and the *Guo yu* 国语 (Sayings of the States), we can see how the Zhou people interpreted the hexagrams in divination in the following chapter.

6. Divinatory Cases in the *Zuo zhuan* 左传 and the *Guo yu* 国语

There are 22 records related to the *Zhou Changes* and other oracular books in the *Zuo zhuan* 左传 (Zuo's Commentary on the *Spring and Autumn Annals*) and the *Guo yu* 国语 (Sayings of the States). These entries can basically be divided into two types: One type cites the hexagram and line statements to shed light on an issue or explicate one's point of view; the other applies the *Zhou yi* or other divinatory books to prognostication. Among the divinatory records, there are different cases: hexagrams with one changing line, with several changing lines, or with no changing line. Now, I will select 13 entries from the 22, these examples representing different cases so as to explain their implications.

I) Citing hexagram texts to account for one's argument

It says in the "First Year of Duke Zhao (of the State of Lu)" (541 B.C.E.) in the *Zuo zhuan*:

> The Marquis of Jin (*Jin hou* 晋侯) wanted to seek a doctor from the State of Qin 秦, the duke of which dispatched a doctor by the name of He 和 to see him. The doctor pronounced: "The illness cannot be cured on account of his excessive sexual indulgence with poison (*gu* 蛊) [...]" Zhao Meng 赵孟, chief

minister of Jin, asked: "What is called *gu*?" Doctor He answered: "*Gu* is that from which indulgence in excessive sex and delusion arise. *Gu* 蛊 is composed by a vessel (*min* 皿) and insects (*chong* 虫). It is also used to refer to spoiled grain [infested with insects]. In the *Zhou yi*, the constituent trigrams of the hexagram Gu [☶☴, Ills to Be Cured, 18] are Gen [☶, symbolizing the youngest son, mountain, and so on] above and Xun [☴, symbolizing the eldest daughter, wind, and so on] below, signifying a woman deluding a young man and also indicating the wind blowing down a mountain. All these refer to the same thing."ccclxxxvi

Here, Doctor He only cited the images of the trigrams in hexagram Gu to analyze the marquis's disease, without the citation of the hexagram's text.

According to the "Sixth Year of Duke Xuan" (603 B.C.E.) in the *Zuo zhuan*,

Manman 曼满, son of a high official of the State of Zheng 郑, told Boliao 伯廖, a prince of Zheng, that he desired to be a minister of Zheng. Upon his desire, Boliao told other people: "He possesses no virtue and is avaricious, which is just like the hexagram Feng [☳☲, Abundance, 55] changing into Li [☲, Cohesion, 30] in the *Zhou yi*, where the description of the situation is much pertinent to his manifestation." [Just as Boliao predicted,] a year later, Manman was killed by people of Zheng.ccclxxxvii

Though Boliao did not directly cite the text of hexagram Feng, his prediction alludes to the statement of the top line [i.e., the changing line] of the hexagram that "even though the person has a luxurious building or mansion, his house is shaded by shadows and there isn't any person in it at all, nor is there any sound in it for three years, which means misfortune."[1]

---

[1] Richard John Lynn, *The Classic of Changes: A New Translation of the I Ching as Interpreted by Wang Bi*. New York: Columbia University Press, 1994, 491, modified.

During the Spring and Autumn period (770-476 B.C.E.), people did not use "nine" or "six" to represent a *yang* (—) or *yin* (--) line, so Boliao employed the style of "hexagram Feng [☰, Abundance, 55] changing into Li [☰, Cohesion, 30]" to indicate that what he cited was the top line statement of hexagram Feng (in that if the top *yin* [--] line changes into its opposite, i.e., a *yang* [—] line, the former [☰] will transform into the latter [☰]). This was a convention for referencing a line statement of some particular hexagram. The following remarks from the "Twenty-ninth Year of Duke Zhao" (513 B.C.E.) of the *Zuo zhuan* can better exemplify this rule:

> In autumn, a dragon descended to the suburb of Jiang 绛, capital of the State of Jin. Wei Xianzi 魏献子 (d. 509 B.C.E.), great official of Jin, inquired of Cai Mo 蔡墨, the official historian of Jin, about his view on this matter. [...] Cai replied: "There is the term dragon in the *Zhou yi* in which it says 'A submerged dragon does not act'[1] in the hexagram Qian's [☰, The Creative, 1] moving to Gou [☰, Encounter, 44], 'A dragon appears in the fields, it is fitting to see the great man'[2] in its Tongren [☰, Fellowship, 13], 'A dragon flies in the sky, it is fitting to see the great man'[3] in its Dayou [☰, Great Holdings, 14], 'A dragon that overreaches should have cause for regret'[4] in its Guai [☰, Resolution, 43], and 'A flight of dragons without a leader appear, it is good fortune'[5] in its Kun [☰☰, The Receptive, 2]. It also says in Kun's [☰☰, The Receptive, 2] moving to Bo [☰☰, Peeling, 23] that 'dragons fight in the fields.'[6] So, if people did not see them every day, who could name it?" [ccclxxxviii]

---

[1] Ibid., 132.
[2] Ibid., 133, slightly modified.
[3] Ibid., 137, slightly modified.
[4] Ibid., 138.
[5] Ibid., 139, slightly modified.
[6] Ibid., 149.

By this record, it can be seen that during the Spring and Autumn period (770-476 B.C.E.) when people applied the *Zhou Changes* to prognostication or arguments, they did not use the "nine" or "six," which are respectively employed to signify a *yang* [—] or *yin* [--] line in the received version of the *Zhou yi*. Here, Cai Mo cited certain text from the *Zhou yi* related to the term "dragon" in order to argue that there were really dragons in ancient times.

When annotating the *Zuo zhuan*, the famous Western Jin (265-316) scholar Du Yu 杜预 (222-285) held that, here, Cai Mo viewed the "Using of Nine" in hexagram Qian [☰] as "Qian [☰] moving to Kun [☷]", i.e. all of the six lines of the former change into their opposites. But Shang Binghe 尚秉和 (1870-1950), a very famous scholar renowned for his emphasis on image-numerology and the prognostic quality of the *Zhou Changes*, argues against Du's view. Shang contends that what Cai illustrated, such as Qian [☰] moving to Gou [☰], to Tongren [☰], to Dayou [☰], to Guai [☰], and Kun [☷] moving to Bo [☷], refers to a case with one changing line, which was a customary rule for the Zhou people. So, the "Using of Nine" certainly does not mean that all the six lines of Qian [☰] change into their opposites, but generally refers to the case where a *yang* line changes into a *yin* line. Mr. Shang further argues: "The reason the 'Using of Nine: A flight of dragons without a leader appear, it is good fortune'[1] affiliated to hexagram Qian [☰] and the 'Using of Six: It is fitting to practice constancy perpetually here'[2] affiliated to hexagram Kun [☷] is that the sages want to let us know the divinatory rules. Thus, they are not prognostic texts." "The statements affiliated to the 'Using of Nine' and the 'Using of Six' were in order to show that 'Nine' and 'Six' signify changing." "It does not mean that one should use these words as pronouncement of the prognostication if all the six lines of these two hexagrams change into their opposites." "The 'Using of Nine' and the 'Using of Six' particularly refer to the formation of one *yang* or *yin* line after three changes in the manipulation of the milfoil stalks."[ccclxxxix] According to the milfoil-stalk method of divination (mentioned in Chapter 5), Shang's point of view is indeed reasonable.

---

[1] Ibid., 139, slightly modified.
[2] Ibid., 151.

Ouyang Xiu 欧阳修 (1007-72) also made similar remarks in his *Yi tongzi wen* 易童子问 (*Questions from a Youth about the Changes*):

> Why does there appear the "Using of Nine" (*yongjiu* 用九) in hexagram Qian [☰] and the "Using of Six" (*yongliu* 用六) in hexagram Kun [☷]? It means that the *Zhou Changes* neither uses "Seven" nor applies "Eight." A *yang* line corresponds to the number of seven whereas the number of nine signifies a *yang* [—] line will change into a *yin* [--] line; a *yin* line is related to the number of eight while the number of six highlights a *yin* line's transforming into a *yang* line. The *Changes* uses "change" in prognostication, hence the sayings of the "Using of Nine" and the "Using of Six."[cccxc]

So, Shang's view coincides with Ouyang's opinion.

According to their perspective, "nine" or "six" in the *Changes* refers to changing, while "seven" or "eight" signifies a lack of change; since the *Zhou Changes* emphasizes changing in divination, "nine" or "six" is employed to represent a *yang* or *yin* line respectively, the rule of which is exposed in hexagrams Qian [☰] and Kun [☷]. In other words, the "Using of Nine" and the "Using of Six" in these two hexagrams demonstrate that, in milfoil divination, when we meet the number of nine or six, the *yang* or *yin* line will change into its opposite in the derivative hexagram, but if we encounter seven or eight, the *yang* or *yin* line will stay the same in both the original and derivative hexagrams.

As the *Zhou yi Cantong qi* 周易参同契 (*Token for the Agreement of the Three According to the Zhou Changes*) indicates, "Although the 'Using of Nine' and the 'Using of Six' do not have concrete line position, they circulate in the six positions of the hexagram" (*er yong wu yaowei, zhouliu xing liuxu* 二用无爻位, 周流行六虚).[cccxci] This means that, in spite of the fact that the "Using of Nine" and the "Using of Six" do not occupy any specific line position in the two hexagrams, the principle of changing manifested by them functions among the six line positions of the hexagrams. If Du Yu's understanding that the "Using of Nine" means all of the six *yang* lines of hexagram Qian [☰] change into *yin* lines, the two "Using" will occupy concrete line positions and will not circulate. But Du Yu indeed thought in this way and thus he contends that the sentence "A flight of dragons without a leader appear, it is good fortune"[1] is the line statement of the "Using of Nine." If it is so, hexagram Qian [☰, The Creative, 1] will possess seven lines. Mr. Shang Binghe thus retorts: "Has anyone from ancient times to present day ever heard of a hexagram including seven lines?"[cccxcii]

It is evident that Du Yu's understanding is incorrect. In spite of this, his interpretation evokes a question for us: If the "Using of Nine" does not mean all of the six lines of the hexagram change into their opposites, how would one express it under that circumstance where all of the six lines really change into their opposites? Mr. Shang Binghe did not give us any direct answer but only said that, in this case, we ought not to prognosticate by the phrase pertaining to the "Using of Nine." But the question is: Even if we do not use this sentence in prognostication, how does one express the case where all of the six lines change into their opposites if we do not call it "Qian [☰] moves to Kun [☷]"? The eminent Song scholar Zhu Xi 朱熹 (1130-1200) might also have encountered difficulty in tackling this problem, thus he stated his view in Chapter 4 of his *Yixue qimeng* 易学启蒙 (Introduction to the Study of the *Changes*): "When all six lines change, in the cases of Qian and Kun, the prognostications of the 'Using of Nine' and the 'Using of Six' are consulted respectively, yet for other hexagrams, the prognostication is the judgment of the resulting hexagram."[cccxciii] This is a compromise of different opinions.

As Du Yu was a famous ancient scholar, his annotation to the "Using of Nine" aroused many debates among later scholars. Though we have used some space to discuss the matter according to the meanings of the *Zuo zhuan*, the problem has not yet been perfectly resolved.

---

[1] Richard John Lynn, *The Classic of Changes: A New Translation of the I Ching as Interpreted by Wang Bi*. New York: Columbia University Press, 1994, 139, slightly modified.

Divinatory Cases in the *Zuo zhuan* 左传 and the *Guo yu* 国语

II) Applying the *Zhou Changes* or other divinatory books to prognostication

1. Several cases with one changing line.
In the "Twenty-fifth Year of Duke Xi" (635 B.C.E.) of the *Zuo zhuan*,

> Count Qin 秦伯 [i.e., Duke Mu of Qin 秦穆公, d. 621 B.C.E.], who then was striving to seek hegemony, deployed his army on the bank of the Yellow River [in order to save King Xiang of Zhou 周襄王 (d. 619 B.C.E.), who was forced to flee to the town Fan 氾 in the State of Zheng 郑 as he was under attacks launched by his younger brother Shudai 叔带 supported by the barbarian army of Rong 戎]. Then Hu Yan 狐偃 (c. 715-629 B.C.E.), prime minister of the State of Jin, advised Marquis Jin 晋侯 [i.e., Duke Wen of Jin 晋文公, 671-628 B.C.E.], who also received King Xiang of Zhou's 周襄王 petition for help: "If you want to be supported by other dukes, the best way is rescuing the King with troops, which is in alignment with righteousness and will suffice for you to win trust from other dukes. It is the height of opportunity for you to be successor of the cause of Marquis Wen 文侯 [805-746 B.C.E., of Jin who had rescued King Ping of Zhou 周平王 and promoted the establishment of the Eastern Zhou dynasty, 770-256 B.C.E.] and thus your trustworthiness will be manifested to other dukes!" [Duke Wen of Jin was not confident enough and] asked the diviner Bu Yan 卜偃 to consult tortoise-shell divination. [Having obtained the auspicious symbols,] Bu Yan pronounced: "It is auspicious, as we get the omen of 'the Yellow Emperor's [*Huang di* 黄帝, 2717-2599 B.C.E., a legendary sage ruler] combating [against the Red Emperor (*Yan di* 炎帝)] at Banquan 阪泉 [where the former defeated the latter]'." [...] [Duke Wen was not assured yet and further asked Hu Yan] to consult the *Zhou yi* through milfoil stalks, whereupon they encountered hexagram Da you 大有 [☲☰, Great Holdings, 14] moving to Kui 睽 [☲☱, Contrariety, 38]. Bu Yan pronounced: "It is also propitious as the related line statement is 'The duke is

feasted by the son of heaven [i.e. the King].'[1] The divination manual tells us that after the enemies had been defeated, the King will present a feast to the duke. What could be more auspicious than this? Additionally, by the images of these two hexagrams, it can be seen that heaven [symbolized by the lower trigram Qian (☰) in the original hexagram Da you (䷍) and alluding to King Xiang of Zhou] transforms into a lake [symbolized by the lower trigram Dui (☱) in the derivative hexagram Kui (䷥)] to meet the sun [symbolized by the upper trigram Li (☲) of both of the hexagrams and alluding to Duke Wen of Jin], which means the King will condescend to meet the duke. Do you still have any doubts? Moreover, the original hexagram Da you [䷍] itself, in which the lower trigram Qian [☰] represents heaven and father, and the upper trigram Li [☲] symbolizes fire and child, which also indicates that the King will condescend to welcome you." [Emboldened by these pronouncements] Duke Wen of Jin left Qin's army aside and led his own army to the capital region [and finally rescued King Xiang of Zhou, who was so moved that he received Duke Wen of Jin with a grand banquet after he returned to the capital].[cccxciv]

It is evident that Bu Yan took both the images and line statement into account in analyzing the hexagrams. However, in his explanation, images played a major role while the statement he chose was the statement affiliated with the changing line.

In the "Twenty-fifth Year of Duke Xiang" (548 B.C.E.) of the *Zuo zhuan*,

Upon the death of Duke Tang of Qi 齐棠公 [a great official of a city], Dongguo Yan 东郭偃 drove his patron Cui Wuzi 崔武子 [a.k.a. Cui Zhu 崔杼, d. 546 B.C.E.], a senior official of the State of Qi 齐, to pay his condolences, where Cui noticed the beauty of Tang Jiang 棠姜, the widow of the deceased and one of the

---

[1] Ibid., modified.

sisters of the driver Dongguo. Cui was so tempted by her beauty that he wanted eagerly to marry her [which was objected to by Donguo for the reason that both Cui and Dongguo share the same original surname Jiang 姜]. [...] Cui [did not drop his intention and] consulted the *Zhou Changes* through milfoil stalks, where he encountered Kun 困 [☱☵, Impasse, 47] transforming into Daguo 大过 [☱☴, Major Superiority, 28]; all the official historians [who, to flatter Cui] pronounced this auspicious, except Chen Wenzi 陈文子 who stated: 'Husband [symbolized by the lower hexagram Kan (☵) of the original hexagram] follows wind [symbolized by the lower trigram Xun (☴) of the derivative hexagram] and wind blows off wife [symbolized by the upper trigram Dui (☱) of both hexagrams], thus this woman ought not to be married! Additionally, the line statement says: 'This person gets trapped by rocks, stands on caltrops, and does not see his wife when he enters his home. This means misfortune.'[1] 'Trapped by rocks' means there is an impasse in the road; 'standing on caltrops' hints that what he relies on hurts him; 'not seeing his wife when he enters his home' means that he will have no place to return." But Cui insisted that "a widow like her will not be so harmful and her former husband had served as the victim!" Then he married her.[cccxcv] [The fact was that, Cheng Wenzi's prediction came true, and both Tang Jiang and Cui Zhu killed themselves two years later.]

By this excerpt, it can be seen that Chen Wenzi at first employed images of the trigrams and then cited the statement of the changing line for further explanation, i.e., taking both images and line statement into account.

In the "First Year of Duke Min" (661 B.C.E.) in the *Zuo zhuan*,

---

[1] Ibid., 431.

> Bi Wan 毕万 divines about his future if he serves as an official of the state of Jin 晋, when he encounters Zhun [䷂, Birth Throes, 3] transforming into Bi [䷇, Closeness, 8]. As diviner Xin Liao 辛廖 interpreted, "It is auspicious. Zhun denotes steadfastness and Bi entering. What will be so auspicious as this! Your family will certainly become prosperous in Jin. [The lower trigram of the original hexagram] Zhen 震 [☳] changes into land [symbolized by the lower trigram Kun 坤 (☷) of the derivative hexagram], chariot [symbolized by trigram Zhen (☳)] follows horse [symbolized by Kun ()], his feet [also symbolized by Zhen (☳)] stand here, the eldest brother [symbolized by Zhen (☳), too] tends him, his mother [☷] protects him, and the multitude [symbolized by trigram Kan (☵) in both of the hexagrams] submit to him. These six aspects do not change and their unity can lead to consolidation, security, and mightiness—these hexagrams are related to the qualities of dukes and marquis. Your ancestors were dukes and your descendants will become dukes, too."[cccxcvi] [Actually, eight generations later, Bi Wan's descendant Wei Si 魏斯 (a.k.a. Marquis Wen of Wei 魏文侯, 472-396 B.C.E.) founded the State of Wei]

It is evident that the diviner here used only the images to prognosticate the future without mentioning a single word of the related line statement.

In the "Twenty-second Year of Duke Zhuang" (672 B.C.E.) in the *Zuo zhuan*,

> Chen people killed the eldest prince Yukou 御寇. [Scared by this event] the younger prince Chen Wan 陈完 [a.k.a. Jingzhong 敬仲] and Zhuan Sun 颛孙 fled to the State of Qi where Jingzhong was appointed to the high office of minister [...]. When Jingzhong was a child, an official historian of Zhou (1046-256 B.C.E.), who brought the *Zhou Changes* with him, was paying a visit to Marquis Chen, i.e., Jingzhong's father. Marquis Chen asked the official historian to perform a prognosis on the future of Jingzhong. They encountered hexagram Guan [䷓,

Viewing, 20] moving to Pi [☷, Obstruction, 12]. The historian interpreted: "This is called 'Viewing the glory of the state, so it is fitting therefore that this one be guest to the king.'[1] Does this mean that he will own a state instead of Chen? Even if this will not happen here, it will certainly occur in another state; even if it will not be realized in his own life, it will happen in later generations after him, and thus his light is far-reaching and will illuminate other places. Kun [☷] is land while Xun [☴] represents wind and Qian [☰] symbolizes heaven. Wind [☴] transforms into heaven [☰] on the land that contains mountains [☶]. There are resources from mountains that are illumined by heavenly lights and reside on land, hence the line statement that 'Viewing the glory of the state, so it is fitting therefore that this one be guest to the king.' The variety of things for his gate and courtyard are substantially exhibited, together with jade and silk. Thus, he is provided with the elegant things from heaven and earth, and hence 'it is fitting therefore that this one be guest to the king.' As hexagram Guan [☷, Viewing, 20] also connotes waiting to see, it means that this will be realized by his descendants! Since wind [☴] blows on the earth [☷], I believe this will occur in another state. If it is another state, it must the state ruled by the Jiang 姜 family, as this family belongs to offspring of the Taiyue 太岳 [an ancient official position in charge of offering sacrifices to spirits of mountain, also referring to Mount Taishan 泰山]. Mountain [☶] is matched to heaven [☰]. As one thing cannot be fully developed in two ends, after the State of Chen declines, his descendants will become prosperous!" [As a result, his prediction came true, in that] by the time the State of Chen was perishing, Chen Wan's fifth generational grandson Chen Huanzi 陈桓子 (a.k.a. Tian Wuyu 田无宇) began to thrive in the Sate of Qi; and by the time of the full collapse of Chen, Chen Chengzi 陈成子 [i.e.

---

[1] Ibid., 263, slightly modified.

Chen Heng 陈恒] launched a coup d'état and obtained the governance of the State of Qi.[cccxcvii]

Here, the official historian started his prognosis by employing the statement of the changing line of the original hexagram Guan [☷☴] and his analysis of the images followed: "Kun [☷] is *tu* 土 (land)"[1] refers to the inner trigram of hexagram Guan "while Xun [☴] represents wind" corresponds to the upper trigram of the original hexagram; "Qian [☰] symbolizes heaven" points to the upper trigram of the transformed hexagram Pi [☷☰]; "Wind [☴] transforms into heaven [☰] on the land which contains mountains [☶]" means that the upper trigram Xun [☴] of the original hexagram turns into the upper trigram Qian [☰] of the derivative hexagram, and line 2, line 3, and line 4 of the transformed hexagram form another trigram [i.e., nuclear trigram] Gen [☶] which symbolizes mountains, hence the term "mountains," as there is no image of "mountain" in the constituent trigrams of either hexagram. This example provides us with an important clue that, as early as the Spring and Autumn period (770-476 B.C.E.), people were applying overlapping trigrams to their interpretations of the images of the hexagrams, and thus it can be seen that this approach had been invented long before. Since in hexagram Pi [☷☰] the outer trigram is Qian [☰] representing heaven, the position of which is above, the inner trigram is Kun [☷] representing land, the position of which is below, and line 2, line 3, and line 4 form the trigram Gen [☶] representing mountains, located on the land and under heaven, hence revealing an image of forests and resources produced from the mountain. Thus, the historian stated: "There are resources from mountains which are illumined by heavenly lights and reside on land." As the trigram Gen [☶] also symbolizes gate and courtyard, Qian [☰] represents heaven and jade while Kun [☷] is associated with silk and earth [See the "Discussion of the Trigrams" (*Shuo gua* 说卦)], hence the words "The variety of things for his gate and courtyard are substantially exhibited, together with jade and silk."

---

[1] In the divinatory examples illustrated in the *Zuo zhuan* 左传 and *Guo yu* 国语, Kun [☷] always symbolizes *tu* 土 (land), which is a little different from the *Shuo gua* 说卦 ("Discussion of the Trigrams") where Kun represents *di* 地 (earth).

Because the hexagram Guan also contains the meaning of waiting to see the future, all the above-mentioned marvelous events will occur for his offspring. As wind [☴] on the land [☷] is movable, hence there occurs the image of another state. The historian contends that if it occurs in another state, the state must be a state governed by the family of Jiang (in that only the Jiang family obtained its enfeoffment behind Mount Taishan, which is close to and matches heaven) and the nuclear trigram Gen [☶] in the transformed hexagram Pi [䷋] be directly under and coordinated with heaven [☰].

In this case, the historian not only quoted the statement of the changing line of the original hexagram but also analyzed the images of both the original and derivative hexagrams to extrapolate his prediction, yet he mainly depends on the images of the derivative hexagram.

In the *Guo yu* 国语 (Sayings of the States), there is no case with one single changing line, while in the *Zuo zhuan,* there are overall 11 cases with one changing line, from which we selected the above-mentioned four cases as representatives. The other seven cases were deciphered in a similar way as those mentioned above, and we will not illustrate them here one after another.

2. Cases with two changing lines. There is no record of such a case in the *Zuo zhuan*, *Guo yu*, or other extant documents dating from the pre-Qin [i.e., before 221 B.C.E.] era.

3. Cases with three changing lines. There is no record of such a case in the *Zuo zhuan*, whereas there are two cases of this kind in the *Guo yu* 国语 (Sayings of the States). Being still a fugitive on account of persecution in his native land a dozen years prior, Chong'er 重耳 (671-628 B.C.E.), a prince of the state of Jin who later was respectfully referred to as Duke Wen of Jin *(Jin Wengong* 晋文公*)*, wished to return, with the help of the state of Qin, to his native land of Jin, when the state was in chaos. But his future hung in the balance. According to the chapter of "Sayings of the State of Jin" (*Jin yu* 晋语):

> The prince [i.e., Chong'er 重耳] did a divination himself and questioned "whether the State of Jin will exist or not?" He obtained hexagram Zhun 屯 [䷂, Birth Throes, 3] transforming

into Yu 豫 [☷☳, Contentment, 16], all eight (*jie ba ye* 皆八也). [The official historians might have seen that the whole image of the original hexagram was such that the chariot symbolized by the inner trigram Zhen (☳) encounters dangers represented by the outer trigram Kan (☵).] All of them [i.e., the official historians] pronounced "inauspiciousness, as it shows obstruction and stagnation and the line indicates taking no-action." But Sikong Jizi 司空季子 (657-570 B.C.E.) said: "It is auspicious, as in the *Zhou yi* both the original and derivative hexagrams pronounce 'It is fitting to establish a state.'[1] If the state of Jin does not exist to assist the king [of Zhou 周 (1046-256 B.C.E.)], how can a state be established? As the question is 'Whether State Jin will exist or not' and the oracle tells us 'It is fitting to establish a state,' it means that you can obtain the task of governing the state. How auspicious it is! Zhen [☳] is chariot, Kan [☵] is water, Kun [☷] is land, Zhun 屯 [☵☳, Birth Throes, 3] connotes abundance of material resources, and Yu 豫 [☷☳, Contentment, 16] designates joy and pleasure. The chariots are presented both inside and outside [in that both the inner trigram of the original hexagram and the outer trigram of the derivative hexagram are Zhen (☳), symbolizing chariot], the multitude of people submit to you [as the inner trigram of Yu (☷☳) is Kun (☷) and line 2, line 3, and line 4 of Zhun () also form a Kun trigram (☷) which is associated with land, multitude, and obedience]; the inexhaustible ever-flowing fountain nourishes you [because line 3, line 4, and line 5 of Zhun (☵☳) and line 2, line 3, and line 4 of Yu (☷☳) can form trigram Gen (☶), symbolizing mountains and the upper trigram of Zhun (☵☳) is Kan (☵), and line 3, line 4, and line 5 of Yu (☷☳) also constitute Kan (☵), the image of water on a mountain representing a fountain or spring]; the land and material resources are abundant and the person is content with his possession [since Yu has the meaning of contentment]. If

---

[1] Richard John Lynn, *The Classic of Changes: A New Translation of the I Ching as Interpreted by Wang Bi*. New York: Columbia University Press, 1994, 152 and 235, slightly modified.

you will not obtain the state of Jin again, what can match these images? Zhen [☳] represents thunder and chariots while Kan [☵] symbolizes labor, water, and the multitude. Thunder and chariots are what is major [i.e., the inner trigram of the original hexagram], with water and multitudes [of the people] [in the outer]. The chariots symbolized by Zhen [☳] exhibit force and power while water, symbolized by Kan [☵], shows the obedience of the civil population. Both the civil and the military are in the possession of one person, which is conceived as the utmost potentiality: hence the hexagram Zhun [䷂]. Its judgment says: 'Zhun consists of fundamentality [*yuan* 元], prevalence [*heng* 亨], benefits [*li* 利], and constancy [*zhen* 贞]. Do not use it as an opportunity to go forth. It is fitting to establish a state.'[1] Its inner trigram is Zhen [☳] representing thunder and the eldest son, hence the term *yuan* (fundamentality); there is the multitude of people who are compliant and convening, hence the term *heng* (prevalence); the terms of 'benefits' and 'constancy' mean that there is Zhen [☳] symbolizing thunder in the inner position, which benefits animate things, and that it is fitting to undertake a great cause with constancy. Meanwhile, the chariot [symbolized by Zhen ☳] moves upward and water [☵] flows downward, illustrating an image of a chariot sinking in water, which presages some obstruction in petty things, hence the statement of 'Do not use it as an opportunity to go forth.' But there is also an image of force and power indicated by one's leadership action followed with the multitude's obedience, hence the words of 'it is fitting to establish a state.'" [In the derivative hexagram Yu (䷏)] Kun [☷] is mother, and Zhen [☳] is the eldest son; even though the mother has become old, the eldest son has been able to undertake tasks, an image of joy and pleasure, hence the name of Yu [䷏, Contentment]. Its judgment of 'It is fitting to establish a state and to send the army into action'[2] displays the

---

[1] Ibid., 152, slightly modified.
[2] Ibid., 235, slightly modified.

internal pleasure when staying in and the external momentum of chariots when marching out. Both the original and transformed hexagrams relate to your returning to the state of Jin and accomplishing your goal [of obtaining the throne]!"[cccxcviii] [As a matter of fact, one year later, Chong'er successfully returned to his native land with the help of the state of Qin's army and then obtained the throne.]

In this case, Sikong Jizi at first interpreted the prognostication via the judgments of both the original and derivative hexagrams, then analyzed the images of both hexagrams in detail, and finally accounted for the judgments of both hexagrams through the images.

We have learned from the previously mentioned case, with one changing line, that when the statements were made use of in pronouncement, the statement that would be employed was that one belonging to the changing line. But in the above-mentioned case with three changing lines, the judgments of both the original and derivative hexagrams will be involved, whereas the line statements are not related. This shows the difference between the case of having one changing line and that of having three changing lines in prognostication.

In this case, a divinatory number appears, as it says, "He obtained hexagram Zhun 屯 [☵☳, Birth Throes, 3] transforming into Yu 豫 [☳☷, Contentment, 16], all eight (jie ba ye 皆八也)." "All eight (jie ba ye 皆八也)" is an issue which merits a detailed discussion.

First of all, let us take a look at the changing lines of the hexagram. As the original hexagram is Zhun 屯 [☵☳, Birth Throes, 3] and the derivative hexagram is Yu 豫 [☳☷, Contentment, 16], apparently the changing lines include line 1, line 4, and line 5. Namely, the bottom line changes from nine to eight [i.e., an old *yang* line changes into a young *yin* line], the fourth line transforms from six to seven [an old *yin* lines transforms into a young *yang* line], and the fifth line changes from nine to eight [an old *yang* line changes into a young *yin* line]. Why does it say, "all eight"?

In order to solve this riddle, earlier scholars have offered various explanations. Some held that, in this prognosis, the diviner first obtained hexagram Zhun 屯 [☵☳] and then got hexagram Yu 豫 [☳☷] at the second time of the manipulation of the milfoil stalks. As neither of the hexagrams has changing lines, the reference is thus made to "all eight." This interpretation is obviously untenable in that, in the previously mentioned divinatory cases, we cannot find any one that refers to two separate manipulations of the milfoil stalks resulting in two hexagrams all offered as a single divination. In the meantime, according to the divinatory cases included in the *Zuo zhuan* and the *Guo yu*, in the Spring and Autumn period (770-476 B.C.E.), every hexagram mentioned with "eight' contains several changing lines, such as seen where "the Eight of Gen [☶, Restraint, 52] means Gen moves to Sui [☶, Following, 17]" in the "Ninth Year of Duke Xiang" (564 B.C.E.) of the *Zuo zhuan* [for the interpretation of this case, please see below], and "obtaining the Eight of Tai [☰, Peace, 11]" in the "Sayings of the State of Jin" of the *Guo yu* [see below] can be taken as evidence.

Another point of view holds that, as both the inner trigram of the original hexagram Zhun [☵] and the outer trigram of the derivative hexagram Yu [☳] are Zhen [☳], and when the former transforms into the latter only the two *yin* lines of Zhen [☳]—i.e., line 2 and line 3 (of the original hexagram)—remain unchanging, i.e., remain eight, which signifies the "all eight." But the problem is that the top line of hexagram Zhun [☵] is also an unchanging line, and its divinatory number is also eight, so, according to this interpretation, why does "eight" only refer to line 2 and line 3, and not line 6? Moreover, in the case of the "Ninth Year of Duke Xiang" (564 B.C.E.) where "the Eight of Gen [☶] means Gen moves to Sui [☶]," in which line 2 is also stable, why does it not say, "He obtained hexagram Gen [☶] transforming into Sui [☶], all eight (*jie ba ye* 皆八也)"? It can be seen that this explanation is also indefensible.

Therefore, scholars of subsequent generations have not been able to explain the real significance of these cases where "eight" is mentioned in the *Zuo zhuan* and the *Guo yu*, as they cannot be thoroughly interpreted by the principle that "nine" and "six" mean changing while "seven" and "eight" signify a lack of change. For this reason, some scholars have had no choice but to ascribe these phenomena to mantic arts of the *Lianshan* (Linked Mountains) and *Guicang* (Return to the Hidden), which, they asserted, use "seven" and "eight" and not "nine" and "six" in divination. But since, long ago, past generations failed to hand down these two books, how can we know this principle? To say the least, even if this argument is foundational, why is only "eight" and not "seven" mentioned in these cases? So, when this assertion came out, it was immediately refuted by others. As we have no other better interpretations for these instances mentioning "eight," we have to leave this question open.

According to the "*Zhou yu* 周语" (Sayings of the Zhou Court) in the *Guo yu*, when Duke Cheng of the State of Jin was to return to his native state to succeed to the position of regional lord, the Jin people made a prognosis for him, obtaining Qian [☰, The Creative, 1] moving to Pi [☷, Obstruction, 12], by which the diviner pronounced: "Though his virtue can match heaven [i.e., he can be the regional lord of the state of Jin], his rule will not be long-lasting and there will be three dukes from the Zhou court to return [to succeed to the throne of the state]." It is evident that line 1, line 2, and line 3 of the original hexagram are moving lines, and thus the inner trigram Qian [☰] of the original hexagram turns into Kun [☷] in the derivative hexagram. As Qian [☰] is associated with heaven and sovereignty while Kun [☷] symbolizes earth and subjects [see the *Shuogua* 说卦 (Discussion of the Trigrams)], which give us the image that heaven changes into earth and sovereign transforms into subject, hence comes the remark of "matching but not long lasting." Because all the three lines of the inner trigram are changing lines, the diviner concluded that there would be three lords succeeding to the throne, one after another.

In this divinatory case, the diviner purely analyzes the images of the original and transformed trigrams without citing related hexagram or line statements, and the analysis of the images is also very succinct.

4. Cases with four changing lines are not available in the *Zuo zhuan* or the *Guo yu*, or other pre-Qin [i.e., before 221 B.C.E.] documents.

5. There is only one divinatory case with five changing lines, which appears in the *Zuo zhuan*, but no case of this kind appears in the *Guo yu*. In the "Ninth Year of Duke Xiang" (564 B.C.E.) of the *Zuo zhuan*:

> Mu Jiang 穆姜 died at the Eastern Palace. Previously, when she was sent, as punishment, to the palace, she had conducted a divination about her future and encountered the Eight of Gen

[☷, Restraint, 52]. The official historian said: "This is called Gen [☶] moves to Sui [☱, Following, 17]. As Sui means 'to be out,' your highness will get out of this palace very soon." But Jiang interpreted it in another way: "No. As it says in the *Zhou Changes* that 'Sui consists of *yuan* 元, *heng* 亨, *li* 利, and *zhen* 贞 and there will be no blame,' in which *yuan* is the leader of man; *heng* is the synthesis of beauty; *li* is coalescence with righteousness; *zhen* is the very trunk of human affairs. (The virtuous man) embodying benevolence is sufficient to be a leader of men, the beautiful virtue in him is sufficient to make men live in accordance with propriety, he engenders fitness in people sufficient to keep them in harmony with righteousness, and his constancy is firm enough to serve as the trunk for human affairs.[1] He who does not tarnish these four virtues will follow the tendency and get out of the place without any blame. But as a woman I took part in a sinister plot and being in an inferior female position I have no benevolence; this cannot match the quality of *yuan*. I disturbed the governance of the state, which cannot be called *heng*; my bad deeds do harm to myself, which cannot be called *li*; I discarded my noble position and became promiscuous, which cannot match the quality of *zhen*. Those who have these four virtues can follow without blame, but I possess none of them, [so] how can I be freed from this place! I have done so many evil things, shouldn't I be blamed? I will have to end my life here and cannot get out of here before my death!"[cccxcix] [As a matter of fact, Mu Jiang was not allowed to leave the palace before her death.]

Mu Jiang (d. 564 B.C.E.) was the wife of Duke Xuan of the state of Lu and Duke Cheng's mother. She committed adultery with the senior official Shusun Qiaoru 叔孙侨如. In the 16th year of Duke Cheng (575 B.C.E.), Mu Jiang and Shusun plotted in vain to overthrow Duke Cheng (r. 590-573 B.C.E.), and thus Mu was forced to move to the Eastern Palace, where she made a divination by the *Zhou yi* to predict her future and encountered the above-mentioned hexagrams.

---

[1] Ibid., 130, slightly modified.

In the case of the *Guo yu*, Sikong Jizi 司空季子 (675-570 B.C.E.) had said that "Zhen [☳] represents thunder and the eldest son, hence the term *yuan* (fundamentality); there is the multitude of people who are compliant and convening, hence the term *heng* (prevalence)," to interpret the terms of *yuan* and *heng* in the judgment of hexagram Zhun 屯 [䷂, Birth Throes, 3]. In the "Twenty-second Year of Duke Zhao" (520 B.C.E.), Zifu Huibo 子服惠伯, a senior official of the state of Lu, also had a similar view that "fundamentality (*yuan*) is the leader of goodness" (which is in alignment with the "Commentary on the Words of the Text")[1]. Their interpretations of the terms of *yuan* and *heng* are largely identical. Therefore, it can be seen that, in as early as the Spring and Autumn period (770-476 B.C.E.), the four terms of *yuan*, *heng*, *li*, and *zhen* had been correlated with the "four virtues," and their interpretation had been established, which was merely cited by Mu Jiang, who was aware that her deeds were not congruent with the four virtues at all, and thus whose interpretation of the hexagrams differs from the official historian's.

In this case, only if line 1, line 3, line 4, line 5, and line 6 change into their opposites can hexagram Gen [䷳] transform into Sui [䷐]. According to the principle of change of the divinatory numbers, line 1 changes from "six" [old *yin*] to "seven" [young *yang*], line 3 from "nine" [old *yang*] to "eight" [young *yin*], line 4 from "six" [old *yin*] to "seven" [young *yang*], line 5 from "six" [old *yin*] to "seven" [young *yang*], and line 6 from "nine" [old *yang*] to "eight" [young *yin*], and only line 2 is "eight" [the number of young *yin*], which remains unchanging. In these five changing lines, line 1, line 4, and line 5 change from "six" to "seven" while line 3 and the top line change from "nine" to "eight." In other words, in this case, there are three lines changing from "six" to "seven" and two lines changing form "nine" to "eight."

Yet, what does the "Eight of Gen [䷳]" mean here? Does the "eight" refer to a changing line? If so, in this case, there are three lines changing from "six" to "seven" and only two lines changing form "nine" to "eight," so why does it not call this case the "Seven of Gen" but the "Eight of Gen"? Some scholars hold that the "Eight of Gen [䷳]" signifies that,

---

[1] Ibid., 130.

when Gen [☶] transforms into Sui [☱], only the second line's divinatory number "eight" remains unchanging and the "Eight of Gen [☶]" means that the divinatory number of line 2 is "eight" while the others are changing lines from "nine" or from "six." If it is really the case that "eight" especially refers to the number of the second yin line of a hexagram which stays stable, though, we cannot account for the previously mentioned case that "hexagram Zhun 屯 [☳, Birth Throes, 3] transforming into Yu 豫 [☲, Contentment, 16], all eight (*jie ba ye* 皆八也)", in which line 2 is also an immobile line, but it was not referred to as "the Eight of Zhun [☳]." Therefore, this point of view is also untenable, and the problem has not yet been resolved.

Under this circumstance, some scholars contend that this reference might belong to the divinatory traditions of the *Lianshan* (Linked Mountains) and the *Guicang* (Return to the Hidden). As these two oracles were lost long ago, the meanings of the "eight" have become an unresolved thousand-year mystery.

The basis for their attributing these interpretations to the traditions of the *Lianshan* and the *Guicang* is that the official historian's pronouncement in Cong'er's case was inauspicious, which might be derived from the *Lianshan* and/or the *Guicang*'s divinatory principle, while Sikong Jizi's pronouncement was auspicious, which was deduced by the divinatory principle of the *Zhou Changes*. In Mu Jiang's case, the official historian's conclusion about her impending good fortune was also based on the *Lianshan* and/or the *Guicang* traditions, but Mu Jiang insisted on turning to the *Zhou yi*, by which she got an opposite prediction.

These scholars' view might originate from Kong Yingda's 孔穎達 (574-648) subcommentary on these cases in the *Zuozhuan zhengyi* 左傳正義 (Correct Meaning of *Zuo's Commentary on the Spring and Autumn Annals*). But if we examine another case related to "eight" in the "Sayings of the State of Jin" (*Jin yu* 晉語) in the *Guo yu*, we can find that this view is not convincing, either. The chapter records:

> In the [lunar] twelfth month, Count Qin 秦伯 [i.e., Duke Mu of Qin 秦穆公 (r. 659-621 B.C.E.)] accepted the prince [i.e., Chong'er who later turned out to be the lord of the State of Jin

and was referred to as Duke Wen of Jin]. [...] Dong Yin 董因, a minister of the state of Qin, met him on the bank of the Yellow River. The prince asked him: "Can I return to the state of Jin [i.e., his native state] and obtain the sovereignty this time?" Dong replied: "... I will do a divination for you." He obtained the eight of Tai [☰☷, Peace, 11] (*de tai zhi ba* 得泰之八) and said: "This is called the intercourse between heaven [symbolized by the lower trigram ☰ which represents the rising *yang* energy] and earth [symbolized by the upper trigram ☷ which represents the falling *yin* energy] and indicates the petty is departing and the great is arriving [the judgment of hexagram Tai].¹ This time you can tide over the difficulties and certainly achieve the sovereign leadership of your native state!"ᶜᵈ

None of the interpretations of the "Eight of Tai" offered by the ancients are reasonable enough. Wei Zhao 韦昭 (204-273), a very famous annotator of the *Guo yu*, avers that this means that the hexagram Tai [☰☷] they encountered has no changing line(s). Many contemporary scholars also follow Wei's view. But if the hexagram Tai [☰☷] indeed has no changing lines, the divinatory number of each of the inner three *yang* lines should be "seven" (young *yang*) and that of the outer *yin* lines ought to be "eight" (young *yin*). According to the convention in divination, as the inner trigram plays a major role, why did Dong Yin not call it the "seven" instead of the "eight" of the hexagram?

Additionally, each hexagram without any changing line appearing in the divinatory cases in the *Zuo zhuan* is referred to through the following: "As far as its hexagram is concerned, we encountered X." [for these cases, please see below] For instance, in the case related to Duke Mu of Qin's sending a punitive expedition against the state of Jin, as mentioned in the "Fifteenth Year of Duke Xi" (645 B.C.E.) of the *Zuo zhuan*, we read that "as far as its hexagram is concerned, we encountered Gu [☶☴]," which has no changing line [for its analysis, please see below]; in the case about the battle at Yanling 鄢陵 between states that Jin and Chu recorded in the "Sixteenth Year of Duke Cheng" (575 B.C.E.), we read that

---

¹ Ibid., 205, slightly modified.

"as far as its hexagram is concerned, we encountered Fu [☷☳]," where, again, there is no moving line. Therefore, it is evident how a hexagram without any changing line is described: "As far as its hexagram is concerned, we encountered X." On the contrary, all the hexagrams with reference to "eight" have changing lines, the testimony of which can be found in the above-mentioned cases. Therefore, Wei Zhao's view that in this case there was no changing line is not correct, and this hexagram ought to be seen as having changing line(s).

Then, other scholars pointed out that the "Eight of Tai" means that line 1, line 2, and line 3 of the hexagram change from "nine" to "eight" while the other three lines remain unchanging, i.e., they still remain "eight." If so, according to the regularity of the divinatory cases in the *Zuo zhuan* and the *Guo yu*, this case should be referred to as "Tai [☷☰] moving to Kun [☷☷]" rather than "Eight of Tai."

Therefore, all of these views are difficult to justify.

Under this circumstance, one scholar pointed out that the "*tai zhi ba* 泰之八" (Eight of Tai) might be the erroneous pronunciation of "*tai zhi bo*" (Tai [☷☰] moving to Bo [☶☷]). But, since in the divinatory cases there are the sayings of "Eight of Gen" and "Zhun 屯 [☵☳, Birth Throes, 3] transforming into Yu 豫 [☳☷, Contentment, 16], all eight (*jie ba ye* 皆八也)," it ought not to be a mistaken pronunciation.

The most noteworthy thing here is that, in this case, Dong Yin cited "the petty is departing and the great is arriving" from the judgment of hexagram Tai to apply it to his prognosis, which undoubtedly demonstrates that, here, Dong was using the *Zhou Changes* rather than the *Lianshan* and the *Guicang*-like divination manuals in the prognostication, which accordingly falsifies the point of view that the divinatory cases related to "Eight" were confined only to the *Lianshan* and the *Guicang*-oriented divinations.

By the above-mentioned three cases related to "Eight," it can be seen that, for all their efforts, the ancients could not find an appropriate answer to its meanings, which forces us to confront a fundamental question: whether the criterion that "nine" and "six" mean changing and "seven" and "eight" designate unchanging was followed by the people in the Spring and Autumn era (770-476 B.C.E.)? Or there might be some other criterion for the use of "eight." This is only a kind of guess on my part. However, it will be necessary to discuss this problem again.

6. Cases with six changing lines. There is no record of such a case in the *Zuo zhuan*, *Guo yu*, or other extant documents dating from the pre-Qin [i.e., before 221 B.C.E.] era.

7. Cases with no changing lines. There are two cases of this kind in the *Zuo zhuan*. In the "Fifteenth Year of Duke Xi" (645 B.C.E.):

> When Duke Mu of Qin (Qin Mugong 秦穆公, d. 621 B.C.E.) was planning to send a punitive expedition against the state of Jin, [the official diviner] Bu Tufu 卜徒父 conducted a milfoil-stalk divination and pronounced: "It is auspicious, as the chariot of the Duke [of Jin] will be destroyed after [our army] has crossed over the Yellow River." [Duke Mu] asked for a detailed explanation and the diviner elaborated: "It is quite auspicious and, after failure occurs three times, the lord of Jin will certainly be captured; as far as its hexagram is concerned, we encountered Gu [䷑, Ills to Be Cured, 18], which says: '[The army] drives its thousand chariots three times and then captures its male fox.' (*Qian sheng san qu, san qu zhi yu, huo qi xiong hu* 千乘三去, 三去之余, 获其雄狐). It is certain that the fox symbolizes its lord. The inner trigram [☴] [representing our side] is wind while the outer trigram [☶] is mountain. As it is now autumn, our side [i.e., wind] blows off the fruits of the woods on the other side [i.e., the mountain] and further obtains its resources; certainly, we can defeat them. Its fruits are blown off and resources are taken away what except losing the war is waiting for them!"[cdi] [Actually, the diviner's prognosis came true.]

In deciphering this hexagram, Bu Tufu's prognosis might be based on the images: From the bottom line to the fourth line of the hexagram [䷑] constitutes a bigger Kan [☵], which symbolizes a river; line 2, line 3, and line 4 form trigram Dui [☱], which denotes destruction; and line 3, line 4, and line 5 comprise trigram Zhen [☳], which represents a chariot—all these trigrams reveal an image that the river is involved with a destruction of chariots, hence the diviner's prognosis that "the chariot of the Duke [of Jin] will be destroyed after (our army) has crossed over the Yellow River." But Duke Mu of Qin still could not understand his analysis well, so he demanded further explanations. As the judgment of the hexagram given by the diviner is not available in the received version of the *Zhou Changes*, it probably came from the *Lianshan*, or the *Guicang*, or some other oracle.

There was not any changing line in this case. In analyzing the hexagram, the diviner at first cited the judgment, and then interpreted the images by which he further testified concerning the judgment that led to his prediction.

In the "Sixteenth Year of Duke Cheng" (575 B.C.E.):

> The armies from the states of Jin and Chu met each other at Yanling 鄢陵, … when Duke Li of Jin (Jin Ligong 晋厉公, d. 573 B.C.E.) made the official historian divine for the possible result of the battle. The historian said: "It is auspicious in that as far as its hexagram is concerned, we encountered Fu [☷, Return, 24] which announces that 'The southern state[1] is poverty-stricken, in shooting the monarch with arrows one can hit his eyes' (*Nanguo cu, she qi yuanwang, zhong jue mu* 南国蹙, 射其元王, 中厥目). Now that the state is in danger and the lord is injured, they will certainly be defeated!" The duke took the diviner's prediction and encouragement.[cdii]

In this case, too, there was not any changing line. The official historian applied the judgment rather than the images of the hexagram to his prediction. The judgment of the hexagram is not available in the received version of the *Zhou Changes*, either, which might again come from the *Lianshan*, or the *Guicang*, or some other oracle prevalent at that time.

---

[1] Translator's note: Here the "southern state" refers to the state of Chu as it was then a state in the southern part of China and south of the state of Jin.

7.
Are the Prognostications Determined Only by the Changing Line(s)?

From the last chapter's 13 examples, especially in regard to the 10 divinatory cases as recorded in the *Zuo zhuan* and the *Guo yu*, it can be seen that, in the Spring and Autumn period (770-476 B.C.E.), there was no fixed formula in prognostication when the *Zhou Changes* was used. For instance, in some cases the divinatory historians pronounced "inauspiciousness," but Sikong Jizi 司空季子 offered an affirmative conclusion (see Chapter 6), and in some cases the divinatory historians pronounced "auspiciousness," but Chen Wenzi 陈文子 provided us with an opposite prediction (see Chapter 6). This is what the predecessors have already asserted: "There isn't any fixed [hermeneutic] rule in prognostications."

According to the so-called *bianzhan* 变占 (literally, prognostication by changing line(s)) principle invented by Zhu Xi 朱熹 (1130-1200), "When only one line changes, we take the statement of the original hexagram's changing line as the prognostication"[cdiii]—this means that there is some fixed rule for divination. But if we take a comprehensive survey of the divinatory cases with one changing line in the Spring and Autumn times (770-476 B.C.E.), it is evident that although in most of these cases the statement of the changing line was taken as the prognostication, the analysis of the images of the related trigrams plays a major role, and some cases also cited the judgment and images of the resulting hexagram. Therefore, the rule invented by Zhu Xi is not completely in alignment with the regulations employed in the Spring and Autumn era. Zhu Xi further asserted: "When two lines change, we take the statements of the two changing lines of the original hexagram as the prognostication, but we take the uppermost line as ruler."[cdiv] There was no case of this kind in the *Zuo zhuan* and the *Guo yu*. This rule might only be words of speculation by Zhu Xi himself.

According to Zhu Xi's argument, "When three lines change, the prognostication is the judgment of the original hexagram and the resulting hexagram, and we use the original hexagram as *zhen* 贞 [the question, or present situation] and the resulting hexagram as *hui* 悔 [the prognostication]."[cdv] One case of this kind is available in the *Guo yu* as illustrated above, in that "he obtained hexagram Zhun 屯 [☷, Birth Throes, 3] transforming into Yu 豫 [☷, Contentment, 16], all eight (*jie ba ye* 皆八也)." where Sikong Jizi 司空季子 concentrated his pronouncement on analysis of images and cited part of the judgment of the original hexagram, and of the resulting hexagram, which share the same phrase, "It is fitting to establish a state." But if the judgment of the original hexagram and that of the derivative are completely different—one declares good fortune while the other states misfortune—we may ask Zhu Xi: How should we draw on the judgment in the divination?

For the case with four changing lines, Zhu Xi advises us to "use the two unchanging lines in the resulting hexagram as the prognostication but take the lower line as the ruler."[cdvi] We have not found any case of this kind in the *Zuo zhuan*, the *Guo yu*, or other extant pre-Qin documents. These remarks are based on nothing but Zhu's arbitrary conjecture.

Zhu Xi went on to assert: "When five lines change, we use the unchanging line of the resulting hexagram as the prognostication."[cdvii] As in the divinatory accounts in the *Zuo zhuan* and the *Guo yu* above, we cannot find evidence that the Zhou (1046-256 B.C.E.) people had this kind of view in divination, and this assumption is obviously not in alignment with the case of "Eight of Gen [☷, Restraint, 52]," which is called by the official historians "Gen [☷] moves to Sui [☷, Following,

17]" (see Chapter 6), where Mu Jiang used the judgment of the latter as the prognostication, which does not conform to Zhu Xi's rule nor use the statement for line 2 [i.e., the unchanging line] of the hexagram that "This one ties itself to the little child and abandons the mature man"[cdviii] as her pronouncement.

Zhu Xi further contended that "when all six lines change, in the cases of Qian [☰, The Creative, 1] and Kun [☷, The Receptive, 2], the prognostications are the 'Using of Nine' and the 'Using of Six,' respectively. For other hexagrams, the prognostication is the judgment of the resulting hexagram."[cdix] No such regulation can be found in the *Zuo zhuan*, the *Guo yu*, or other pre-Qin documents. Therefore, what Zhu Xi asserted was nothing but his own conjecture.

Based on these considerations, it seems that the so-called *bianzhan* 变占 [literally, prognostication by changing line(s)] method invented by Zhu Xi cannot be brought into accord with the real prognostications recounted in the *Zuo zhuan* and the *Guo yu*; some rules invented by Zhu Xi were merely based on his personal speculations.

As a matter of fact, according to the accounts of the divinatory cases archived historically, there are no fixed rules for the interpretation of the hexagrams and lines in divination. Such predictions tended to be determined by the diviner's own understanding of the statements. The most obvious example is the case considered above, of Mu Jiang, who encountered hexagram Sui [☱, Following, 17], the judgment of which is "Sui consists of *yuan* 元, *heng* 亨, *li* 利, and *zhen* 贞 and there will be no blame"—an apparently auspicious phrase—but she contends: "Those who have these four virtues can follow without blame, but I possess none of them, [so] how can I be freed from this place! I have done so many evil things, shouldn't I be blamed? I will have to end my life here and cannot get out of here before my death!"[cdx]

In Mu Jiang's opinion, the prediction is finally determined by virtues of the divined: Even if the evildoers get an auspicious hexagram in divination, they will not have a propitious outcome. Deduction from this principle suggests that even though virtuous people may obtain an inauspicious hexagram in divination, a fortunate result will wait for them. If this is the case, though, and cultivation of virtues will suffice, is there then any need for them to use divination?

Some people may offer a completely new interpretation according to specific conditions of the matter in question. For example, in the "Divination" (*bushi* 卜筮) chapter of Wang Chong's 王充 (27-c. 97) *Lun heng* 论衡 (Discourses Weighed in the Balance), there is a legend:

> The State of Lu was to send a punitive expedition against the State of Yue. The people of Lu divined about the outcome in advance and encountered "The Caldron breaks its feet,"[cdxi] which Zi Gong 子贡 (520-446 B.C.E.) — one of the seventy-two brilliant disciples of Confucius — pronounced "inauspicious," as he was thinking that armies march on foot; now that the feet were broken, they would not win. But Confucius pronounced it "auspicious" and his reasoning was that "The Yue people live near water and the army uses ships but not feet to march on." The outcome was that the former really defeated the latter.[cdxii]

As is evident, Zi Gong's prediction was based on the line statement while Confucius's judgment was based on the particular condition of the matter.

In this way, the fortune or misfortune of the judgment or line statement of a hexagram obtained in divination will not be of any significance, in that the fortune or misfortune depends on the interpreter's insights. If the diviner wants to pronounce the oracle fortunate, he or she can find reasons for the good fortune; and if it is seen as unfortunate, then one can find reasons for declaring misfortune. The renowned Qing scholar Ji Xiaolan's 纪晓岚 (1724-1805) interpretation can also exemplify this uncertainty:

> When Ji was young, he once participated in an imperial examination held at his native town. His tutor divined about the result for him in advance and got the third line of hexagram Kun [䷮, Impasse, 47], the statement for which is that "This one suffers Impasse between rocks and caltrops, he enters his home but does not see his wife. This means misfortune."[cdxiii] Based on the statement, his teacher pronounced it "inauspicious," while Ji himself contended that "though the

statement tells us 'he enters his home but does not see his wife, which means misfortune,' as I have not been married, does this statement have anything to do with me? In my opinion, in this examination, I might get the second place while the first place might be taken by a person whose surname is Shi 石 (rock) or whose surname contains the 'rock' signifier, or radical."[cdxiv]

As expected, Ji gained the second place while the first place was obtained by a person whose surname was Shi, and the third place was awarded to a person whose surname was Mi 米, the pictograph of which is like a caltrop.[cdxv] This is certainly a fabricated story. But, we can see from this story that even until the Qing dynasty (1616-1912) people did not completely rely on the judgment and/or line statement(s) in their prognostications, and sometimes only depended on their improvisations based on the judgment and/or line statement(s).

Additionally, in the divinatory cases in the *Zuo zhuan* and the *Guo yu* mentioned above, some ancient people directly got rid of the judgments and line statements altogether and depended only on images to interpret their hexagrams. Later diviners also followed this trend. For example, the Northern Qi (*Bei qi* 北齐, 550-577) expert on the *Changes* Zhao Fuhe 赵辅和 once met a person asking for a diviner to divine about his father's disease. They encountered hexagram Tai [☷☰, Peace, 11], at which the diviner pronounced great auspiciousness and stated that his father would recover very soon. After the person had gone, Zhao told the diviner: "The image of hexagram Tai [☷☰] is that Qian [☰] is located in the lower position while Kun [☷] resides in the upper position; as the former symbolizes father and the latter earth, the whole image is that father goes into the earth [i.e., an image of burial and death], so is there any reason for the pronouncement of auspiciousness?"[cdxvi]

In this case, the diviner evidently used the judgment of hexagram Tai as the prognostication and pronounced auspiciousness while Zhao Fuhe depended only on the images of the hexagram that led to a pronouncement of misfortune. For the same hexagram, the prediction by the judgment and that by the images led to completely opposite conclusions, which makes us wonder who was right and who was wrong, as well as what course to follow!

AN INTRODUCTION TO THE *ZHOU YI* (BOOK OF CHANGES)

By the time of the Western Han dynasty, Jing Fang 京房 (77-37 B.C.E.) employed the *Najia* 纳 divinatory system in divination, which attaches the 10 heavenly stems and 12 earthly branches to the hexagrams. This mantic art is said to have been invented by Western Han scholars and exerted far-reaching influences on later generations in both the academic circle and the field of commoners interested in divination.

In the *Najia* system, the 64 hexagrams are permuted into "eight palaces," and thus each palace comprises eight hexagrams, with a pure hexagram [i.e., the hexagram resulting from the doubling of two identical trigrams] as the leader of the palace. Please see Fig. 7. 1.

Palace / Generational line	Qian	Zhen	Kan	Gen	Kun	Xun	Li	Dui
	Top line	Top line	Top line	Top line	Top line	Top line	Top line	Top line
Line 1	Gou	Yu	Jie	Bi	Fu	Xiaoxu	Lü	Kun
Line 2	Dun	Jie	Zhun	Daxu	Lin	Jiaren	Ding	Cui
Line 3	Pi	Heng	Jiji	Sun	Tai	Yi	Weiji	Xian
Line 4	Guan	Sheng	Ge	Kui	Dazhuang	Wuwang	Meng	Jian
Line 5	Bo	Jing	Feng	Lü	Guai	Shihe	Huan	Qian
Wandering soul (line 4)	Jin	Daguo	Mingyi	Zhongfu	Xu	Yi	Song	Xiaoguo
Returning soul (line 3)	Dayou	Sui	Shi	Jian	Bi	Gu	Tongren	Guimei

Figure 7. 1. The Sixty-four Hexagrams in the Eight Palaces

Are the Prognostications Determined Only by the Changing Line(s)?

Each palace is attributed to one of the Five Agents, each hexagram has a generational line (*shiyao* 世爻) and a response line (*yingyao* 应爻),[1] and by some regularities each line is attached with a heavenly stem and an earthly branch, which also has its five-agent attribution.[2] Based on the five-agent relationship between a line and the palace it belongs to, the six-relative (*liuqin* 六亲) attribution of the line in terms of "father or mother," "elder or younger brother," "wife or wealth," "son or grandson," and "official or ghost" can be determined.[3] (For the affiliation of the earthly branches in the hexagrams Qian [☰] and Kun [☷], as well as their six-relative attributions, please see Fig 7. 2.)

乾为天 Qian [☰] is heaven
父母戌土、世 Father or mother *xu* earth、[4]Generation
兄弟申金、 Elder or younger brother *shen* metal、
官鬼午火、 Official or ghost *wu* fire、
父母辰土、应 Father or mother *chen* earth、 Response
妻财寅木、 Wife or wealth *yin* wood、
子孙子水、 Son and grandson *zi* water、、[5]

坤为地 Kun [☷] is earth
子孙酉金、、世 Son or grandson *you* metal、、 Generation
妻财亥水、、 Wife or wealth *hai* water、、

---

[1] Translator's note: If the generational line is line 1, the response line will be line 4; if the former is line 2, the latter will be line 5; if the former is line 3, the latter will be line 6; if the former is line 4, the latter will be line 1; if the former is line 5, the latter will be line 2; and if the latter is line 6, the latter will be line 3.
[2] The twelve branches from the first to the last and their five-agent attributes are as follows: *zi* 子 water, *chou* 丑 earth, *yin* 寅 wood, *mao* 卯 wood, *chen* 辰 earth, *si* 巳 fire, *wu* 午 fire, *wei* 未 earth, *shen* 申 metal, *you* 酉 metal, *xu* 戌 earth, and *hai* 亥 water.
[3] Translator's note: For instance, the bottom line of hexagram Qian [☰] is affiliated with the earthly branch *zi* 子 which belongs to water, as Qian [☰] belongs to the Qian palace which belongs to metal; since metal produces water, the bottom line of the hexagram is just like the later generation of the palace, and thus this line will be marked as "son or grandson."
[4] In the table, "、" represents a *yang* line (—).
[5] In the table, "、、" represents a *yin* line (--).

兄弟丑土、、 Elder or younger brother *chou* earth 、、
官鬼卯木、、 应 Official or ghost *mao* wood 、、 Response
父母巳火、、 Father or mother *si* fire 、、
兄弟未土、、 Elder or younger brother *wei* earth 、、

Figure 7. 2. Hexagrams Qian [☰] and Kun [☷] attached with six-relative attributions and the twelve branches

Additionally, this system also takes into consideration the "six spirits" of "green dragon" (*qinglong* 青龙) (attributed to Wood), "rosefinch" (*zhuque* 朱雀) (Fire), "Ursae Minoris" (*gouchen* 勾陈) (Earth), "winged snake [i.e., Andromedae]" (*tengshe* 螣蛇) (Earth), "white tiger" (*baihu* 白虎) (Metal), and "black tortoise" (*xuanwu* 玄武) (Water). In actual divination, the "generational line" and "response line" play the major role. I did not do any textual research on whether this mantic art is believable or not. What I know is that Jing Fang himself was killed by the emperor of his time. I do not know whether, having invented the *Najia* divinatory system, he had predicted this sticky end of himself.

Unfortunately, the *Najia* system in actual divinations provided sophists with more convenience. For instance, when Zhao Fuhe (just mentioned above) was analyzing a hexagram obtained by a person whom he questioned concerning his father's illness and encountered hexagram Qian [☰] changing into Jin [䷢], Zhao spoke some words of comfort to him. But after the person had left, he told other people that Jin [䷢] is the "Wandering Soul" (*you hun* 游魂) of the Qian [☰]; Qian represents father, so now that the father changes into the "wandering soul," would he not die? Here Zhao Fuhe abandoned both the images and line statement, and purely used the *Najia* technique to account for the hexagram.[cdxvii]

As another example tells us that when two Ming (1368-1644) scholars, Hu Yun 胡斎 and Yuan Qishan 袁杞山, toured Jinling 金陵 [i.e., today's Nanjing 南京, capital of Jiangsu Province] and stayed at a Daoist temple called Shenle guan 神乐观, the abbot was strictly scolding one of his disciples for the loss of a gold cup. The two scholars felt pity for the disciple and divined about it; they got hexagram Bo [䷖, Peeling, 23] transforming into Yi [䷚, Nourishment, 27] and told the abbot that the cup was not lost and could be rediscovered if he had some person dig five inches underneath the surface of the southwest corner of the temple. As was recorded, "The abbot followed their words and got the cup."[cdxviii]

The compiler of this story might have made use of the images and the *Najia* theory in order to make it up: The upper trigram of hexagram Bo [䷖] is Gen [☶], which is like a covered bowl or cup; according to the *Shuogua* 说卦 (Discussion of the Trigrams), Gen [☶] is also associated with stillness while the inner trigram [☷] represents earth. The whole image is that of a cup in the earth; in divination, the inner trigram plays a major role. Since the inner trigram is Kun [☷], which references the southwest, they suggested that the abbot dig at the southwest corner; as in the *Najia* system, hexagram Kun [䷁] belongs to the fifth palace, hence the "five inches." As the cup had just been missed, the story's fabricator certainly would not stupidly suggest digging five feet.

By these several cases mentioned above, it can be seen that from the pre-Qin times [i.e., before 221 B.C.E.] to the Qing dynasty (1616-1912), there were no fixed regularities for one to follow in the interpretation of the hexagrams for divination. Some employed the judgment and line statements in prognostication; some completely relied on images; some interpreted the judgment or line statement in this way while others took advantage of an opposite way; some took both images and statements into consideration. For the same hexagram, the deduction by images and interpreting by statements may lead to completely opposite predictions. And still, some abandoned both the images and statements but purely extrapolated meaning based on the *Najia* system, while some took both the images and the *Najia* theory into account. As there is not any fixed routine to abide by, the principle invented by Zhu Xi — prognostication by changing line(s) — simply served as a reference rather than as a formula for later diviners.

8.
A Brief Introduction to the Studies of the *Changes* in the Past Dynasties (I)

In the early Zhou dynasty (1045-256 B.C.E.), the *Zhou Changes* was kept by divinatory officials one generation after another, as a result of which commoners had no opportunity to access it. Through the Spring and Autumn era (770-476 B.C.E.), it seems to have been the same case. The most obvious testimony of this can be seen in the "Second Year of Duke Zhao" (*Zhao gong er nian* 昭公二年) (540 B.C.E.) in the *Zuo zhuan* 左传 (Zuo's Commentary on the *Spring and Autumn Annals*): "Marquis Jin dispatched Mr. Han Xuan 韩宣 [d. 514 B.C.E.], one of the six great officials of the state of Jin, to visit the State of Lu. When Han browsed the books collected by the Great Historian [in the library of the state], he came across the *Yi xiang* 易象 (literally, Images of the *Changes*) and *Lu chunqiu* 鲁春秋 (Spring and Autumn Annals of the State of Lu, i.e., the History of the State of Lu) and exclaimed: 'The Zhou rituals are all preserved in the State of Lu!'"[cdxix] As this suggests the high-ranking persons like Han Xuan could find the *Images of the Changes* only in the state library of Lu, this means that even the marquis of the state of Jin had no right to own it, let alone that other officials and common folk would be allowed the same. It is also mentioned in the "Twenty-second Year of Duke Zhuang"

(672 B.C.E.) in the *Zuo zhuan* that "Bringing the *Zhou Changes* with him, some historian of Zhou paid a visit to Marquis Chen,"[cdxx] which signifies that Marquis Chen might not have the book, himself.

However, elaborations upon the *Zhou yi*, such as monographs like the "Discussion of the Trigrams" (*Shuo gua* 说卦), might have come into existence in the Spring and Autumn period (770-476 B.C.E.) or even earlier. Otherwise, why are the images of the eight trigrams drawn upon by over 20 divinatory cases in the *Zuo zhuan* and the *Guo yu* so coherent? Additionally, there seem to have been some monographs explaining the basic meanings—similar to the "Commentary on the Judgments" (*Tuan zhuan* 彖传), the "Commentary on the Images" (*Xiang zhuan* 象传), and the "Commentary on the Words of the Text" (*Wenyan zhuan* 文言传)— in that explications of the four key words *yuan* 元, *heng* 亨, *li* 利, and *zhen* 贞, which are in alignment with the "Commentary on the Words of the Text," are by and large identical to the interpretations of the same words cited by Mu Jiang 穆姜 in the divinatory cases in the *Zuo zhuan* and the *Guo yu* (see Chapter 6). In the meantime, the concise interpretations for some hexagrams and trigrams—such as that "Zhun [☳, Birth Throes, 3] denotes steadfastness and Bi [☵, Closeness, 8] entering" and "Kun [☷] symbolizes security and Zhen [☳] mightiness" in the case of the "First Year of Duke Min" in the *Zuo zhuan* (see Chapter 6)—most possibly came from some monograph explicating the meanings of the hexagrams and trigrams.

Until the Warring States period (475-221 B.C.E.), the range of the spread of the *Zhou Changes* enlarged, but its flowing into the commoners' society should at earliest have occurred in the late Spring and Autumn era. The commentaries on the *Zhou yi*—such as the "Commentary on the Judgments" (*Tuan zhuan* 彖传), the "Commentary on the Images" (*Xiang zhuan* 象传), the "Commentary on the Words of the Text" (*Wenyan zhuan* 文言传), and the "Commentary on the Appended Phrases" (*Xici zhuan* 系辞传)—had taken form during the Warring States period. Since this topic has been discussed in Chapter 2, we will not here explore it in detail. Intellectuals at that time, like Zhuang zi 庄子 (369-286 B.C.E.), had asserted that "the *Changes* is that which discourses on *yin* and *yang*" (in the "Under Heaven" [*Tianxia* 天下] chapter of the *Zhuang zi*), and Xun zi 荀子 (c. 313-238 B.C.E.) began to cite words from the basic text and the commentaries to demonstrate his own points of view (in the "Criticizing Physiognomy" [*Feixiang* 非相] and "Great Strategies" [*Da lüe* 大略] chapters in the *Xun zi*). But then the *Zhou yi* still did not enjoy an exalted academic position when the must-read items for intellectuals included the *Book of Poetry*, the *Book of History*, the *Book of Rituals*, and the *Book of Music* rather than the *Book of Changes*. This state of affairs was ongoing until the unification of China by the Qin dynasty (221-206 B.C.E.), when all the sages's books valued by Confucians were ruined and only the *Changes*, by virtue of its divinatory attributes, survived.

This also means that, after the Qin had unified the world under heaven [i.e., China], the *Zhou Changes* was still considered to be a divination manual and did not have a high academic position. It is thanks to this that it survived the infamous "burning of the books" in 213 B.C.E. But not until the Western Han dynasty (206 B.C.E.-9 C.E.) did the *Zhou Changes* override the other five Confucian classics of the *Poetry*, *History*, *Rituals*, *Music*, and *Spring and Autumn Annals*, and turn out to be the head of the six scriptures. Ban Gu 班固 (32-92) praised it as the "origin of the great Dao [Way]"[cdxxi] and Yang Xiong 扬雄 (53 B.C.E.-18 C.E.) also contended that "in the Six Classics the *Changes* is the greatest and most comprehensive."[cdxxii] Then the *Changes* experienced a meteoric rise, and the commentaries on it, such as the "Commentary on the Judgments" (*Tuan zhuan* 彖传), the "Commentary on the Images" (*Xiang zhuan* 象传), the "Commentary on the Words of the Text" (*Wenyan zhuan* 文言传), and the "Commentary on the Appended Phrases" (*Xici zhuan* 系辞传), were also canonized.

Why did the Western Han people raise the *Changes* to such a high position? To answer this question, we need to talk about the relationship between Confucius and the *Zhou yi*.

According to traditional discourse, the "Ten Wings" (*Shiyi* 十翼) — including the "Commentary on the Judgments" (Part I and Part II), the "Commentary on the Images" (I and II), the "Commentary on the Words of the Text," the "Commentary on the Appended Phrases (I and II), the "Discussion of the Trigrams" (*Shuogua* 说卦), the "Orderly Sequence of the Hexagrams" (*Xu gua* 序卦), and the "Hexagrams in Irregular Order" (*Zagua* 杂卦) — were composed by Confucius. This statement originated from Sima Qian 司马迁 (145-90 B.C.E.) in his *Shiji* 史记 (Historical Records) and Ban Gu 班固 (32-92) in the *Han shu* 汉书 (History of the Western Han Dynasty [206 B.C.E.-9 C.E.]), as the former alleged: "In his later years, Confucius was fond of the *Changes* and put the *Tuan zhuan*, *Xici zhuan*, *Xiang zhuan*, *Shuo gua*, and *Wenyan zhuan* in order."[cdxxiii]

However, were the "Ten Wings" originally written by Confucius? This question was primarily raised by Ouyang Xiu 欧阳修 (1007-1072) in his *Yi tongzi wen* 易童子问 (Questions from a Youth about the *Changes*), where he insisted that from the *Xici zhuan* to the *Zagua*, the above-mentioned commentaries were not Confucius's writings in that these works were heterogeneous. He further asserted, "It will be not strange if we think they [the Ten Wings] came from various scholars who had studied the *Changes* in ancient times and gathered material unsystematically to support their own theories; if they were composed by one single person, they are no more than repetitious and contradictory writings; it will be a great fallacy if we contend they were composed by the Sage! What Confucius composed includes the *Changes* and the *Spring and Autumn Annals* whose language is concise but whose meanings are profound. I do not know why the Sage's discourses are so repetitious, heterogeneous, and contradictory [in the Ten Wings]."[cdxxiv]

Not only in the words, but also in the contents, Ouyang Xiu found various contradictory places in the related commentaries: "Now that the 'Commentary on the Words of the Text' in the beginning has said that *yuan* 元 (fundamentality), *heng* 亨 (prevalence), *li* 利 (benefits), and *zhen* 贞 (constancy) are the four virtues of hexagram Qian [☰, The Creative, 1], it also states in a later paragraph that 'the *yuan* of Qian manifests prevalence at the beginning while *lizhen* 利贞 [here the term means it is beneficial to keep constancy or constancy can lead to benefits] is a matter of human nature and emotions [which means that if one can control one's emotions, one's innate nature will be felt, whereby one can be in alignment with the Dao [Way] of heaven demonstrated by the *yuan* of hexagram Qian], here they are not the four virtues! It is ridiculous if we think these two statements were composed by one single person."[cdxxv] As for the invention of the eight trigrams, the "Commentary on the Appended Phrases" (*Xici zhuan* 系辞传) tells us that "The Yellow River brought forth a diagram [which was referred to as the *he tu* 河图 (Yellow River Chart)], and the Luo River brought forth writings [which was called the *luo shu* 洛书 (Luo River Diagram)], and on the basis of these things the sages invented the eight trigrams";[cdxxvi] while, in another part, the commentary indicates that "when in ancient times Lord Bao Xi [i.e., Fu Xi] ruled the world as sovereign, he looked upward and observed the images in heaven and looked downward and observed the models that the earth provided. He observed the patterns on birds and beasts and what things were suitable for the land. Nearby, adopting them from his own person, and afar, adopting them from other things, he thereupon made the eight trigrams in order to become thoroughly conversant with the virtues inherent in the numinous and the bright and to classify the myriad things in terms of their true, innate natures";[cdxxvii] but according to the "Discussion of the Trigrams," the sage "observed the changes between *yin* and *yang* and so established the trigrams."[cdxxviii] Ouyang Xiu contends that "it will be unreasonable if we think these three sayings come from one single person."[cdxxix]

He also discovered problems in the style of the writing and claimed that the words of "What does it mean" (*he wei ye* 何谓也) in the "Commentary on the Words of the Text" and the "The Master said" (*zi yue* 子曰) in the "Commentary on the Appended Phrases" are the words of the discoursing teacher and that the "Discussion of the Trigrams" and "Hexagrams in Irregular Order" are but out of divinatory documents. Nonetheless, Ouyang still maintained that the "Commentary on the Judgments" and the "Commentary on the Images" had been authored by Confucius.

Following Ouyang Xiu's view, the Song (960-1279) scholar Zhao Rumei 赵汝梅 in his *Zhou yi Jiwen* 周易辑闻 (An Unofficial History of the *Zhou Changes*) suspected that the "Discussion of the Trigrams," the "Orderly Sequence of the Hexagrams," and the "Hexagrams in Irregular Order" might have been interpolated into the Ten Wings by Han (206 B.C.E.-220 C.E.) Confucians and that the "Commentary on the Appended Phrases" was not Confucius's, but his disciples' writings, in that "The Master (i.e., Confucius) said" (*zi yue* 子曰) was frequently noted in this portion.

The Yuan 元 (1271-1368) scholar Wang Shenzi 王申子 (fl. 1313) in his *Da yi jishuo* 大易辑说 (Collected Discussions of the Great *Changes*) also judged that the "Orderly Sequence of the Hexagrams" was not made up of Confucius's remarks. With strong evidence that some words in the

"Commentary on the Images" were cited from Zeng zi's 曾子 (505-435 B.C.E.) [a renowned disciple of Confucius] discourses in his *Zhusi kaoxin lu* 洙泗考信录 (Textual Research on Confucius's Life Story), the Qing scholar Cui Shu 崔述 (1740-1816) further concluded that the "Commentary on the Judgments" and the "Commentary on the Images" were not Confucius's writings, either, and that they "must have been authored by the people later than Zeng zi."

These views of the Song, Yuan, and Qing scholars aroused later scholars' attention to this issue, and in particular, the wide-ranging discussions and textual research of contemporary scholars have fundamentally overturned the traditional view that the "Ten Wings" were composed by Confucius.

However, are the references in Sima Qian's *Shiji* 史记 (Historical Records) and Ban Gu's *Han shu* 汉书 (History of the Western Han Dynasty [206 B.C.E.-9 C.E.]), that Confucius composed the *Commentaries on the Changes*, completely untenable? I do not think so. Because it was merely 200 years, or slightly more, from Confucius's (551-479 B.C.E.) time to the early Han (206 B.C.E.-220 C.E.), scholars like Sima Qian and Ban Gu, who had a strong sense of responsibility to historical materials, would not have fabricated a story, and so what they recorded must have had grounds. Both the "Biographies of Confucius's Disciples" (*Zhongni dizi liezhuan* 仲尼弟子列传) in the *Shiji* and the "Biographies of the Confucians" (*Rulin zhuan* 儒林传) in the *Han shu* listed a detailed line of transmission of the *Changes* coming down from Confucius. Despite some trivial differences in these two lists of the names of those who passed on the *Changes*, the final successor in the early Han was the same person Tian He 田何. As the Han people paid much attention to transmission lines, if they did not possess certain testimonies, could Sima Qian and Ban Gu have dared to fabricate them?

Since Confucius was from the State of Lu and had been a high-ranking official of the state, he must have seen the "*yi xiang* 易象 (literally, Images of the *Changes*) and *Lu chunqiu* 鲁春秋 (*Spring and Autumn Annals of the State of Lu*, i.e., the *History of the State of Lu*)" seen by Han Xuan. And particularly as these two books embody the Zhou rituals [and it is well known that Confucius had paid much attention to the Zhou rituals], wouldn't Confucius have read them? So, the

A Brief Introduction to the Studies of the *Changes* in the Past Dynasties (I)

"Biographies of the Confucians" in the *Han shu* recounted that Confucius "based himself on the *Lu chunqiu*, illustrated the events of the twelve dukes, and judged their deeds by the Dao [Way] of Kings Wen (1152-1056 B.C.E.) and Wu (c. 1087-1043 B.C.E.) [i.e., kingly way, *wangdao* 王道] in order to establish a law for sovereigns. The events stopped in the fourteenth year of Duke Ai 哀公 (481 B.C.E.), when the unicorn was captured [a token that Confucius would die soon and his discourses in person would end]. It seems that Confucius in his later years was so fond of the *Changes* that the bindings of his copy of the *Changes* had been broken three times and he further made comments in it."[cdxxx] It is evident that Confucius's composition of the *Spring and Autumn Annals* was extremely related to the *Lu chunqiu* 鲁春秋. And it was not irresponsible to talk about his being so in favor of the *Changes*, either, because Confucius had said: "Give me few more years, so that even though I began to study the *Changes* at age fifty I will not make big mistakes!"[cdxxxi] This is testimony to the fact that Confucius became interested in the *Changes* in his later years. In the meantime, according to *The Analects of Confucius*, Confucius had cited the third line statement of hexagram Heng [䷟, Perseverance, 32] that "this one does not persevere in maintaining his virtue, so he might have to bear the shame of it,"[cdxxxii] and added, "This can be inferred without prognosis." (13:22) This can assure us that Confucius had indeed studied the *Zhou Changes* and had applied it to divination.

    It is reasonable for a person like Confucius, who in his later years had traveled to a variety of states and tried in vain to persuade the dukes to accept his discourses, to become devoted to the *Zhou yi* and add commentaries on it. So, the assertions in the *Shiji* and the *Han shu* that Confucius had commented on the *Changes* must have evidence. As previously indicated, according to the divinatory cases accounted in the *Zuo zhuan* (Zuo's Commentary on the *Spring and Autumn Annals*) and the *Guo yu* (Sayings of the States), at least by the Spring and Autumn era (770-476 B.C.E.), a unified interpretation of the images of the trigrams had come into existence, and the notes and interpretations to the hexagram and line statements might have appeared, too. Confucius should have sorted out these notes and interpretations just as he had selected and arranged the *Poetry*. Now that Confucius had used to advocate transmitting the ancient kingly way without writing anything of his own, he might have made some oral elaborations upon these interpretations of and notes to the *Changes*, as the "Household of Confucius" (*Kongzi shijia* 孔子世家) section in the *Shiji* asserted that "then the discourses on the Six Classics in the *Zhong guo* 中国 (literally, Middle Kingdom, i.e., China) were synthesized by Confucius."[cdxxxiii] This assertion should be tenable.

In this case, we can surmise that, on the basis of his predecessors's discourses on the *Changes*, Confucius had extended some oral interpretations, and after that his disciples and later Confucians took down these notes with certain acts of polishing and supplements, and by the early and mid-Warring States period (475-221 B.C.E.), the main part of the *Commentaries on the Changes* took form—which reflected Confucius's thought, but with the name of Confucius borrowed by later Confucians.

As a reaction to the First Emperor of Qin's burning of Confucian books and burial of Confucians, the Western Han (206 B.C.E.-9 C.E.) raised the position of Confucianism, and by the reign of Emperor Wu (r. 140-87 B.C.E.), Confucianism turned out to be the sole orthodoxy. Until 136 B.C.E., the Erudites of the Five Confucian Classics (*wujing boshi* 五经博士), including the *Classic of Changes*, were established. The early Han scholars must have known Confucius's comments on the *Changes*. Since the sage had made elaborations on the *Zhou Changes*, the academic position of the *Changes* would become higher in the name of Confucius. This might be the root cause of the *Changes*' leap to being the first of the Five Confucian Classics in the Western Han dynasty (206 B.C.E.-9 C.E.).

According to the "Biography of Liu Xin (50 B.C.E.-23 C.E.)" (*Liu Xin zhuan* 刘歆传) in the *Han shu*, after the burning of Confucian books by the Qin (221-206 B.C.E.), "there was only the divination-oriented *Changes* under heaven"[cdxxxiv] in the beginning of the Han. It was not until the time of Emperor Hui (r. 195-188 B.C.E.), when the proscription of Confucian books was abolished, that the Confucian books such as the *History*, the *Poetry*, the *Rituals*, and the *Spring and Autumn Annals* were brought to light again. But in the early Han, only Tian He 田何 was transmitting the *Changes*.

Later, the Han *Changes* gradually became divided into three schools: in addition to Tian He's *Changes* scholarship, there was Jiao Yanshou's 焦延寿 *Yi* learning, correlating the *Changes* with omens and anomalies, and also Fei Zhi's 费直 Ancient Text[1] tradition. By the time Ban Gu (32-92) was writing the *Han shu* 汉书 (History of the Western Han Dynasty [206 B.C.E.-9 C.E.]), *Changes* scholarship had been divided into 13 schools. Tian He transmitted the *Changes* to Ding Kuan 丁宽, who passed it down to Tian Wangsun 田王孙, who further passed it down to Shi Chou 施仇, Meng Xi 孟喜, and Liang Qiuhe 梁丘贺, whose approaches were simultaneously allowed to be the orthodoxies in the late period of Emperor Xuan (r. 73-49 B.C.E.) despite the differences in the meanings of the *Changes* that they offered.

Why did the original single teaching eventually turn into several different schools? The reason is that when *Changes* scholarship loomed large in the Western Han, especially by the reign of emperors Xuan (r. 73-49 B.C.E.) and Yuan (r. 48-33 B.C.E.), those who could be conversant with one classic were not only exempt from taxes and military service, but could also be given an official position—and some scholars like Zhou Ba 周霸 from Lu 鲁, Heng Hu 衡胡 from Ju 莒, and Zhufu Yan 主父偃 from Linzi 临淄 had become high-ranking officials on account of their mastery of the *Changes*. Then some people began to study the *Changes* so as to obtain promotion, and more and more people followed this trend and extended their novel views on it. As the "Biographies of the Confucians" (*Rulin zhuan* 儒林传) of the *Han shu* 汉书 stated, a person called Zhao Bin 赵宾, who came from Shu 蜀 (now Sichuan Province), "maintains such novel and quibbling arguments that other scholars could not refute them, but had to say that Zhao's views did not conform to ancient teachings."[cdxxxv] It was also reported that Meng Xi 孟喜 (fl. c. 50 B.C.E.) had tampered with the traditional teachings, due to which he lost an opportunity to be the Erudite of the *Classic of Changes*.

It can be seen that even in the early Western Han (206 B.C.E.-9 C.E.), the meanings of the basic text of the *Zhou yi* had begun to be distorted. Although most later scholars think Han scholars' interpretations of the

---

[1] Translator's note: In the Han dynasty (206 B.C.E.-220 C.E.), there were basically two traditions of the *Changes*, the so-called New Text (*jinwen* 今文) and the Ancient Text (*guwen* 古文): the former tends to give tedious interpretations and correlate the emperor or sovereign's good or bad governance with the natural good omens or anomalies, and dominated in the Western Han (206-B.C.E.-9 C.E.), while the latter gravitated to concise explanations of the classic and was prevalent in the Eastern Han (25-220).

Changes are faithful, as a matter of fact, in the early Western Han, there were some scholars who made up novel and quibbling interpretations and deviated from their teacher's discourse. But the Western Han people by and large esteemed the original meanings of the classic, and additionally, as it was not very long from the formation of the *Zhou Changes* to the Western Han dynasty, the original meanings of the hexagram and line statements were not completely lost. Particularly because all of the three schools of Shi Chou's 施雠 (fl. c. 50 B.C.E.), Meng Xi's 孟喜 (fl. c. 50 B.C.E.), and Liangqiu He's 梁丘贺 (fl. c. 60 B.C.E.) scholarship on the *Changes* were based on Tian He's learning, they occupied a very significant position among the 13 schools and were given pride of place in the "Art and Literature Treatise" (*Yiwen zhi* 艺文志) section of the *Han shu* (History of the Western Han Dynasty), exerting formidable influence on the Han (206 B.C.E.-220 C.E.) Confucians.

Since they had been lost long before, what we can see of Shi Chou's, Meng Xi's, and Liangqiu He's *Changes* are now only fragments in some books collected by the Han, Tang (618-907), or Song (960-1279) scholars. Now we examine some of the fragments so as to demonstrate some features of the scholarship on the *Changes* in the Western Han dynasty.

A transitional figure between the Northern and Southern Song dynasties, Zhu Zhen 朱震 (1072-1138) in his *Hanshan Yizhuan* 汉上易传 (Commentary on the *Changes* by Zhu Zhen [1072-1138]), when interpreting the bottom line statement of hexagram Sheng [䷭, Climbing, 46] that "It is right that this one climbs"[cdxxxvi] (*yunsheng* 允升), said: "In Shi Chou's version, it is '靱升', the former character meaning 'advancing.'"[cdxxxvii] This conforms to both the *Shuowen* 说文 (Explanation of Simple and Composite Characters) and *Han jian* 汗简 [a collection of ancient Chinese characters], which point out that in the ancient version of the *Zhou yi*, the term was "靱升." This is the single extant entry of Shi Chou's interpretations of the *Changes*.

There is no reference to Liang Qiuhe's *Changes* in extant documents.

So far as Meng Xi's *Changes* is concerned, as it still existed in the Tang dynasty (618-907) and additionally it was often quoted by Xu Shen 许慎 (c. 58-147) in his *Shuowen* 说文 (Explanation of Simple and Composite Characters), some legacy of his learning is available to us. According to these documents, Meng's *Changes* contains many variants in contrast to the received version of the *Changes*—such as that hexagram Jin 晋 [☷☲, Advance, 35] in the former was written as "曆", Xun 巽 [☴☴, Compliance, 57] as "篹", Gen 艮 [☶☶, Restraint, 52] as "㠯", and so on. "亢龙" (*kang long*) (A dragon that overreaches) in the top line statement of hexagram Qian [☰, The Creative, 1] of the received version corresponds to "忼龙" in Meng's version. So it was with the version in the Tang (618-907) scholar Tang Yuandu's 唐元度 *Jiujing ziyang* 九经字样 (The Pictograms of the Characters in the Nine Classics) and the Song scholar Guo Zhongshu's 郭忠恕 (d. 977) *Han jian* 汗简 [a collection of ancient Chinese characters]. Therefore, it was not correct for one contemporary scholar to interpret "亢" [literally, excessiveness] as "沆" [pond]. There are many other variants in Meng's version, and we will not list them one by one here.

The Tang scholar Lu Deming 陆德明 (c. 550-630) also cited Meng's *Changes* many times in his *Jingdian shiwen* 经典释文 (Exegetical Texts of the Classics). For instance, he tells us that the term *rizhong zeze* 日中则昃 [as soon as the sun reaches the meridian it declines] in the "Commentary on the Judgments" of hexagram Feng [☳☲, Abundance, 55] in the received version is "日中则稷" in Meng's version of the *Changes*. Coincidently, the character *ze* 昃 in the sentence of "*wuwu, ri xiaze nai kezang* 戊午, 日下昃乃克葬" [on the day of *wu* (the fifth heavenly stems) *wu* (the seventh earthly branches), the body was buried while the sun was declining] in the "Fifteenth Year of Duke Ding" (*Ding gong shiwu nian* 定公十五年) (495 B.C.E.) of the *Zuo zhuan* (Zuo's Commentary on the *Spring and Autumn Annals*) was also the character *ze* 昃 in the *Gongyang zhuan* 公羊传 (Gongyang's Commentary on the *Spring and Autumn Annals*), but in *Guliang zhuan* 谷梁传 (Guliang's Commentary on the *Spring and Autumn Annals*) the character *ze* 昃 became *ji* 稷. This is the evidence indicating in the Spring and Autumn period (770-476 B.C.E.) that these two characters shared the same meaning and could replace each other. Since Meng's *Changes* as transmitted from Tian He 田何 used the character "稷," it is tenable that Tian He's version of the *Changes* can be traced back to the later Spring and Autumn period and that the "Commentary on the Judgments" (*Tuanzhuan* 彖传) might date from the early Warring States period (475-221 B.C.E.).

According to the "Preface" to the *Jingdian shiwen* 经典释文 (Exegetical Texts of the Classics), Shi Chou's and Liangqiu He's *Changes* were lost in the chaos that occurred in the fifth year of Yongjia (311 CE). It also says in the "Treatise on Classics and Literature" (*Jingji zhi* 经籍志) of the *Sui shu* 隋书 (History of the Sui Dynasty [581-618]) that: "Lianqiu's, Shi's, and Gao's *Changes* disappeared in the Western Jin dynasty [266-316]."[cdxxxviii] Only Meng's *Changes*, owing to its being passed down by his family ancestors through five generations to the illustrious scholar of the Eastern Han, Yu Fan (164-233), survived to the Tang dynasty (618-907), but it was scattered into fragments in the tumultuous Six Dynasties (229-589). It was further lost in the Tang dynasty and was completely lost by the Song era (960-1279).

According to the *Han shu* (History of the Western Han Dynasty [206 B.C.E.-9 C.E.]), besides the above-mentioned three schools of the *Changes*, Jing Fang's 京房 (77-37 B.C.E.) discourse was also officially recognized as the orthodoxy of the *Changes*. The "Biographies of the Confucians" (*Rulin zhuan* 儒林传) of the *Han shu* tells us that, during the reign of Emperor Cheng (r. 32-7 B.C.E.), the renowned scholar Liu Xiang 刘向 (77-6 B.C.E.) was commissioned to check different versions of the *Changes*; he found that all of the other schools of *Changes* similarly originated from Tian He 田何 except for Jing Fang's tradition, which was much different from them. Jing Fang's original surname was Li, which was changed into Jing by himself on the basis of the theory of pitch pipes. He received his *Changes* from Jiao Yanshou 焦延寿, and his learning is characterized by the analysis of omens and anomalies in terms of *najia* 纳甲 (attaching the heavenly stems and earthly branches into the hexagrams), eight-palace (*bagong* 八宫), generation-response (*shiying* 世应), manifest-latent (*feifu* 飞伏), and five-planet (*wuxing* 五星) systematics. According to the "Art and Literature Treatise" of the *Han shu*, Jing Fang's works at that time included *Mengshi Jing Fang* 孟氏京房 (Jing Fang's *Changes* Based on Meng Xi's *Yi* Learning) (11 chapters), *Zaiyi Menshi Jing Fang* 灾异孟氏京房 (Analysis of Omens and Anomalies by Jing Fang's and Meng Xi's Theories) (66 chapters), and *Jingshi Duan Jia* 京氏段(殷)嘉 (Jing Fang's and Yin Jia's Scholarship on the *Changes*) (12 chapters). By the Sui dynasty (581-618), there were still 10 separate writings by Jing Fang (amounting to 73 chapters) on the *Changes*.

However, there left only five (amounting to 23 chapters) of his writings in the Tang dynasty (618-907).

What Han people cited from Jing Fang's works was referred to as *Jing Fang Yizhuan* 京房易传 (Jing Fang's Commentary on the *Changes*), most of which was related to the analysis of omens and anomalies, and mainly cited in the "Five Agents Treatise" (*Wuxing zhi* 五行志) of the *Han shu*. But the text cited by the *Jingdian shiwen* 经典释文 (Exegetical Texts of the Classics) [hereafter *Shiwen*] and the *Zhou yi jijie* 周易集解 (Collected Explanations of the *Zhou Changes*) [hereafter *Jijie*], compiled by the Tang scholar Li Dingzuo 李鼎祚, is totally different from the Han people's quotations. According to the *Shiwen*, the term "*guanwo duoyi* 观我朵颐" (watching my moving jaw[cdxxxix]), the bottom line statement in the received version of the *Zhou yi* for hexagram Yi [䷚, Nourishment, 27], was "观我榣颐" in Jing Fang's version; the character "*kan* 坎" of the received version of hexagram Xikan [䷜, The Constant Sink Hole, 29] is "㱃"—which means danger and sinking in Jing's version. By the *Jijie*, in Jing Fang's opinion, the term "*jiyu baoshang* 系于苞桑" (tying it to a healthy, flourishing mulberry[cdxl]) in the fifth line statement of hexagram Pi [䷋, Obstruction, 12] means that "mulberries can make contributions to man's food and clothing while the sages also have an all-covering virtue like heaven and an all-sustaining quality like earth. So, the author of the *Book of Changes* used this as a metaphor."[cdxli] When annotating hexagram Wu Wang [䷘, No Errancy, 25], Jing Fang contended that this term refers to "the year of drought when everything is dead and there is not any hope."[cdxlii] According to the *Shiwen*, Jing Fang interpreted the sentence of "*guzhi yi leiting* 鼓之以雷霆" (It [the Dao] arouses things with claps of thunder and thunderbolt[cdxliii]) like this: "*ting* 霆 (thunderbolt) is the surplus of *lei* 雷 (thunder) and can prop up generations of the myriad things."[cdxliv] All these views are ingenious. It is regrettable that the legacy of Jing Fang's *Changes* occupies only a little part of the *Shiwen* and the *Jijie*—there are, overall, 50 to 60 entries, from which it is difficult for us to discern a full perspective of Jing Fang's scholarship on the *Changes*.

At that time, in addition to the above-mentioned, officially recognized four schools of the *Changes*, among the people there were two schools of Fei's and Gao's *Changes*. According to the "Art and Literature

Treatise" of the *Han shu*, when Liu Xiang was checking Shi's, Meng's, and Liangqiu's versions of the *Changes* in contrast to the Ancient Text of the *Changes* collected in the secret imperial library, he discovered that they might have missed the term of *"wujiu* 无咎*"* (there is no blame) and *"huiwang* 悔亡*"* (regret vanishes), whereas Fei's text was the only one identical to the secret Ancient Text version.

What is called Fei's text refers to the *Classic of Changes* passed down by Fei Zhi 费直 (the progenitor of the Ancient Text tradition of the *Changes* in the Western Han dynasty). Fei's teaching was not officially recognized as orthodoxy. As it says in the "Biographies of the Confucians" of the *Han shu*, Fei Zhi "was well versed in divination and his *Changes* had no tedious sentence by sentence explanations, and he only made use of the Ten Wings to interpret the basic text of the *Changes*."[cdxlv]

As a matter of fact, preliminary textual research demonstrates that Fei's *Changes* had also adopted images and numbers. So, the assertion made by the "Biographies of the Confucians" of the *Han shu* might not be comprehensive. This will be mentioned again later.

Fei's version of the *Changes* was different from Shi's, Meng's, and Liangqiu's New Text version. The *Jingji zhi* 经籍志 (Treatise on Classics and Literature) of the *Sui shu* 隋书 (History of the Sui Dynasty [581-618]) tells us: "His version is completely comprised of ancient characters, which was named as the Ancient Text *Changes*."[cdxlvi] It should be noted that, in the Han dynasty (206 B.C.E.-220 C.E.), the classical studies were divided into New Text studies and Ancient Text studies. In the field of *Changes* scholarship, Fei's lineage belongs to the Ancient Text tradition while Shi's, Meng's, Liangqiu's, and Jing's were attributed to the New Text discourses.

The Ancient Text tradition of the *Changes* transmitted by Fei Zhi was not influential when he was alive. Later, along with the exacerbation of the strife between the two schools of the New Text and the Ancient Text, Fei's *Changes* loomed large and was passed down. This will also be discussed in a later part of the book.

The earliest materials related to the explanations of the basic text and the Ten Wings of the *Zhou yi* we can see today date back to the Western Han. Therefore, the Western Han scholarship on the *Changes* occupies a relatively important position in the history of *Yi* (Changes) learning. Meng's and Jing's *Changes* in particular exerted most significant influences upon the later generations' studies of the *Changes*, in that the former had been viewed as the authentic ancient *Changes* by later scholars and was transmitted to the Tang dynasty while the mantic arts related to Jing Fang's *feifu* 飞伏 (manifest and latent hexagrams) and *najia* 纳甲 (equating the lines of the hexagrams with the heavenly stems and earthly branches) were extensively spread period by period.

The Eastern Han dynasty (25-220) witnessed the prevalence of the "prophetic-apocryphal texts" (*chenwei* 谶纬) and works, which tended to force associations of the Confucius classics with these texts. Though there had been a grand occasion when Zhang Xing 张兴 was teaching Liangqiu's 梁丘 *Changes* and there were nearly 10,000 disciples, in general, Shi's, Meng's, Liangqiu's, and Jing's *Changes*, which had once been in full flourish in the Western Han, declined in the Eastern Han. Thanks to Ma Rong's 马融 (79-166) and Xun Shuang's 荀爽 (128-190) subcommentaries and Zheng Xuan's 郑玄 (127-200) annotations to it, Fei's *Changes* was widely transmitted in the Eastern Han.

Han *Changes* scholarship, relatively systematically compiled by Qing (1616-1912) scholars, include Zheng Xuan's 郑玄 (127-200), Xun Shuang's 荀爽 (128-190), and Yu Fan's 虞翻 (164-233) *Changes*. Zheng's and Xun's *Changes* were based on Fei Zhi's 费直, while Yu Fan's originated from Meng Xi's 孟喜 approaches.

As representatives of Han *Changes*, these three *Changes* will be briefly introduced as follows.

The "Biography of Zheng Xuan" of the *Houhan shu* 后汉书 (History of the Eastern Han Dynasty [25-220]) tells us that Zheng Xuan had presented over a million words of annotations on all of the Confucian classics while he was young. His exegesis is characterized by taking advantage of both the Ancient Text and New Text traditions. Adopting both the *huti* 互体 (overlapping trigrams) (see Chapter 3) and the *xiaoxi* 消息 (waxing and waning hexagrams) (see Chapter 4) approaches in searching the images of the trigrams or hexagrams, he made use of "*yaochen* 爻辰" [literally, line-month, correlating the earthly branches, which correspond to the 12 pitch pipes and 12 lunar months, with the hexagrams] theory.

In Zheng's *yaochen* theory, the 12 lines of both hexagrams of Qian 乾 [☰] and Kun 坤 [☷] are equated with 12 lunar months. Thus, the bottom line (*chujiu* 初九) of Qian corresponds to *zi* 子 [the 11th lunar month], the second line (*jiu er* 九二) to *yin* 寅 [the first lunar month], the third (*jiu san* 九三) to *chen* 辰 [the third lunar month], the fourth line (*jiu si* 九四) to *wu* 午 [the fifth lunar month], the fifth line (*jiu wu* 九五) to *shen* 申 [the seventh lunar month], and the top line (*shang jiu* 上九) to *xu* 戌 [the ninth lunar month], while the bottom line (*chu liu* 初六) of Kun corresponds to *wei* 未 [the sixth lunar month], the second line (*liu er* 六二) to *you* 酉 [the eighth lunar month], the third line (*liu san* 六三) to *hai* 亥 [the 10th lunar month], the fourth line (*liu si* 六四) to *chou* 丑 [the 12th lunar month], the fifth line (*liu wu* 六五) to *mao* 卯 [the second lunar month], and the top line (shang liu 上六) to *si* 巳 [the fourth lunar month]. (Please see Figure 8. 1.)

Figure 8. 1. Zheng's *Yaochen* Configuration[1]

Zheng made use of these associations and the terms of the 28 lunar lodges, four directions, Five Agents (*wuxing* 五行), *gua-qi* 卦气 (correlating trigrams and hexagrams with the seasonal points), and the 12 animals to account for the hexagram and line statements.

---

[1] As is often the case with traditional Chinese charts and diagrams representing geographical space, the north is located at the bottom of the figure. So it is with the following figures in the chapter.

A Brief Introduction to the Studies of the *Changes* in the Past Dynasties (I)

Now we employ some notes from the *Zhou yi Zhengshi zhu* 周易郑氏注 (Zheng Xuan's Annotations to the *Zhou Changes*) and briefly analyze the features of Zheng's *Changes*. When interpreting the fifth line statement of hexagram Tai [☷☰, Peace, 11] that "the sovereign Yi gave his younger sister in marriage. As a result, there were blessings and fundamental good fortune,"[cdxlvii] Zheng explains: "[According to the *yaochen* theory,] the fifth line [of this hexagram] corresponds to *mao* 卯 [the second lunar month], mid-spring, when the ten thousand things are given birth. Birth results from marriage, and the month of mid-spring is the high time for marriage. There will be blessings and fundamental good fortune if the wedding is held in the month of mid-spring."[cdxlviii] Here, Zheng Xuan applied his *yaochen* theory to the explanation of the line statement. He also employs this theory to explain the association with the 12 animals. For instance, when interpreting the top line statement of hexagram Kan [☵☵, The Constant Sink Hole, 29] that "here it is as if for bonds two- and three-ply cords were used, or...,"[cdxlix] Zheng says, "According to the *yaochen* theory, the top line is *si* 巳, which means snake. The coiling of a snake looks like a two- and three-ply cord."[cdl] Another instance is in regard to the second line statement of hexagram Mingyi [☷☲, Suppression of the Light, 36] that "Suppression of the Light finds this one wounded in the left thigh,"[cdli] where Zheng Xuan interprets: "The second line of the hexagram corresponds to *you* 酉, which refers to west [metal and the right, opposite to destroys the left, i.e., wood symbolized by trigram Zhen (☳), an overlapping trigram formed by line 3, line 4, and line 5 of the hexagram, hence the terms of 'wound' and 'left' in the line statement]."[cdlii]

However, a salient feature of the *yaochen* theory is its combination with the images or simulacra of stars and asterisms when explaining the hexagram and line statements. By Zheng's annotations, it can be seen that he used to consider the shape of certain asterisms and the associated earthly branch in order to interpret the hexagram and line statements. For instance, when interpreting the statement for line 4 of hexagram Kan [☵☵, The Constant Sink Hole, 29], that "for a cup of wine and food bowls two, use plain earthenware. Receive the dipper [with wine] through the window, and in the end there will be no blame,"[cdliii] Zheng Xuan annotates: "The fourth line of the hexagram corresponds to *chou* 丑, which is associated to the lodge of *dou* 斗 [Dipper] in the sky and signifies pouring wine [see Figure 8.2.]; above the Dipper is the constellation of *jian* 建, whose shape looks like a bowl; above *jian* is the lodge of *bian* 弁 [literally, a kind of man's cap used in ancient times], the shape of which looks like that of plain earthenware. [...]"[cdliv] [In this way, the images of "food bowl" (*gui* 簋), "earthenware" (*fou* 缶), and "dipper" (*shao* 勺) were found, respectively.]

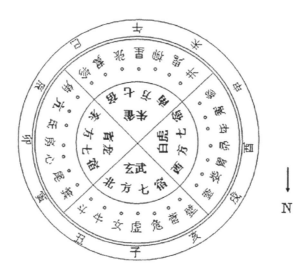

Figure 8. 2. The Twelve Earthly Branches and the Twenty-eight Lunar Lodges

Zheng Xuan also drew upon the names of some constellations in his annotations. For instance, when interpreting the second line statement of hexagram Kun [☷, Impasse, 47] that "this one has Impasse in his food and drink,"[cdlv] Zheng Xuan annotates: "*Wei* 未 is equated with *tianchu* 天厨 [literally, heavenly kitchen, i.e., Draco], an image of food and drink."[cdlvi] This means that, according to the *yaochen* theory, the bottom line of this hexagram is matched to *wei* 未, which corresponds to the constellation of "heavenly kitchen." As there are food and wine in a kitchen, hence the image of food and wine [which were extended as a feoff, not large enough for the subject to use, in the situation of Impasse. The second line mounts over the bottom line, which signifies that the subject of line 2 lived on the income from the small feoff symbolized by line 1, hence the second line statement]. Here is another example: when accounting for the statement for line 1 of hexagram Bi [☲☷, Closeness, 8] that "this one has whole-hearted sincerity like an earthenware pot filled,"[cdlvii] Zheng says: "Its *yaochen* is at *wei* 未 which is associated with the Eastern Well [*dongjing* 东井, i.e., Gemini]. The water in the well is drawn by the earthenware pot [in ancient times]."[cdlviii]

There are some other annotations of this kind in Zheng's exegesis, which will not be cited here one by one. Zheng's extant annotations are not fully intact; in particular, there are only around a dozen of the *yaochen*-oriented cases available. However, of all the Han commentators on the *Changes* using the *yaochen* tradition, only Zheng Xuan's annotations by the *yaochen* theory are relatively well preserved, and so we have discussed them in the above-mentioned part. Nonetheless, in his annotations in this genre, there are many forced associations that certainly are not particularly convincing.

Many scholars in the past held that the *yaochen* approach was used only by Zheng Xuan, and some Qing (1616-1912) scholars even contended that this approach was invented by Zheng. Actually, that is not the case. The correlation between the 12 lines of hexagrams Qian [☰] and Kun [☷] with the 12 lunar months, and the association between the 12 lunar months and the Five Agents, had been employed by Western Han (206 B.C.E.-9 C.E.) people. As it says in the "Treatise on the Pitch Pipes and Calendar" (*Lüli zhi* 律历志) of the *Han shu* 汉书 (History of the Western Han Dynasty), "The Three Concordances (*santong* 三统) [a kind of calendar used since late Western Han] means that heaven bestows energy, earth transforms the myriad things, and humans attune themselves to the natural order. [...] The 6th lunar month matches the bottom line of Kun [☷] and is correlated with *wei* 未; the 1st lunar month corresponds to line 3 of Qian [☰] when everything is vibrant and gathers at *yin* 寅, which belongs to Wood;"[cdlix] and "There are twelve pitch pipes, of which six are attributed to *yang* and the other six to *yin*. [...] Change and action never stand still but keep flowing all through the six vacancies. It starts from *zi* 子 in the 11th lunar month [...], arrives at *chou* 丑 in the 12th lunar month [...], at *yin* 寅 in the 1st lunar month [...], at *mao* 卯 in the 2nd lunar month [...], at *chen* 辰 in the 3rd lunar month [...], at *si* 巳 in the 4th lunar month [...], at *wu* 午 in the 5th lunar month [...], at *wei* 未 in the 6th lunar month [...], at *shen* 申 in the 7th lunar month [...], at *you* 酉 in the 8th lunar month [...], at *xu* 戌 in the 9th lunar month [...], and at *hai* 亥 in the 10th lunar month."[cdlx] Therefore, there were such kinds of correlations in the Western Han dynasty.

The equation of the *yaochen* with stars and constellations might not have been devised by Zheng Xuan himself. Study of the origin of this correlation may assure us that Zheng might have received this theory from his predecessors. It is known that Zheng Xuan learned the *Changes* from Ma Rong 马融 (79-166), who used to draw upon heavenly configurations in his *Changes* interpretations. For example, according to the *Jingdian shiwen* 经典释文 (Exegetical Texts of the Classics) compiled by Lu Deming 陆德明 (c. 550-630), when interpreting the "Commentary on the Judgments" regarding hexagram Wuwang [☰, No Errancy, 25], that "*Tianming bu you* 天命不佑[右]" (literally, not to be blessed by the will of heaven), Ma Rong stated: "*Tian bu you xing* 天不右行" (literally, heaven [symbolized by the upper trigram ☰] does not rotate to the right (or counterclockwise) [*you* 右])."[cdlxi] When interpreting the second line statement of hexagram Mingyi [☷, Suppression of the Light, 36] that "Suppression of the Light finds this one wounded in the left thigh,"[cdlxii] Ma tells us: "The sun runs to the right [or clockwise] along with heaven."[cdlxiii] In his *Zhou yi zhengyi* 周易正义 (Correct Meaning of the *Zhou Changes*), Kong Yingda 孔颖达 (574-648) cites Ma Rong's annotation to the words of "The number of the great expansion is fifty [milfoil stalks]. Of these we use forty-nine"[cdlxiv] in the "Commentary on the Appended Phrases" like this: "The *Changes* has *Taiji* [literally, Supreme Ultimate] which refers to the Northern Asterism. The Supreme Ultimate produces two modes, which in turn produce the sun and moon, which go on to produce the four seasons, which in their turn produce the Five Agents, from which are produced the twelve lunar months, which finally produce the twenty-four seasonal points. The Northern Asterism stays motionless while the rest forms the forty-nine [i.e., 2 + 2 + 4 + 5 + 12 + 24 = 49] as the manifestation of its function in motion."[cdlxv] Though there are not so many words as Zheng used, the heavenly configurations, the Five Agents, and the 12 lunar months related to Zheng's *yaochen* theory are all mentioned here. So, Zheng's *yaocheng* theory might have originated from Ma Rong's teaching. As what Ma Rong transmitted was Fei Zhi's 费直 *Changes*, his teaching might be traced back to Fei Zhi's teaching. Fei's *Changes* includes some contents equating the eight trigrams with asterisms, and the heavenly stems and earthly branches, as well, which can be seen in the works *Fei's Yilin* 费氏易林 (Forest of *Changes* by Fei Zhi) and *Fei's Fenye* 费氏分野 (Field Allocation Taught by Fei Zhi) as compiled by Ma Guohan 马国翰 (1794-1857) in his *Yuhan shan fang ji yishu* 玉函山房辑佚书 (Collection of Lost Texts from the Treasury Chamber 'Jade Slipcase'). Therefore, in the "Biographies of the Confucians" of the *Han shu* 汉书 (History of the Western Han Dynasty [206 B.C.E.-9 C.E.]) the assertion that Fei Zhi "uses only the Ten Wings to explain and discuss the basic text of the *Changes*"[cdlxvi] might not be comprehensive. Additionally, having explained and discussed (*jieshuo* 解说) the basic text, he must have had his own elaborations upon it; could he possibly have simply made a direct copy of the Ten Wings after the basic text to serve as his "explanations and discussions"?

Moreover, it says in the "Opening up the Regularities of the [Hexagram] Qian" (*Qian zao du* 乾凿度) of the *Yi wei* 易纬 (Apocrypha of the *Changes*): "Heaven and earth are illuminating and clear; the sun, moon, and stars are hung, the eight trigrams are in order, the calendar and pitch pipes are tuned, and the five planets rotate in their orbits respectively."[cdlxvii] This is evidence indicating that, at least in the Western Han dynasty, the equations of the heavenly configurations, the eight trigrams, the calendar, and pitch pipes had come into existence. Furthermore, in the beginning, the *Zhou Changes* were taken care of by the Official Historians (*taishi* 太史) who were in charge of heavenly patterns and the calendar, as is stated in the "Monthly Ordinances" (*yue ling* 月令) of the *Li ji* 礼记 (Record of Ritual): "then order the Official Historian to attend to the classics and laws, observe the motions of the sun, moon, stars, and lunar lodges."[cdlxviii] Therefore, the approach to the *Zhou Changes* based on heavenly configurations might have come into existence long before and might be one of the lost methods used by the Official Historians of Zhou. This can be surmised since there are remarks such as "looking up, the sage observed the configurations of Heaven";[cdlxix] "[Lord Bao Xi] looked upward and observed the images in heaven";[cdlxx] "Heaven hung images in the sky and revealed good fortune and bad, and the sages regarded these as meaningful signs";[cdlxxi] and "As a book, the

Changes is something which is broad and great, complete in every way. There is the Dao [Way] of Heaven in it, the Dao of Man in it, and the Dao of Earth in it"[cdlxxii] in the "Commentary on the Appended Phrases" (*Xici zhuan* 系辞传), and, additionally, "One looks to the pattern of Heaven in order to examine the flux of seasons"[cdlxxiii] in the "Commentary on the Judgments" (*Tuan zhuan* 彖传) regarding hexagram Bi [☶☲, Decoration, 22]. The authors of the Ten Wings, when they were sorting out the lost discourses of their predecessors, must have read the documents of ancient people who used heavenly images to account for the *Changes*. Furthermore, in the hexagram and line statements, there is indeed a great deal of material related to astronomical observation. For instance, the hexagram and line statements of Feng [☳☲, Abundance, 55] very possibly came from a complete record of a total solar eclipse. If we further take the following quoted remarks into consideration—that "(the sages) determined what the Dao of Heaven was, which they defined in terms of *yin* and *yang*"[cdlxxiv] in the "Discussion of the Trigrams" (*Shuogua zhuan* 说卦传) and "In Heaven this [process] creates images"[cdlxxv]—we can conclude that the hexagrams and lines, and the statements of the *Zhou Changes*, must have absorbed the achievements of contemporary astronomical observations.

So, though the full features of Zheng Xuan's approach to the *Changes* cannot be fully viewed, we can discern part of it through the extant dozen interpretive examples. It is evident that, in *Changes* scholarship, the legacy of the Han people really has its own value as a reference that inspires us to probe into the origin of the *Zhou Changes*, and thus it is necessary to engage in related further discussions and textual research.

In the late Eastern Han dynasty (25-220), another famous expert in *Changes* scholarship who followed Fei Zhi's tradition was Xun Shuang 荀爽 (128-190), whose courtesy name is Ciming 慈明. According to the preface to the *Jingdian shiwen* 经典释文 (Exegetical Texts of the Classics) compiled by Lu Deming 路德明 (c. 550-630), by the Tang dynasty (618-907), there were still 10 *juan* 卷 (literally, scrolls, i.e., chapters) of Xun Shuang's annotations to the *Changes*, which were lost in later dynasties. Three chapters of his annotations to the *Changes* were collected by Ma Guohan 马国翰 (1794-1857) in his *Yuhan shan fang ji yishu* 玉函山房辑

佚书 (Collection of Lost Texts from the Treasury Chamber 'Jade Slipcase'). They were also collected in Hui Dong's 惠栋 (1697-1758) *Yi Hanxue* 易汉学 (Han Scholarship on the *Changes*) and Zhang Huiyan's 张惠言 (1761-1802) *Zhou yi Xunshi jiujia* 周易荀氏九家(Nine Masters' [Interpretations Collected] of the *Zhou Changes* from Xun's Family).

Interpreting the basic text and the Ten Wings of the *Zhou Changes* by the *rising and falling* (*shengjiang* 升降) of *yin* and *yang* characterizes Xun Shuang's approach to the *Changes*. Here are some examples. In interpreting the "Commentary on the Images" regarding the bottom line of hexagram Qian [☰, The Creative, 1] that "'a submerged dragon does not act': the *yang* force is below,"[cdlxxvi] Xun Shuang elaborates: "As the force of the bottom *yang* line is weak and its position is humble, though it has qualities of *yang*, it still hides beneath [the surface of the earth], hence the term 'does not act.'"[cdlxxvii] For the "Commentary on the Images" pertaining to hexagram Tai [☷, Peace, 11] that "'Heaven and Earth perfectly interact:' this constitutes the image of Peace,"[cdlxxviii] Xun says: "The force of Kun [☷] ascends in order to accomplish the Dao [Way] of Heaven while the force of Qian [☰] descends so as to fulfill the Dao of Earth. If the two forces do not interact, there will be stagnation and obstruction. Now that they perfectly interact, prevalent peace comes into being."[cdlxxix] For the "Commentary on the Judgments" related to hexagram Heng [☷, Perseverance, 32] that "'it would be fitting should one set out to do something here,' for when something ends, there is always another beginning,"[cdlxxx] Xun explains, "The force of Qian [☰] ends at the lower position and then begins and rises to the fourth line position whereas the force of Kun [☷] ends at the upper position and begins and falls to the bottom line position."[cdlxxxi] For the "Commentary on the Judgment" of hexagram Da zhuang [☷, Great Strength, 34] that "strength is the result of action taken by the hard and strong,"[cdlxxxii] he states: "Qian [☰] signifies hardness and Zhen [☷] movement. As the force of *yang* rises from below and moves energetically, so the strength is manifested."[cdlxxxiii]

He also employed interactions of the *yin* and *yang* forces to account for the changes of the lines. For instance, in his view, the words that "Kun is perfectly compliant, but the way it takes action is strong and firm; it is perfectly quiescent, but its virtue is square and solid"[cdlxxxiv] in the "Commentary on the Words of the Text" regarding hexagram Kun [☷, the Receptive, 2] indicate that "the nature of Kun [☷] is extremely quiescent; when it is stimulated by *yang*, its force moves and spreads to the four directions."[cdlxxxv] In addition to this point, when interpreting the remarks in the "Commentary on the Appended Phrases" that "looking up, the sage observed the configurations of Heaven, and looking down, he examined the patterns of Earth. Thus he understood the reasons underlying what is hidden and what is clear,"[cdlxxxvi] he elaborates: "It means that if the force of *yin* rises to the position of *yang* [i.e., higher position] the configurations of Heaven will take shape, whereas if the force of *yang* descends to the position of *yin* [lower position] the patterns of Earth will be formed. 'What is hidden' refers to those things which are invisible in heaven and on earth, meaning hexagram Pi [☲, Stagnation, 12] transforms into Weiji [☵, Incompletion, 64]; 'What is clear' refers to the myriad things in order between Heaven and Earth which can be seen by eyes and heard by ears, signifying hexagram Tai [☳, Peace, 11] changes into Jiji [☱, Completion, 63]."[cdlxxxvii]

He contends that *yin* and *yang*, as symbolized by hexagrams Kun [☷] and Qian [☰] respectively, represent the source and origin of heaven and earth, which generate the myriad things. In annotating the remarks of "it conceives and spreads brightness and grandness—so that things in all their different categories can prevail as they should"[cdlxxxviii] in the "Commentary on the Judgments" pertaining to hexagram Kun [☷, The Receptive, 2], he states: "That the second line of Qian [☰] moves to the fifth line position of Kun [☷] means 'conceiving' while the fifth line of the latter moving to the second line position of the former is called 'spreading,' and the bottom line of the latter moving to the fourth line position of the former means 'brightness' while the fourth line of the former moving to the bottom line position of the latter signifies 'grandness.' [In this way] Heaven and Earth intercourse and the ten thousand things are generated."[cdlxxxix] So, in Xun's mind, since hexagrams Qian and Kun represent the intercourse of Heaven and Earth, which gives rise to the myriad things, the other six trigrams of Kan [☵], Li [☲], Gen [☶], Zhen [☳], Dui [☱], and Xun [☴] are also generated by it. This idea is evident in his interpretation of the remarks of "Water flows to where it is wet; fire goes toward where it is dry. Clouds follow the dragon; wind follows the tiger" in the "Commentary on the Words of the

Text"[cdxc] as pertaining to the fifth line of hexagram Qian [☰, The Creative, 1], where he says: "*Yang*'s moving to Kun [☷] gives rise to Kan [☵] and as Kun is pure *yin* it symbolizes 'wet'; *Yin*'s moving to Qian [☰] results in Li [☲] and since Qian is pure *yang* it represents 'dry.' 'Dragon' refers to a king, represented by line 2 of Qian [☰] moving to the position of line 5 of hexagram Kun [☷], and then the upper trigram Kun [☷] of the latter hexagram will transform into Kan [☵] [which symbolizes 'clouds']; 'Tiger' is a token of a prince, resulting from the moving of line 5 of hexagram Kun [☷] to the second line position of hexagram Qian [☰], by which line 2, line 3, and line 4 will form trigram Xun [☴] [which symbolizes wind] and follow the third *yang* line above it. The third *yang* line represents the prince of the lower body [trigram]."[cdxci] Then he interprets the sentence of "the great man is someone whose brightness is consonant with the sun and the moon"[cdxcii] in this way: "It means that the fifth line of Kun [☷] moves to the second line position of Qian [☰], then the lower trigram of the latter will transform into Li [☲] which is the sun; [in the meantime,] the second line of the latter moves to the fifth line position of the former, then the upper trigram will change into Kan [☵] which is the moon."[cdxciii] This means that, in his view, the trigrams Li [☲] and Kan [☵] result from the interchange of the position of line 2 of hexagram Qian [☰] and the position of line 5 of hexagram Kun [☷]. So it is with the other trigrams, in that when he interprets the "Commentary on the Judgments" pertaining to hexagram Jie [䷧, Release, 40] that "When Heaven and Earth allow Release, thunder and rain play their roles; when thunder and rain play their roles, all the various fruits, shrubs, and trees burgeon forth,"[cdxciv] he says: "Intercourse and communication of Qian [☰] and Kun [☷] give rise to hexagram Jie [䷧]; as Kan [☵] is in the lower position [which symbolizes falling rain] while Zhen [☳] is in the upper position [which represents thunder], 'thunder and rain play their roles.'"[cdxcv]

This kind of approach to the *Changes* through the rising and falling, as well as the interaction of, of *yin* and *yang* used by Xun Shuang exerted great influence upon later scholars. For example, when he interprets the fourth line statement of hexagram Tai [䷊, Peace, 11] that "fluttering, one does not use riches to deal with his neighbors. Without admonishing them, he has their faithfulness," Wang Bi 王弼 (226-249) tells us: "Qian

[☰] is happy to arise and return to its own place, and Kun [☷] is happy to descend and return to its own place."[cdxcvi] This understanding was obviously derived from Xun's theory. But Wang deliberately avoided the terms of "rising and falling" (*sheng jiang* 升降) and replaced them with "arising and returning" (*shangfu* 上复) and "descending and returning" (*xiafu* 下复) in order to show his dislike of the Han people's images-and-numbers approach.

It is on the basis of his "rising and falling" and the interaction of *yin* and *yang*, as well as his idea that Qian [☰] and Kun [☷] produce, like children, the other six trigrams, that he was supposed by later scholars to have been the first one who began to discuss hexagram changes (*guabian* 卦变). As we have mentioned his thoughts on hexagram changes (see Chapter 4), we will not discuss it here again.

Finally, let us introduce Yu Fan's 虞翻 (164-233) scholarship on the *Changes*.

A late Eastern Han (25-220) scholar, Yu Fan's courtesy name was Zhongxiang 仲翔. Meng Xi's tradition of the *Changes* had been transmitted for five generations by his ancestors and himself. He wrote the *Zhou yi zhu* 周易注 (Annotations to the *Zhou Changes*). Possessing high moral character, he did not believe in immortality. Once when Sun Quan 孙权 (182-252), then the king of the kingdom Wu 吴, was discussing immortality with Zhang Zhao 张昭 (156-236), a high-ranking official of Wu, Yu Fan pointed with his finger to Zhang and said: "The persons you are referring to are all dead people; are there actually any immortals in the real world?"[cdxcvii]

In my view, the most distinctive feature of Yu Fan's scholarship on the *Changes* is manifested in his *najia* 纳甲 (attaching the heavenly stems to the eight trigrams) theory (see Fig. 8. 3.) and *guabian* 卦变 (hexagram changes) theory.

The *najia* approach is that which correlates moon phases with the eight trigrams and heavenly stems so as to demonstrate the waxing and waning of *yin* or *yang* energy and tell us to "be like the moon in the sky: do not lose one's time."[cdxcviii] Regarding the sentence that "of images that are suspended above and emit brightness, none are greater than the sun and the moon"[cdxcix] in the "Commentary on the Appended Phrases" (*Xici zhuan* 系辞传), he explains: "It means that the position and phases in

A Brief Introduction to the Studies of the *Changes* in the Past Dynasties (I)

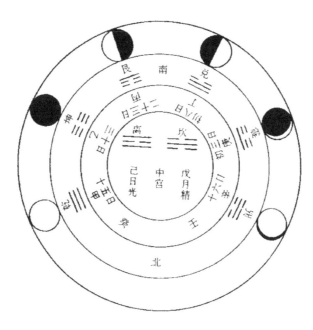

Figure 8. 3. Correlation of the Moon Phases, Eight Trigrams, and Heavenly Stems

the sky of the sun and the moon manifest the images of the eight trigrams. When night falls on the 3rd day of a lunar month, a crescent as an image of trigram Zhen 震 [☳] appears in the west of the vault marked by the heavenly stem *geng* 庚 (the 7th heavenly stem). When night falls on the 8th day of a lunar month, a waxing gibbous moon as an image of trigram Dui 兌 [☱] appears in the south symbolized by the heavenly stem *ding* 丁 (the 4th heavenly stem). When night falls on the 15th day of a lunar month, a full moon as an image of trigram Qian 乾 [☰] appears in the east marked by *jia* 甲 (the first heavenly stem). When day breaks on the 17th day of a lunar month, a waning gibbous moon as an image of trigram Xun 巽 [☴] appears in the west marked by *xin* 辛 (the eighth heavenly stem). When day breaks on the 23rd day of a lunar month, a waning crescent moon as an image of trigram Gen 艮 [☶] appears in the south symbolized by *bing* 丙 (the third heavenly stem). On the night of the 30th day of a lunar month, the moon disappears in the east of *yi* 乙 (the second heavenly stem), an image of Kun 坤 [☷]. On the midnight between the 30th day and the 1st day of the next lunar month, the moon symbolized by Kan 坎 [☵] is located at the position of *wu* 戊 (the 5th heavenly stem) opposite to the zenith. At noon, the sun as image of Li 离 [☲] always hangs in the zenith which is marked by *ji* 己 (the sixth heavenly stem)."[d] [For the correlation between the heavenly stems and directional positions, please see Fig. 8. 4.] On the basis of this interpretation, the Southern Song scholar Zhu Zhen 朱震 (1072-1138) summarizes in his *Zhou yi guatu shuo* 周易卦图说 (Illustrations of the Hexagrams and Trigrams of the *Zhou Changes*): "Why is it called *Najia*? It set up *Jia* 甲 [the initial heavenly stem] as a symbol of the ten heavenly stems. Qian 乾 [☰] is attached with *jia* 甲 and *ren* 壬 (the ninth heavenly stem); Kun 坤 [☷] is affiliated with *yi* 乙 and *gui* 癸 (the 10th heavenly stem), Zhen 震 [☳] with *geng* 庚, Xun 巽 [☴] with *xin* 辛, Kan 坎 [☵] with *wu* 戊, Li 离 [☲] with *ji* 己, Gen 艮 [☶] with *bing* 丙, and Dui 兑 [☱] with *ding* 丁. The sages looked up and observed the motions of the sun and the moon and equated them with the eight trigrams, and thus the meanings of the eight trigrams and the ten heavenly stems were brought into light." In this way, the waning and waxing of *yin* and *yang* symbolized by the eight trigrams are well illustrated by the waxing and waning of the moon.

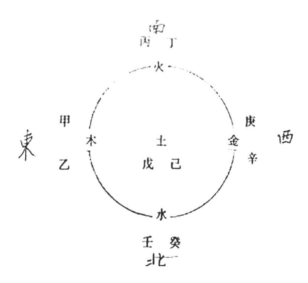

Figure 8. 4. Correlation of the Heavenly Stems and Directional Positions

The *najia* method has been credited to Jing Fang (77-37 B.C.E.); but when interpreting the fourth line statement of hexagram Zhongfu [☲, Inner Trust, 61] that "the moon is about to wane from full,"[di] Meng Xi 孟喜 says: "It refers to the 16th day of a lunar month."[dii] This demonstrates that this method dates from more ancient times. I cannot help believing that it might have taken form when scholars were sorting out the legacies of the pre-Qin period, interpreting the *Changes* by motions of celestial bodies and via the waxing and waning of *yin* and *yang* forces. It seems likely, since we can see related resources in the "Commentary on the Judgments" regarding hexagram Gu [☲, Ills to be Cured, 18], that "'it will be effective during three days before and three days after the day of *Jia*' means that with its ending a thing starts all over again: such is the way Heaven operates,"[diii] and in the *Tuan* commentary pertaining to hexagram Bo [☲, Peeling, 23], that "the noble man holds in esteem how things ebb and flow, wax and wane, for this is the course of Heaven."[div] These words indicate that there were indeed materials applying the waning and waxing of the moon to the exegesis of the *Changes*.

With its abundant knowledge of astronomy, the *najia* theory exerted great influence upon later scholars. For instance, the Eastern Han (25-220) scholar Wei Boyang 魏伯阳, a famous Eastern Han Daoist priest traditionally viewed as the progenitor of the Alchemical Daoism, in his *Zhou yi cantong qi* 周易参同契 (Token for the Agreement of the Three According to the *Zhou Changes*), adopted this theory to explicate alchemical refinery, which occupies an im portant position in the history of Chinese science and technology.

As was previously mentioned, Jing Fang mainly applied the *najia* system to divination (see Chapter 7).

Additionally, Yu Fan was known for his rigidity in his scholarship on the *Changes*. He accounted for hexagram changes by rising (*sheng* 升) and falling (*jiang* 降) (of *yin* and *yang* lines), ascending (*shang* 上) and *xia* 下 (descending) (of *yin* and *yang* energy), lateral linkage, and waxing and waning (of *yin* and *yang* forces) (see chapters 3 and 4). He gave top priority to images of the hexagrams and trigrams, and interpreted the hexagram and line statements through images that were considered to have preserved the tenor of Western Han (206 B.C.E.-25 C.E.) approaches to the *Changes*. Although his blind adherence to the images contains far-fetched associations, his discourses regarding the mutations between "Nine" and "Six," the *gua-qi* theory, and the waxing and waning schema, must have been transmitted by masters, one generation after another, which therefore might indeed consist of ancient approaches passed down from the Western Han.

Eastern Han people were used to drawing upon the *gua-qi* system to interpret the *Changes*. So it is with Yu Fan. This theory reportedly originated from the Western Han scholar Meng Xi 孟喜, but Jing Fang 京房 (77-37 B.C.E.) also made use of it, as it says in the "Biography of Jing Fang" of the *Han shu* 汉书 (History of the Western Han Dynasty): "His theory is adept in prognostication by anomalies and mutations, equating the sixty-four hexagrams with the phenological phenomena of wind, rain, cold, and warmth of a whole lunar year, and its efficacy is manifest in each aspect."[dv] This system was comparatively well preserved in the "Consultations Charts" (*Jilan tu* 稽览图) of the *Yi wei* 易纬 (Apocrypha of the *Changes*)[dvi].

The salient feature of the *gua-qi* theory is its equating the four hexagrams of Kan 坎 [☵], Zhen 震 [☳], Li 离 [☲], and Dui 兑 [☱] with the four seasons of winter, spring, summer, and autumn, respectively. Then, the 24 lines of the four hexagrams were correlated to the 24 calendrical divisions. Namely, the six lines from the bottom to the top of hexagram Kan 坎 [☵] correspond to "Winter Solstice" (*dongzhi* 冬至, 22nd solar term), "Lesser Cold" (*xiaohan* 小寒, 23rd solar term), "Great Cold" (*dahan* 大寒, 24th solar term), "Beginning of Spring" (*lichun* 立春, first solar term), "Rainwater" (*yushui* 雨水, second solar term), and "the Waking of Insects" (*jingzhe* 惊蛰, third solar term), respectively. The six lines from the bottom to the top of hexagram Zhen 震 [☳] are associated with "Vernal Equinox" (*chunfen* 春分, fourth solar term), "Pure Brightness" (*qingming* 清明, fifth solar term), "Grain Rain" (*guyu* 谷雨, sixth lunar term), "Beginning of Summer" (*lixia* 立夏, seventh solar term), "Grain Full" (*xiaoman* 小满, eighth solar term), and "Grain in Ear" (*mangzhong* 芒种, ninth solar term), respectively. The six lines of hexagram Li 离 [☲] from the bottom to the top are equated with "Summer Solstice" (*xiazhi* 夏至, 10th solar term), "Slight Heat" (*xiaoshu* 小暑, 11th solar term), "Great Heat" (*dashu* 大暑, 12th solar term), "Beginning of Autumn" (*liqiu* 立秋, 13th solar term), "Limit of Heat" (*chushu* 处暑, 14th solar term), and "White Dew" (*bailu* 白露, 15th solar term), respectively. The six lines from the bottom to the top of hexagram

A Brief Introduction to the Studies of the *Changes* in the Past Dynasties (I)

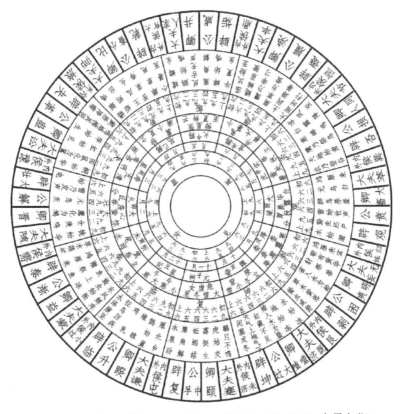

Figure 8. 5. Chart of Six Days and Seven Divisions (*liuri qifen* 六日七分)

Dui 兑 [☱] correspond to "Autumnal Equinox" (*qiufen* 秋分, 16th solar term), "Cold Dew" (*hanlu* 寒露, 17th solar term), "Frost's Descent" (*shuangjiang* 霜降, 18th solar term), "Beginning of Winter" (*lidong* 立冬, 19th solar term), "Light Snow" (*xiaoxue* 小雪, 20th solar term), and "Great Snow" (*daxue* 大雪, 21st solar term), respectively (see Fig. 8. 5.)

One solar term is further divided into three periods, which are referred to as "initial phenology" (*chu hou* 初候), "middle phenology" (*zhong hou* 中候), and "final phenology" (*mo hou* 末候), respectively. As one solar term consists of 15 days, one phenology, or pentad, governs five days. In this way, the 24 calendrical divisions are further divided into 72 pentads. The *gua-qi* theory further equates the other 60 hexagrams (other than the above-mentioned four hexagrams of Kan [☵], Zhen [☳], Li [☲], and Dui [☱]) with the 365 and 1/4 days of the year, and thus one hexagram governs 6 and 7/80 days:

(365+1/4) days × 1/60 = (6 + 7/80) days

This is the provenance of what is called the "six days and seven divisions" (*liuri qifen* 六日七分) in the *qua-qi* theory.

These 60 hexagrams are arrayed in a special order, starting from Zhongfu 中孚 [䷼, Inner Trust, 62] and ending with Yi 颐 [䷚, Nourishment, 27] [see the outermost ring of Fig. 8. 5], and equated with the 24 calendrical divisions [the fifth ring] and 72 pentads [the seventh ring] in terms of the "initial hexagram," "middle hexagram," and "final hexagram," and further repeated in the titles of duke (*gong* 公), sovereign (*bi* 辟), marquis (*hou* 侯), great official (*dafu* 大夫), and lower minister (*qing* 卿) [the outermost ring].

Each of the 72 pentads has its own name. These names had already appeared in the "Monthly Ordinances" (*Yue ling* 月令) in the *Li ji* 礼记 (Record of Ritual), which carefully displays the transformations of some creatures and phenomena in the natural world along with the shifts of the 24 seasonal points. For instance, the first line of Kan hexagram 坎 [䷜] rules the "Winter Solstice." For the half month from "Winter Solstice" (*dongzhi* 冬至, 22nd solar term), its initial phenology is "earthworms curl up" (*qiuyin jie* 蚯蚓结); its middle phenology is "moose shed their horns" (*mijiao jie* 麋角解); and its final phenology is "spring water in movement" (*shuiquan dong* 水泉动). The initial hexagram for this half month is Zhongfu 中孚 [䷼], which is associated with "duke" (*gong* 公) and governs 6 and 7/80 days; the related middle hexagram is Fu 复 [䷗], which is "sovereign" (*bi* 辟) and governs the next 6 and 7/80 days, the sum being 12 and 14/80 days; its final hexagram is Zhun 屯 [䷂], which is "marquis" (*hou* 侯) and governs the next 6 and 7/80 days, the sum adding up to 18 and 21/80 days. The second line of hexagram Kan 坎 [䷜] corresponds to "Lesser Cold" (*xiaohan* 小寒, 23rd solar term), the initial phenology of which is "wild geese begin to migrate toward north" (*yan beixiang* 雁北乡) and the initial hexagram of which is Zhun 屯 [䷂], too (as three phenologies govern 15 days while the above-mentioned three hexagrams of Zhongfu, Fu, and Zhun rule 18 and 21/80 days, the initial pentad of this seasonal point still corresponds to Zhun). The next phenologies one after another include "magpies begin to build nests" (*que shichao* 鹊始巢), "pheasants begin to chirp" (*zhi gou* 雉雊), "chickens begin to hatch" (*ji ru* 鸡乳), … and so on.

Obviously, the 72 phenologies manifest the knowledge of ancient Chinese people regarding the changes of natural phenomena along with the shifts of the seasonal points in detail, such as "dormant insects begin to come out of hibernation" (*zhechong shizhen* 蛰虫始振), "swan geese come from the south" (*hongyan lai* 鸿雁来), "grasses and trees bud" (*caomu mengdong* 草木萌动), "peaches begin to bloom" (*tao shi hua* 桃始华), "thunder rumbles" (*lei nai fasheng* 雷乃发声), "lightning flashes" (*shi dian* 始电), "cuckoos flap" (*mingjiu fu qi yi* 鸣鸠拂其羽), "mole crickets sing" (*louguo ming* 蝼蝈鸣), "Pinellia ternate grows" (*banxia sheng* 半夏生), "it often rains cats and dogs" (*dayu shixing* 大雨时行), "cicadas cry" (*hanchan ming* 寒蝉鸣), "grass and trees wither" (*caomu huang luo* 草木黃落), "water begins to freeze" (*shui shi bing* 水始冰), "ground begins to freeze" (*di shi dong* 地始冻), "people shut doors in winter" (*bise er cheng dong* 闭塞成冬), and so on. By their contents, it can be seen that some give an account of bird migration, such as "swallows come from the south" (*xuanniao zhi* 玄鸟至), the initial phenology of "Vernal Equinox" (*chunfen* 春分, fourth lunar term) equated with the bottom line of hexagram Zhen 震 [☳], and "swallows return south" (*xuanniao gui* 玄鸟归), the midphenology of "White Dew" (*bailu* 白露, 15th solar term) corresponding to the top line of hexagram Li 离 [☲]. Some display the appearance or disappearance of some natural phenomenon, such as "rainbows begin to appear" (*hong shi jian* 虹始见), the final phenology of "Pure Brightness" (*qingming* 清明, fifth solar term) associated with the second line of hexagram Zhen 震 [☳], and "rainbows hide and disappear" (*hong cang bu jian* 虹藏不见), the initial phenology of "Light Snow" (*xiaoxue* 小雪, 20th solar term) equated with the fifth line of hexagram Dui 兑 [☱].

In short, the 72 phenologies display the shifts of seasonal points based on the movement of the sun in the zodiac band. If the *yaochen* theory used by Zheng Xuan originated from ancient Chinese people's astrological knowledge, the schema of *gua-qi* was no more than their knowledge of the solar calendar.

Though the *gua-qi* theory is not testified to in the extant pre-Qin documents, like the *yaochen* and *najia* theories, it might not have been originally invented by the Han (206 B.C.E.-220 C.E.) people. As it says in the "Commentary on the Appended Phrases" (*Xici* 系辞), "of things that serve as models for images, none are greater than Heaven and Earth. Of things involving the free flow of change, none is greater than the four seasons,"[dvii] and in the "Commentary on the Images" (*Xiang zhuan* 象传) in regard to hexagram Ge [䷰, Radical Change, 49] that "Inside the Lake [☱], there is Fire [☲]: this is the image of Radical Change. In the same way, the noble man orders the calendar and clarifies the seasons,"[dviii] the author(s) of the two commentaries might have seen the legacy from the past associating calendrical knowledge with the *Zhou Changes*. Moreover, the "Discussion of the Trigrams" (*Shuogua* 说卦) explicitly points out: "Dui 兑 [☱, Joy] here means autumn at its height, something in which the myriad things all find cause to rejoice. This is why it says: 'makes them happy then in Dui,'"[dix] which can assure us that by the date of composition of the commentary, or earlier, ancient people had correlated Dui [☱] to autumn. The "Commentary on the Images" of hexagram Fu [䷗, Return, 24] also tells us: "Thunder [☳] in the Earth [☷]: this constitutes the image of Fu. In the same way, the former kings closed the border passes on the occasion of the winter solstice, and neither did merchants and travelers move nor sovereigns go out to inspect domains."[dx] According to the *gua-qi* schema, hexagram Fu [䷗] is equated with the winter solstice. In the Western Han dynasty (206 B.C.E.-9 C.E.), on winter and summer solstices, officials would take holidays, and it was understood to have been a long-standing practice to do so. As it says in the "Biography of Xue Xuan" (*Xue Xuan zhuan* 薛宣传) of the *Han shu* 汉书 (History of the Western Han Dynasty), "At winter solstice and summer solstice, officials would be ordered to take holidays. This custom had been established long before."[dxi] Yan Shigu's 颜师古 (581-645) commentary tells us: "On winter and summer solstices, officials did not inspect or conduct official business, so they took a holiday."[dxii] Since the quote states that the custom was long established, it is probable that pre-Qin times also practiced it. It is evident that when the "Commentary on the Images" was being composed, hexagram Fu [䷗] had been associated with winter solstice. In the meantime, as is accounted in the "Commentary on the Appended Phrases" (*Xici* 系辞), "Thus the stalks needed to form Qian [☰] number 216, and the stalks needed to form Kun [☷] number 144. In all, these number 360 and correspond to the days of a year's cycle,"[dxiii] which is also in alignment with the *gua-qi* theory.

Therefore, the *gua-qi* system might also be a legacy of ancient official historians who were also in charge of the calendar, which can be supported by the account in the "Monthly Ordinances" (*Yueling* 月令) of the *Li ji* 礼记 (Record of Ritual) that "the official historian pays a visit to the Son of Heaven [i.e., the king] and says: 'Such and such a day is the 'Beginning of Winter.'"[dxiv] On the basis of their predecessors' achievements, Han people probably supplemented and sorted out the system so as to make it more perfect.

Most of the scholars in the past contended that the *yaochen* and the *gua-qi* approaches were made up by Han people, due to their absence in the divinatory cases in the *Zuo zhuan* 左传 (Zuo's Commentary on the Spring and Autumn Annals) and the *Guo yu* 国语 (Sayings of the States). Actually, what the divinatory cases in the two books reflected were very narrow. If we conclude that the approaches of *najia* 纳甲 (correlating the heavenly stems and earthly branches with the hexagrams), *feifu* 飞伏 (manifest and latent), and *shiying* 世应 (generation and response), and so on, were invented by the Han people, we might be able to make a reasonable case for such a claim based on the partial, early evidence; whereas, it would be improper if we want to discern all of the contents of the ancient *Changes* merely through these two dozen examples. For instance, when Han Xuan 韩宣 [d. 514 B.C.E.] found the *Yi xiang* 易象 (Images of the *Changes*) and *Lu chunqiu* 鲁春秋 (*Spring and Autumn Annals* of the State of Lu) in the official historian's library of the state, he realized that "the [records of the] Zhou rituals were all preserved in the State of Lu,"[dxv] but there was not any divinatory case in the *Zuo zhuan* and the *Guo yu* elucidating the Zhou rituals. Therefore, although there was not any mention of the associations between the *Zhou Changes* and calendars, as well as heavenly configurations, we cannot deny that there were these correlations used by the official historians in the Spring and Autumn era (770-476 B.C.E.). Additionally, the equating of the trigram Dui [☱] with mid-autumn in the *Shuogua* 说卦 (Discussion of the Trigrams) is an ironclad proof that, during or before the Warring States period (475-221 B.C.E.), there were such kinds of correlation. More importantly, as the *Shuogua* was a product collecting the images of the *Changes* used by the antecedents, this kind of association must have earlier origins.

In spite of this, we believe that in the beginning the correlation was not so complex, and after incessant expansions, amplifications, inventions, and even forced associations by the successors of Tian He 田何, who was teaching the *Changes* in the early Han dynasty, these associations that are available to us at present were gradually accomplished in the Eastern Han dynasty (25-220). Therefore, like *yaochen* and *najia*, *gua-qi* is still an important facet for us to use in exploring Han approaches to the *Changes*.

Additionally, Eastern Han people also applied the *mengqi* 蒙气 (atmospheric haze), *shi'er qinchen* 十二禽辰 (12 animals), and other correlations to the exegesis of the *Changes*, which will not be introduced here one by one.

Generally speaking, though the scholarship on the *Changes* in the Eastern Han dynasty was not so flourishing as it was in the Western Han, the comparatively systematic Han tradition we can see today was only the legacy of the Eastern Han scholars, among which Yu Fan's scholarship on the *Changes* was the most complete. For this reason, from the Tang dynasty (618-907) onward, Yu's scholarship turned out to be the main avenue for later scholars to use in exploring the Han tradition of the *Changes*, exerting great influence upon the studies of the *Changes* in later generations.

According to the divinatory cases recorded in the *Zuo zhuan* and the *Guo yu*, the interpretations of the *Changes* by the people in the Spring and Autumn (475-221 B.C.E.) were very concise and succinct. For example, they held that "Zhun [☳, Birth Throes, 3] signifies solidification and Bi [☷] entering"[dxvi] while "Kun [☷] symbolizes security and Zhen [☳] mightiness"[dxvii] (see Chapter 6). Therefore, they used to employ one term to expose the meaning and quality of a hexagram or trigram. In the early Western Han (206 B.C.E.-9 C.E.), Tian He 田何 might still have preserved this tradition. For instance, according to the "Biographies of the Confucians" (*Rulin zhuan* 儒林传) in the *Han shu* 汉书 (History of the

Western Han Dynasty), Ding Kuan 丁宽, one of Tian's renowned disciples, "was also known as General Ding [in that he had been a general who helped the imperial court and a prince to resist the insurgency organized by seven other princes in 154 B.C.E.], who composed his *Yi shuo* 易说 (An Explanation of the *Changes*) which contains 30,000 words that just displayed explanations of the words and basic meanings (of the hexagrams)."[dxviii] But from the establishment of the Erudit100s of the "Five Confucian Classics" (136 B.C.E.) on to the era of Emperor Ping 平帝 (r. 1 B.C.E.-6 C.E.), a period of less than one and a half centuries, the situation was that "the explanation of a single classic was over a million words and the number of the great masters (i.e., officially endorsed famous teachers) was over a thousand."[dxix] According to the "Biography of Zhang Xing 张兴" in the *Houhan shu* 后汉书 (History of the Eastern Han Dynasty [25-220]), when Zhang Xing was teaching Liangqiu He's 梁丘贺 tradition of the *Changes*, his pupils numbered up to 10,000. During that time when the academic atmosphere was filled with the ethos of exegetical tediousness, Zhang's discourse absolutely could not merely contain "30,000 words" (like Ding Kuan's explanations).

Then, the *Zhou Changes*, the sole classic which in 213 B.C.E. survived the "burning of books" by the Qin dynasty (221-206 B.C.E.), was transmitted only by Tian He 田何 in the early Han, whereas over a century later in the academic circle, besides the New Text tradition, there appeared that of the Old Text; besides the teacher's teaching lineage, there emerged the teaching from one generation to another within a single family, and then different subgroups appeared within these lineages. Consequently, there developed a situation such that "the teachings of the classics were divided into many schools and each school contains several sects … though the pupils had tried their best to study, they could hardly grasp them, and later they became suspicious of them and unaware of the correct meanings."[dxx] There was a later point of view expressed by the editors of the *Siku qushu* 四库全书 (Complete Collection of the Four Treasuries) concerning the Han people's scholarship on the classics: "the teachers' transmission was passed down from one generation after another. Not only did they transmit their exegesis without any deviation, but they also adhered faithfully to what they heard from their teachers in respect to division of chapters and sections, as well as the paraphrasing of terms." It seems that this point of view does not fit with the reality of that time, though. Rather, it ought to be the case that (the transmission of each classic), just "like a stem which generated branches, branches continue to generate smaller branches. As a result, branches and leaves turned out to be exuberant while the root was gradually neglected."[dxxi] As the snowball of the *Changes* scholarship became bigger and bigger, and the image-numerology became more and more complex, it would inextricably collapse. Therefore, the New Text tradition of the Western Han (206 B.C.E.-9 C.E.) *Changes* declined in the Eastern Han dynasty (25-220) and the Old Text tradition of the Eastern Han *Changes* faded out in large part in the early Tang dynasty (618-907). The main reason for the declining and withering was probably the tediousness and inconsistency of the image-numerology of the Han people's *Changes*.

Under this circumstance, Wang Bi's 王弼 (226-249) scholarship on the *Changes* stood out.

Taking Fusi 辅嗣 as his courtesy name, Wang Bi came from Wei 魏 (220-265), one of the Three Kingdoms. The *Zhou yi zhu* 周易注 (Commentaries on the *Zhou Changes*), *Zhou yi lüeli* 周易略例 (General Remarks on the *Zhou Changes*), *Lao zi zhu* 老子注 (Commentaries on the *Lao zi*), and *Lao zi weizhi lüeli* 老子微指略例 (General Remarks on the Purports of the *Lao zi*) were composed by him. He found that when Han people were explaining the *Changes*, they always sought the images behind the statements and habitually attempted to force a fit between them. Additionally, besides the images of the eight trigrams illustrated in the *Shuogua* 说卦 (Discussion of the Trigrams), Han people also supplemented a good number of "lost images" (*yi xiang* 逸象). So far as I can see, the nine masters' collected interpretations of the *Zhou Changes* from Xun's family exposed 31 "lost images" (see *Jingdian shiwen* 经典释文 [Exegetical Texts of the Classics]), which were adopted into the *Zhou yi benyi* 周易本义 (Original Meaning of the *Zhou Changes*) by Zhu Xi 朱熹 (1130-1200); Yu Fan 虞翻 (164-233) and his ancestors had transmitted Meng Xi's tradition of the *Changes* for five generations, all of whom added up to 331 "lost images," nearly 10 times more than the exposition of Xun's family, some of which present ancient meanings that are unlike Yu's self-invented contents. We can imagine that the number of the images adopted by the Han people at that time might be several times more than the number of extant images illustrated by Yu Fan. This approach to the *Changes*, with so many such tedious and multitudinous images to be associated with the hexagram and line statements, drove the *Zhou Changes* into a corner.

On this account, when interpreting the *Zhou Changes*, Wang Bi with one stroke swept away the Han tradition that blindly adheres to image-numerology and devoted much attention to the attainment of "Ideas." He set forth a new point of view that "getting the ideas is in fact a matter of forgetting the images, and getting the images is in fact a matter of forgetting the words." He argued that "images are the means to express ideas, and words are the means to explain the images. To yield up ideas completely, there is nothing better than the images, and to yield up the meaning of the images, there is nothing better than words. The words are generated by the images, and so one can ponder the words and so observe what the images are. The images are generated by ideas, and so one can ponder the images and so observe what the ideas are. The ideas are yielded up completely by the images, and the images are made explicit by the words. Thus, since the words are the means to explain the images, once one gets the images, he forgets the words, and since the images are the means to allow us to concentrate on the ideas, once one gets the ideas, he forgets the images."[dxxii]

Here Wang Bi clearly laid out his understanding about the "images" of the *Changes*. From his perspective, the "images" are no more than a means to get the "ideas," and with the help of the "images" one can get the "ideas" of the *Zhou Changes*; once a person has gotten the "ideas," he should forget, or in other words, not rigidly adhere to, the "images." To demonstrate this point, he gives us a vivid example: "The rabbit snare exists for the sake of the rabbit; once one gets the rabbit, he forgets the snare. And the fish trap exists for the sake of fish; once one gets the fish, he forgets the trap."[dxxiii] In other words, "although the images were established in order to yield up ideas completely, as images they may be forgotten. Although the trigrams were doubled in order to yield up all the innate tendencies of things, as trigrams they may be forgotten."[dxxiv]

Therefore, so far as the "forgetting of the images" is concerned, in Wang's view, it does not mean that we should discard the "images," but signifies that once we have gotten the "ideas," we need not stick to the "images" and be constrained by them. In regard to the defect of the Han people who tended to search for some "images" behind each term of the hexagram and line statements of the *Zhou Changes*, Wang Bi criticizes them in this way: "If the concept involved really had to do with dynamism [as in the case of Qian ☰], why must it only be presented in terms of the horse? And if the analogy used really has to do with compliance [as in the case of Kun ☷], why must it only be presented in terms of the cow? If its lines really do fit with the idea of compliance, why is it necessary that Kun represent only the cow; and if its concept really corresponds to the idea of dynamism, why is it necessary that Qian represent only the horse? Yet there are some who have convicted Qian of horsiness. They search the 'images' of the trigram. They may have come up with a horse, but Qian itself got lost in the process! And then this spurious doctrine spread everywhere, even to the extent that one cannot keep account of it! When the 'overlapping hexagram' method proved inadequate, such people went on further to the 'hexagram change' method, and when this 'hexagram change' method proved inadequate, they pushed on ever further to the 'five elements' method, for once they lost sight of what the images originally were, they had to become more and more intricate and clever. Even though they sometimes might have come across something [concerning the images], they got absolutely nothing of the concepts."[dxxv] Considering the reason for the emergence of this situation, Wang Bi holds that "this is all due to the fact that, by concentrating on the images, one forgets about the ideas."[dxxvi] On the basis of this perspective, his recognition about the "images" rose to a new level: "If one were instead to forget about the images in order to seek the ideas they represent, the concepts involved would then become evident as a matter of course."[dxxvii]

At first sight, it seems that Wang's view—"to yield up ideas completely, there is nothing better than the images, and to yield up the meanings of the images, there is nothing better than words"—is inconsistent with his statement that "if one were instead to forget about the images in order to seek the ideas they represent, the concepts involved would then become evident as a matter of course." As a matter of fact, as was previously indicated, the "ideas" (*yi* 意) in Wang's eyes refer to the intellectual content of each of the 64 hexagrams, whereas the "concepts" (*yi* 义) represent the sublimation and comprehensive summary of the essence conceived in each instance of one kind of trigram or hexagram image. Thus, he asks, "If the concept involved really had to do with dynamism [as in the case of Qian ☰], why must it only be presented in terms of the horse? And if the analogy used really has to do with compliance [as in the case of Kun ☷], why must it only be presented in terms of the cow?" The "concept" (*yi* 义) is an abstraction of the associations based on the same kind of image. As far as the "concept" is concerned, it can be expressed by the multifarious associations based on the same kind of image [or trigram]; in return, these associations can comprehensively attest to the "concept," just as Wang Bi tells us that "this is why anything that corresponds analogously to an idea can serve as its image, and any concept that fits with an idea can serve as corroboration of its nature."[dxxviii] Therefore, in understanding the "images," Wang Bi made a further step forward: When seeking an idea, if one blindly adheres to those concrete associations with a trigram, even though he has found all the correspondence between the words and the images, it does not mean that he has gotten the kernel essence of the "images." That is, "Even though they sometimes might have come across something [concerning the images], they got absolutely nothing of the concepts;"[dxxix] only if one does not blindly stick to those specific associations [images] of the trigrams [i.e., forgetting the images] can he closely grasp the core and essence, i.e., the "concept" of a trigram or hexagram. Compared with Han scholarship, Wang Bi no doubt made progress in this respect. But the sublimation of his comprehension of the "images" of the *Changes* also opened a convenient door for later scholars to interpret the *Changes* at random, and particularly, his idea established a theoretical foundation for Song (960-1279) scholars who approached the *Changes* on the basis of "principle" (*li* 理). Therefore, though his new understanding of the "images" of the *Changes* makes certain contributions to the accusation of the Han people for their affiliating their complex imagery to the hexagram and line statements, his cognition is not commensurate with the remarks in the "Commentary on the Appended Phrases,"[dxxx] that "the eight trigrams make their pronouncements in terms of images, and the line texts and Judgments address themselves to us in terms of the innate tendencies of things." So, from "pondering the images to observe what the ideas are" (*xun xiang yi guan yi* 寻象以观意) to "forgetting about the images in order to seek the ideas they present" (*wang xiang yi qiu yi* 忘象以求意), Wang

Bi drew at will his exegesis of the *Changes* into his metaphysical idealist orbit and associated Lao zi 老子 (c. 571-471 B.C.E.) and Zhuang zi's (369-286 B.C.E.) 庄子 Daoist views, which are regarded as "ideas" by him, with the hexagram and line statements of the *Zhou Changes*.

Even so, his *Zhou yi zhu* 周易注 (Commentaries on the *Zhou Changes*), due to its exegetical conciseness and opposition to Han people's prolixity, infused energy and vitality into the scholarship on the *Changes* and deserves to be called a valuable work. For example, he thought the second line statement of hexagram Qian [☰, The Creative, 1], that "when there appears a dragon in the fields, it is fitting to see the great man," means that "it has come out of the depths and abandoned its hiding place; this is what is meant by 'there appears a dragon.' It has taken up a position on the ground; this is what is meant by 'in the fields.' With virtue [*de* 德] bestowed far and wide, one here takes up a mean [*zhong* 中] position and avoids partiality [*pian* 偏]. Although this is not the position for a sovereign, it involves the virtue of a true sovereign. If it is the first line, he does not reveal himself; if the third, he makes earnest efforts; if the fourth, he hesitates to leap; if the top line, he is overreaching. Fitness to see the great man [*daren* 大人] lies only in the second and the fifth lines."[dxxxi] For the fourth line statement of the hexagram that "hesitating to leap, it still stays in the depths, so suffers no blame," he tells us: "To leave the topmost line in the lower trigram and occupy the bottom line of the upper trigram signifies the moment when the Dao [Way] of Qian undergoes a radical change. Above, one is not in Heaven [symbolized by the fifth and top lines of the hexagram]; below, one is not in the fields [Earth, symbolized by the bottom and second lines of the hexagram]; and in between one is not with Man [symbolized by the third line of the hexagram]. Here one treads on the dangerous territory of the double strong [i.e., the third and the fourth *yang* lines] and so lacks a stable position in which to stay. This is truly a time when there are no constant rules for advancing or retreating. Drawing close to an exalted position [the ruling fifth line], one wishes to foster the Dao involved, but forced to stay in a lower position, this is not something his leap can reach. One wishes to ensure that his position here remains quiescent, for this is not a secure position in which to stay. Harboring doubts, one hesitates and does not dare determine his own intentions. He concentrates on preserving his commitment to the public good, for advancement here does not lie with private ambitions. He turns his doubts into reflective thought and so avoids error in decisions. Thus, he suffers no blame."[dxxxii]

Easily understood on account of its conciseness, his interpretations were in alignment with the hermeneutic style of the "Commentary on the Words of the Text" (*Wenyan* 文言) and similar to the disposition of "simple interpretations to disclose general meanings"[dxxxiii] (*xungu ju dayi* 训诂举大谊) prevalent in the early Han dynasty (206 B.C.E.-220 C.E.). Therefore, when Wang's *Zhou yi zhu* came out, it very quickly became in vogue and dealt a tremendous blow to the tradition of the Han *Changes* scholarship. As Zhao Shixiu 赵师秀 (1170-1219), a famous poet in the Northern Song dynasty (1127-1279), remarked, "When Wang Bi's *Changes* became prevalent, the Han tradition of the *Changes* was assaulted."[dxxxiv] However, it also occasioned criticism immediately. For example, in the "Treatise on Classics and Literature" (*Jing ji zhi* 经籍志) of the *Sui shu* 隋书 (History of the Sui Dynasty [581-618]) in the "Catalogue Attributed to the *Changes*" (*yi lei* 易类), there was "a book called *Zhou yi nan Wang Fusi yi* 周易难王辅嗣义 (Questioning and Reproaching Wang Bi for His Meanings of the *Zhou Changes*) written by Gu Yi 顾夷, provincial governor of Yangzhou 场州 in the Eastern Jin dynasty (317-420), et al."[dxxxv] Until the early Tang dynasty (618-907) when Wang's commentaries were established as the *Zheng yi* 正义 (Correct Meaning) of the *Changes*, according to the "Treatise on Art and Literature" (*Yiwen zhi* 艺文志) of the *Tang shu* 唐书 (History of the Tang Dynasty [618-907]), there were scholars elaborating on Wang Bi's discourse at that time, such as Yin Hongdao 阴弘道 who composed the *Zhou yi xinzhuan shu* 周易新传疏 (A Subcommentary on the New Commentaries [i.e., Wang Bi's Commentaries] on the *Zhou Changes*), Xue Rengui 薛仁贵 (614-683) who wrote the *Zhou yi xinzhu benyi* 周易新注本义 (Original Meaning of the New Commentaries on the *Zhou Changes*), Xuan Pin 宣聘 who authored the *Zhou yi xiang lun* 周易象论 (Discussions on the Images of the *Zhou Changes*), Dong Xiangzhu 东乡助 who composed the *Zhou yi wuxiang shiyi* 周易物象释疑 (Clearing up Doubts About the Images of Objects in the *Zhou Changes*), and Cui Liangzuo 崔良佐 (fl. 732), a recluse who authored the *Yi wang xiang* 易忘象 (Forgetting the Images of the *Changes*). From the Jin (265-420) through the Qing (1616-1912) dynasties, some scholars highly valued his theory while others were critics of his hermeneutics. Particularly, in the early Tang dynasty, Emperor Taizong 太宗 (r. 626-649) commissioned certain scholars to compile the *Wujing zhengyi* 五经正义 (Correct Meaning of the Five Classics), among which the *Zhou yi zhengyi* 周易正义 (Correct Meaning of the *Zhou Changes*) adopted Wang Bi's commentaries, which turned out to be the standard text in civil examinations from the Tang (618-907) through the Song (960-1279) dynasties. For this reason, Wang's commentaries exerted extremely significant influences upon later generations of scholars' research and made him an important figure in the history of *Changes* studies in China.

In my opinion, in the early Western Han (206 B.C.E.-9 C.E.), people interpreted the *Changes* in a simple way, which by and large inherited the primary hermeneutical means employed by the Spring and Autumn (770-476 B.C.E.) people. Later, the interpretations became more and more complicated: besides methods of "overlapping trigrams" (*huti* 互体) and "hexagram changes" (*guabian* 卦变), Jing Fang (77-37 B.C.E.) further raised *najia* 纳甲 (attaching the heavenly stems and earthly branches to the hexagrams), "eight palaces" (*bagong* 八宫), "five elements" (*wuxing* 五行), "generation" (*shi* 世), and "response" (*ying* 应) for the explanations of the *Zhou Changes*. Later, the methods of *yaochen* 爻辰 (correlating the earthly branches, which correspond to the 12 pitch pipes and 12 lunar months, with the hexagrams) and *gua-qi* (equating the trigrams and hexagrams with the seasonal points) were also supplemented. It was acceptable that Wang Bi abandoned the above-mentioned methods of *najia*, *bagong*, and so on, credited to Jing Fang, due to their absence in the ancient divinatory cases of the Spring and Autumn period; yet, as the "overlapping trigrams" (*huti* 互体) can evidently be found in the *Zuo zhuan* 左传 (Zuo's Commentary on the Spring and Autumn Annals) and the "hexagram changes" (*guabian* 卦变) had been mentioned in the "Commentary on the Judgments" (*Tuan zhuan* 彖传) and the "Commentary on the Appended Phrases" (*Xici zhuan* 系辞传), these approaches might not have been invented by the Han people. So, Wang's abolition of these two methods shows his extreme attitude to image-numerology. Additionally, though Wang Bi got rid of image-numerology, considering the origin of his *Changes* scholarship, it could be traced back to Fei Zh's 费直 tradition of *Changes,* which also took image-numerology into consideration. Though the original, intact copy of Fei Zhi's *Changes* is not available today, some fragments of it were collected by Ma Guohan 马国翰 (1794-1857) in his *Yuhan shan fang ji yishu* 玉函山房辑佚书 (Collection of Lost Texts from the Treasury Chamber 'Jade Slipcase'), by which it can be seen that Fei's *Changes* also contains image-numerology. Moreover, some features of Fei's *Changes* can also be discerned in Xun Shuang's 荀爽 (128-190) annotations to the *Changes*, the progenitor of whose *Yi* learning was Fei Zhi. As previously indicated in this chapter and in Chapter 4, Xun Shuang valued the positions of lines, rising and falling of the *yin* or *yang* force, the quality of softness or hardness of a hexagram, and held "hexagram changes," "waxing and waning," and *gua-qi* theory in high esteem, by which we can infer that there must have been image-numerological factors in Fei's *Changes.* Furthermore, when interpreting the judgment of hexagram Fu [☷☳, Return, 24], that "The Dao [way] that he goes out and comes back on is such that he returns after seven days,"[dxxxvi] Wang Bi tells us: "From the time the *yang* material force begins to undergo Bo [☶☷, Peeling] until its completion and then on to the time it arrives in Fu [☷☳, Return] is commonly seven days."[dxxxvii] Kong Yingda 孔颖达 (574-648) further comments in his *Zhou yi zhengyi* 周易正义 (Correct Meaning of the *Zhou Changes*): "[Here Wang Bi] also made use of the meaning of 'six days and seven divisions' (*liuri qifen* 六日七分), mentioned in the *Yi wei* (Apocrypha of the *Changes*), in a way that was identical to the point of view of Zheng Xuan 郑玄 (127-200) who annotated the apocrypha; but Wang here omitted Zheng's detailed interpretation and concrete remarks."[dxxxviii] If Kong Yingda's subcommentary is correct, Wang had indeed brought image-numerological learning into his exegesis. Additionally, as was previously introduced, when he interpreted the fourth line statement of hexagram Tai [☷☰, Peace, 11] that "fluttering, one does not use riches to deal with his neighbors. Without admonishing them, he has their faithfulness,"[dxxxix] Wang Bi 王弼 (226-249) tells us: "Qian [☰] is happy to arise and return to its own place, and Kun [☷] is happy to descend and return to its own place."[dxl] This was obviously derived from Xun's theory of the intercourse between *yin* and *yang* forces through rising and falling. It is evident that Wang Bi did not thoroughly abandon image-numerology when he was interpreting the *Changes*. In the meantime, as he held *yin-yang* and positions within each hexagram in the highest esteem, the images had always been kept in his mind, and he did not dare to interpret the *Changes* at will. Because his exegesis was often mixed with Daoism, later scholars have always accused him of taking the *Changes* to address principle. As a matter of fact, "taking the *Changes* to address principle" (*yi yan li* 以易言理) is not necessarily wrong in that the "Discussion of the Trigrams" (*Shuogua* 说卦) had made use of it to expose principle and almost the entire "Commentary on the Words of the Text" (*Wenyan* 文言) reveals principles of human affairs (*renshi* 人事). Additionally, in the early Han, Ding Kuan's concise interpretation of the *Changes* in a simple way also contains elements that disclose principle. Wang Bi's inappropriateness rested in his forcing a fit between Daoism and the *Zhou Changes* and drawing on the *Changes* to discourse on his metaphysics. For example, when interpreting the "Commentary on the Judgment" regarding hexagram Qian [☰, The Creative, 1], that "how great is the fundamental nature of Qian! The myriad things are provided their beginnings by it, and, as such, it controls Heaven. It allows clouds to scud and rain to fall and things in all their different categories to flow into forms,"[dxli] Wang Bi tells us: "The term *tian* [Heaven] is the name for a form, a phenomenal entity; the term *jian* 健 [strength and dynamism: the quality of Qian] refers to that which uses or takes this form. Form is an encumbrance of a thing..."[dxlii] These remarks, evidently stamped with Daoism, are obviously not in alignment with the original meaning of the commentary. This shows the unworthy aspect of his commentaries.

Generally speaking, there is both something to be gained and lost in Wang Bi's scholarship on the *Changes*; as the gain is more than the loss, we should affirm his contribution in this regard.

In the Northern and Southern Dynasties (420-589), the classical studies were also divided into "Northern learning" and "Southern learning," respectively. The former took Zheng Xuan's 郑玄 (127-200) tradition of *Changes* while the latter viewed Wang Bi's commentaries as the orthodoxy. Of course, according to the "Catalogue Attributed to the *Changes*" (*yi lei* 易类) in the "Treatise on Classics and Literature" (*Jing ji zhi* 经籍志) of the *Sui shu* 隋书 (History of the Sui Dynasty [581-618]), some of the dynasties took both of them: "Liang 梁 (502-557) and Chen 陈 (557-589) took both Zheng Xuan's and Wang Bi's commentaries as the official learning, while Qi 齐 (479-502) only admitted Zheng's ideas."[dxliii]

It was not until the establishment of the Sui dynasty (581-618), when China was unified again, that the "Southern learning" flourished, whereas the "Northern learning" declined. During that time, according to the "Catalogue Attributed to the *Changes*" (*yi lei* 易类) in the "Treatise on Classics and Literature" (*Jing ji zhi* 经籍志) of the *Sui shu* 隋书 (History of the Sui Dynasty [581-618]), the scholarship on the *Zhou Changes* also followed this trend, resulting in "the prevalence of Wang's commentaries and fading out of Zheng's learning, which is close to extinction at present."[dxliv] It can be seen that during that period, Wang Bi's commentaries predominated while Zheng's *Changes* was sharply declining.

In the early Tang dynasty (618-907), [in order to legitimize his rule] Emperor Taizong 太宗 (r. 627-649) commissioned Kong Yingda 孔颖达 (574-648) to put together a team of scholars to compile the *Wujing zhengyi* 五经正义 (Correct Meaning of the Five Classics), among which the *Zhou yi zhengyi* 周易正义 (Correct Meaning of the *Zhou Changes*) chose the commentaries of Wang Bi (who had commented the text of the *Zhou Changes* and the Commentaries on the images and judgments) and Han Kangbo 韩康伯 (fl. c. 350) (who had interpreted the *Xi ci* 系辞 [Commentary on the Appended Phrases], *Shuo gua* 说卦 [Discussion of the Trigrams], *Xugua* 序卦 [Orderly Sequence of the Hexagrams], and *Za gua* 杂卦 [The Hexagrams in Irregular Order] of the Ten Wings in the metaphysical way prevailing at his time) and Kong Yingda's sub-commentaries as the main body of the book. From the Tang through the Song dynasty (960-1279), because this book was established as the standard text for civil examinations, it exerted far-reaching influence on the Tang and Song Confucians.

There was a chapter called *Zhou yi zhengyi juanshou* 周易正义卷首 (Introduction to the *Correct Meaning of the Zhou Changes*), which likely was among the earliest introductions to the *Zhou Changes* that we can currently see. It discussed eight issues related to the *Zhou yi* studies at that time: 1) on the three names of the *Changes*; 2) on the person who doubled the trigrams to form the hexagrams; 3) on the names of the *Changes* in the three dynasties (of Xia 夏, Shang 商, and Zhou 周); 4) on the authorship of the hexagram and lines statements; 5) on the division of the two sections of the text; 6) on Confucius's Ten Wings; 7) on the persons who had transmitted the *Changes*; and 8) on the first person who added the term "Classic" (to the *Changes*).

By the discussion of these eight issues, it can be seen that Kong Yingda basically followed the traditional points of view. For example, for the authorship of the hexagram and line statements, he argued that "the hexagram statements were composed by King Wen while the line statements were attached by the Duke of Zhou. Both Ma Rong 马融 (79-166) and Lu Ji 陆绩 (187-219) had this point of view, which we will follow and appropriate here."[dxlv] For the authorship of the "Ten Wings," he said: "Former Confucians share the same point of view that the 'Ten Wings' were composed by Confucius. ... So, here we still follow their point of view."[dxlvi] Regarding the persons who had transmitted the *Changes*, he holds that: "after the 'Ten Wings' were composed by Confucius, the Dao [Way] of the *Changes* became illuminating [and the *Changes* were transmitted successively in later dynasties]."[dxlvii]

But regarding the interpretation of the name of the *Zhou yi* 周易, he does not agree with Han scholars' words and set forth his own idea that "the '*Zhou* 周' in the *Zhou yi* 周易 refers to the place of Qiyang 岐阳 [the birthplace of the Zhou (1045-256 B.C.E.) dynasty] and thus the name of Zhou was used to differentiate itself from the Yin 殷 (c.1600-1046 B.C.E.) [the dynasty that was replaced by the Zhou dynasty]."[dxlviii]

However, the part that should arouse the most attention from us is his discussion "on the three names of the *Changes*." After he had cited the thee meanings of the *Changes* [i.e., "easiness" (*yi* 易), "change" (*bian yi* 变易), and "no change" (*buyi* 不易)] from the "Opening up the Regularities of the [Hexagram] Qian" (*Qian zao du* 乾凿度) of the *Yi wei* 易纬 (Apocrypha of the *Changes*), Kong Yingda elaborated upon the statement in the chapter that "things with form were generated from the formless" by noting: "The three meanings of the *Changes* only rested in existence (*you* 有); yet existence came from non-existence (*wu* 无) while principle (*li* 理) encompasses non-existence."[dxlix] He further quoted some evidence from the *Qian zao du* and viewed "easiness" (*yi* 易) as "chaos" (*hundun* 浑沌): "*Hundun* refers to the state under which the myriad things were fused chaotically without any separation; as it was invisible, intangible, and inaudible; it was called 'easiness' (yi 易)."[dl] In the meantime, in Kong's view, the *Zhou Changes* was composed of principle, which "encompasses both existence and non-existence," and the images, which "only dwell in existence": "The principle of the *Changes* encompasses both existence and non-existence while the images of the *Changes* only dwell in [the realm of] existence. The reason for it might be that the sages' composition of the *Changes* originally aimed to show the way of edification, and the way of edification depends on existence [i.e., concrete approaches]."[dli] He cited some related remarks from the "Commentary on the Appended Phrases" (*Xici zhuan* 系辞传) to support his view: "The 'Dao' [Way] in the phrase 'what is prior to physical form pertains to the Dao'[dlii] refers to nonexistence while the 'concrete objects' (*qi* 器) in 'what is subsequent to physical form pertains to concrete objects [the phenomenal world]'[dliii] refers to existence. The former lies in the body of the Dao while the latter dwells in physical objects and their functions."[dliv] Here, Kong Yingda distorted the original meaning of these remarks in the "Commentary on the Appended Phrases" (*Xici zhuan* 系辞传), through the use of which he wanted to demonstrate his argument that "the Dao [Way] is nothing but nonexistence."[dlv] Yet, there are some other remarks in the *Xici zhuan* that can refute his wrong idea that *yi* 易 (easiness or change) is the invisible and intangible "chaos." The *Xici zhuan* explicitly tells us: "The *Changes* is [no more than] images. *Image* means 'the making of semblances.'"[dlvi] In other words, the *Changes* was nothing but what Kong called the images which "only rest in [the realm of] existence."[dlvii] So far as his point of view that "the Dao [Way] is but nonexistence" is concerned, as it says in the *Xici zhuan* that "[The reciprocal process of] one *yin* and one *yang* is called the Dao"[dlviii] and Kong admitted that *yin-yang* refers to *qi* (material force)—as he stated that "in terms of *qi*, it [the Dao] exists in *yin-yang*" (*yi qi yan zhi, cunhu yin-yang* 以气言之，存乎阴阳)—seeing as how the Dao is that which embodies *qi* (material force), the Dao still belongs to "existence" rather than "nonexistence."

But by drawing upon the *Yi wei* (Apocrypha of the *Changes*), Kong Yingda's view of the *Changes* as an invisible and intangible "chaos"—which encompasses both existence and nonexistence—brought the *Zhou Changes* into Wang Bi's nonexistence-based idealism, a circumstance with consequences which, though passively received, were far-reaching for later scholars. Meanwhile, Kong's argument inspires us to recognize that a large part of Wang Bi's views highly valuing "nonexistence" (*wu* 无, also translated as "no being" or nonactuality") might have absorbed ideological nourishment from the *Apocrypha of the Changes*. It was remarks from Kong, that "existence came from non-existence and principle encompasses non-existence," and that "the principle of the *Changes* encompasses both existence and non-existence," which, to a large extent, inspired the Song (960-1279) people who created a new approach to the *Changes* by "principle" (*li* 理). To this end, Zhu Xi 朱熹 (1130-1200) and Lu Jiuyuan 陆九渊 (1139-1193) opened a debate on this issue. Therefore, the influence of the "Introduction to the *Correct Meaning of the Zhou Changes*" as an earlier overview of the *Zhouyi*, upon later *Changes* scholarship, cannot be neglected.

Besides the subcommentary on Wang Bi's commentaries, the *Correct Meaning* also took views from the *Apocrypha of the Changes* of the Han people, and from other predecessors' comments, such as those of Zi Xia 子夏 [one of Confucius's renowned disciples], and most of these views were based on textual research. Also, this commentary further developed the positive aspect of Wang Bi's commentaries. For example, when interpreting the judgment of hexagram Qian [☰, The Creative, 1] as "fundamentality [*yuan* 元], prevalence [*heng* 亨], fitness [*li* 利], and constancy [*zhen* 贞],"[dlix] the *Correct Meaning* unequivocally points out: "Things have ten thousand images and man has ten thousand affairs. If we only stick to one affair the images of the ten thousand things cannot be included; if we confine ourselves to one image, the myriad things cannot be epitomized. Therefore, there are names with both apparent and hidden meanings and there are words with both simple and complex implications, which should neither be sought by one single example nor be identified by one single classification. So, the 'Commentary on the Appended Phrases' says 'Rising and falling without any consistency, the hard and soft lines change one into the other, something for which it is impossible to make definitive laws, since they are doing nothing but keeping pace with change'[dlx] and Han Kangbo said 'we should not establish a fixed law.'"[dlxi] These words adequately manifested the positive function of Wang Bi's commentaries that upheld "getting the idea is in fact a matter of forgetting the images"[dlxii] and blamed the Han people for their inappropriately associating each word of the basic text of the *Zhou*

Changes with an image. In the meantime, it set forth an argument that "images" are "metaphors": "What the *Changes* contains are but images. Sometimes it takes the image of a specific object, such as the 'submerged dragon' and the 'dragon appearing in the fields' in [the bottom and second line statements respectively of] hexagram Qian [☰, The Creative, 1] and '[from] frost to solid ice' and 'dragons fighting in the fields' in [the bottom and top line statements respectively of] hexagram Kun [☷, The Receptive, 2], so as to reveal the significance of a hexagram or a line. Sometimes it draws upon the images of various things or events, such as 'going after deer without a forester' and 'yoked horses pulling at odds' in [the third and fourth line statements respectively of] hexagram Zhun [☳, Birth Throes, 3], so that the meanings of the lines are brought to light. There are many cases of this kind in the *Changes*. Sometimes it directly takes human affairs, rather than images of objects, to disclose the meanings of a line, such as the third line statement of hexagram Qian [☰, The Creative, 1] that 'The noble man makes earnest efforts throughout the day'[dlxiii] and the third line statement of hexagram Kun [☷, The Receptive, 2] that 'One who effaces his own prominent qualities here will be able to practice constancy.'[dlxiv] According to the sage's intention, when images were suitable, he would take images; when human affairs were more fitting (to the situation), he would draw on human affairs."[dlxv] These points of view were truly valuable at that time.

Nevertheless, it must be admitted that the *Correct Meaning* also has drawbacks. For example, although it simultaneously took up other predecessors' interpretations, seldom had it gone beyond Wang Bi's commentaries and even appeared as a defender of Wang Bi's commentaries; it seems that without Wang's exegesis, the interpretation (of the basic text of the *Changes*) would not be established. For instance, for the judgment of hexagram Gu [☶, Ills to Be Cured, 18] that "Gu is such that it provides the opportunity for fundamental prevalence, and so it is fitting to cross the great river, but it will be suitable for three days before the day of *Jia* 甲 [the initial stem of the ten heavenly stems, namely, *Jia* 甲, *Yi* 乙, *Bing* 丙, *Ding* 丁, *Wu* 戊, *Ji* 己, *Geng* 庚, *Xin* 辛, *Ren* 壬, and *Gui* 癸 which form a cycle of 10 days] and for three days after the day of *Jia* 甲."[dlxvi] The *Correct Meaning* elaborates on the days in this way:

Mr. Chu 褚, Mr. He 何, and Mr. Zhou 周 arrived at a consensus with the view of Mr. Zheng 郑 (玄) who averred that the day of *Jia* refers to the day by which time a new law has been initiated, and "three days before the day of *Jia*" refers to *Xin* 辛 [literally, new], which means turning over a new leaf, and "three days after the day of *Jia*" refers to the day of *Ding* 丁, which means urging again and again (*dingning* 丁宁). It is noteworthy that Wang Bi contends that *Jia* here means "a newly initiated law"[dlxvii] rather than the day for the initiation of law. And additionally, for the "three days before the day of *Geng* 庚 and three days after the day of *Geng* 庚" mentioned in the fifth line statement of hexagram Xun [䷸, Compliance, 57], Wang Bi told us that "for an order to be given is what *Geng* [law issued] means,"[dlxviii] and he also holds that "*Jia* and *Geng* both mean the issuing of orders."[dlxix] Therefore, the above-mentioned Confucians did not pay attention to the purport of Wang Bi's exegesis, and provided their heretical views, which are not advisable.[dlxx]

Through the above-mentioned words, it can be seen that although the emperor ordered the establishment of Wang Bi's commentaries as the orthodoxy, Chu's, He's, and Zhou's *Changes*, treated as commensurate with Zheng Xuan's exegesis, were still permissibly propagated. Therefore, Zheng Xuan's discourse on the *Changes* was still exerting a certain influence at that time. However, if one's exegesis deviated from Wang Bi's hermeneutical purport, it would be viewed as heresy by Kong Yingda. This reminds us of the basic reason for the withering away of Zheng's *Changes*. Moreover, there were originally no interpretations from Hang Kangbo for the fifth paragraph of the "Discussion of Trigrams" (*Shugua* 说卦) that "The Divine Ruler [*shangdi*] comes forth in Zhen [☳, Quake] and sets all things in order in Xun [☴, Compliance]…"[dlxxi] [Disregarding other scholars' interpretations at hand,] Kong Yingda adopted Wang Bi's commentaries on the second line statement of hexagram Yi [䷩, Increase, 42] that "The king uses this opportunity to make offering of this one to the Divine Ruler [*di*]." [According to Wang Bi, this sentence means that "The Divine Ruler (*di*) is the master of all living things, the patriarch who sets Increase in motion and who 'comes forth in *Zhen* (☳, Quake) and sets all things in order in *Xun* (☴, Compliance)."'[dlxxii] This assimilation was felt to be an extreme exegesis and became an object of ridicule for later scholars.

For all this, the *Correct Meaning* as a work of the Tang people on the *Changes* was of high academic value for later scholars wishing to study previous *Changes* scholarship, and especially significant to the studies of the *Changes* scholarship from the Wei (220-265) to the Jin (265-420) dynasties.

In the early Tang dynasty, another famous work was Lu Deming's 陆德明 (c. 556-630) *Jingdian shiwen* 经典释文 (Exegetical Texts of the Classics), the second *juan* 卷 (chapter) of which is the *Zhou yi yinyi* 周易音义 (Pronunciation and Meaning in the *Zhou Changes*). Though the text of the *Zhou yi yinyi* was based on Wang Bi's version of the *Changes*, according to the "Prefatory Notes" (*Xulu* 序录) of the *Shiwen* 释文 (Exegetical Texts), there were over 20 renowned scholars' works on the *Changes* before the Jin dynasty (265-420) still existing at that time. The *Shiwen* broadly adopted various schools' interpretations. It is regrettable that the citations were overly succinct. Despite this, the *Shiwen* can still provide us with precious material for research on the Han *Yi* tradition.

In the prosperous Tang dynasty (618-907), since most intellectuals converted to Buddhism, they offered very few innovative perspectives on the *Changes*. Besides the *Correct Meaning* and the *Shiwen* 释文, the extant and relatively valuable *Changes*-oriented works include Li Dingzuo's 李鼎祚 *Zhou yi jijie* 周易集解 (Collected Explanations of the *Zhou Changes*), Shi Zheng's 史徵 *Zhou yi koujue yi* 周易口诀义 (Meanings of the Pithy Formulae of the *Zhou Changes*), and Guo Jing's 郭京 *Zhou yi juzheng* 周易举正 (An Illustration of the Correct Meanings of the *Zhou Changes*).

Here, we will particularly introduce the value of Li Dingzuo's 李鼎祚 *Zhou yi jijie* 周易集解 (Collected Explanations of the *Zhou Changes*).

We do not have any way to know the detailed life story of Li Dingzuo, and what we can know of him is that he completed the *Zhou yi jijie* in 762, which collected the related entries of all the famous works on the *Changes* available at that time. In the "Author's Preface," he claims that this book aims to "expunge Wang Bi's unorthodox comments and to add

Zheng Xuan's lost images"[dlxxiii] to the analysis of the *Yi jing*, in which he adopted the related annotations of over 35 scholars, including Zi Xia 子夏 [one of the 72 famous disciples of Confucius], Meng Xi 孟喜, Jiao Gan 焦赣, Jing Fang 京房 (77-37 B.C.E.), Ma Rong 马融 (79-166), Xun Shuang 荀爽 (128-190), Zheng Xuan 郑玄 (127-200), Liu Biao 刘表 (142-208), He Yan 何晏 (d. 249), Song Zhong 宋衷, Yu Fan 虞翻 (164-233), Lu Ji 陆绩 (187-219), Gan Bao 干宝 (d. 336), Wang Su 王肃 (195-256), Wang Bi 王弼 (226-249), Yao Xin 姚信, Wang Yi 王廙, Zhang Fan 张璠, Xiang Xiu 向秀 (c. 227-272), Hou Guo 侯果 [a scholar in the early Tang dynasty], and Shu Cai 蜀才 [a scholar in the early Tang dynasty]. Thanks in large measure to this work, we can discern and explore the Han scholarship on the *Changes*. Therefore, the editors of the *Siku quanshu* (Complete Collection of the Four Treasuries) assessed the value of this book in "The Changes" (*yi lei* 易类) of the classical category (*Jing bu* 经部) as follows: "With the thriving of Wang Bi's learning, the Han *Changes* faded out. Over a thousand and several hundred years later, it is only thanks to the existence of this book that today's learners can discern the original meanings of the hexagram and lines. (On this account,) it was undoubtedly a precious representative of ancient literature!"

The Han people's *Changes* had become so decadent in the Tang (618-907) and the Five Dynasties (907-960) that it was left without anybody to care for it. Fortunately, Lu Deming and Li Dingzuo excerpted some part of the Han *Changes*, which, from today's perspective, is the great contribution made by the Tang people to the study of the *Changes*.

9.
A Brief Introduction to the Studies of the *Changes* in the Past Dynasties (II)

The Song dynasty (960-1279) witnessed the renewed flowering of *Changes* scholarship again.

The *Changes*-related works of the Song people were abundant, and they particularly gave attention to the inventions and illuminations of the *tu shu* 图书 (chart or diagram).

The so-called *tu* 图 and *shu* 书 mainly refer to the *he tu* 河图 (Yellow River Chart) and the *luo shu* 洛书 (Luo River Diagram), which were manufactured by the Song people so as to associate them with former scholars' commentaries on the *Changes*. Speculations concerning these charts and diagrams brought the two into mutual engagement, and thus more and more charts and diagrams were spawned. From the Song (960-1279) through the Qing (1616-1912) dynasties, the number of these charts and diagrams reportedly mounted to several thousand, and thus a new branch of the *Changes* studies took form, which was referred to as the "*he tu*- and *luo shu*-based learning (*tushu zhi xue* 图书之学)."

Now let us discuss the cause of the rise of the charts and diagrams invented by the Song people, and their contents. The terms *he tu* and the *luo shu* were derived from the sentence in the "Commentary on the

Appended Phrases" (*Xici* 系辞) that "the Yellow River brought forth a chart, and the Luo River brought forth a diagram, and the sages regarded these things also as ruling principles."[dlxxiv]

There really were the terms "*he tu*" in the pre-Qin [i.e., before 221 B.C.E.] documents. For example, it says in the "Deathbed Testament" (*Gu ming* 顾命) of the *Shang shu* 尚书 (Classic of History): "The big jade, the barbarian jade, the [map of the] celestial globe, and the River Chart (*he tu* 河图) were displayed in the east."[dlxxv] Additionally, according to the *Analects of Confucius*, Confucius once sighed and said: "The phoenix does not come and the river gives forth no chart, [the arrival of which was regarded as portents that heralded the rise of a Saviour sage.] It is all over with me [which means Heaven does not intend to let me play a Sage's part!]" (9:8).

But there was not any reference to the pattern of the chart at that time. Though the "Commentary on the Appended Phrases" told us that the sages' composition of the *Changes* was based on the *he tu* and the *luo shu*, all the commentators on the *Changes* from the Han (206 B.C.E.-220 C.E.) through the Six Dynasties (229-589) had never described or illustrated their specific configurations. And the Tang scholars such as Lu Deming 陆德明 (c. 550-630), Kong Yingda 孔颖达 (574-648), and Li Dingzuo 李鼎祚 did not disclose their details, either.

Though Han scholars like Liu Xin 刘歆 (50 B.C.E.-23 C.E.), Kong Anguo 孔安国 (156-74 B.C.E.), Yang Xiong 扬雄 (53 B.C.E.-18 C.E.), and Ban Gu 班固 (32-92) mentioned the terms *he tu* and *luo shu* in their works, they only superficially referred to them and did not reach a consensus on their meanings. Additionally, the *Zhushu jinian* 竹书纪年 (Bamboo Annals), *Li ji* 礼记 (Record of Ritual), *Huainan zi* 淮南子 [written by the intellectuals surrounding Liu An 刘安 (179-122 B.C.E.), then the king of the state of Huainan], "Opening Up the Regularities of the [Hexagram] Qian" (*Qian zao du* 乾凿度) of the *Yi wei* 易纬 (Apocrypha of the *Changes*), *Lun heng* 论衡 (Discourses Weighed in the Balance), and *Baihu tong yi* 白虎通义 (Comprehensive Discussions at the White Tiger Hall) also mentioned *he tu* and *luo shu*, but they merely touched upon the terms through generalities. Among these scholars and works, only Zheng Xuan 郑玄 (127-200) told us that *he tu* has nine chapters and *luo shu* contains six chapters when he commented on these two terms in the "Commentary on the Appended Phrases" (*Xi ci* 系辞),[dlxxvi] by which it can be seen that they ought to be made up of articles rather than the charts related to the *Changes*. Moreover, Zheng's interpretation might originate from some apocrypha that came out later and certainly could not be viewed as evidence.

During the period of Taiping xingguo 太平兴国 [literally, State of Great Peace and Prosperity, a goal to be realized by the second emperor of the Song dynasty] (976-984), the famous Daoist Chen Tuan 陈抟 (871-989) was reportedly transmitting the so-called *he tu* (Yellow River Chart), *luo shu* (Luo River Diagram), *Xiatian tu* 先天图 (Chart of the Former Heaven Sequence), and so on. We do not know from where Chen Tuan obtained these miraculous and complex diagrams. According to [the famous early Qing (1616-1912) scholar] Huang Zongxi's 黄宗羲 (1610-95) *Yixue xiangshu lun* 易学象数论 (Discussion of Images and Numbers in *Changes* Scholarship), Chen Tuan passed them down to Chong Fang 种放, who further passed them down to Li Gai 李溉, who further passed them down to Xu Jian 许坚, who further passed them down to Fan Echang 范谔昌, who further passed them down to Liu Mu 刘牧. On the basis of the *he tu* and the *luo shu*, Liu Mu wrote the *Yishu gouyin tu* 易数钩隐图 (Investigation into the Hidden: Illustrations of *Changes* Numerology), by which Chen Tuan's diagrams began to be known by common intellectuals. Chen Tuan transmitted the *Xiantian tu* (Chart of the Former Heaven Sequence) to Chong Fang 种放, who further transmitted it to Mu Xiu 穆修, who further transmitted it to Li Zhicai 李之才, who further transmitted it to Shao Yong 邵雍 (1011-77), [one of the five founders of the Neo-Confucianism prevailing from the Song dynasty to the end of imperial China] who wrote the famous *Huangji jingshi* 皇极经世 (Supreme Principles That Rule the World). Additionally, based on the *Taiji tu* 太极图 (Diagram of the Supreme Ultimate) passed down to him by Mu Xiu 穆修, Zhou Dunyi 周敦颐 (1017-73) [one of the five founders of the Neo-Confucianism] wrote the famous *Taiji tu shuo* 太极图说 (An Explanation of the "Diagram of the Supreme Ultimate"). All of these works forced associations between these diagrams and the meanings of the *Changes*. As a result, the learning of the diagrams took a form that exerted great influence upon later scholars' approaches to the *Changes*. It is evident that the *he tu* and the *luo shu*-based learning originated from [religious] Daoism.

Later, Zhu Xi (1130-1200) wrote the *Zhou yi benyi* 周易本义 (Original Meaning of the *Zhou Changes*), in the very beginning of which nine charts were illustrated, including the *he tu*, the *luo shu*, "Fuxi's Sequence of the Eight Trigrams" (*Fuxi bagua cixu* 伏羲八卦次序), "Fuxi's Positioning of the Eight Trigrams" (*Fuxi bagua fangwei* 伏羲八卦方位), "Fuxi's Sequence of the Sixty-four Hexagrams" (*Fuxi liushi si gua cixu* 伏羲六十四卦次序), "Fuxi's Positioning of the Sixty-four Hexagrams" (*Fuxi liushi si gua fangwei* 伏羲六十四卦方位), "King Wen's Sequence of the Eight Trigrams" (*Wenwang bagua cixu* 文王八卦次序), "King Wen's Positioning of the Eight Trigrams" (*Wenwang bagua fangwei* 文王八卦方位), and "The System of Hexagram Changes (*guabian* 卦变) of King Wen's Sixty-four Hexagrams." The authenticity of these charts and diagrams was further affirmed by Zhu Xi, though some later scholars knew the error—for fear of Zhu's authoritative position, and being afraid of the accusation of interference with politics [as from the Yuan dynasty (1271-1368) onward, Zhu Xi's exegesis of the classic, among other things, was authorized as the standard text for civil examinations], few of them dared to point it out. On this account, from the Yuan (1271-1368) and Ming (1368-1644) dynasties onward, more and more charts and diagrams proliferated, such that most later scholars had to illustrate the charts like the *he tu* and the *luo shu* in the beginning of their works interpreting the *Changes*. Thus, it seems that these charts had become an important component of the *Zhou Changes*. Some scholars even claimed that the *Zhou yi* was derived from the *he tu* and the *luo shu* rather than the other way around.

Now, we will select four of the nine charts illustrated in the beginning of the *Zhouyi benyi* 周易本义 (Original Meaning of the *Zhou Changes*), as follows:

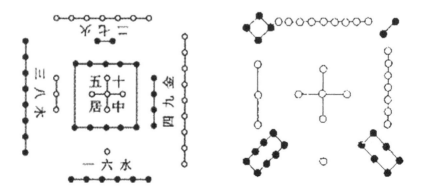

Figure 9.1. Yellow River Chart (*he tu*)   Figure 9.2. Luo River Diagram (*luo shu*)

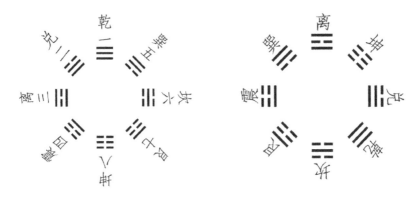

Figure 9.3. Fuxi's Positioning of the Eight Trigrams

Figure 9.4. King Wen's Positioning of the Eight Trigrams[1]

As indicated above, though the terms *he tu* and *luo shu* had been mentioned in the *Xici* (Commentary on the Appended Phrases), there was not any evidence at all that the *he tu* and the *luo shu* included there, by which the sages reportedly invented the eight trigrams, were just the same as the Song people's *he tu* made up of 55 dots (among which there are 30 black ones and 25 white ones) and *luo shu* with 45 dots (among which there are 25 white ones and 20 black ones). These charts were not available in the pre-Qin (before 221 B.C.E.) documents and cannot be found in the *Changes*-related works from the Han (206 B.C.E.-220 C.E.) through Tang (618-907) dynasties.

In spite of this, in view of the numbers and distributions of the white and black dots, these two charts might not have been fabricated out of thin air by the Song people but derived from some predecessors' commentaries on the *Changes*.

The distribution of the 55 black and white dots of the Song people's *he tu* might have been inspired by a paragraph of the *Xici* (Commentary on the Appended Phrases), which says: "Heaven is one, and Earth is two; Heaven is three, and Earth is four; Heaven is five, and Earth is six; Heaven is seven, and Earth is eight; Heaven is nine, and Earth is ten. Heaven's

---

[1] As is often the case with traditional Chinese charts and diagrams representing geographical space, the north is located at the bottom of these illustrations.

numbers are five, and Earth's numbers are five. With the completion of these two sets of five places, each number finds its match. Heaven's numbers come to twenty-five, and Earth's numbers come to thirty. The total sum of Heaven's and Earth's numbers is fifty-five. These [numbers] indicate how change and transformation are brought about and how gods and spirits are activated." [dlxxvii]

In the meantime, as it says in the "Treatise on Pitch Pipes and Calendar" (*Lüli zhi* 律历志) of the *Han shu* 汉书 (History of the Western Han Dynasty [206 B.C.E.-9 C.E.]):

> Heaven produces water with one; Earth produces fire with two; Heaven produces wood with three; Earth produces metal with four; Heaven produces Earth with five. The Five Agents destroy each other [i.e., Wood destroys Earth; Earth destroys Water; Water destroys Fire; Fire destroys Metal; Metal destroys Wood], and thus a cycle is generated.[dlxxviii]

According to "Opening Up the Regularities of the [Hexagrams] Qian and Kun" (*Qiankun zao du* 乾坤凿度) in the *Yi wei* 易纬 (Apocrypha of the *Changes*) [prevalent in the late Western Han (220 B.C.E.-9 C.E.)]:

> Heaven was established on one. One was the source of numbers. With the match-up of earth, six was produced and thus Heaven's number [of one] and Earth's number [of six] were completed, the combination of which led to the quality [of water]. Then the match-up between the heavenly number of three and earthly number of eight, that between heavenly seven and earthly two, that between heavenly five and earthly ten, and that between heavenly nine and earthly four, [together with the match-up of the heavenly one and earthly six in the beginning,] formed the five agents of Water, Wood, Fire, Earth, and Metal, respectively [a cycle of mutual production]. Wood corresponds to benevolence (*ren* 仁), Fire to etiquettes (*li* 礼), Earth to trustworthiness (*xin* 信), Water to wisdom (*zhi* 智), and Metal to propriety (*yi* 义). Additionally, it says in the *Wanming jing* 万名经 (Canon of the Ten Thousand Names): "Water and Earth simultaneously contain virtues of wisdom and trustworthiness respectively;

Wood and Fire simultaneously possess virtues of benevolence and bounty. The five innate virtues are equated with the [five] relationships [between parents and children, husband and wife, the superior and the inferior, elder and younger brothers or sisters, and friends]."dlxxix

Here, not only can we see the origin of the Song people's *he tu*, but we also get to know how the Western Han people associated the five agents with the five virtues. From Zheng Xuan's 郑玄 (127-200) perspective, "Heavenly one produces water in the north; Earthly two produces fire in the south; Heavenly three produces wood in the east; Earthly four produces metal in the west; Heavenly five produces earth in the center. [...] Earthly six completes water in the north and combines with heavenly one; Heavenly seven complete fire in the south and fuses with earthly two; Earthly eight completes wood in the east and conflates with heavenly three; Heavenly nine completes metal in the west and merges with earthly four; Earthly ten completes earth in the center and incorporates with heavenly five."dlxxx Yu Fan's 虞翻 (164-233) argument regarding the qualities of these numbers is identical with Zheng Xuan's.dlxxxi

These predecessors'—and especially Zheng Xuan's—exegeses of these numbers could enable us to see the origin of the Song people's *he tu* more clearly.

For the arrangement of the 45 black and white dots in the *luo shu*, there was a very striking feature: the numbers in any series of three, whether taken vertically, horizontally, or diagonally, all add up to 15. Additionally, the black dots representing the earthly numbers were all placed at the four corners. The "Discussion of the Charts" (*Tu shuo* 图说) in the *Zhouyi benyi* 周易本义 (Original Meaning of the *Zhou Changes*) summarized this feature of the diagram in this way: "The *luo shu* might take the image of a tortoise, which had nine dots on its head and treaded on one dot, with three on the left and seven on the right, with two and four on its shoulders, with six and eight as its rear feet."dlxxxii

Yet, according to "Opening Up the Regularities of the [Hexagram] Qian" (*Qian zao du* 乾凿度) in the *Yi wei* 易纬 (Apocrypha of the *Changes*), "The merging of the *yin* and *yang* (numbers) resulting in fifteen is called the Dao [Way] in the *Changes*. That *yang* changes from seven to nine and *yin* changes from eight to six also lead to fifteen [i.e., 7+8=15; 9+6=15]."dlxxxiii "So, the Great One (*tai yi* 太一) took these numbers to move in the nine palaces in which all the numbers in any series, whether perpendicular, horizontal, or diagonal, add up to 15."dlxxxiv From Zheng Xuan's 郑玄 (127-200) perspective:

> [Here] *Taiyi* was the name of the Spirit of the Northern Asterism. When it rests at its original place, it is called the Great One. [...] The four cardinal directions and the four corners are called [eight] palaces as the names of residences of the spirits of the eight trigrams. [...] The Great One goes down and moves to the palaces of the eight trigrams. After it has moved through four palaces, it returns to the center, which is the residence of the Spirit of the Northern Asterism. There are overall nine palaces. Generally speaking, it comes out from *yang* and enters from *yin*. As *yang* starts from *zi* 子 [the 1st earthly branch, corresponding to north] and *yin* from *wu* 午 [the 7th earthly branch, equated with south], when the Great One travels through the nine palaces, it starts from the palace of Kan 坎 [☵, north], which corresponds to the Middle Son. Then it moves to the palace of Kun 坤 [☷, southwest], which corresponds to the Mother; then it moves to the palace of Zhen 震 [☳, east], which corresponds to the Eldest Son; then, it further moves to the palace of Xun 巽 [☴, southeast], which corresponds to the Eldest Daughter. So far it has completed a half of the way and returns to the central palace and takes a rest there. Then it moves to the palace of Qian 乾 [☰, northwest], which corresponds to the Father; then it moves to the palace of Dui 兑 [☱, west], which corresponds to the Youngest Daughter; then, it moves to the palace of Gen 艮 [☶, northeast], which corresponds to the Youngest Son; then, it moves to the palace of Li 离 [☲, south], which corresponds to the Middle Daughter. Now the circuit is completed and it returns and takes a rest in the purple palace [i.e., the central palace], the residence of the Great One or Heavenly One. Its travel starts from the palace of Kan [☵, north] and ends at the

palace of Li [☲, south], and the number starts from one (which corresponds to trigram Kan [☵] and north)."dlxxxv

Taking references from the positions (and directions) of the eight trigrams and taking the above-mentioned explication by Zheng Xuan into consideration, the Qing scholar Hu Wei 胡渭 (1633-1714) made a tabulation in his *Yitu Mingbian* 易图明辨 (A Clarifying Critique of the Illustrations Associated with the *Changes*) as follows[dlxxxvi]:

Xun 巽 四 (Four)	Li 离 九 (Nine)	Kun 坤 二 (Two)
Zhen 震 三 (Three)	Center 五 (Five)	Dui 兑 七 (Seven)
Gen 艮 八 (Eight)	Kan 坎 一 (One)	Qian 乾 六 (Six)

This tabulation clearly exposes the provenance of the 45 black and white dots in the Song people's *luo shu*, which was fabricated according to Zheng Xuan's explanation of the above-mentioned words from "Opening Up the Regularities of the [Hexagram] Qian" (*Qian zao du* 乾凿度) in the *Yi wei* 易纬 (Apocrypha of the *Changes*).

But the *he tu* and the *luo shu* we see today come from Cai Yuanding's 蔡元定 (1135-98) view, which was followed by Zhu Xi 朱熹 (1130-1200) and set at the beginning of his *Zhou yi benyi* 周易本义 (Original Meaning of the *Zhou Changes*). However, here the names of the two charts were confused and opposite to what was originally taught by Liu Mu, who wrote the famous *Yishu gouyin tu* 易数钩隐图 (Investigation into the Hidden: Illustrations of *Changes* Numerology), by which Chen Tuan's diagrams begun to be known by common intellectuals. That is, the *he tu* we see today was called *luo shu* by Liu Mu, whereas the *luo shu* in Zhu Xi's work was referred to as *he tu* by Liu Mu. Because these charts were allegedly passed down from Chen Tuan, there had been two different points of view concerning their names at that time.[dlxxxvii]

Zhu Xi argued that the *he tu* and the *luo shu* belong to the "Changes of Naturalness of Heaven and Earth" (*tiandi ziran zhi yi* 天地自然之易). Apart from this, there are "Fu xi's *Changes*," "King Wen and the Duke of Zhou's *Changes*," and "Confucius's *Changes*."[dlxxxviii] Thus, the differences between "Fuxi's Positioning of the Eight Trigrams" and "King Wen's Positioning of the Eight Trigrams" were brought to light.

The chart of "Fuxi's Positioning of the Eight Trigrams" was actually based on Shao Yong's 邵雍 (1011-77) "Chart of the Former Heaven Sequence" (*Xiantian tu* 先天图), and thus it was also called the "Eight Trigrams' Positions of the Former Heaven" (*Xiantian bagua fangwei* 先天八卦方位), in which Qian 乾 [☰] is located at the south point (in the chart), Kun 坤 [☷] at the north point, Li 离 [☲] at the east point, Kan 坎 [☵] at the west point, Zhen 震 [☳] at the northeast point, Xun 巽 [☴] at the southwest point, Gen 艮 [☶] at the northwest point, and Dui 兑 [☱] at the southeast point (see Fig. 9.3).

The chart of "King Wen's Positioning of the Eight Trigrams" is also called the "Eight Trigrams' Positions of the Latter Heaven" (*Houtian bagua fangwei* 后天八卦方位), which was described in the "Discussion of the Eight Trigrams" (*Shuogua* 说卦)[dlxxxix] (see also Fig. 9.4).

As with the *he tu* and the *luo shu*, before the Song dynasty (960-1279), from the Han (206 B.C.E.-220 C.E.) through the Tang dynasty (618-907), no one explicitly mentioned the appellation of "positions of the former heaven." It was not until the Song dynasty that the "Chart of the Former Heaven Sequence" (*Xiantian tu* 先天图) came out of Daoism and was taken into Zhu Xi's *Zhou yi benyi* (Original Meaning of the *Zhou Changes*). There were both followers and dissenters among later scholars, and particularly the Qing (1616-1912) scholars launched endless debates on this issue and failed to come to any consensus.

But if we take some sayings from the "Discussion of the Trigrams" (*Shuogua* 说卦) and take the Han (206 B.C.E.-220 C.E.) people's commentaries into consideration, we can find that the Song people's reference to "Positions of the Former Heaven" was not groundless.

It says in the "Discussion of the Trigrams": "Li [☲] is fire, is the sun, [...] is the trigram of Qian [☰]."[dxc]

When interpreting the sentence of "in terms of the concepts of *yin* and *yang*, it refers to the sun [corresponding to *yang*] and the moon [*yin*]"[dxci] in the *Xi ci*, Xun Shuang 荀爽 (128-190) tells us: "Qian [☰]

resides at (the position of) Li [☲] and corresponds to the sun while Kun [☷] resides at (the position of) Kan [☵] and corresponds to the moon."[dxcii] When interpreting the last sentence of the "Commentary on the Words of the Text" (*Wenyan* 文言) regarding hexagram Kun [䷁, The Receptive, 2] that "(Black-and-yellow refers to how Heaven and Earth are mixed together.) Heaven is black and Earth is yellow,"[dxciii] he argues: "Heaven [symbolized by ☰] signifies *yang* which starts from the northeast [...]; Earth [symbolized by ☷] signifies *yin* which starts from the southwest."[dxciv] Here, "northeast" and "southwest" obviously refer to Zhen [☳, symbolizing the emergence of *yang* from the bottom line] and Xun [☴, symbolizing the emergence of *yin* from the bottom line], respectively. Xun Shuang's views must have their grounds, as [we can see] in the "Sayings Explained" (*Quanyan xun* 诠言训) of the *Huainanzi* 淮南子 [credited to the intellectuals surrounding and serving Liu An (179- 122 B.C.E.), a king of the State of Huainan in the Western Han dynasty (206 B.C.E.- 9 C.E.)] that "*Yang qi* arises in the northeast and culminates in the southwest. *Yin qi* arises in the southwest and culminates in the northeast. From their inception, the evolutions of *yin* and *yang* are synchronized."[dxcv] Therefore, it is evident that, in the early Western Han dynasty, this kind of view had come into being—which was exactly in alignment with the positions of Zhen [☳] on the northeast and Xun [☴] on the southwest in the chart of the "Eight Trigrams' Positions of the Former Heaven" (*Xiantian bagua fangwei* 先天八卦方位).

When annotating the sentence "The bright ones [i.e., the sun and the moon] shine from beginning to end, the positions of the six lines form, each at its proper moment"[dxcvi] in the "Commentary on the Judgment" (*Tuan zhuan* 彖传) regarding hexagram Qian [䷀, The Creative, 1], Xun Shuang 荀爽 (128-190) linked it with the related trigrams: "Qian [☰] arises from (the position of) Kan [☵] (on the north), [waxes through the east,] and culminates in Li [☲] (on the south), whereas Kun [☷] arises from Li [☲] (on the south), [accumulates through the west,] and culminates in Kan [☵] (on the north). And thus Kan [☵] and Li [☲] are the homes of Kun [☷] and Qian [☰], and the residences of *yin* and *yang* (respectively)."[dxcvii]

When annotating hexagram Tongren [䷌, Fellowship, 13], the *Jiujia yi* 九家易 (Nine Schools' *Changes*) says: "Qian [☰] resides at [the position of] Li [☲], and both of them correspond to the sun."[dxcviii] In Xun

Shuang's view, "Qian [☰] resides at [the position of] Li [☲], and thus they [i.e., Qian and Li] share the same location."[dxcix]

These annotations remind us of a divination ordered by Duke Huan of the State of Lu in the "Second Year of Duke Min" (660 B.C.E.) of the *Zuo zhuan* (Zuo's Commentary on the *Spring and Autumn Annals*): "Then, he further ordered the diviner to divine about it by yarrow stalks and encountered Dayou [䷍, Great Holdings, 14] transforming into Qian [䷀, The Creative, 1]. The diviner said: 'He will become as noble as his father and will be venerated as the sovereign.'"[dc] According to the "Discussion of the Trigrams" (*Shuogua* 说卦), Qian [☰] "is the sovereign, is father."[dci] In this divination, the upper trigram Li [☲] transformed into Qian [☰], which is associated with the sovereign and father. By the "Trigrams' Positions of the Former Heaven," Qian [☰] is located at south, whereas in the chart of the "Trigrams' Positions of the Latter Heaven" Li [☲] is also located at south. Based on this identity, here "he [symbolized by Li (☲), the upper trigram of the original hexagram] will become as noble as his father [symbolized by Qian (☰), the upper trigram of the derivative hexagram]" would seem to mean that "Qian [☰] resides at (the position of) Li [☲], and both of them correspond to the sun"[dcii] or "Qian [☰] resides at [the position of] Li [☲], and thus they share the same location."[dciii]

As indicated above, we believe that in the Han (206 B.C.E.-220 C.E.), and even in the Spring and Autumn period (770-476 B.C.E.), in the use of the *Changes*, there might have been a view that "Qian [☰] arises from [the position of] Kan [☵] (on the north), [accumulates through the east,] and culminates in Li [☲] [on the south], whereas Kun [☷] arises from Li [☲] [on the south], [accumulates through the west,] and culminates in Kan [☵] [on the north]" to reveal the changes and transformations between (*yin* and *yang* energies symbolized by) the eight trigrams. Therefore, the positions of the "Trigrams of the Former Heaven" were not arbitrarily made up by the Song people.

On the basis of the above-mentioned documents and material, we have made a preliminary survey of the Song people's *he tu*, *luo shu*, and the "Eight Trigrams' Positions of the Former Heaven."

Additionally, in the spring of 1977, at Shuanggudui 双古堆, Fuyang County, Anhui Province, the tomb was excavated of the Western Han (206 B.C.E.-9 C.E.) Marquis Ruyin 汝阴侯, whose name was Xiahou Zhao 夏侯灶 (d. 165). Among the unearthed relics, there was a divinatory board referred to by the excavators as "Divinatory Board of the Great One with Nine Palaces" (*Taiyi jiugong zhanpan* 太乙九宫占盘) (see Fig. 9.5). According to the excavation bulletin, "[the elements on] the obverse side of the divinatory board were arranged according to the attributes of the eight trigrams and Five Agents (of Water, Fire, Wood, Metal, and Earth). The names of the nine palaces and the number of days each palace governs were identical to those exhibited in the chart (see Fig. 9.7) illustrated at the very beginning of the chapter of 'Nine Palaces and Eight Winds' (*Jiugong bafeng* 九宫八风) of the *Lingshu jing* 灵枢经 [an acupuncture-oriented canon, an integral part of the famous *Huangdi neijing* 黄帝内经 (Yellow Emperor's Canon of Internal Medicine)], whereas the permutation of numbers on the round plate (see Fig. 9. 6) is in accordance with the *he tu* and the *luo shu*."[dciv] On this round plate, there were four equiangular lines crossing at the center of the circle where the numbers of "one" (*yi* 一) corresponding to the sovereign (*jun* 君) and "nine" (*jiu* 九) corresponding to the common people (*baixing* 百姓) formed a pair, "two" (*er* 二) and "eight" (*ba* 八) constituted a pair, "three" (*san* 三) corresponding to the prime minister (*xiang* 相) and "seven" (*qi* 七) equated with the senior general (*jiang* 将) were considered to be a pair, and "four" (*si* 四) and "six" (*liu* 六) were seen as a pair. [These pairs are in alignment with the pairs of numbers in the *luo shu*.] There are four characters of *li* 吏 (official), *zhao yao* 招摇 [i.e., Big Dipper], and *ye* 也 around the center. The number of the characters, i.e., four, together with the center of the circle as one, will add up to five, similar to the distributions of the five white dots in the center of the *luo shu*.

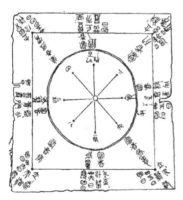 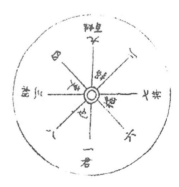

Figure 9.5. Divinatory Board of the Great One with Nine Palaces Figure

9.6. The Round Plate

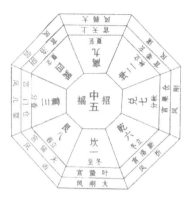

Figure. 9.7. Nine Palaces and Eight Winds

Therefore, it can be seen that the permutation of the numbers on this divinatory board coincides with [the distributed numbers of the white and black dots of] the *luo shu* [rather than the *he tu*]. This irrefutably verifies that, in the early Western Han, or earlier than that time, there were charts like the *luo shu*. The Song people's *luo shu* was actually modeled on the charts similar to the "Divinatory Board of the Great One with Nine Palaces" (*Taiyi jiugong zhanpan* 太乙九宫占盘). This further demonstrates that the Song people's *he tu* and *luo shu* were not groundless, and just how cogent the Qing scholar Hu Wei's 胡渭 (1633-1714) textual research was! If we are still suspicious of it, another piece of solid evidence is that it says in the "Treatise on the Rites and Rituals" (*Liyi zhi* 礼仪志) of the *Jiu Tangshu* 旧唐书 (Old Book of Tang [618-907]) that: "In the 3rd year of Tianbao 天宝 (744), an occultist called Su Jiaqing 苏嘉庆 submitted a memorandum to the emperor and asked to set up an altar for the noble Spirits of Nine Palaces, ... where [the Spirit in] the southeast is called *zhaoyao* 招摇, that in the east is called *Xuanyuan* 轩辕, that in the northeast *taiyin* 太阴 (Senior Yin), that in the south *tianyi* 天一 (Heavenly One), that in the center *tianfu* 天符, that in the north *taiyi* 太一 (Great One), that in the southwest *sheti* 摄提, that in the west *xianchi* 咸池, and that in the northwest *qinglong* 青龙 (Green Dragon); and with [the number of] five in the center, it should have nine dots on its head and tread on one dot, with three on the left and seven on the right, with two and four in the upper part, with six and eight in the lower part···."[dcv] [The distribution of the numbers is in alignment with that in the *luo shu*.]

It can be seen, by the charts of the *he tu*, *luo shu*, and the "Eight Trigrams' Positions of the Former Heaven" (*Xiantian bagua fangwei* 先天八卦方位), and so on, the *Zhou yi* studies in the Song dynasty (960-1279) entered into a new period of great florescence, which exerted far-reaching influences upon the realm of thought at that time.

According to Mr. Qiu Hansheng's 邱汉生 (1912-1992) research, all the famous Neo-Confucians, such as Cheng Yi 程颐 (1033-1107), Lu Xiangshan 陆象山 (1139-93), and Zhu Xi 朱嘉 (1130-1200), commented on the *Zhou Changes*.[dcvi] In this regard, one of the origins of the Neo-Confucianism dominating China's realm of thought for over 700 years came from the Song people's elaborations on the principles conceived in the *Changes*. Mr. Qiu holds that some of the Neo-Confucian concepts [and categories]—such as Dao 道 (Way), *wuji* 无极 (non-ultimate), *taiji* 太极 (supreme ultimate), *yin-yang* 阴阳, *wuxing* 五行 (Five Agents), *dong jing* 动静 (movements and stillness), *xing ming* 性命 (nature and fate), *shan e* 善恶 (good and evil), *de* 德 (virtue), "*ren* 仁, *yi* 义, *li* 礼, *zhi* 智, *xin* 信" (benevolence, propriety, ritual, wisdom and trustworthiness), *zhu jing* 主静 (advocating quiescence), *gui shen* 鬼神 (ghosts and spirits), *si sheng* 死生 (life and death), *wuwei* 无为 (inaction), *wuyu* 无欲 (unselfishness), *zhong* 中 (centrality or the Mean), *shun* 顺 (compliance), and so on—came from the Song people's commentaries on the *Zhou Changes*, and particularly from the parts on the "Ten Wings."[dcvii]

Additionally, there was reportedly a school related to image-numerology in Neo-Confucianism, which can further demonstrate the connection between the *Zhou Changes* and Neo-Confucianism (*lixue* 理学, literally, Learning of Principle).

A careful study of Neo-Confucianism demonstrates that its salient feature was its discourses on the *Changes* by the concept of *li* 理 (principle).

In order to account for this point, now we set up *Cheng shi Yizhuan* 程氏易传 (Cheng Yi's Commentary on the *Changes*) as an example, so as to view how the Neo-Confucian made use of the "principle" in his elaboration on the *Changes*.

Cheng Yi 程颐 (1033-1107), whose courtesy name was Zhengshu 正叔, came from (Yichuan 伊川 County,) Luoyang City, and was referred to as Mr. Yichuan 伊川 by intellectuals [and therefore *Cheng shi Yizhuan* was also called *Yichuan Yizhuan*]. He learned the *Changes* from Zhou Dunyi 周敦颐 (1017-73) when he was young and completed his *Yi zhuan* (Commentary on the *Changes*) in his later years.

Just like Wang Bi 王弼 (226-49), whose commentary took the *Zhou Changes* as a tool for discourse on his metaphysics, Cheng Yi also employed it as a tool to extend his thought on "principle."

In Cheng Yi's *Yi zhuan*, the "images" of the *Zhou Changes* were derived from the "principle" that could universally regulate the Dao (Way) of Heaven and Earth.

For example, when interpreting the bottom line statement of hexagram Qian [☰, The Creative, 1] "A submerged dragon does not act,"[dcviii] Cheng Yi tells us: "The principle is formless, so its meaning is manifested with the help of image."[dcix] Regarding the meaning of the first sentence of the *Xi ci* (Commentary on the Appended Phrases), "As Heaven is high and noble and Earth is low and humble, so it is that Qian [☰] and Kun [☷] are defined,"[dcx] Cheng Yi contends, "Events contain the principle and things possess forms. ... Only after the principle came into being were there the images in which the positions were established."[dcxi]

Then, he annotated the sentence of *"yi yu tiandi zun, gu neng milun tiandi zhi dao* 易与天地准, 故能弥纶天地之道" (literally, The *Changes* is a paradigm of Heaven and Earth, and so it shows how one can fill in and pull together the Dao of Heaven and Earth[dcxii]) in this way: "'*Mi* 弥' means 'universality' (*bian* 遍) and '*lun* 纶' the principle (*li* 理). ... '*Milun* 弥纶' signifies the 'universal principle' (*bianli* 遍理)."[dcxiii] This point of view was evidently adopted from the famous Western Han scholar Jing Fang's (77-37 B.C.E.) exegesis, as the latter commented on these terms as such: "'*Mi* 弥' means universality and '*lun* 纶' the knowledge."[dcxiv] Here, Cheng Yi replaced the "knowledge" with "principle" and continued to extend his point of view: "(As one can) universally regulate the Dao (Way) of Heaven and Earth (according to the principle), ... he is able to understand the reasons underlying what is hidden and what is clear. 'What is hidden' refers to the principle and 'what is clear' corresponds to the images. 'Understanding the reasons underlying what is hidden and what is clear' means 'knowing the whys and wherefores of the principle and things.'"[dcxv]

In Cheng's commentary on the *Changes*, the "principle" is not only the root of the images and *yin* and *yang* forces, but also the source and origin of the myriad things of Heaven and Earth. When interpreting the sentence "In its capacity to produce and reproduce, we call it 'change,'"[dcxvi] he contends: "Lao zi also held that 'Three produces the myriad things,' which has the same meaning as this sentence. The principle (produces things) naturally in this way, and 'the way of Heaven is perfect and endless' (*weitian zhi ming, wumu buyi* 维天之命, 于穆不已) [a verse from the *Book of Poetry*] was also an expression of the function of the principle."[dcxvii]

In Cheng Yi's view, even the root cause for the divinatory capacity of the *Zhou Changes* was also because there was the "principle" functioning (behind it). As it says in the *Xi ci*, "This is why when the noble man would act in a certain way or would try to do something, he addresses his doubts to the *Changes* in terms of words. The charge that it receives comes back to him like an echo, with no distance or concealment to it. In consequence, one knows of things to come. The *Changes* as such has to be the thing most capable of perfect subtlety in the world, for what else could possibly be up to this!"[dcxviii] From Cheng's perspective, "the reason for why there were answers in divinations and the ghosts and spirits could enjoy the sacrifices was also because there exists the principle. Although the tortoise and milfoil stalks have no emotions, why a hexagram could be formed and why the hexagrams could forebode fortune or misfortune was merely because there was this principle. Since there was this principle, when one addresses his doubts, he will get a response. But if one is selfish and disorders the images of the trigrams and hexagrams, he will not get an answer, in that the principle will not be there. The reason for why it can echo is because today's principle and the principle established before are no more than the same principle. The offering of sacrifices and the ghosts and spirits' absorption of them also depend on the same principle. As long as I have prayed in accordance with this principle, they will enjoy the sacrifices. Not two or three principles are allowed, as there is only one principle."[dcxix]

In the meantime, as the root of the myriad things of Heaven and Earth and the principle by which the *Zhou Changes* takes images in divination, the principle, in Cheng's opinion, is also an eternal and unchangeable supreme law of the world. When interpreting the sentence in the *Xi ci* "Being utterly still it does not initiate movement, but when stimulated it is commensurate with all the causes for everything that happens in the world,"[dcxx] he tells us: "The heavenly principle is complete in every way, which will not change with Yao's 尧 [a legendary sage ruler] sagaciousness or Jie's 桀 [the last emperor of the Xia dynasty (c. 2100-c. 1600 B.C.E.), a notorious tyrant] tyranny. The eternal principle threading through the relationships between the father and son, between the superior and inferior, will not change. Has it ever had any movement? The stimulation is not from the external world, but from the internal world. ... Here it only refers to the affairs related to man's duties and responsibilities."[dcxxi]

It was because this "principle" was viewed as the unchangeable supreme law that Cheng Yi in his *Yizhuan* sometimes referred to the principle as the "mandate of heaven" (*tianming* 天命). For instance, when interpreting the judgment of hexagram Cui [䷬, Gathering, 45] "To use a sacrificial beast means good fortune,"[dcxxii] he contends, "This means the subject should act in a timely manner and obey the principle, so the 'Commentary on the Judgment' (*Tuan* 彖) of the hexagram says that this means the one should 'obey the mandate of Heaven.'[dcxxiii]"[dcxxiv]

Meanwhile, this "principle" was "abstracted from the (principles conceived in one's) person and encompasses all of the concrete principles"[dcxxv] (*jinqu zhu shen, bai li jieju* 近取诸身, 百理皆具), and this principle "inherent in everything can accrue along with the application of it" (*wei guyou cili, er yiu shang chongzhang zi* 谓故有此理, 而就上充长之).[dcxxvi] After Cheng Yi foisted the "principle" into his *Yi zhuan* (Commentary on the *Changes*), he indeed expanded it and constantly elaborated on this "principle" with spiritual and ontological significance as his point of departure in his exegesis of the *Zhou Changes*, which, to some extent, let his commentary come to be his principle-oriented work. To put it in a nutshell, this "principle" in his commentary, after all, might to a large extent be an extension based on Kong Yingda's 孔颖达 (574-648) assertion that "the principle of *Changes* comprehensively encompasses (the realms of both) existence and non-existence."[dcxxvii] (*Yi li beibao youwu* 易理备包有无)

Nonetheless, as an interpretive work of the *Changes*, on the basis of the popular exegetic approaches referred to as "yielding" (*cheng* 承),

"mounting" (*cheng* 乘), "neighboring" (*bi* 比), "response" (*ying* 应), and "basing" (*ju* 据), Cheng Yi in his commentary explains some images of the trigrams and hexagrams and sets forth his novel idea in regard to the "hexagram changes" (*guabian* 卦变) theory discussed time and again by his predecessors. For example, when interpreting the "Commentary on the Judgment" regarding hexagram Bi [☶☲, Decoration, 22] that "one looks to the pattern of man in order to transform and bring the whole world to perfection,"[dcxxviii] he tells us:

> This hexagram took the image that "there is fire [symbolized by the lower trigram Li (☲)] under mountain [☶]," and, according to the "hexagram changes" theory, "the soft [i.e., the second *yin* (- -) line] comes (from the top) to decorate the *yang* lines [i.e., the bottom and the third lines] (in order to form a pattern)" (*rou lai wen gang* 柔来文刚) and "the hard *yang* line goes up (from the second position) to the top to decorate the soft lines [line 4 and line 5] (in order to form a pattern)" (*gang shang wen rou* 刚上文柔). The formation of some hexagrams was based on the meanings and images of the two constituent trigrams, such as: hexagram Zhun [☵☳, Birth Throes, 3], which was based on the image of "taking action [symbolized by the lower trigram Zhen ☳] in the midst of danger [symbolized by the upper trigram Kan ☵]"[dcxxix] and the meanings of "clouds [☵] and thunder [☳]"[dcxxx]; hexagram Song [☰☵, Contention, 6], which adopted the meanings of "strength [symbolized by the upper trigram Qian ☰] and danger [symbolized by the lower trigram Kan ☵]"[dcxxxi] and the image that "heaven [☰] and water [☵] operate in contrary ways."[dcxxxii] Some hexagrams treated a single line as the cause for the completion of these hexagrams, such as: hexagram Xiaoxu [☴☰, Lesser Domestication, 9] in which "a weak line [i.e., line 4] obtains an appropriate position [as a *yin* line in a *yin* position], so those above and those below [i.e., the other five *yang* lines] respond to it"[dcxxxiii]; hexagram Dayou [☲☰, Great Holdings, 14] in which "a weak line [i.e., the fifth *yin* line] obtains the noble position and there practices the Mean and enjoys greatness, as that

above and those below [i.e., the other five *yang* lines] all respond to it."[dcxxxiv] Some hexagrams took both the meanings of the two constituent trigrams and significance of waxing or waning into consideration, such as hexagram Fu [☷☳, Return, 24] in which "Thunder [☳] in the Earth [☷]: this constitutes the image of Return [signifying the waxing of the *yang* energy and waning of the *yin* energy][dcxxxv] and hexagram Bo [☶☷, Peeling, 23] in which "The Mountain [☶] is attached to the Earth [☷]: this constitutes the image of Peeling [indicating the waxing of the *yin* force and waning of the *yang* force]."[dcxxxvi] Some took both the images of the two constituent trigrams and exchange of positions of two lines, such as hexagram Yi [☴☳, Increase, 42] in which the meanings of "wind" [symbolized by the upper trigram Xun ☴] and "thunder" [represented by the lower trigram Zhen ☳] were adopted and the "diminution for those above and Increase for those below"[dcxxxvii] was also taken into account, and hexagram Sun [☶☱, Diminution, 41] in which the meanings of "mountain" and "lake" referred to in "below the Mountain [☶], there is the Lake [☱]"[dcxxxviii] were adopted and the significance of "Diminution for those below and increase for those above"[dcxxxix] was also taken into consideration. Some took both the images of the two constituent trigrams and the significance of lines, such as hexagram Kuai [☱☰, Resolution, 43] in which "the hard and strong [i.e., the five *yang* lines] take decisive action against the soft and weak [i.e., the top *yin* line]"[dcxl] and hexagram Gou [☰☴, Encounter, 44] in which the soft [i.e., the bottom *yin* line] encounters the hard [i.e., the other five *yang* lines]."[dcxli] Some took the utility as the means of forming the hexagrams, such as hexagram Jing [☵☴, The Well, 48] where "the (lower) trigram Xun [☴ symbolizing wooden cask] goes into the Water [the upper trigram ☵] and raises the Water"[dcxlii] and hexagram Ding [☲☴, The Cauldron, 50] where "above Wood [☴], there is Fire [☲]."[dcxliii] Additionally, hexagram Ding [☲☴] also took the shape and picture of the hexagram as the image. Some took the pictographic shape of the hexagram as the image, such as in hexagram Yi [☶☳,

Nourishment], which looks like one's mouth, and hexagram Shihe [☲☳, Bite Together, 21], where it seems that "there is something between the cheeks"[dcxliv] [or there is a hard thing in one's mouth and he/she has to bite it through]. All this manifests the significance of the formation of the hexagrams.[dcxlv]

For the formation and nomination of each hexagram, Cheng Yi sets forth his views as indicated above, among which there are really many ingenious understandings. But when criticizing former scholars' views, he tends to lapse into arbitrariness, as he continues to assert that: "All the other sixty-two hexagrams are derived from Qian [☰, The Creative, 1] and Kun [☷, The Receptive, 2]. Some former Confucians were not intelligent enough and held that hexagram Bi [☶☲, Decoration, 22] was originally derived from hexagram Tai [☷☰, Peace, 11], … as a matter of fact, Qian [☰, symbolizing the Father] and Kun [☷, the Mother] initially changed into the six trigrams corresponding to the six children, and the eight trigrams were doubled and the sixty-four hexagrams were produced. Therefore, all the hexagrams were derived from Qian [☰] and Kun [☷]."[dcxlvi]

Here, Cheng Yi's assertion that "Qian [☰, symbolizing the Father] and Kun [☷, the Mother] initially changed into the six trigrams corresponding to the six children"[dcxlvii] is not so persuasive, in that it says in the *Xi ci* (Commentary on the Appended Phrases) that "in change there is the great ultimate. This is what generates the two modes [the *yin* and *yang*]. The two basic modes generate the four basic images and the four basic images generate the eight trigrams,"[dcxlviii] by which it can be seen that the "eight trigrams"—including Qian [☰] and Kun [☷]—are derived from the "four basic images" rather than supporting Cheng Yi's view that in the beginning Qian [☰] and Kun [☷] were generated and then they changed into the other six trigrams. In the meantime, in the course of his statements, he often jumps to conclusions without necessary examinations. For instance, he avers that in the "Commentary on the Judgments" (*Tuan* 彖) , "All the hexagrams whose fifth line is a *yin* line were referred to as 'the soft advances and moves upward (from the below)' (*rou jin er shang xing* 柔进而上行)."[dcxlix] Actually, in the "Commentary on the Judgments" (*Tuan* 彖), those hexagrams which have a fifth *yin* line are not always marked with "the soft advances and moves upward (from the below) (*rou jin er shang xing* 柔进而上行)," which we will not illustrate here one by one.

On the whole, although the volume of Cheng Yi's *Yizhuan* contains over 10,000 Chinese characters and has exerted great influence upon later scholars, it can only be viewed as a Neo-Confucian work. The value of its research on the *Zhou Changes* itself is far from that of Zhu Xi's 朱熹 (1130-1200) *Zhou yi benyi* 周易本义 (Original Meaning of the *Zhou Changes*).

The Song (960-1279) person who contributed the most to the study of the *Changes* was Zhu Xi, whose courtesy names include Yuanhui 元晦, Zhonghui 仲晦, and Huian 晦庵. His most important work on the *Changes* was his *Zhouyi ben yi* 周易本义 (Original Meaning of the *Zhou Changes*, hereafter *Benyi* 本义 [Original Meaning]).

Although Zhu Xi also discourses on *li* 理 (principle) and *qi* 气 (material force) when interpreting the *Changes*, the radical difference between Zhu Xi in his *Original Meaning* and Cheng Yi in his *Yizhuan*, from the famous Song scholar Wang Yinlin's 王应麟 (1223-79) view, is that: "Cheng Yi held that once one get the meanings of the *Changes*, the images and numbers are included, whereas Zhu Xi avers that one has to be aware of images and numbers before he speaks of the principle, and otherwise there would be no solid evidence supporting his assumptions, so his illusory principle is apt to deviate from the correct path."[dcl]

The valuable point of the *Original Meaning* just dwells on this aspect. For example, when interpreting the sentence in the *Xi ci* (Commentary on the Appended Phrases) "Being utterly still it does not initiate movement, but when stimulated it is commensurate with all the causes for everything that happens in the world,"[dcli] Cheng Yi holds that: "The heavenly principle is complete in every way … The stimulation is not from the external world but from the internal world.[dclii] … Here it only refers to the affairs related to man's duties and responsibilities,"[dcliii] whereas, as an objector to Cheng Yi in this regard, Zhu Xi clearly argues that this sentence and that of "exploring principles to the utmost and making human nature and even man's destiny fully developed"[dcliv] (*Qiongli jinxing yizhiyu ming* 穷理尽性以至于命) "originally spoke of (the function of) the *Changes* rather than human affairs,"[dclv] reflecting the frankness of him as a commentator.

In the exegesis of the *Zhou Changes*, the *Original Meaning* provides many extraordinary insights. For example, when interpreting the meanings of the judgment of hexagram Qian [☰, The Creative, 1] of "*yuan* 元, *heng* 亨, *li* 利, and *zhen* 貞," the *Jijie* 集解 (Collected Explanations) [compiled by the Tang scholar Li Dingzuo 李鼎祚] cites Zixia's 子夏 [one of the famous disciples of Confucius] (507 B.C.E.-?) commentary that "*yuan* means the beginning (*shi* 始), *heng* prosperity (*tong* 通), *li* harmony (*he* 和), and *zhen* rectitude (*zheng* 正),"[dclvi] whereas the *Original Meaning* avers that "*yuan* designates greatness (*da* 大), *heng* prosperity (*tong* 通), *li* appropriateness (*yi* 宜), [and] *zheng* rectitude and steadfastness (*zheng er gu* 正而固)."[dclvii] Here, it seems that Zhu Xi's interpretation was different from former scholars' view, but when interpreting the "Commentary on the Judgment" of the hexagram "How great is the *Qianyuan* 乾元! The myriad things are provided their beginnings by it,"[dclviii] Zhu Xi contends that "*yuan* means greatness (*da* 大) and beginning (*shi* 始), and *Qianyuan* 乾元 refers to the great beginning (*dashi* 大始) of the heavenly virtue."[dclix] When interpreting the sentence in the commentary that ensued, the *Original Meaning* also views *yuan* 元 as the "beginning" (*shi* 始) and regards *zhen* 貞 as "end" (*zhong* 終).[dclx]

Because there were not so many words in ancient times, one word was often polysemic. Therefore, when interpreting the *Zhou Changes*, Zhu Xi usually did not stick to one single meaning of a word. Though his interpretation of the *yuan* 元 here as "greatness" might not be correct, his not blindly adhering to one single meaning of a word is commendable.

Here are some other examples. When interpreting the "Commentary on the Judgment" regarding hexagram Zhen [☳, Quake, 51] that "*chu keyi shou zongmiao sheji* 出可以守宗廟社稷" [literally, When one goes forth, this one may thereby be entrusted with the maintenance of the ancestral temple[dclxi]], he argues that the character *chu* 出 was a misprinted character of *chang* 鬯 (the fragrant wine).[dclxii] For the meaning of *wujiu* 无咎 [literally, there is no blame] in the third line statement of hexagram Jie [☵, Control, 60], Zhu Xi argues that "here the meaning of the *wujiu* differs from the *wujiu* in other line statements, [as] here it means *wusuo guijiu* 无所归咎 (there is no one else to blame)."[dclxiii] For the "Commentary on the Image" (*Xiang* 象) of the hexagram Zhongfu [☱☴, Inner Trust, 61] that "Above the Lake [☱], there is Wind [☴]: this constitutes the image of Inner Trust. In the same way, the noble man evaluates criminal punishments and mitigates the death penalty,"[dclxiv] the *Original Meaning* says: "Wind [☴] motivates Water [☵], which receives the motivation: this is the image of Inner Trust. 'Evaluating criminal punishments and mitigating the death penalty' is the implication of the Inner Trust."[dclxv] There are many examples of this kind of innovative interpretation in the *Original Meaning*, which we will not be illustrating one after another here.

Although the *Original Meaning* contains many insights, it also absorbed its predecessors' strong points. Here are two examples. For the character of "*pei* 沛" in the third line statement of hexagram Feng [☳☲, Abundance, 55], the *Original Meaning* adopts Wang Bi's 王弼 (226-49) view that "this character was (originally) printed as 旆 which refers to pennant or curtain."[dclxvi] For the character "*shun* 順" in the "Commentary on the Image" of hexagram Sheng [☷☴, Climbing, 46], the *Original Meaning* takes Wang Su's 王肅 (195-256) view and regards it as a variant of the character "*shen* 慎."[dclxvii] This sort of excellent exegesis from former scholars is frequently available in the *Original Meaning*.

It is particularly noteworthy that, during the course of the interpretation of the *Zhou Changes*, if the meanings of some line statements were not understandable, Zhu Xi would frankly admit it—and if he had any doubts about the meanings of the "Ten Wings," he would honestly raise his suspicions in the *Original Meaning*. Here are some examples. For the meaning of the fourth line statement of hexagram Mingyi [☷☲, Suppression of the Light, 36] "This one enter into the left side of the belly and so obtains the heart of [him who effects] Suppression of the Light, this by leaving his gate and courtyard,"[dclxviii] the *Original Meaning* admits that "we don't know the real meaning of this line statement,"[dclxix] unlike Cheng Yi (1033-1107), whose far-fetched explanation of its meaning is "both the right hand and right foot (rather than the left hand and left foot) are oft-used by man. ... Here the 'left' refers to a hidden place out of the way."[dclxx] Zhu Xi also admitted that he could not account for the characters of *yi* 亿, *jiuling* 九陵 [literally, very high mountain], and *qiri* 七日 [literally, seven days] in the second line statement of hexagram Zhen [☳, Quake, 51]. When interpreting the fourth line statement of hexagram Kun [☱, Impasse, 47] "This one comes slowly, so slowly, for he suffers Impasse at the metal-clad cart. Although there is humiliation, he should bring about a successful conclusion,"[dclxxi] the *Original Meaning* tells us: "the 'metal-clad cart ought to be attached to the second line, as I believe (the lower trigram) Kan [☵] has the image of wheels (of the cart), but I do not know the detailed image of the fourth line."[dclxxii] He also frankly admitted that he was not aware of the meaning of the fourth line statement of hexagram Xiaoguo [☳, Minor Superiority, 62] and the meaning of the "Commentary on the Image" of this line, and "leaves the question open and waits for those who know the real meaning of it."[dclxxiii] Additionally, Zhu Xi doubted that "*heng* 亨" in the "Commentary on the Judgment" of hexagram Bi [☶, Decoration, 22] was a redundant character. So it is with the characters of "*zhi* 之" in the "Commentary on the Judgment" of hexagram Jian [☶, Gradual Advance, 53] and "*xian* 贤" in the "Commentary on the Image" of the hexagram, where he also thought that there might be some lost character(s) after "*shan* 善 (good)". Moreover, he honestly admitted that he does not know the real meaning of the character "*ji* 极" (in the "Commentary on the Image") in the bottom line of hexagram Weiji [☲, Ferrying Incomplete, 64] and found that "it does not rhyme and I suspect it might be '*jing* 敬 (veneration)'. But I am not sure, and let us leave the question open."[dclxxiv]

This kind of prudent attitude to seek truth and "leave questions open" was also very valuable.

Meanwhile, Zhu Xi was well aware that the *Zhou Changes* was originally a book of divination in ancient times. On this account, in order to make his *Original Meaning* indeed restore the original divinatory significance of the *Zhou Changes*, Zhu Xi not only wrote a chapter called "Clarifying Milfoil-stalk Divination" (*ming shi* 明筮) in the *Original Meaning*, but also composed another related chapter called the "Etiquette for Milfoil-stalk Divination" (*Shi yi* 筮仪) in the book and often specially referred to its divinatory utility when interpreting the *Zhou Changes* so as to rectify the original meaning of the work.

For instance, when interpreting the judgment of hexagram Qian [☰, The Creative, 1] of "*yuan* 元, *heng* 亨, *li* 利, and *zhen* 贞," Zhu Xi argues that: "This manifests the subtle intention of the sages' for composing the *Changes* to instruct people in prognosis and develop the things and enterprises. (The function of the judgments of) other hexagrams are similar to this."[dclxxv] When annotating the bottom line statement of the hexagram, the *Original Meaning* holds that "when some person encounters hexagram Qian [☰, The Creative, 1] with this line as a changing line, he should observe the image of this line and take the statement of this line as the prognostication."[dclxxvi] When annotating the fifth line statement of the hexagram, the *Original Meaning* tells us: "The instruction of this line in divination is identical to that of the second line in divination."[dclxxvii] Additionally, he insists that the "noble man" (*junzi* 君子) in the third line statement of the hexagram "refers to the one who seeks instructions from divination by the *Zhou Changes*."[dclxxviii] When interpreting the other hexagrams, the *Original Meaning* often provides similar remarks in order to expose its divinatory utility to the readers.

Although Zhu Xi intended to clarify the original divinatory significance of the *Zhou Changes* through his *Original Meaning*, in the "Treatise on Art and Literature" (*Yiwen zhi* 艺文志) of the *Han shu* (History of the Western Han Dynasty [206 B.C.E.- 9 C.E.]), the 13 schools of the *Changes* did not include divinatory methods and the works related to mantic arts in the name of the *Zhou Changes* were attributed to the catalog of "(Divination by) Tortoise Shells and Milfoil Stalks" (*Shigui lei* 蓍龟类). Therefore, it is evident that the Han people distinguished the works interpreting the connotations of the *Changes* from those explicating divinatory methods and that these two aspects might not be mixed in one book. This was the reason Wang Bi 王弼 (226-49) and other Han (206 B.C.E.-220 C.E.) scholars did not specially mention "divinatory etiquettes" and "divinatory methods" in their works.

Zhu Xi believed in the learning of the *he tu* 河图 (Yellow River Chart) and the *luo shu* 洛书 (Luo River Diagram) and illustrated nine charts in the very beginning of the *Original Meaning,* which played an important role in the spread of *Changes*-oriented charts. This was Zhu Xi's loss, which has been elaborated upon in the beginning of this chapter.

Appropriating charts and diagrams to interpret the *Zhou Changes* was not initially undertaken by the Song people, as this approach had been employed by former scholars. For instance, according to the "Treatise on the Classics and Literature" (*Jingji zhi* 经籍志) of the *Sui shu*

隋书 (History of the Sui Dynasty [581-618]), there were works called the *Zhou yi qiankun san xiang* 周易乾坤三象 (Three Images of Hexagrams Qian [☰] and Kun [☷] of the *Zhou Changes*) and *Zhou yi xintu* 周易新图 (New Charts for the *Zhou Changes*) in the Liang dynasty (502-557); in the "Treatise on Art and Literature" (*Yiwen zhi* 艺文志) of the *Tang shu* 唐书 (History of the Tang Dynasty [618-907]), there was a book called *Dayan xuantu* 大衍玄图 (Mysterious Charts for the Grand Expansion [Divinatory Method by Milfoil Stalks]). Among the Song people's charts, the one called the chart for "the System of Hexagram Changes of King Wen's Sixty-four Hexagrams" (*Wen wang liushisi gua guabian tu* 文王六十四卦卦变图), illustrated in the beginning of the *Original Meaning*, reveals the derivation and changes of the 64 hexagrams. In spite of the fact that there are some inaccuracies in describing the relationships between the hexagrams in the chart, this is undoubtedly a product of the sorting out and expansion of former scholars' discourses on the *Changes* and was inspiring to later scholars when it came to disclosing the relationships among the 64 hexagrams. Therefore, this kind of chart can play an active role in the study of the *Zhou Changes*. But the Song people's other charts, such as the so-called *he tu* 河图 (Yellow River Chart) and *luo shu* 洛书 (Luo River Diagram), can only add an air of mystery to the *Zhou Changes* and cannot be helpful in explicating the original purport of the book, and additionally they easily contribute to far-fetched ideas discussed by later scholars, thus making them be more abstruse and absurd.

But the charts of "Fuxi's Sequence of the Eight Trigrams" (*Fuxi bagua cixu* 伏羲八卦次序) and "Fuxi's Sequence of the Sixty-four Hexagrams" (*Fuxi liushisi gua cixu* 伏羲六十四卦次序) illustrated in the very beginning of the *Original Meaning* reflect the Song people's misunderstanding about the *Zhou Changes*.

Here, we just take the chart of "Fuxi's Sequence of the Eight Trigrams" (*Fuxi bagua cixu* 伏羲八卦次序) as an example to demonstrate the mistakes made.

8	7	6	5	4	3	2	1
Kun [☷]	Gen [☶]	Kan [☵]	Xun [☴]	Zhen [☳]	Li [☲]	Dui [☱]	Qian [☰]
Senior *Yin* (━ ━)		Junior *Yang* (━ ━)		Junior *Yin* (━━)		Senior *Yang* (━━)	
Yin (━ ━)				*Yang* (━━━)			
The Supreme Ultimate							

This chart was established by Zhu Xi 朱熹 (1130-1200), who accepted Shao Yong's 邵雍(1011-77) discourses.

According to this chart, the Supreme Ultimate (*Taiji* 太极) produced the two modes (of *Yin* [━ ━] and *Yang* [━]); the two modes further produced the four images (of Junior *Yin* [⚎], Junior *Yang* [⚍], Senior *Yin* [⚏], and Senior *Yang* [⚌]); the four images further produced the eight trigrams. Following this binary style of production, in the "Fuxi's Sequence of the Sixty-four Hexagrams" (*Fuxi liushisi gua cixu* 伏羲六十四卦次序), next to the eight trigrams were the 16 tetragrams; the 16 tetragrams further produced the 32 quintuplet grams, which further produced the 64 hexagrams.

This kind of procedure of production was purely fabricated by Shao Yong, the basis of which could not be found in either the basic text of or the commentaries on the *Zhou Changes* at all. Additionally, if the eight trigrams were produced through three steps of the "Supreme Ultimate," "Two Modes," and "Four Images" before the formation of the eight trigrams, how could the "Two Modes" and "Four Images" be established?

The famous early Qing scholar Huang Zongxi 黄宗羲 (1610-95) accused Shao Yong and Zhu Xi of the mistakes shown in these two charts in the chapter of "Chart of the Former Heaven Sequence" (*Xiantian tu* 先天图) of his *Yixue xiangshu lu* 易学象数论 (Discussion on Images and Numbers in *Changes* Scholarship). As he points out, "that 'in change there is the Supreme Ultimate which generates the two modes [the *yin* and *yang*]'[dclxxix] refers to the Dao (Way) of one *yin* and one *yang*. One *yang* encompasses the overall 192 *yang* lines (of the sixty-four hexagrams) and one *yin* is a summary of the overall 192 *yin* lines (of the sixty-four hexagrams). It divided the 384 lines rather than two lines (of *yin* and *yang*) into two modes. 'The two modes generate the four images,'[dclxxx] the so-called senior *yang*, senior *yin*, junior *yang*, and junior *yin*, indicating that Qian [☰] belongs to 'senior *yang*' and Kun [☷] to 'senior *yin*'; [and that] Zhen [☳], Kan [☵], and Gen [☶] belong to 'junior *yang*' while Xun [☴], Li [☲], and Dui [☱] are attributed to 'junior *yin*.' In other words, the trigram with three *yang* lines exhibits the image of 'senior *yang*,' that with three *yin* lines the image of 'senior *yin*,' that with one *yang* line and two *yin* lines the image of 'junior *yang*,' and that with one *yin* lines and two *yang* lines the image of 'junior *yin*.' That is to say, the eight trigrams constitute the four images, hence the remarks of 'when the eight trigrams formed ranks, the [basic] images were present there within them'[dclxxxi] and 'the eight trigrams make their pronouncements in terms of images.' Therefore, my assertion indeed can be verified by the words in the *Zhou Changes*."[dclxxxii]

Huang Zhongxi's argument was absolutely correct. It is regretful that Zhu Xi, who was so erudite and rigid, made such mistakes.

When discussing the divinatory method, Zhu Xi denied predecessors' *guoshe fa* 过揲法 (counting-off-stalk method) and set forth his own *guale fa* 挂扐法 (dangling-and-clamping-stalk method). Although the result is the same from both methods, the latter does not accord with the description related to milfoil-stalk divination in the "Commentary on the Appended Phrases" (*Xi ci* 系辞). This point was particularly mentioned in the chapter discussing divination by milfoil stalks (see Chapter 5).

In the exegesis of the basic text of and commentaries on the *Changes*, Zhu Xi sometimes also employs the terms of "principle" (*li* 理) and "material force" (*qi* 气).

In short, as an influential work on the *Changes*, despite the abovementioned loss and drawbacks, the *Original Meaning* still deserves to be called a valuable *Changes*-oriented opus.

Additionally, the other relatively valuable works written by the Song people include Zhang Zais' 张载 (1020-78) *Yi shuo* 易说 (A Discussion of the *Changes*), Chen Guan's 陈瓘 (1057-1124, whose courtesy name was Liaozhai 了斋) *Liaozhai Yishuo* 了斋易说 (Liaozai's Discussion of the

Changes), Zhu Zhen's 朱震 (1072-1138 aka Mr. Hanshang 汉上) *Hanshang Yizhuan* 汉上易传 (Commentary on the *Changes* by Hanshang), Zheng Gangzhong's 郑刚中 (1088-1154) *Zhouyi kuiyu* 周易窥余 (Discerning the Remnant Discussions on the *Zhou Changes*), Yang Wanli's 杨万里 (1127-1206, a. k. a. Chengzhai 诚斋) *Cehngzhai Yizhuan* 诚斋易传 (Chengzhai's Commentary on the *Changes*), Lü Zhuqian's 吕祖谦 (1137-81) *Guyi yinxun* 古易音训 (Pronunciation and Exegesis of the Ancient *Changes*), Wei Liaoweng's 魏了翁 (1178-1237) *Zhou yi yaoyi* 周易要义 (Essential Meaning of the *Zhou Changes*), Zhao Rumei's 赵汝楳 *Zhou yi jiwen* 周易辑闻 (An Unofficial History of the *Zhou Changes*), and Yu Wan's 俞琬 (1258-1314) *Zhou yi jishuo* 周易集说 (Collected Discussions on the *Zhou Changes*) and *Du Yi juyao* 读易举要 (Essentials of Reading the *Changes*), and so on. All of these works present their own unique views. For example, when interpreting the sentence of "*yi yu tiandi zun, gu neng milun tiandi zhi dao* 易与天地准, 故能弥纶天地之道" (literally, The *Changes* is a paradigm of Heaven and Earth, and so it shows how one can fill in and pull together the Dao of Heaven and Earth[dclxxxiii]), diametrically different from Cheng Yi's opinion that here "'*Mi* 弥' means 'universality' (*bian* 遍) and '*lun* 纶' the principle (*li* 理). … '*Milun* 弥纶' signifies the 'universal principle' (*bianli* 遍理),"[dclxxxiv] Zhang Zai contends that "this term (of '*Milun* 弥纶') must be created by Confucius. '*Mi*弥' designates seaming and patching while '*lun* 纶' means dealings and businesses, which are attributed to human affairs (*renshi* 人事)."[dclxxxv] His argument that "the sages wrote a book of law [i.e., the *Book of Changes*] in order to enable people to know what to do. This is the significance of the *Changes*"[dclxxxvi] reflects his gravitation toward applying the *Changes* to discourses on human affairs. He does not agree with Kong Yingda's 孔颖达 (574-648) view that "change" was an invisible and intangible "chaos," either, and argues that "the *Changes* was composed so as to be manifested to man, just like Heaven hung images in the sky so as to reveal good fortune and bad."[dclxxxvii] "As Heaven and Earth change and transform, the sages created the *Changes* so as to reveal the model of these changes and transformations."[dclxxxviii] When interpreting the sentence of "Looking up, the sages observed the configurations of Heaven, and, looking down, they examined the patterns of Earth. Thus they understood the reasons underlying what is hidden (*you* 幽) and what is clear (*ming* 明),"[dclxxxix] being highly critical of Han Kangbo's 韩康伯 view that "here '*you* 幽' (what is hidden) and '*ming* 明' (what is clear) refer to intangible and tangible representations respectively"[dcxc] and Kong Yingda's argument that "intangible things are attributed to '*you* 幽' and the tangible '*ming* 明,'"[dcxci] Zhang zai contends that "Both the configurations of Heaven and the patterns of Earth are visible under light (*ming* 明), and, without light, both of them are (invisible in) darkness (*you* 幽). This is the reason underlying what is *you* 幽 (darkness) and what is *ming* 明 (light). All things can be seen under light; otherwise, they will be invisible. The visibility of the things relies on light, but if we cannot see them, it does not mean they do not exist. This is the ultimate reality. But those heresies lapsed into emptiness and a void because they only grasped what is *ming* 明 but lost what is *you* 幽, and thus their views were one-sided."[dcxcii]

Zhang Zai attributed Han Kangbo's 韩康伯 and Kong Yingda's discourses to heresies. Additionally, diametrically opposed to Han's and Kong's other points of view that "existence (*you* 有) must be generated from non-existence (*wu* 无)"[dcxciii] and "existence came out of non-existence,"[dcxciv] Zhang Zai avers that "if *Qi* (material force) contracts things [will] come to be visible and tangible, which shows the function of Li [☲] symbolizing brightness; if *Qi* disperses things will seem to be invisible and intangible, under the circumstance of which the Li [☲] symbolizing brightness will not function. Under the state of its contraction, shouldn't we call it existence? Under the circumstance of its dispersion, should we abruptly call it non-existence? Therefore, it [the *Changes*] just says that, through looking up and down, the sages understood the reasons underlying *you* 幽 (darkness) and *ming* 明 (light) rather than *you* 有 (existence) and *wu* 无 (non-existence)."[dcxcv]

Confronted with the influential discourses of Han Kangbo and Kong Yingda at that time, Zhang Zai raised his point of view that "heaven only manipulates and activates the *Qi* (material force), stimulates and generates the myriad things, and has no heart to show solicitude for the myriad things,"[dcxcvi] by which it becomes evident that he insists *Qi* (material force) is the substance that constitutes the myriad things. This was really praiseworthy in the Song people [as most of them consider principle, or heart-mind, to be the root of the universe].

Another example is Yang Wanli's 杨万里 (1124-1206) *Chengzhai Yizhuan* 诚斋易传 (Chengzhai's Commentary on the *Changes*), which tends to make use of examples from Chinese history to support his opinions. As a matter of fact, because the *Zhou Changes* was composed for the sake of man, many hexagram and line statements—such as the third line statement of hexagram Qian [☰, The Creative, 1] that "the noble man makes earnest efforts throughout the day, and with evening he still takes care; though in danger, he will suffer no blame;"[dcxcvii] the fourth line statement of hexagram Kun [☷, The Receptive, 2], "Tip up the bag, so there will be no blame, no praise;"[dcxcviii] the top line statement of hexagram Xu [☰, Waiting, 5], "when entering the pit, one finds that three uninvited guests have arrived. If one treats them with respect, in the end, there will be good fortune;"[dcxcix] the bottom line statement of hexagram Qian [☷, Modesty, 15], "The noble man is characterized by the utmost Modesty and because of that may cross the great river. This means good fortune;"[dcc] and so on—discuss how to deal with and get along with others [under different circumstances]. But most of the Song people tended to deliberately employ the *Zhou Changes* to discuss principle, heart-mind, and the Dao (Way) of heaven, and thus distorted its original purport. The focal point of Yang Wanli in his book was to align it with human affairs. This was also very praiseworthy at that time.

The Song people left abundant works on the *Changes* to us. Due to space limitations, we have only introduced several of them, as mentioned above. So, the list is far from being complete. Despite this, we can also discern some basic characteristics of the Song people's scholarship on the *Changes*.

A comprehensive survey shows that, as its striking feature, it was the *tushu zhi xue* 图书之学 (*he tu* and *luo shu*-based learning) of the Song *Changes* scholarship that exerted far-reaching influences. So, we have focused on the discussion of that here. However, these charts and diagrams were invented on the basis of former scholars' discourses or through simulating similar charts created by ancient people. Some of them were even derived from misunderstandings of the basic text of and commentaries on the *Zhou Changes*, and thus only some particular charts are of certain significance for the exploration of the meanings of the *Changes*.

Therefore, the *tushu zhi xue* 图书之学 (*he tu* and *luo shu*-based learning) in general was not valuable to the explication of the original meaning of the *Zhou yi*.

On the basis of the Song (960-1279) scholarship on the *Changes*, most of the scholars in the Yuan dynasty (1271-1368) continued to elaborate on the charts and diagrams or discourse on human nature and "principle." According to the introduction of *Changes* studies of the time by the *Siku quanshu zongmu tiyao* 四库全书总目提要 (Annotated General Catalogue of the *Complete Collection of the Four Treasuries*), Huang Ze 黄泽 (1259-1346) was one of the scholars whose arguments were cogent and insightful. He authored the *Yixue lanshang* 易学滥觞 (Origin of *Changes* Studies), in which he faults Wang Bi 王弼 (226-49) for his "abandoning all the images and numbers,"[dcci] thus drifting into abstruse commentary, and condemns Han (206 B.C.E.-220 C.E.) Confucians for their entire gravitation toward images and numbers, and thus becoming lost in redundancy. He insists that, before interpreting the *Yi jing*, we should at first clarify the symbols of the *Changes*, and, as far as prognostication is concerned, we ought to base ourselves on the rules dwelling in the divinatory cases in the *Zuo zhuan* 左传 (Zuo's Commentaries on the *Spring and Autumn Annals*). Huang's point of view is even-handed and tenable. Particularly, he gives us many novel understandings about the archaic meanings of the *Zhou Changes*.

Another noteworthy figure was Wang Shenzi 王申子 (fl. 1313), who wrote the *Da Yi jishuo* 大易缉说 (Collected Discussions of the Great *Changes*), which shows his emphasis on the images of the *Changes* and, additionally, he avers that the "Orderly Sequence of the Hexagrams" (*Xu gua* 序卦) was not composed by Confucius—and thus he resolutely abandons the exegesis of this chapter.

At that time, as the study of the *he tu* and *luo shu*-based charts and diagrams occupied a very important position, Qian Yifang 钱义方 wrote the *Zhou yi tushuo* 周易图说 (Discussion of the Illustrations Related to the *Zhou Changes*), in which he discusses in detail the charts and diagrams invented by the Song people and argues that all these later illustrations were composed to illuminate the *Changes* rather than it being the other way around. In this way, he criticizes the Song people's view that the *he tu* and the *luo shu* be attributed to the "changes of naturalness of Heaven and Earth"[dccii] (*tiandi ziran zhi yi* 天地自然之易). This was commendable at that time. But he himself also invented 27 *Changes*-oriented charts and diagrams based on former illustrations. He became embroiled in these new charts and diagrams, which offered no value at all for the study of the *Zhou Changes*.

After the Song dynasty (960-1279), the one who openly refuted the *he tu* and *luo shu*-based learning was the Yuan scholar Chen Yingrun 陈应润 (14th century), who composed the *Zhou yi yaobian yiyun* 周易爻变义蕴 (Meaning and Essence of the Line Transformations in the *Zhou Changes*). In his eyes, the charts and diagrams related to the so-called "Former Heaven" were adulterated with the alchemical refinement theory conceived in the *Cantong qi* 参同契 (Token for the Agreement of the Three According to the *Zhou Changes*), which was after all not the original meaning of the *Zhou Changes*. He contends that the directions and positions of the eight trigrams could be determined only by the related description in the "Discussion of the Trigrams" (*Shuo gua* 说卦); and that the explanation of the "Non-Ultimate" (*wuji* 无极), "Supreme Ultimate" (*taiji* 太极), "two forces (of *yin* and *yang*)" (*erqi* 二气), "Five Agents" (*wuxing* 五行), and so on, was only Zhou Dunyi's 周敦颐 (1017-73) own point of view and could not be grounded in the exegesis of the *Changes*. When people were holding the *he tu* and *luo shu*-based learning in high esteem, Chen Yinrun condemned the charts and diagrams—such as the "Former Heaven's Sequence of the Eight Trigrams"—as being without credit. This is also extremely estimable.

In the early Ming dynasty (1368-1644), Hu Guang 胡广 (1370-1418) was ordered by the Yongle 永乐 emperor (r. 1402-24) to put together a work called the *Zhou yi daquan* 周易大全 (Great Comprehensive [Compilation of] the *Zhou Changes*) [which was completed less than a year after it was commissioned]. This book mainly adopted Cheng Yi's 程颐 (1033-1107) commentary and Zhu Xi's 朱熹 (1130-1200) *Benyi* 本义 (Original Meaning). Additionally, Hu Guang also appropriated other Song scholars' works, such as Dong Kai's 董楷 (fl. 1265-74) *Zhou yi zhuan yi fulu* 周易传义附录 (Appended Discussions to [Cheng Yi's] Commentary and [Zhu Xi's] Original Meaning of the *Zhou Changes*), Dong Zhenqing's 董真卿 (fl. ca. 1330) *Zhou yi huitong* 周易会通 (A Comprehensive Compilation on the *Zhou Changes*), Hu Yigui's 胡一桂 (1260-1346) *Zhou yi benyi fulu zuanshu* 周易本义附录纂疏 (Appended Sub-commentaries to [Zhu Xi's] *Original Meaning of the Zhou Changes*), and Hu Bingwen's 胡炳文 (1250-1333) *Zhou yi benyi tongshi* 周易本义通释 (A Thorough Explanation of [Zhu Xi's] *Original Meaning of the Zhou Changes*). All these works were subcommentaries or expansions of Cheng Yi's commentary and Zhu Xi's *Original Meaning*. This determined the Ming people's upholding of the Song people's scholarship on the *Changes* and exhibited their biases on the issue of *Yi* learning.

Therefore, there were few insightful interpretative works completed on the *Changes* during the almost 300-year span of the Ming dynasty (1368-1644), among which the relatively famous work was Lai Zhide's 来知德 (1525-1604) *Zhou yi jizhu* 周易集注 (Collected Commentaries on the *Zhou Changes*).

With 29 years of steadfast efforts, Lai Zhide, whose courtesy name was Yixian 矣鲜, at last yielded this magnum opus. Based on some idea conceived in the "Commentary on the Appended Phrases" (*Xi ci* 系辞) and taking reference from the purport manifested in the "Orderly Sequence of the Hexagrams" (*Xu gua* 序卦), he originally created two new terms: *zonggua* 综卦 (inverse hexagrams) and *cuogua* 错卦 (interchanging hexagrams).

The *zonggua* 综卦 (inverse hexagrams) had also been called *fandui gua* 反对卦 (inverted hexagrams) by former scholars, that is, "pairs of hexagrams that were linked because each of them appeared to have been formed by turning the other one upside-down."[dcciii] For example, the *zonggua* 综卦 (inverse hexagram) of hexagram Sui [☱☳, Following, 17] is hexagram Gu [☶☴, Ills to Be Cured, 18], and vice versa. So it is with the relationship between hexagrams Zhun [☵☳, Birth Throes, 3] and Meng [☶☵, Juvenile Ignorance, 4], and that between hexagrams Xu [☵☰, Waiting, 5] and Song [☰☵, Contention, 6], and so on (see Chapter 3).

Actually, the theory of *zonggua* (inverse hexagrams) was an expansion of (the regularities revealed by) the "Commentary on the Judgments" (*Tuan* 彖), as it says in the commentary regarding Sui [☱☳, Following, 17] that "the hard [i.e., ☳] comes and takes a place below the soft [i.e., ☱]" (*gang lai er xia rou* 刚来而下柔),[dcciv] whereas in the commentary regarding Gu [☶☴, Ills to Be Cured, 18], it comes to be understood that "the hard [i.e., ☶] ascends and the soft [i.e., ☴]

descends" (*gang shang er rou xia* 刚上而柔下),[dccv] by which the inversion of the pair of hexagrams is clearly manifested.

The so-called *cuogua* 错卦 (interchanging hexagrams) were referred to by the Han (206 B.C.E.-220 C.E.) people as *pangtong gua* 旁通卦 (laterally linked hexagrams)—that is, "pairs of hexagrams that were related by virtue of having opposite lines (*yin* vs. *yang*) in all six positions."[dccvi] For instance, hexagrams Qian [☰, The Creative, 1] and Kun [☷, The Receptive, 2] can form a pair of *cuogua* 错卦 (interchanging hexagrams), and similarly, hexagrams Tongren [☰, Fellowship, 13] and Shi [☷, The Army, 7] can also constitute a pair of *cuogua* 错卦 (interchanging hexagrams).

Additionally, there were also so-called cardinal *zonggua* 综卦 (inverse hexagrams), diagonal *zonggua* 综卦, and the mixture of the two kinds, as well as cardinal *cuogua* 错卦 (interchanging hexagrams), diagonal *cuogua* 错卦, and the mixture of the two kinds. All these kinds of relationships termed *zonggua* 综卦 (inverse hexagrams) and *cuogua* 错卦 (interchanging hexagrams) were painstakingly speculated upon and brought out by him. Although it was unavoidable that there would be forced associations in his system, it was indeed unprecedentedly significant for the exhibition of the orderly sequence of the 64 hexagrams and the interrelationship between them, and thus was praised as the "ultimate study."[dccvii] (*juexue* 绝学)

But his self-partiality displayed in the self-preface of his opus occasioned criticism from the Qing 清 (1616-1912) people, who ridiculed him as "being extremely arrogant."[dccviii]

Other *Changes*-oriented works by the Ming people—such as Huang Daozhou's 黄道周 (1585-1646) *Yixiang zheng* 易象正 (Rectification of the Images of the *Changes*), He Kai's 何楷 (1594-1645) *Gu Zhou yi dinggu* 古周易订诂 (Rectification and Phonetic and Semantic Exegesis of the Ancient *Zhou Changes*), and Zhang Cizhong's 张次仲 (1589-1676) *Zhou yi wanci kunxue ji* 周易玩辞困学记 (Notes about the Phrases of the *Zhou Changes* from Learning in Difficulty)—were also well-grounded.

But, generally speaking, over the span of the Ming dynasty (1368-1644), the majority of the scholars' *Changes* studies treaded on the Song people's path, drawing new charts and diagrams related to the *Changes* or employing the *Changes* in order to explicate "principle." Especially after the reign of Emperor Shenzong 神宗 (r. 1573-1620), heart/mind-oriented theories adulterated the study of the *Changes*, and even the Chan 禅 sect of Buddhism was also applied to the exegesis of the *Changes*, such that there were thousands of newly invented charts and diagrams, whereas few paid attention to the interpretations of the basic text of the *Zhou Changes*. Therefore, it is no wonder that the famous scholar of the classical studies, Pi Xirui 皮锡瑞 (1850-1908), concluded that "the Ming dynasty was the most declining period of the classical studies."[dccix] In regard to the Ming people's studies of the *Changes*, this verdict is not untenable.

After the decline during the Ming dynasty, the scholarship on the *Changes* entered into a new fluorescence in the Qing dynasty (1616-1912).

The collapse of the Ming dynasty [and the establishment of the Qing dynasty by Manchus] greatly stimulated the intellectuals at that time who were forced to think of the lessons to be taken from the destruction of the Ming. Therefore, the Ming-Qing transitional period witnessed a relative freedom and activity in intellectual circles, and "the talented savants abruptly and painstakingly began to rectify the shallowness of the prevalent ethos, criticize the loss at the present and show their favor of the ancient, and abandon emptiness and value solidness in order to realize the retrieval of a good environment, resulting in a quick and complete change [in academic circles]."[dccx] Under these circumstances, in the early Qing dynasty, the Han (206 B.C.E.-220 C.E.) tradition of *Changes* scholarship was revived.

But in the beginning of the Qing era, the Song (960-1279) tradition of *Changes* scholarship still dominated. The reappearance of the Han tradition of *Changes* scholarship immediately occasioned assaults from the proponents of the Song *Yi*, and therefore there appeared the Han-Song controversy.

Confronted with this situation and for the convenience of rule, Emperor Kangxi 康熙 (r. 1661-1722) took a relatively wise attitude. As was mentioned above, Emperor Taizong of Tang 唐太宗 (r. 627-49) singly gravitated to Wang Bi's 王弼 (226-49) commentary on the *Zhou Changes* and neglected Zheng Xuan's 郑玄 (127-200) approaches to the *Changes* when he commissioned Kong Yingda 孔颖达 (574-648) and his team to compile the *Wujing zhengyi* 五经正义 (Correct Meaning of the Five

Classics); Emperor Yongle 永乐 (r. 1402-24) took up only Cheng Yi's 程颐 (1033-1107) and Zhu Xi's 朱熹 (1130-1200) exegesis of the *Zhou Changes* when he ordered Hu Guang 胡广 (1369-1418) and his team to put together the works of *Wujing daquan* 五经大全 (Great Comprehensive Compilation of the *Five Classics*), which consequently led to the prejudices and vulgarity of the Ming Confucians. Unlike these two emperors, Kangxi, who recognized the controversy, took an eclectic approach and ordered Li Guangdi 李光地 (1642-1718) to compile a synthetic work called *Zhou yi zhezhong* 周易折中 (A Balanced Compendium on the *Zhou Changes*), which "adopted the theories conceived in the charts and diagrams and numbers upheld in (Zhu Xi's) *Yixue qimeng* 易学启蒙 (Introduction to the Study of the *Changes*) without excessively talking about the *he tu* and the *luo shu* which obscured the origin of divination and images, and put Cheng Yi's *Yizhuang* 易传 (Commentary on the *Changes*) in the first place followed with (Zhu Xi's) *Original Meaning* without abandoning the apocrypha and the *huti* 互体 (overlapping trigrams) approach exposing the usage of line transformations. Those interpretations which might not be commensurate with Cheng Yi or Zhu Xi's views but could actually illuminate the meaning of the classic were also included, disregarding their discrepancies. [...] All the different views formed in the past several hundred years were synthesized in this book."[dccxi]

The fluorescence of *Yi* studies in the Qing dynasty and the phenomena of vying Han and Song traditions were really closely related to Kangxi's policy of integration when it came to the scholarship on the *Changes*.

Emperor Qianlong 乾隆 (r. 1735-95) further carried forward this policy and ordered a group of scholars led by Fuheng 傅恒 (c. 1720-70) to compile a work later referred to as the *Zhou yi shuyi* 周易述义 (Narration of the Meaning of the *Zhou Changes*), which "merged the variety of the views, selected the essentials without illustrating the names nor distinguishing the gains from loss, [...] aiming to reveal its practicality."[dccxii] Moreover, Fuheng clearly reflected to the emperor: "We officials obediently observed your order, balanced Han and Song traditions of the *Changes*, explored its in-depth essence so as to determine both Wang Bi and Zheng Xuan's strong and weak points, and thus there will be no discrepancies regarding the meaning of the age-old *Changes*."[dccxiii]

Clearly, no matter the reconciliation of the different views by Li Guangdi 李光地 (1642-1718) in *Zhouyi zhezhong* 周易折中 (A Balanced Compendium on the *Zhou Changes*) or the balance of Han and Song traditions by Fuheng 傅恒 in his *Zhouyi shuyi* 周易述义 (Narration of the Meanings of the *Zhou Changes*), the fundamental objective of Kangxi and Qianlong was one of convenience for their rule.

Now, let us take a look at how the work claims itself to be "comprehensively including the variety of interpretations from the Han (206 B.C.E.-220 C.E.) to the present and taking their quintessence."[dccxiv] For example, when interpreting the judgment of hexagram Zhun [☵, Birth Throes, 3] that "Zhun consists of fundamentality [*yuan* 元], prevalence [*heng* 亨], fitness [*li* 利], and constancy [*zhen* 贞]. Do not use this as an opportunity to go forth. It is fitting to establish a chief,"[dccxv] the *Zhou yi shuyi* 周易述义 (Narration of the Meanings of the *Zhou Changes*) tells us: "The inner trigram is Zhen [☳] and outer trigram Kan [☵], [an image of] taking action [symbolized by ☳] and encountering danger [☵], hence the name of Zhun. In the midst of the hexagram, the overlapping trigrams include Gen [☶, formed by line 3, line 4, and line 5] and Kun [☷, formed by line 2, line 3, and line 4]. Zhen [☳] designates the beginning of the *yang* energy, and Kun [☷] means submissiveness and compliance,[dccxvi] hence the term of *yuanheng* 元亨; Kan [☵] moistens the lower and Gen [☶] curbs it, hence the term of *zhen* 贞 (constancy); Kun [☷] is the multitude[dccxvii] [of people] and Zhen [☳] takes command of them,[dccxviii] hence the words of 'going forth' [*you youwang* 有攸往]; but they are prevented by Gen [☶], which means the situation should not be used [as an opportunity to take action]; the bottom line gains the [support of] the commoners [symbolized by Kun ☷], hence the term of *hou* 侯 [chief],[dccxix] and the nature of the fifth line is identical to that of the bottom line, so '[it is fitting to] establish [a chief].'[dccxx] During these hard times, the first thing is to secure the people, and [this one] must be committed to humane governance with benevolent heart, nourish them in quiescence in accordance with the time and the place, and he must be circumspect and not be anxious to achieve quick success, crave for greatness, or send troops."[dccxxi]

Clearly, the above-mentioned interpretations associating the hexagram statement with the images [symbolic representations] of the trigrams one by one followed the Han people's hermeneutic approaches, whereas the following words of "During these hard times, the first thing is to secure the people, and [this one] must be committed to humane governance with benevolent heart [...]" obviously held the Song people's tone in the exegesis of the *Changes*.

Through the two generations of Kangxi's 康熙 and Qianglong's 乾隆 advocacy of the fusion of Han and Song traditions, at last the Han scholarship on the *Changes* was established after its revival; this led to the situation under which the two branches of the Han and Song traditions competed with each other and coexisted throughout the entire Qing dynasty, which eventually became the era to comprehensively synthesize the achievements of the past dynasties in regard to the *Changes*.

A general survey of the nearly 300 years of the Qing dynasty (1616-1912) manifests that men of talent in *Changes* studies came out in succession, and accordingly there emerged abundant works related to *Changes* scholarship. Merely according to the "Treatise on Literature and Arts" (*Yiwen zhi* 艺文志) of the *Qingshi gao* 清史稿 (Draft of History of the Qing Dynasty [1616-1912]), there were over 150 *Changes*-oriented works produced, including over 1,700 *juan* 卷 (literally, scrolls, i.e., chapters), at that time. That which actually constituted the academic feature of the scholarship on the *Changes* of the time was the Qing Confucians' compilation, collation, and textual research on the works and fragments of some renowned scholars from the Han (206 B.C.E.-220 C.E.) through the Six Dynasties (222-589), and particularly their collation and compilation of the Han *Changes* scholarship ought to be viewed as their outstanding contributions.

During the reigns of emperors Shunzhi 顺治 (r. 1644-61) and Kangxi 康熙 (r. 1661-1722), most intellectuals, suppressed by literary inquisition, did not dare to be embroiled into politics, and had to force themselves to be immersed in compilations, textual research, and exegesis of ancient books, and particularly during the reign of Emperor Qianglong 乾隆 (r. 1735-95), along with the accomplishment of the *Siku quanshu* 四库全书 (Complete Collection of the Four Treasuries), a large amount of ancient books came out, and the exponents of the Han *Yi* tradition gained the upper hand.

The first one who specially collected the lost writings of the Han *Changes* scholarship was the Song scholar Wang Yinglin 王应麟 (1223-96), who intently searched for the lost documents of Zheng Xuan 郑玄 (127-200) and compiled one *juan* (chapter) of the *Zhou yi Zheng Kangcheng zhu* 周易郑康成注 (Zheng Xuan's Commentary on the *Changes*). The Qing scholar Hui Dong 惠栋 (1697-1758) carried on his cause and continued to supplement the omissions and lost writings, and composed one *juan* of the *Zengbu Zhou yi Zheng zhu* 增补周易郑注 (Supplement to Zheng Xuan's Commentary on the *Changes*) and one *juan* of the *Zhou yi Zheng Kangcheng yaochen tu* 周易郑康成爻辰图 (*Zhou Changes*-based Diagram of *yaocheng* Invented by Zheng Xuan). But his most famous work ought to be seen as the *Yi Hanxue* 易汉学 (Han Scholarship on the *Changes*). There were overall eight *juan* in this book, among which Meng Xi's 孟喜 *Changes* occupied two *juan*, Yu Fan's 虞翻 (164-233) *Changes* one *juan*, Jing Fang's 京房 (77-37 B.C.E.) two *juan*, Zheng Xuan's 郑玄 (127-200) one *juan*, and Xun Shuang's 荀爽 (128-190) one *juan*, and the last *juan* was his differentiation of the Song people's *he tu* (Yellow River Chart) and *luo shu* (Luo River Diagram) from the Han tradition of *Changes* scholarship. This was a book systematically introducing the outlines of the works of the famous experts in *Changes* scholarship in the Han dynasty (206 B.C.E.-220 C.E.), which played a significant role in the exegesis and spread of Han scholarship on the *Changes*.

Additionally, in his *Zhou yi shu* 周易述 (Description of the *Zhou Changes*), Hui Dong mainly dwelled on Yu Fan's 虞翻 (164-233) *Changes* and took Zheng Xuan's 郑玄 (127-200), Xun Shuang's 荀爽 (128-190), and Gan Bao's 干宝 (d. 336) approaches to the *Changes* as references; and on the basis of these scholars' discourses, he also presented his own subcommentaries. Although the table of contents shows 40 *juan*, it actually only contains 23 *juan*, among which 21 *juan* are interpretations of the basic text of and the "Commentaries on the *Changes*" (*Yi zhuan* 易传), and the other two *juan* are named "Subtlety of the *Changes*" (*Yi weiyan* 易微言), being selected words from the variety of scholars' views. Unfortunately, it was an unfinished work.

After Hui Dong, another Qing scholar called Zhang Huiyan 张惠言 (1761-1802) made a larger-scale compilation and collation of ancient intellectuals' annotations to the *Changes*. He compiled nine *juan* of *Zhou yi Yushi yi* 周易虞氏易 (The Meaning of the *Zhou Changes* Based on the Interpretations of Yu Fan), two *juan* of *Yushi xiaoxi* 虞氏消息 (Waxing and Waning of the Hexagrams Based on the Interpretations of Yu Fan), two *juan* of *Yushi yili* 虞氏易礼 (Rituals of the *Changes* Based on the Interpretations of Yu Fan), two *juan* of *Yushi yishi* 虞氏易事 (Events of the *Changes* Based on the Interpretations of Yu Fan) and *Yushi yiyan* 虞氏易言 (Words of the *Changes* Based on the Interpretations of Yu Fan), one *juan* of *Yushi yihou* 虞氏易候 (Meteorology of the *Changes* Based on the Interpretations of Yu Fan), two *juan* of *Yushi yibian biao* 虞氏易变表 (Table of Interchangeability of the Hexagrams Based on the Interpretations of Yu Fan), two *juan* of *Zhou yi Zhengshi zhu* 周易郑氏注 (Zheng Xuan's Annotation to the *Changes*), one *juan* of *Zhou yi Xunshi jiujia yi* 周易荀氏九家易 (The Meaning of the *Zhou Changes* Based on the Interpretations of the Nine Scholars from Xun's Family), one *juan* of *Yitu tiaobian* 易图条辨 (Detailed Discrimination of the Illustrations Associated with the *Changes*), three *juan* of *Yiwei lüeyi* 易纬略义 (A Brief Introduction to the Meaning of the Apocrypha of the *Changes*). He also compiled fourteen *juan* of *Yiyi bielu* 易义别录 (Supplement to the Meaning of the *Changes*), which include one *juan* of Meng Xi's 孟喜 *Changes*, one *juan* of Yao Xin's 姚信 *Changes*, one *juan* of Zhai Zixuan's 翟子玄 (an early Tang [618-907] scholar) *Changes*, one *juan* of Shu Cai's 蜀才 (a scholar in the early Tang dynasty [618-907]) *Changes*, one *juan* of Jing Fang's 京房 (77-37 B.C.E.) *Changes*, one *juan* of Lu Ji's 陆绩 (187-219) *Changes*, two *juan* of Gan Bao's 干宝 (d. 336) *Changes*, one *juan* of Ma Rong's 马融 (79-166) *Changes*, one *juan* of Song Zhong 宋衷 (a scholar of the late Three Kingdoms period [220-280]) and Liu Jingsheng's 刘景升 (142-208) *Changes*, one *juan* of Wang Su's 王肃 (195-256) *Changes*, one *juan* of Dong Yu's 董遇 (a scholar of the late Three Kingdoms period [220-280]) *Changes*, one *juan of* Wang Yi 王廙 (276-322) and Liu Huan's 刘瓛 (434-89) *Changes*, and one *juan* of Zixia's 子夏 (one of Confucius' excellent disciples) *Changes*.

With proper attribution and some textual research and subcommentaries, Zhang Huiyan 张惠言 (1761-1802) divided the works of most eminent scholars from the Han (206 B.C.E.-220 C.E.) through the Six Dynasties (222-589) into different subsections, which allowed the ancient *Changes* existing as dispersed in different documents to be systematically exhibited in the presence of the readers and provided later scholars who wanted to engage in the study of ancient *Changes* scholarship with great facilities.

In the interpretive documents of the *Changes* collected by Zhang Huiyan, Yu Fan's scholarship on the *Changes* was the most detailed and substantial; this was considered to be the most complete exploration and collation of the Han scholarship on the *Changes*, so much so that the famous Qing scholar Ruan Yuan 阮元 (1764-1849) held that Zhang's work made the Han *Yi* tradition, particularly Yu Fan's scholarship on the *Changes* which had been lingering on in a steadily worsening condition over 1,400 years after Yu Fan (164-233), "clearly come to light again, which is really a grand event!"[dccxxii]

Following Zhang Huiyan's path, Zeng Zhao 曾钊 (1793-1854) wrote the *Zhou yi Yushi yi jian* 周易虞氏易笺 (Notes on the Meaning of the *Zhou Changes* Based on [the Interpretations of] Yu Fan), Li Rui 李锐 (1768-1817) composed the *Zhou yi Yushi lüeli* 周易虞氏略例 (General Remarks on the *Zhou Changes* Based on [the Interpretations of] Yu Fan), and Hu Xianglin 胡祥麟 (d. 1823) wrote his *Yushi yi xiaoxi tuoshuo* 虞氏易消息图说 (An Explanation of the Diagram of Waxing and Waning Conceived in Yu Fan's *Changes* Scholarship). All these works provided further collation and exegesis on Yu Fan's *Changes*. Additionally, taking Yu Fan's "laterally linked hexagrams" (*pangtong* 旁通) and Xun Shuang's 荀爽 (128-190) "rising (of *yang*) and falling (of *yin*)" approaches into his interpretations of the *Changes*, Jiao Xun 焦循 (1763-1820) composed the *Yi zhangju* 易章句 (Sentence by Sentence Interpretation of the *Changes*), *Zhou yi bushu* 周易补疏 (Supplemented Subcommentaries on the *Zhou Changes*), *Yihua* 易话 (Remarks on the *Changes*), and *Yitu lüe* 易图略 (An Outline of the Diagrams of the *Changes*). Moreover, all of the following works—including Wu Yiyin's 吴翊寅 *Yi hanxue kao* 易汉学考 (Textual Research on [Hui Dong's] *Han Scholarship on the Changes*); *Yi hanxue shicheng biao* 易汉学师承表 (Table of the Lineages and Affiliations of the Scholars Mentioned in [Hui Dong's] *Han Scholarship on the Changes*); Dai Tang's 戴棠 *Zhengshi yaochen bu* 郑氏爻辰补 (Supplement to Zheng

Xuan's *Yaochen* Theory); He Qiutao's 何秋涛 (1844 *jinshi*) *Zhou yi yaochen shen Zheng yi* 周易爻辰申郑义 (An Extension of the Meaning of Zheng Xuan's *Yaochen* Theory); Fang Shen's 方申 outputs of *Zhujia Yixue bielu* 诸家易学别录 (Supplement to the Variety of Scholars' Study of the *Changes*), *Yushi Yixue huibian* 虞氏易学汇编 (A Compilation of Yu Fan's Scholarship on the *Changes*), *Zhou yi huti xiangshu* 周易互体详述 (A Detailed Description of the *Huti* [Overlapping Trigrams] Approach to the *Zhou Changes*), and *Zhou yi guabian juyao* 周易卦变举要 (Essentials of Hexagram Transformations of the *Zhou Changes*); Yu Yue's 俞樾 (1821-1907) *Zhou yi huti zheng* 周易互体徵 (Evidence for the *Huti* [Overlapping Trigrams] Approach to the *Zhou Changes*), and the part of "The Classic of Changes" (*Yi jing* 易经) in Pi Xirui's 皮锡瑞 (1850-1908) *Jingxue tonglun* 经学通论 (A Comprehensive Discussion of Classical Studies)—provided meticulous and in-depth textual research on, exegesis, and collation of the Han scholarship on the *Changes*, and shed much significant light on the approaches of *guabian* 卦变 (hexagram changes), *xiaoxi* 消息 (waxing and waning) [exposed by the 12 sovereign hexagrams], and *huti* 互体 (overlapping hexagrams). Prior to their efforts, Ma Guohan 马国翰 (1794-1857) had devoted his entire life to searching for and collecting the ancient documents before the Song dynasty (960-1279), most of which were not publicly transmitted for a long time, and at last he accomplished his *Yuhan shanfang jiyi shu* 玉函山房辑佚书 (Collection of Lost Texts from the Treasury Chamber 'Jade Slipcase'), in which the part of *Yixue* 易学 (Scholarship on the *Changes*) includes the discourses of the Western Han (206 B.C.E.-9 C.E.) scholars of Ding Kuan 丁宽 (a famous disciple of Tian He 田何 [fl. c. 200 B.C.E., the progenitor of the teaching of the *Changes* after the foundation of the Han dynasty (206 B.C.E.-220 C.E.)]), Han Ying 韩婴 (a famous early Western Han [206 B.C.E.-9 C.E.] scholar), and the nine masters serving Liu An 刘安 (179-122) [king of the State of Huainan 淮南], as well as the *Changes*-oriented texts of Shi Chou 施雠, Liangqiu He 梁丘贺, and Fei Zhi 费直. Particularly, in this book he compiled as many as three *juan* of Fei Zhi's 费直 *Changes*-related works, including one *juan* of his *Yizhu* 易注 (Commentary on the *Changes*), one *juan* of *Yilin* 易林 (Forest of the *Changes*), and one *juan* of *Zhouyi fenye* 周易分野 (Distinction of the *Zhou Changes*).

Through the successive efforts of these Qing Confucians, the Han tradition of the *Changes* scholarship was brought to light again after 1,500 years of eclipse. Thanks to their achievements, today we can systematically study this tradition and explore its exegetical and image-numerological features. Without their efforts, we do not know how much time we would waste in being devoted to searching for these characteristics among such a tremendous number of ancient documents. Therefore, the compilations of, collations of, and subcommentaries on the ancient *Changes*-related works before the Tang dynasty (618-907), and especially the Han *Changes* scholarship, by Qing Confucians significantly contributed to the studies of *Yi* learning in China.

Besides the above-mentioned works, Qing Confucians also made detailed textual research on and emendation of predecessors' *Changes*-oriented outputs and also achieved a fair amount in these respects. For instance, their textual research on the Song (960-1279) people's *he tu*- and *luo shu*-oriented learning and the "Former Heaven Sequence of the Eight Trigrams" reflected their matter-of-fact attitude. From their perspective, as the *Zhou Changes* survived the "burning of books" (213 B.C.E.) of the Qin dynasty (221-206 B.C.E.), if the charts and diagrams really existed at that time, they would not have been lost separately and only preserved by Daoists to be later disclosed by Chen Tuan 陈抟 (871-989) in the Song dynasty. Therefore, Wang Fuzhi 王夫之 (1619-92) wrote the *Zhou yi baishu* 周易稗疏 (A Detailed Commentary on the *Zhou Changes*), Mao Qiling 毛奇龄 (1623-1716) composed the *Tushu yuantuan bian* 图书原舛编 (Real Original Sources for the *He tu* and the *Luo shu*), Huang Zongxi 黄宗羲 (1610-95) wrote the *Yixue xiangshu lun* 易学象数论 (Discussion of Images and Numbers in *Changes* Scholarship), and Huang Zongyan 黄宗炎 (1616-86) composed the *Tushu bianhuo* 图书辨惑 (Straightening Out the Confusing Points Related to the *He tu* [Yellow River Chart] and the *Luo shu* [Luo River Diagram]), by which they gave solid evidence in order to refute the fallacy of the *Tushu* (Yellow River Chart and Luo River Diagram) learning. More significantly, Hu Wei 胡渭 (1633-1714) published his *Yitu mingbian* 易图明辨 (A Clarifying Critique of the Illustrations Associated with the *Changes*), by which he specially examined the provenance of the *tu shu* learning alleged by Song (960-1279) people. In particular, on the basis of Zheng Xuan's 郑玄 (127-200)

related annotations, he drew a chart (see the above-mentioned discussion related to Song scholarship on the *Changes*) by which he conclusively manifested the origin of the so-called *luo shu* and solved a big mystery in the study of *Changes* scholarship.

In regard to the emended works, Qing scholars also contributed a lot, such as through Ruan Yuan's 阮元 (1764-1849) *Zhou yi jiaokan ji* 周易校勘记 (Notes from Emendating the *Zhou Changes*), Ding Jie's 丁杰 *Zhou yi Zhengzhu houding* 周易郑注后定 (A Determined Version of Zheng Xuan's Commentary on the *Zhou Changes*), and so on.

As synthesizers of the achievements in *Changes* studies by periods, Qing Confucians also accomplished a great cause—that is, the completion of the *Siku quanshu* 四库全书 (Complete Collection of the Four Treasuries) [hereafter *Siku*] during the reign of the Qianlong 乾隆 emperor (r. 1735-95), accompanying which the *Siku quanshu zongmu* 四库全书总目 (General Catalogue of the *Complete Collection of the Four Treasuries*) was also issued.

Because the *Siku quanshu* was the largest-scale collation of ancient documents after Liu Xiang 刘向 (77-6 B.C.E.) and Liu Xin 刘歆 (50 B.C.E.-23 C.E.) of the Han dynasty, the *Siku quanshu zongmu* (hereafter *Zongmu* [General Catalog]) turned out to be the largest booklist up through contemporary time, which contains as many as 200 *juan*. Under the "Classical Category" (*Jingbu* 经部), the first one was the six *juan* of "The Changes" (*yi lei* 易类) and four *juan* of *Cun mu* 存目 [the list of books whose names existed but whose real contents were not included in the *Siku* on account of their violating contemporary prohibitions or their incongruence with the orthodox ideology]. This overall 10 *juan* of *Changes*-related philology was also affiliated with the compendiums of the books collected in the *Siku*, which include the respective authorship, number of *juan*, abstract, and a brief evaluation of each book by the editors of the *Siku*.

Although there had always been different comments on the academic value of the *Zongmu* (General Catalogue), for the part related to "The Changes" (*yi lei* 易类), we think the evaluations are in general acceptable as reference materials for today's research on *Changes* scholarship.

For example, the editors of the *Siku* summarized the malpractice of the over 2,000 years of study of *Changes* scholarship in this way: "The way of the *Changes* is broad and great. It encompasses everything, including astronomy, geography, music, military methods, phonetics, numerical calculation, and even alchemy. All these fields drew upon the *Changes* to establish their theories, and those who were in favor of different views further associated these theories with the *Changes*, so the *Changes*-related discourses proliferated more and more."[dccxxiii] The editors also hold that "the 'Commentary on the Images' (*Xiang* 象) affiliated to each of the sixty-four hexagrams contains the words like, 'In the same way, the noble man [...],' and that affiliated to each line, always admonishes the questioner, by which the sage's intentions can been seen. [Each of] the other [commentaries] only reflected one aspect of the *Changes*, and thus was not the origin of it."[dccxxiv] (All of these views are insightful and pertinent.)

When briefly reviewing each of the books collected in the *Siku*, the editors usually could hit on their valuable points and identify authenticity based on textual research. For example, when introducing the Song scholar Zhu Yuansheng's 朱元升 (d. 1273) *San yi beiyi* 三易备遗 (Memorandum for the Three Kinds of *Changes*), they give textual evidence regarding the names of *xian tian* 先天 (Former Heaven), *hou tian* 后天 (Latter Heaven), and *zhong tian* 中天 (Mid Heaven): "According to Gan Bao's 干宝 (d. 336) *Zhou li zhu* 周礼注 (Commentary on the *Zhou Rituals*), Fuxi's 伏羲 *Changes* represented the small completion and was called the *xian tian* [i.e., the earlier stage], Shennong's 神农 *Changes* mid-completion and the *zhong tian* [the mid-term stage], Yellow Emperor's *Changes* the great completion and the *hou tian* [the final stage]. So the *zhong tian* was also an ancient term rather than a new one."[dccxxv] When evaluating Yu Wan's 俞琬 (1258-1314) *Du Yi juyao* 读易举要 (Essentials of Reading the *Changes*), they say:

> Shi Xuan 史璿 told us that as Ge [䷰, Radical Change, 49] was the 49th hexagram [in the received version of the *Zhou Changes*], a number corresponding to the number of Great Expansion, [as it says in the 'Commentary on the Appended Phrases' (*Xi ci* 系辞), "the number of the great expansion is fifty [yarrow stalks], of which we use forty-nine,"[dccxxvi]] [in which the

concept of four seasons was adopted]¹, so the "Commentary on the Judgment" (*Tuan* 彖) regarding the hexagram has the remarks related to the "four seasons"[dccxxvii]; and because Jie [䷻, Control, 60] was the 60th hexagram, the number representing a sexagenary cycle (of a year made up of the four seasons), the 'Commentary on the Judgment' regarding this hexagram also refers to the "four seasons"[dccxxviii] As a matter of fact, these are nothing but coincidences through which Shi Xuan 史璿 tried to discern the sage's idea as conceived in the composition of the *Changes*. Yu Wan 俞琬 continued to draw upon this point of view, which was absolutely not the original purport."[dccxxix]

When briefly introducing one of the Yuan (1271-1368) scholar Bao Ba's 宝巴 *Changes*-oriented works, they point out: "The preface (of the work) was shallow and not like the works of an intellectual at all. So, this work might have been taught by some occultist and coincidentally shared the same name as the lost Bao Ba's book. The Ming (1368-1644) people like to make pseudographs and thus borrowed Bao Ba's name as the author of the preface in order to allude to it."[dccxxx]

When briefly evaluating the *Zhou yi daquan* 周易大全 (Great Comprehensive [Compilation] of the *Zhou Changes*) put together by the Ming Confucian Hu Guang 胡广 (1370-1418) and his associates, as commissioned by the Yongle 永乐 emperor (r. 1402-24), the editors provided us with a criticism of it with deep grief: "Over the two hundred years (of the Ming dynasty), it was taken as the standard for civil examinations and graced with a preface written by the emperor himself. It was evident that it was due to the existence of this book that the early Ming Confucians' classical studies were short of vitality, and it was also due to its existence that later Ming Confucians were inevitably obstinate and superficial. [...] The ancient commentaries and sub-commentaries after all ought not to be abolished. Even while the Ming dynasty was in its prime, some far-sighted personage began to worry about abuses of it. Looking at this compilation, we can see that it indeed can remind us of gains and losses [in the compilation of ancient documents] in the past thousands of years."[dccxxxi]

---

¹ For the detail of the Great Expansion, please see Chapter 5.

When introducing the Qing scholar Wang Xinjing's 王心敬 (aka Fengchuan 丰川, 1656-1738) *Fengchuan Yishuo* 丰川易说 (Discussion of the *Changes* by Fengchuan), the editors tell us: "As the *Changes* was a book discoursing on human affairs, the waxing and waning of *yin* and *yang* were just borrowed as signs. So, it was said that 'This is why the *Changes* as such consists of images, and the term *image* means the making of semblances.'[dccxxxii] If one could not clearly see the waxing and waning of *yin* and *yang*, it means that the signs were not true in his mind. If one only blindly followed the traces of the waxing and waning of *yin* and *yang* without any self-awareness of human affairs, what he would understand [about the *Changes*] would be like running after a shadow."[dccxxxiii] "If the *Changes* has nothing to do with images, how would the meanings be formed? If the *Changes* is not related to divination, why were the yarrow stalks provided there?"[dccxxxiv] "Generally speaking, the *Changes* scholarship from the Han (206 B.C.E.-220 C.E.) through the Tang (618-907) put a premium on word by word exegesis, whereas the Song-Ming (960-1644) *Changes* scholarship tended to display cleverness [and fantasy]. Although the former might not reveal the real meaning of the *Changes*, the *Changes* was still existing there, while the latter adulterated the *Changes* and made it die out."[dccxxxv] All these remarks clearly reflect the editors' academic point of view.

Because the person who was actually in charge of the editing of the *Siku* was Ji Yun 纪昀 (1724-1805), at that time, the persons who participated in the editing of the "Classical Category" (*Jingbu* 经部) included Dai Zhen 戴震 (1724-77). Both of them were renowned scholars already and fully gravitated toward the Han *Changes* tradition; and thus, this tradition was highly esteemed and received high evaluations in the *Zongmu* (General Catalogue), whereas the exponents of the Song *Changes* traditions were often ridiculed as occasion served. For example, when briefly introducing Cheng Yi's 程颐(1033-1107) *Yizhuan* (Commentary on the *Changes*), they say: "Mr. Shao Yong 邵雍 (1011-77) elaborated on the *Changes* by numbers while Mr. Cheng Yi makes use of this commentary to explicate the principle. The former elucidates the Dao [Way] of heaven while the latter pays attention to human affairs. When composing books, each of the ancient people might attempt to just air his own views [and all their views could form a whole], but sectarianists [like Song Confucians] must blindly defend discourses of their teachers. This deviated from the original purport of former Confucians!"dccxxxvi When commenting on Zheng Ruxie's 郑汝谐 (aka Donggu 东谷, 1126-1205) *Donggu Yi yizhuan* 东谷易翼传 (Appended Commentaries to Donggu's *Changes*), the editors also voice their own opinions: "In the course of interpreting the classics, Zhu Xi 朱熹 (1130-1200) also modified a lot of Cheng Yi's 程颐 (1022-1107) exegesis and then contributed his final version. More explications of the classic, more profoundness of the sage's essential ideas (dwelling in the classics) would be found. Being immersed in former Confucians' discourses, once one's understandings were identical to them, he would further clarify them, and once his insight was different from theirs, he would speak out and shed light on his own idea. This kind of attitude also contributes to former Confucians' achievements. Therefore, one should not blindly adhere to one former Confucian's views in that this kind of attitude could only strengthen sectarianism."dccxxxvii Here is another example: When evaluating the [Yuan (1271-1368)-Ming (1368-1644) transitional figure Zhao Cai's 赵采] *Zhou yi Cheng-Zhu zhuan yi zhezhong* 周易程朱传义折中 (Synthesis of [Cheng Yi's] Commentary and [Zhu Xi's] Original Meaning of the *Zhou Changes*), they tell us: "Although this book focused on Song (960-1279) learning, it also adopted 'images and numbers' (*xiangshu* 象数), 'hexagram changes' (*guabian* 卦变) and 'overlapping trigrams' (*huti* 互体) approaches [dominating in Han learning]. So, it preserved considerable ancient meanings rather than merely ardently adhering to one person's speeches."dccxxxviii

There are many examples of this kind in "The *Changes*" (*Yi lei* 易类) of the *Zongmu* (General Catalog). The editors every now and then criticized Song people's sectarianism, even for some very famous works of the Song experts at the *Changes*, such as Cheng Yi's 程颐 *Yizhuan* 易传 (Commentary on the *Changes*) and Zhu Xi's 朱熹 *Benyi* 本义 (Original Meaning), they just referred to their layout but without any word about their contents, gain, or loss. This unfair attitude also belonged to sectarianism, which ought not to be adopted by scholars.

It was on account of the editors' inclination toward the Han tradition, and despising the Song approaches, that when evaluating Song Confucians' works, they tended to be overly critical and short of sufficient evidence for such criticism. For example, the Song scholar Lin Guangshi's

林光世 (aka Shuicun 水村 [literally, watery village], fl. 1259) *Shuicun Yi jing* 水村易镜 (Mirror of the *Changes* by Shuicun) "was mainly based on the remarks in the 'Commentary on the Appended Phrases' (*Xi ci* 系辞) and held that, when interpreting the *Changes*, the intellectuals lost the significance of looking upward and downward [in order to observe the heavenly configurations and earthly patterns like Fuxi 伏羲]. As I [the author of the book, i.e., Lin Guangshi] lived in a coastal city, I could observe and verify heavenly configurations, by which I was enlightened concerning the constellations allotted to the eight palaces of Heaven [symbolized by ☰], Marsh [☱], Fire [☲], Thunder [☳], Wind [☴], Water [☵], Mountain [☶], and Earth [☷], which naturally correspond to the sixty-four hexagrams, and so I associate the constellations with the hexagrams." For this feature of the book, the editors criticize: "The star map he illustrated displayed his far-fetched associations and the interpretations of the *Changes* from ancient times to present had never been so ridiculous as his. When Baoxi 包牺 [i.e., Fuxi 伏羲] looked up and observed the heavenly configurations, he aimed to measure the waning and waxing manifested in the rotations [of the heavenly planets]; never had he invented trigrams and hexagrams modeled on the constellations,"[dccxxxix] and the editors continued to speak sarcastically in saying: "Later Chen Tu 陈图 composed his *Zhou yi qiyuan* 周易起元 (Exploring the Origin of the *Zhou Changes*), in which he associated the famous mountains and rivers with the sixty-four hexagrams and called it [Fuxi's 伏羲] 'observing the earthly patterns.' According to this analogy, they will not stop until the patterns on birds and beasts are associated with the hexagrams!"[dccxl]

Lin Guangshi's 林光世 view that there was a natural correspondence between the constellations of the eight palaces and the 64 hexagrams, through which he forced the associations between them in star maps, of course contains elements of absurdity, but it was not strange, in that from ancient times to the present the "school of meteorological observation" (*cehou pai* 测候派) has always been a big school that tends to interpret the *Changes* by the images formed by the constellations. Their words of "When Baoxi [i.e., Fuxi] looked up and observed the heavenly configurations, he aimed to measure the waning and waning manifested in the rotations (of the heavenly planets); never had he invented trigrams and hexagrams modeled on the constellations," seems to lack evidence.

The original text related to this interpretation was from the "Commentary on the Appended Phrases" (*Xi ci* 系辞): "When in ancient times Lord Baoxi ruled the world as sovereign, he looked upward and observed the images in heaven and looked downward and observed the patterns that the earth provided. He observed the patterns on birds and beasts and what things were suitable for the land. Nearby, adopting them from his own person, and afar, adopting them from other things, he thereupon made the eight trigrams."[dccxli] Taking a thorough view of these words, we can see that the purpose of Fuxi's "observing the images in heaven" does not only refer to "measuring the waxing and waning," but really has the meaning of "inventing the trigrams modeled on the constellations."[dccxlii] And through the following words of "He observed the patterns on birds and beasts and what things were suitable for the land. Nearby, adopting them from his own person, and afar, adopting them from other things, he thereupon made the eight trigrams," it is evident that the author of the *Zhou Changes* contends that Fuxi manufactured the eight trigrams through adopting the images from his own person and other things. Since it says in the "Commentary on the Appended Phrases" (*Xi ci* 系辞) that "the term *image* means 'the making of semblances,'"[dccxliii] "The sages had the means to perceive the mysteries of the world and, drawing comparisons to them with analogous things, made images out of those things that seemed appropriate,"[dccxliv] and "[Baoxi] looked upward and observed the images in heaven,"[dccxlv] so we cannot completely deny that there were contents of "inventing the trigrams modeled on the constellations." Of course, those far-fetched star maps in the *Shuicun Yi jing* 水村易镜 (Mirror of the *Changes* by Shuicun) were quite another thing.

Although the editors had academic prejudices of esteeming the Han tradition of *Changes* scholarship and denigrating the Song tradition, through their brief introductions to former scholars' *Changes*-related works and evaluations of gains and losses in these works, it can be seen that their comprehension of *Changes* scholarship was relatively solid and contains certain insights. Their reviews of some books (e.g., the Ming people's *Zhou yi daquan* 周易大全 [Great Comprehensive Compilation of the *Zhou Changes*]) indeed contain incisive understandings and still ought to be affirmed today.

Although the Qing dynasty (1616-1912) ruled for less than 300 years, it occupied an extremely important position in the history of *Changes* scholarship in China.

If the two millennia of studies of *Changes* scholarship were divided into two traditions of Han (206 B.C.E.-220 C.E.) and Song (960-1279), then the Qing (1616-1912) Confucians, with their academic style encouraging diverse thinking and the abundance of their *Changes*-oriented works, turned out to be the synthesizers and summarizers of these two traditions as well as a variety of other schools. Particularly, their exploration and collation of the Han *Changes* scholarship, which had been fading out for one and a half thousand years before their shedding of light on them, will now live forever in the history of *Changes* scholarship.

PART II

Some Prefaces and Speeches Related to the Scholarship on the *Changes*

10.
A Preface to the *Najia shifa* 纳甲筮法 (Three-Coin Method of Divination)[dccxlvi]

"One looks to the *pattern* of Heaven in order to examine the flux of the seasons, and one looks to the *pattern* of man in order to transform and bring the whole world to perfection"[dccxlvii] (*guanhu tianwen yi cha shibian, guanhu renwen yi hua cheng tianxia* 观乎天文以察时变; 观乎人文, 以化成天下). This is the definition of the term *wenhua* 文化 (literally, pattern and transformation, generally translated as *culture*). Just as the German philosopher Ernst Cassirer (1884-1945) pointed out when he was discussing the intrinsic quality of man, man is far less a "social" and "rational" animal than a "symbolic" animal—that is, a kind of animal applying symbols to cultural creation. From his perspective, animals can give only conditioned reflexes to signals, whereas humans can transform these signals into symbols of self-conscious significance and make use of them to create culture. Only through activities of cultural creation can man become human in the true sense; culture is no more than the externalization and objectification of humans and is nothing but the actualization and embodiment of symbolic activities.[dccxlviii]

As the crystallization of Chinese national wisdom, the *Zhou Changes* best expressed this point. It was by employing heavenly patterns and seasonal fluxes that the *Zhou Changes* epitomized and transformed the innumerable natural signals into the eight trigrams "in order to [let people] become thoroughly conversant with the virtues inherent in the numinous and the bright, and to classify the myriad things in terms of their true, innate natures,"[dccxlix] from which the always vivifying flow of *Changes*-oriented culture was initiated. The mantic arts inspired by the *Zhou Changes* just attempted to seek out the formulae that could accurately reexhibit the capacity and dynamic condition of human activities through various explicit symbols of the eight trigrams, and cycles of the implicit producing and destroying mechanisms among the Five Agents, to be used to calculate the fortune or misfortune of future activities.

It can be easily seen that, from milfoil-stalk divination to the Najia 纳甲 [attaching the 10 heavenly stems and 12 earthly branches to the 64 hexagrams according to certain regulations] *shi fa* 筮法 (Method of Divination) [traditionally credited to Jing Fang 京房 (77-37 B.C.E.)]—which makes use of three coins to obtain hexagram(s)—it was the objects represented by the image-numerological symbols of the eight trigrams that provided different divinatory methods with the force for their emergence, evolution, and transformation. In the course of remaking nature and society, man does not only remake the external world so as to make it cater to his demands, but also gradually changes the contents and realm of his life in order to seek a style by which he can know and expose the world. The mantic arts derived from the *Zhou Changes* just represent different styles by which one can know and expose the world formed in the course of practices by ancient Chinese sages and worthies. In China, the course of perfection of ancient people's cognition might be seen, in some sense, as the course of perfection of the divinatory methods derived from the *Zhou Changes*.

Formerly, intellectuals used to praise the profundity of the milfoil-stalk divination and criticize the art of *Najia* for its shallowness, venerating the former's solemnity and reproaching the latter for its randomness. And at last, they were always felt to be esteeming the past over the present. Actually, the *Najia* method has its own significance!

Today, in this book [i.e., *Najia shifa* 纳甲筮法], we only introduce general operational modes of the *Najia* divinatory method and illustrate some divinatory cases, past and present. In the future, we will approach it from the perspective of cultural history and explore this method and its calculating system, adopting the heavenly stems and earthly branches to the hexagrams that came into being and spread throughout history. In my opinion, the value, vitality, and reason that the stems-and-branches-based symbolic system—which attempted to reproduce the scene of man, nature, and society— endured and was handed down from age to age lies in the fact that it is not a fixed and static formula, but a dynamic formula that can actively manifest human capacities for action. Through unfixed positions of lines and hexagram changes, it adequately expresses the changeability of events and man's initiative, sociality, and creativity. In the symbols of hexagrams and lines [affiliated with heavenly stems and earthly branches] of the *Najia* system, man is not only the subject who imposes influences on them, but also their inventor and the creative source in the manipulation of the system. Not only does it take the elements of *ri* 日 (day) [expressed by a combination of the heavenly stems and earthly branches], *yue* 月 (month) [also expressed by the combination of the heavenly stems and earthly branches], and *liu shen* 六神 (six spirits) [equated with the six lines of a hexagram according to certain rules] symbolizing objective powers into consideration, but it also takes the *liu qin* 六亲 (six-relative) representing human relationships into account. Through the terms *jin shen* 进神 (advancing spirit [element]), *tui shen* 退神 (retreating spirit [element]), *yuan shen* 元神 (producing spirit [element]), and *ji shen* 忌神 (destroying spirit [element]), it exhibits the tendency of the unity of the objective body of the hexagram and the subjective body of the questioner, as well as the tendency of the unity of day, month, *yong shen* 用神 (the spirit [element] pertaining to the question), and *shi yao* 世爻 (generational line). In terms of the spirits of *sui jun* 岁君 (sovereign of the year), *yue jiang* 月将 (general of the month), *ri chen* 日辰 (day) [expressed by earthly branches], *fei* 飞 (manifest), and *fu* 伏 (latent), it embodies ancient people's constant explorations, which tell us that the body of related hexagrams is a temporal continuum of the event and human behavior, a channel of time connecting man and spirits, and connecting the subjective and the objective; it is the best style of consultation to guarantee human security and fortune. We might as well regard these hexagrams [affiliated with heavenly stems and earthly branches] as the abstraction reflecting the questioner's personal mentality, which, as a system of information conveyed by the hexagrams, usually was viewed as a driving force for us to react to the past, change the present, and look into the future. The load capacity of these hexagrams is very large, encompassing the expressions of politics, economy, morality, belief, knowledge, customs, self-worth, and so on. In short, the *Najia* method can disclose multifarious layers of human culture, turning out to be the summarizer and synthesizer of these layers. Therefore, as the embodiment of the *Zhou Changes*' symbolic culture, the hexagrams (with their attached heavenly stems and earthly branches) not only positively display the essence of human culture but also give us different overviews of its various layers with distinctive modes. To be sure, different interpreters of these hexagrams will give different analyses, which leaves broad space for sophism, superstition, and ridiculous presumption, which can be frequently seen in the ancient people's (analysis of) divinatory cases illustrated in the book.

11.
A Postscript to the *Najia shifa* 纳甲筮法 (Three-Coin Method of Divination)[dccl]

In recent years, there more and more people have been paying attention to the *Zhou Changes*. But the attention might be far from the real formation of a "fever" of *Zhou Changes* studies. For instance, looking at the achievements in *Changes* scholarship from 1985-95, it can be seen that there were few works on *Changes* scholarship, and the research on the newly unearthed *Changes*-related documents and comparative studies of foreign and domestic methodologies on the *Yi jng* has not been well accomplished, either. As very few magnum opuses or articles on these topics can be seen so far, how can we say the "fever" of *Changes* studies has arrived?

First of all, the so-called "fever" ought to start from the "1st International Conference on the *Zhou Changes*," which was approved by the State Education Commission and held at Shandong University in Jinan in December 1987. The conference received active responses at home and abroad and was reported by many media outlets, including major journals, newspapers of China, and CCTV (China Central Television). The complete success of the conference was not only embodied by the participants' sufficient exchanges of views and discussions on the subjects and orientations of *Changes* scholarship, but also manifested by the attention to *Zhou yi* studies from Chinese commoners who knew of the conference through mass media. Therefore, this conference can be considered the starting point of the *Zhou Changes* fever. Under this circumstance, on the one hand, there appeared a happy situation that encouraged serious and rigorous research and discussions on *Changes* scholarship, but on the other hand, an unsatisfactory phenomenon also came into being: Soon after the conference, taking advantage of people's attention to the *Zhou Changes*, some people claimed that they had resolved the millennial mystery of the *Zhou Changes*. Some alleged that they had decoded the millennial mystery of the eight trigrams; some then claimed they had deciphered the mystery of the *he tu* 河图 (Yellow River Chart) and *luo shu* 洛书 (Luo River Diagram). But soon there was no news whatsoever from these self-styled discoverers, who disappeared along with the short life of their theories.

Later, the real pivot of the "fever"—prognostics—loomed large, this actually referring to the method of divination of the *Zhou Changes*, or more concretely, the *Najia* 纳甲 method of divination (together with other mantic arts, including the *Meihua yi shu* 梅花易数 [Plum-blossom Numerology of *Changes*], *Si zhu mingli* 四柱命理 [Four-pillar Theory about One's Destiny, a.k.a. Chinese Astrology], and so on). In the pre-Qin [i.e., before 221 B.C.E.] times, the *Zhou Changes* was indeed considered to be a book of divination. Thanks to this attribution, it survived the notorious "burning of Confucian books" (213 B.C.E.) due to the tyranny and ignorance of the Qin (221-206 B.C.E.) and was transmitted successfully. For instance, there were many divinatory cases recorded in the *Zuo zhuan* 左传 (Zuo's Commentary on the *Spring and Autumn Annals*) and the *Guo yu* 国语 (Sayings of the States), and the prognostications came true later. By the Western Han dynasty (206 B.C.E. -9 C.E.), the *Zhou Changes* was esteemed as the "first of the five Confucian classics" and the "source of the great Dao (Way)," and the Western Han people even felt it was irreverent to call it the *Zhou Changes* and thus began to refer to it as the *Yi jing* 易经 (Classic of Changes). But along with its veneration and elevation, a strange thing occurred: Its basic text (together with the "Ten Wings") was stealthily separated from its function of divination. Its exegetical works were classified to the section of the "Thirteen Schools of the *Changes*,"[dccli] the first section for the "Five

Confucian Classics" scholarship, in the "Treatise on Art and Literature" (*Yiwen zhi* 艺文志) of the *Han shu* 汉书 (History of the Western Han Dynasty [206 B.C.E.-9 C.E.]), whereas the works related to its divinatory method were classified under the section of the "Fifteen Schools of the Tortoise-shell and Milfoil-stalk Divination"[dcclii] or that of the "Eighteen Schools of Miscellaneous Divination,"[dccliii] which were arranged after the sections of the "Calendars"[dccliv] and the "Five Elements."[dcclv] So, here the position of its divinatory function dropped significantly! Apparently, this trick was played by intellectuals who had the bad habit of disparaging each other, or else it resulted from the literati's spurning and attacking occultists at that time. But this kind of classification was followed from the Western Han through the Qing (1616-1912) dynasties. For example, in the *Siku quanshu zongmu* 四库全书总目 (General Catalog of the Complete Collection of the Four Treasuries) compiled by the Qing scholars, the monographs on the text of the *Zhou Changes* and its image-numerology were listed in "The Changes" (*Yi lei* 易类) of the "Classical Section" (*Jing bu* 经部) while the works related to divination were attributed to "The Arts of Calculation" (*Shushu lei* 术数类). Therefore, even at present, people tend to despise divination, which might be the result both of people's fury against those who like to cheat for money through divination and the impact formed in the history that still functions in our memory.

After divination turned out to be prognostics, it aroused tremendous attention and interest. The attitudes from the academic circle to this phenomenon are not unanimous: Some affirm its value, some think it to be worthless, and others contend that we should study it from academic perspectives. As the famous scholar Mr. Feng Youlan 冯友兰 (1895-1990) said in his congratulatory letter to the "1st International Conference on the *Zhou Changes*" held at Shandong University in 1987, "When studying the *Zhou Changes*, we certainly should focus on its philosophy. But since the *Zhou Changes* was originally a divination manual and some contents of its philosophy were related to its divinatory method, I suggest we should also investigate the divinatory methods associated with it."[dcclvi] Mr. Ren Jiyu 任继愈 (1916-2009), president of the Association of Chinese Philosophy, held: "As a book of divination, the method of divination of the *Zhou Changes* is quite noteworthy. We may take materials related to divination, domestic and abroad, employed by minorities or primitive tribes, and compare them with divinatory methods related to the *Zhou Changes*, by which we can certainly achieve more discoveries than ancient people could. This will help us precisely grasp features of the *Zhou Changes*' method of divination and thereby make a breakthrough in the study of the *Zhou Changes*."[dcclvii]

Those who denied the divinatory value of the *Zhou Changes* were also divided into two factions. One faction firmly believed that the *Zhou Changes* was exclusively a philosophical literature that has nothing to do with divination; the other felt that it seemed to be inappropriate to not admit its relationship with divination, in that the "Treatise on Arts and Literature' (*Yiwen zhi* 艺文志) of the *Han shu* 汉书 (History of the Western Han Dynasty [206 B.C.E.-220 C.E]) told us "the (*Zhou*) *Changes* was a book of divination,"[dcclviii] but the Han Confucians regarded its divination as dregs and consider the study of its text (including the "Ten Wings") as the orthodoxy.

In my opinion, as a cultural phenomenon that has continued for thousands of years, divination of the *Zhou Changes* indeed merits a particular study. Otherwise, if we blindly suppress and disparage it, the result will inevitably run counter to our desire. Therefore, I ventured to make a brief introduction to and discussion of the *Najia* method of divination, which has so far become the focus of people's attention, and present my own point of view on the mechanism of calculation from this divinatory system. The name of the essay I wrote for this purpose was originally "Causerie about Divination Method" (*Shifa mantan* 筮法漫谈). To my surprise, after it was published in the academic journal *Zhouyi yanjiu* 周易研究 (Studies of Zhouyi), it aroused intensive response, and a great number of readers sent letters contending that, as an academic journal, although theoretical studies ought to occupy the main contents of the *Zhouyi yanjiu*, it should also take both image-numerology and philosophical connotations into consideration. Therefore, I had to continue to write these essays and form a serial. As in these articles I added some teaching materials related to the *Najia* method of divination, I renamed them "Lectures on the *Najia* Divination Method" (*Najia shifa jiangzuo* 纳甲筮法讲座), which were serially published in the *Zhouyi yanjiu*. It was before their publication that the serial was formally designated the *Najia shifa* 纳甲筮法 (Three-Coin Method of Divination).

A Postscript to the *Najia shifa* 纳甲筮法 (Three-Coin Method of Divination)

In my opinion, when studying divinatory methods, we should absolutely not merely evaluate ourselves by the standard for occultists who are skilled in mantic arts, but also explore the essence and profundity of divination, study its significance for human affairs, and further experience the extraordinary realm of ceaseless creativity conceived in the *Changes* by the standard for superior men who benefit the world without showing themselves off, and whose virtues are broad and can transform the world. To my way of thinking, this is not by an unchangeable eternal state, but by the ceaseless changeability manifested through transformations of its trigrams and hexagrams, the *Changes* interprets our always changing world. This is the reason its eyes always keep vigilant. If we always keep its vigilant eyes in mind, we should carefully, honestly, and objectively investigate the principles conceived in the *Changes*, explore the mechanism of calculation of its divinatory system, and further release unprecedented new discussions on this cultural phenomenon. This meets not only the demands of the times but also the demands of academic conscientiousness.

According to former works of divination, almost all the divinations completely came true. Therefore, most people believe prognostications are surely efficacious, but this is not true. Now that our actual predictions are often inefficacious, there are probably problems in three respects: 1) The mechanism of the calculation of this divinatory system transmitted by ancient people is not rigorous enough; 2) the diviner is not proficient enough; 3) the questioner has evil intentions. Therefore, in my view, the prognostications are not absolutely but relatively efficacious, and it is generally not reliable when some ancient and contemporary authors of the divinatory books claim that their predictions always come true.

Some of the materials and divinatory cases used in this book came from the notes taken down in the 1960s, when I was practicing the *Najia* method of divination. Due to the poor conditions at that time, the origin of some materials was not recorded, and thus the provenance of some divinatory cases was not provided, for which I ask the readers to forgive me.

And now, a scene around 1954 reappears in my mind: In a room only 18 square meters in size, my younger brother and I were reading books and doing homework on the only square table in my family's home while my youngest brother was doing homework on another smaller table below the square one, when my mother was busy doing housework or was sitting on the bed and conceiving a bright future for her children. Past events have faded like a puff of smoke. The old poor house has by now been dismantled, and my loving mother has left us forever.

> Being not filial enough, I could only show my grief through three bows;
> Lingering in sorrow, I am not able to express my lament by six poems.

This elegiac couplet for my mother just expresses my mood at this very moment, when it had been five years since my mother passed away. I would like to make use of the publication of this book to commemorate my mother and console her spirit for her unselfish love.

Liu Dajun
On November 10, 1994, at my study room called *Yunqian shuzhai* 运乾书斋

12.
Opening Speech at the "International Conference on Confucianism and *Changes* Studies"[1]

My respectable leaders, distinguished guests, and participants, ladies and gentlemen:

Under various levels of officials' concerns and support, and through preparation for over a year, the "International Conference on Confucianism and *Changes* Studies," co-sponsored by the Laoshan Scenic Area Administration Committee of Qingdao City and the Center for Zhouyi & Ancient Chinese Philosophy of Shandong University, is now inaugurated! On behalf of the Preparatory Committee, I am extending the most earnest gratitude to all levels of officials and scholars concerned

---

[1] The "International Conference on Confucianism and *Changes* Studies" was held solemnly in Qingdao, and lasted from August 15 to 18, 2005. This academic activity, cosponsored by the Center for Zhouyi & Ancient Chinese Philosophy of Shandong University and the Administration Committee of Laoshan Scenic Area in Qingdao City, aimed to further promote *Changes* scholarship and Confucianism studies so as to revitalize traditional Chinese culture. Over 150 experts and scholars from the United States, Australia, Brazil, South Korea, Hong Kong, Taiwan, and Mainland China participated in the conference.

who supported the conference and extending the warmest welcome to the participants and specialists!

Following the vigor at the turn of the 20th and 21st centuries, the world today presents more strongly the momentum with which multipolar cultures and civilizations coexist and move forward. As one of the most distinctive civilizations to be counted, the great and ancient Chinese civilization has become an important pole in world civilizations. Along with rapid economic development, Chinese people's aspiration for the revitalization of Chinese culture becomes more and more urgent. To expand traditional Chinese culture so as to make it show its due contributions and values, and shine brilliantly in the development of contemporary China and the whole world, has undoubtedly become scholars' unshrinking responsibility and sacred task at present. In the organism of traditional Chinese culture, *Yi* learning and Confucianism constitute the most important components. The former has always been praised as the unexhausted source of Chinese civilization and is valued as the "origin of the great Dao (Way)," the depth and scope of its influence being unrivaled by other traditional Chinese schools; the latter is regarded as the stem of Chinese civilization, which has for all time been active as the orthodoxy at the center of politics and culture in various dynasties for over 2,000 years and has permeated all layers of traditional Chinese culture. We can say without any exaggeration that, without the *Changes* and Confucianism, there would not be a core and main body in traditional Chinese culture. Therefore, in spreading traditional Chinese culture, the expansion of the *Changes* and Confucianism is an indispensable work. Today, in that so many native and overseas scholars gather on invitation to meet at the beautiful coastal city of Qingdao, we are certain to reach the joint purpose of promoting traditional Chinese culture, including *Yi* learning and Confucianism. This just manifests the significance and value of the conference.

Because the conference relates to *Changes* studies and Confucianism, we have to speak of Confucius here. The relationship between Confucius and the *Yi zhuan* (Commentaries on the *Changes*) has always been a focus argued over by *Yi jing* experts and Confucian scholars. Lacking convincing materials in the past, the relationship between Confucius and the *Yi zhuan* has been veiled. Yet, the *Yi zhuan* of the silk manuscripts excavated at Mawangdui and published in the 1990s recorded the discussions between Confucius and his disciples on the *Changes*. These manuscripts can attest to the fact that Confucius studied the *Changes* and took actions according to the principles conceived in the *Changes*, which can verify the assertions of Si-ma Qian 司马迁 (145-90 B.C.E.) and Ban Gu 班固 (32-92) that Confucius "became interested in the *Changes* in his late years"[dcclix] and studied the *Changes* in such an earnest way that "the thong threading together [of] the bamboo slips (of his copy) broke three times."[dcclx] This evidence directly refutes the historical doubts. The Mawangdui silk version of *Yi zhuan* opened a new perspective for us to clarify how the *Zhou Changes* was adopted into the Confucian system and turned out to be a treasure connecting Heaven and Man. By this combination, we can see that Confucianism, even in its primordial form, possessed the all-adoptive and creative spirit, and Confucianism at its very beginning had established inseparable relations with the *Changes*. By the Western Han (206 B.C.E.-9 C.E.) dynasty, with its salient feature connecting Heaven and Man and its abundance of attendant philosophical connotations, the *Zhou Changes* was valued by Confucian scholars as the first of the Five Confucian Classics, becoming an indispensable element of Confucian studies in later dynasties, which further gave rise to the combination and interpenetration between *Changes* studies and Confucianism in their pursuit of value. It was even more the case in the Song (960-1279) and Ming (1368-1644) dynasties; and particularly, the *Yi zhuan* provided a holistic metaphysical system for Song and Ming Neo-Confucianism. Without any exaggeration, we can say that each brilliant Neo-Confucian was a brilliant specialist in the *Changes*. By modern and contemporary times (1840-1949), scholars such as Zhang Taiyan 章太炎 (1869-1936), Xiong Shili 熊十力 (1885-1968), Ma Yifu 马一浮 (1883-1967), Mo Zongsan 牟宗三 (1909-95), and Feng Youlan 冯友兰 (1895-1990) were well versed in both the *Changes* and Confucianism. Nowadays, when research fields are divided into more and more disciplines, we find that many scholars who engage in Confucianism studies tend to disregard *Changes* studies, and vice versa. This obviously does not conform to the original pattern of Confucianism, nor is it in alignment with the paradigmatic correlation between the *Yi jing* and Confucianism, either. Based on this understanding, the Center for Zhouyi and Ancient Chinese Philosophy and the Laoshan Scenic Area Administration Committee have decided to cosponsor this international academic conference to provide a platform for scholars at home and abroad engaging in *Changes* studies and Confucianism, and establish a preliminary basis for further comprehensive studies.

But, since modern times (1840-1919), traditional Chinese culture represented by Confucianism has landed in a predicament. Where China should head for has become an issue perplexing Chinese people for over 200 years, hence the presence of a series of opinions and trends of thought such as "overall occidentalization," "oriental ideology being the foundation with occidental thought being the auxiliary agent," and "occidental thought being the foundation with oriental ideology being the auxiliary agent." So far, since China has stepped into modernization and globalization, how Confucian culture should reestablish its subjectivity in the presence of the forceful occidental culture to exert its function and realize its value in the development of Chinese civilization and the progress of human history has become a great and important issue with which we are confronted. Undoubtedly, it is not only a logical demand of the development of Confucianism itself, but also an inevitable demand of today's development of the world and of China, in that we should adapt ourselves to the requirements of the times and creatively transform Confucianism; that is, give forth new interpretations to modernize it.

Therefore, we must give forth modern interpretations to the original contents of Confucianism so as to create modern Confucian metaphysics to merge Confucianism and modernity. The modernization of Confucianism set forth by present scholars ought to be a kind of modernity generated from the continuity of Chinese history and innateness of its culture, and ought to be a modernization of Confucianism itself rather than a modernity in which the Confucian tradition is purely interpreted by modern concepts and methods, causing the loss of the inherent spirit of Confucianism. Equally important, not only do Confucianism studies need modernization, but also *Changes* studies demand modernization. Modernization of both Confucianism and the *Yi jing* is necessary and inevitable. Since the later period of last century, the most significant historical event in the academic circle was the excavation of a great number of lost manuscripts of the pre-Qin (before 221 B.C.E.), Qin (221-206 B.C.E.), and early Han (206 B.C.E.-220 C.E.) times. The Mawangdui silk version of *Zhou Changes*, the Fuyang 阜阳 bamboo-slip version of the *Zhou Changes*, the manuscripts on the bamboo slips unearthed at Wangjiatai 王家台 and Guodian 郭店 in 1990s, as well as the manuscripts on the bamboo slips of Chu collected in Shanghai Museum, reveal many valuable contents concerning Confucian theories of heart-mind and human nature, the outlook of the mandate of heaven and cosmology, and the Five Classics, including the *Changes*. These materials opened a new academic world for us, allowing the academic circle to review Confucian civilization based on rites and music, and the ideology, sects, and evolution of primary Confucianism, as well as various problems related to studies of Confucianism, which are expected to lead us to more definite conclusions. As one contemporary scholar claimed, "The time to reappraise the significance and value of the Six Classics and early Confucianism has arrived."[dcclxi] We should take this opportunity and probe into these valuable materials to achieve more in Confucian culture, Confucian ideology, the transmission and evolution of the *Changes*' original meanings, and to differentiate the new script connotations from those of the ancient script. This research will certainly deepen our understanding of the original Confucian Classics, which could enhance and expand our understanding and grasp of the entire history of Chinese ideology, Confucianism studies, and Chinese philosophy, as well as give rise to historical changes in academic perspectives, ideas of value, and research approaches, and constitute a contemporarily unique academic style, thereby shedding light on and exploiting Confucian and *Changes*' contemporary significance and value.

The modern significance and value of Confucianism and the *Yi jing* are subjects of the times, which relate to both the present time and the future, to both China and the world. Today, the survival and development of human beings in the world are confronted with severe challenges. Just as British historian Arnold J. Toynbee said, "Since human beings' position in nature obtained superiority, human beings' survival has never been so endangered as it is today."[dcclxii] Not only is this point reflected in the relationship between humans and nature, but also in interpersonal relationships, and has been manifested as environmental pollution, conflicts of civilization, polarization of wealth and poverty, moral deterioration, spiritual crisis, and so on. It is reported that all these problems result from the Western worldview and mode of thinking separating the subject from object, and from its utilitarian rationalism.

Occidental civilization has been subjected to suspicion and challenges. Different from the occidental civilization, oriental Confucian culture's worldview advocates for the unity of Heaven and Man, and its mode of thinking is characterized by holism; it attaches importance to man's moral cultivation and enhancement of man's realm of life and seeks mutual participation between Heaven and Man as well as interpersonal harmony. It has always been permeated with deep humanistic concerns. All these features have become a valuable source of thought to tackling man's crisis of survival. The ideal of "all-inclusion by which various things obtain their full development"[dcclxiii] conceived in the *Yi jing* may enhance man's spiritual realm and broaden man's mind, and bring forth an idea for the coexistence of different nationalities with different cultures; the idea of "harmony with different opinions"[1] set forth by Confucius provides a platform for dialogue and communication for us to deal with the conflicts between different civilizations. The moral doctrine of "Never do to others what you would not like them to do to you"[2] creates a guideline for the establishment of global ethics; the ultimate concern of pacifying one's person and firmly establishing one's destiny upheld by Confucianism gives us precious sources of thought to solve a spiritual crisis; and so forth. As a matter of fact, in recent years, influences of Confucianism and the *Yi jing* have become more and more powerful. They are functioning in various fields, such as in international relationships, economic trade, social administration, and so on, arousing attention from all corners of the world. To reexamine, redefine, and unite the abundant cultural resources of Confucianism and the *Yi jing*, and make them adapt to the times, could not only relieve the variety of crises occurring today in the world and thereby make contributions to the future development of human beings, but also enhance the competitive ability and force of cohesion of Chinese peoples, being of theoretical and realistic significance for the upsurge of the Chinese economy and the harmony of the whole society.

---

[1] Roger T. Ames and Henry Rosemont, Jr. (trans.), *The Analects of Confucius: A Philosophical Translation* (13:23). New York: Ballantine Books, 1998, 168-169, modified.

[2] Arthur Waley (trans.), *The Analects* (15:23). Beijing: Foreign Languages Teaching and Research Press, 1997, 207.

Opening Speech at the "International Conference on Confucianism and Changes *Studies*"

Three years ago, in 2002, the Center for Zhouyi and Ancient Chinese Philosophy of Shandong University and the Laoshan Scenic Area Administration Committee successfully cosponsored the "Cross-strait Conference on Chinese Philosophy and *Changes* Studies," where over 200 people participated in the conference and the atmosphere was friendly and ardent. Today, we again cosponsor this conference related to the subjects of Confucianism and *Changes* studies. Of course, we may also discuss other subjects in which the participants are interested. It is my hope that each participant, according to the spirit of "sincerity," voices out his or her points of view about various issues concerning Confucianism and the *Yi jing* so as to make the conference a complete success. Now, let me announce that the "International Academic Conference on Confucianism and *Changes* Studies" is formally inaugurated! May all the attending officials, all the distinguished guests, and all the scholars be healthy and peaceful, and achieve more in their research fields; as it says in the *Yi jing*: "Heaven will help him as a matter of course; this is good fortune!"[1] May the conference find complete success! Thank all of you for your attendance!

---

[1] Richard John Lynn, *The Classic of Changes: A New Translation of the I Ching as Interpreted by Wang Bi*. New York: Columbia University Press, 1994, 226.

13.
A Preface to Mr. Liu Junzhu's *Yi jing and Contemporary Life* (《易经》与现代生活)

Through the historical development of *Changes* studies, it can be seen that the *Zhou Changes* has experienced an evolution from being a manual of divination to a book of wisdom concerning the unity of Heaven and Humanity. In other words, the profound connotations conceived in the *Zhou Changes* itself were not manifested with divination but were gradually disclosed. As it says in the "Treatise on Art and Literature" (*Yiwen zhi* 艺文志) of the *Han shu* 汉书 (History of the Western Han Dynasty [206 B.C.E.-9 C.E.]), "The Dao (Way) of the *Changes* was profound, which was completed by three sages [Fu Xi, King Wen, and Confucius (551-479 B.C.E.)] and experienced three antiquities."[dcclxiv] Therefore, the *Zhou Changes* was not composed by one person at one time but was formed over a relatively long history. During this course, the *Zhou Changes* realized its transformation from a book of divination to being a work of learning concerning Heaven and humanity. It was Confucius who played a crucial role in this transformation. The relationship between Confucius and the *Zhou Changes* has been a much-discussed issue in Chinese academic history. Although it was recorded in the *Analects of Confucius*, *Shi ji* 史记 (Historical Records) and the *Han shu* 汉

书 (History of the Western Han Dynasty [206 B.C.E.-9 C.E.]) that Confucius had studied the *Changes*, because the *Zhou Changes* was a book of divination which was not in alignment with the Confucian spirit, many intellectuals denied this fact and even argued that Confucius had nothing to do with the *Changes*. The excavation of the Mawangdui silk manuscript of the *Zhou Changes* provided new evidence for us to use in clarifying this history. The chapter of "Essentials" (*Yao* 要) not only clearly recorded the discussions on the *Changes* between Confucius and his disciples, but also highlighted Confucius's views on the relationship between its mantic attributes and the academic quality of the *Zhou Changes*, since Confucius said: "As for the *Changes*, I do indeed put its prayers and divinations last, only observing its virtue and righteousness."[1] This is to say, Confucius did not aim to study mantic art, but to explore the virtues and righteousness of the *Changes* conceived in the book. The *Zhou Changes* obtained an entirely new significance in Confucius's eyes and realized a kind of transformation of the hermeneutic field of vision from a dimension of man's life by external exploration, through resorting to gods and spirits in divination, to a dimension of internal pursuit in terms of personal virtue and good deeds. Although there were also records of explanations of the *Changes* based on virtues in the *Zuo zhuan* 左传 (Zuo's Commentary on the *Spring and Autumn Annals*) and the *Guo yu* 国语 (Sayings of the States), it was through Confucius's elaboration on the *Yi jing* from perspectives of virtue that made the *Zhou Changes* enhanced to be a book of wisdom. The excavation of the Mawangdui silk manuscript of *Yi zhuan* (Commentaries on the *Changes*) further demonstrated that there were various interpretive texts in pre-Qin [i.e., before 221 B.C.E.] times. It was these lost manuscripts that manifested the infinite meanings and essences of the *Zhou Changes*. The received version of the *Yi zhuan*, also known as the "Ten Wings," was the most outstanding representative of this transformation. Not only did the "Ten Wings" establish the hermeneutic style by which the hexagrams and the statements can be mutually interpreted to clearly reveal the relationship between images and hexagram and line statements in theory; it also interpreted the meanings and essence conceived in the basic text of the *Zhou Changes*

---

[1] Edward L. Shaughnessy, *I Ching: The Classic of Changes*. New York: Ballantine Books, 1996, 241, slightly modified.

as the Dao (Way) of Heaven, Earth, and Man, endowing the *Zhou Changes* with the characteristics of ceaseless creativity, changeability, timeliness, and ideals of humanistic cultivation, to finally interpret the *Zhou Changes* as a kind of learning which was extremely broad, including everything, and to accomplish a leap for the academic quality of the *Zhou Changes*. Since then, both the image-numerological school and the meanings and principles school developed on the basis of the received version of *Yi zhuan* and could not surpass it. This shows the great significance of the "Ten Wings."

After the "Ten Wings" came out, the intellectuals who studied the *Changes* could be generally affiliated either with the image-numerological school or the meaning and principle school. As the editors of the *Siku quanshu* 四库全书 (Complete Collection of the Four Treasuries) assert, "The *Changes* is that which elaborates on the Dao (Way) of Heaven so as to illuminate human affairs. The divinatory cases noted down in the *Zuo zhuan* 左传 (Zuo's Commentary on the *Spring and Autumn Annals*) might preserve the lost methods of the official diviners, while the Han (206 B.C.E.-220 C.E.) Confucians expounded images and numbers which were not far from the ancient times. But the image-numerology was then transformed and led to the prevalence of Jing Fang 京房 (77-37 B.C.E.) and Jiao Yanshou's 焦延寿 *Changes* which finally lapsed into prophesy, and then it was further transformed into the *Changes* of Chen Tuan 陈抟 (871-989) and Shao Yong 邵雍 (1011-1077), who endeavored to explore changes and transformations of the natural world, when the *Changes* began to be separated from people's daily lives. Wang Bi 王弼 (226-249) completely swept away images and numbers, and discoursed on the *Changes* in Daoist terms, which then transformed into the approach of Hu Yuan 胡瑗 (993-1059) and Cheng Yi 程颐 (1033-1107), who explicated Neo-Confucianism through their interpretations of the *Changes*; the tradition further transformed into the approach of Li Guang 李光 (1078-1159) and Yang Wangli 杨万里 (1127-1206), who supported their opinions with examples from Chinese history. This gradually gave rise to disputes on the *Changes*. These two schools which include the above-mentioned six sects then launched attacks against each other."[dcclxv] These affiliations of different schools and sects quite conform to historical facts. The image-numerological school took form in the Western Han dynasty (206 B.C.E.-9 C.E.), and treated images and numbers as the first task in research on the *Changes*, attaching importance to the clarification of the qualities of imagery and numerology of the *Changes*. The extremity of this tendency gave rise to the forced associations between image-numerology and the hexagram and line statements, and masked the Dao (Way) communicating Heaven and Man under the image-numerological network. Wang Bi's scholarship on the *Changes* marked the emergence of the meanings and principles school, which considered the exposition of the meanings and principles conceived in the *Changes* to be the most important duty, and paid attention to the explication of these connotations. The extremity of this tendency led to an overreading of the meanings and principles implicit in the lines of the text and commentaries. Consequently, rootless and empty words were spawned, and the great Dao (Way) of Heaven and humanity fell into language games. In my opinion, image-numerology and meanings-principles are two inseparable aspects of the *Changes*, in which the former is the body while the latter reflects its function. Without images and numbers, the *Changes* would lose its foundation and could not be called the *Changes*; without meanings and principles, the *Changes* would lose its fundamental aim and could not be referred to as a classic. In the history of *Changes* studies, the distinction between these two schools has been to manifest each school's unique feature and gravitation, but this does not mean that there has not been any compatibility between them. As different schools, both have advantages and disadvantages, and in the history of *Changes* scholarship they add radiance and beauty to each other, showing their own particular splendors. From today's perspective, the diversity of the schools and sects of *Changes* scholarship only manifested the broadness of the Dao (Way) of the *Changes*. As the Song (960-1279) Neo-Confucian Hu Yuan 胡瑗 (993-1059) asserts, the *Changes* could "fully reveal the profound meanings of Heaven and Earth and the thread running through human affairs,"[dcclxvi] which not only discloses the broad academic purpose and field of vision of the *Changes* but can also be regarded as the general feature of the evolution of the study of the *Changes*. Ancient people created the radiant *Changes* scholarship, explaining layer by layer the subtle Dao (Way) of *Changes* that could not only reach the metaphysical, infinite realm of Heaven and Earth, but also touch our mundane life; their genuine understanding about the universe, society, and life was thereby infused into our daily life. The work not only has a general concern about the cosmos, but also an ultimate concern about humanistic study. None of these contents is merely a fussy, empty argument but instead is a real manifestation of the significance of the cosmic life at present.

The reason the *Changes* could maintain its vigorous vitality in the past was related to its ability to guide and prompt the progress of China over time. If the *Changes* is still expected to maintain its vitality, it must be able to respond well to what is happening today and what will happen in the future, and to draw sustenance from reality. Corresponding to the multiple paths of contemporary development, today's research on the *Changes* also shows a diversity in which people are engaging in new exegesis of the *Zhou Changes* from multidisciplined perspectives such as philosophy, historiography, literature, art, management, physics, mathematics, astronomy, biology, and so on, attempting to discover some thought congruent with modernity from the ancient *Changes*, both to revitalize it and guide contemporary social life and to push human civilization forward, as well. This magnum opus of Mr. Liu Junzhu 刘君祖 is a substantial achievement of contemporary study on the *Changes* and holds this belief. As Mr. Liu has been very diligently studying the *Changes* for over two decades and has experienced all aspects of life through his insights inspired by the *Changes*, the contemporary business management, organizational management, business policymaking and so on involved in this book are closely associated with contemporary social relations. Closely grasping the pulse of times, his book sheds light on the profound connotations of the advancement of virtue, changing along with time, and the fulfillment of the great cause related to the Dao (Way) of the *Changes* in contemporary life. Although this work is not completely based on a traditional hermeneutic style, it follows traditional image-numerological and meaning-principle approaches, and through analyzing the hexagram and line statements and the complexity of different permutations of the hexagrams, it contributes incisive discussions on various levels of contemporary social life, including historical trends, international situations, decision making for enterprises, business management, family relationships, ways to manage one's life in the world, and so on, which are pertinently, intricately, and perfectly associated with the thoughts conceived in the *Changes*. I am filled with admiration for the clarity of his style of writing, the sharpness of his eye, and the profundity of his understanding of the *Changes*. The views that "in the course of research on some learning, instead of only taking its theory into consideration, we must take contemporary things, events, and new experiences to verify it"[dcclxvii] and "the whole book of the *Yi jing* seems to be a highly-compacted data bank in which the sophisticated hexagram and line statements hide abundant information"[dcclxviii] reflect his feelings and experiences resulting from many years of research on the *Changes*. Mr. Liu and I have been keeping in touch for many years, over the course of which I have come to respect his moral quality and admire his academic achievements. Now, before his new book called *Yijing yu xiandai shenghuo* 易经与现代生活 (The *Yi jing* and Contemporary Life) comes out, I am pleased to add these words to the book, which can both show my feeling after my reading of the manuscript and be regarded as a preface to satisfy his request.

Liu Dajun
In May 2006, in my study room called *Yunqian shuzhai* 运乾书斋

14.
Characteristics of the *Yi* Studies in the 20th Century: A Preface to the *Collected Quintessential Articles of the Yi Studies of the Past Century and Decade* (1900-2009)[dcclxix]

From the outset of the 20th century, traditional Chinese academia and culture were impacted by Occidental academia and culture, hence the lingering arguments regarding the priority of the East or West, and on the superiority of the Ancient or Present. Discussions on the legitimacy of Chinese philosophy are no more than the succession of the arguments of the past century. "Philosophy" and "religion"—which were originally concepts loaned from Occidental culture—are unavoidably involved in the above-mentioned arguments, whereas the unique learning of traditional Chinese culture, such as the studies of Confucian Classics, exegetics, and philology, experienced unprecedented changes in the reforms of the times.

Chinese ideology and culture are rooted in Confucianism, the lifeline of which is the study of Confucian Classics. Among the system of the

Confucian Five Classics and Four Books, the *Yi jing* (the Classic of Changes) is positioned as the first and has always been venerated as the fountainhead and source of the running water of Chinese culture, the influence of which is saturated in each layer of traditional Chinese culture and thus has molded the quality of Chinese culture. As Mr. Feng Youlan 冯友兰 (1895-1990) asserted: "The *Yi jing* is a spiritual phenomenology of Chinese civilization."[dcclxx] The three-millennium-long history of the development of the culture of the *Yi* studies turns out to be the most representative miniature of the development of Chinese culture. The study of the *Changes* in the 20th century is located in the great swirl of the arguments about the West and East, modernity and antiquity. In the times when Chinese culture was experiencing an entire transformation, the study of the *Changes* also met a change never before encountered in the past 3,000 years. In reviewing the *Changes* studies of the 20th century, we can find two most important events: One was that the scholars impacted by Western academia broke traditional research modes and launched new studies through new academic perspectives and historical concepts; the other was that some extremely valuable archaeological manuscripts were excavated, which presented new literature to us, exhibiting rich contents of the earlier *Changes* scholarship that could enable us to unravel a great number of unresolved problems of the past.

First, the impact of Occidental academia led to the renovation of historical concepts and a changing of academic approaches to the study of the *Changes*, and scholars broke ancient research paradigms embodied by terms of image-numerology, meaning-principle, Han tradition, Song tradition, Classics, and apocrypha, and toiled in new research fields, such as the study of the text (*jing* 经) and commentaries (*zhuan* 传) of the *Zhou yi*, philosophy conceived in the *Zhou yi*, the relationship between natural science and the *Zhou yi*, the history of *Changes* scholarship, and so on. In the study of the text and commentaries of the *Zhou yi*, the achievements of the *Gu shi bian* 古史辨 (Debates on Ancient History) school that was active in the 1930s particularly represent this tendency. They unraveled the sacred halo around the *Zhou yi*, relegated it to being just one book of the ancient literature, and objectively studied its quality, time of composition, authorship, and origin. These studies in light of new historical horizons became the core of the *Yi* studies in the early half of the 20th century.

Scholars such as Gu Jiegang 顾颉刚 (1893-1980), Yu Yongliang 余永梁, Gu Moruo 郭沫若 (1892-1978), Qian Mu 钱穆 (1895-1990), Qu Wanli 屈万里 (1907-79), and Li Jingchi 李镜池 (1902-75) engaged in novel research and discussions on the authors, time of completion, and qualities of the text and commentaries of the *Zhou yi*. Among them, the most eminent is Gu Jiegang, who made use of oracular inscriptions on bones and tortoise shells of the Shang dynasty and argued that the time of completion of the hexagram and line statements ought to have been the beginning of the Western Zhou dynasty (1046-771 B.C.E.). Later studies just supplement this point of view but could not override or subvert it. After the May 4th Movement (1919), along with the beginning of the dissemination of Marxism in China, a number of scholars began to study the *Zhou yi* from the angle of materialism. Among them were scholars like Guo Moruo 郭沫若 (1892-1978). Although he regarded the *Zhou yi* as containing historical materials, as did the *Gu shi bian* 古史辨 (Debates on Ancient History) school (as far as the time of publication is concerned, Guo Moruo's point of view about the history of the Shang and Zhou dynasties conceived in the *Zhou yi* was published even earlier than Gu Jiegang's), he exposed the political and social structure as well as the spiritual production of the Shang and Zhou dynasties from materialistic conceptions of history. In spite of the fact that the discussions in some of these studies are not rigorous enough and some conclusions are overextrapolated, they opened a new domain of discourse for *Yi* studies, which not only greatly pushed forward the studies of the earlier *Changes* but also improved the study of the history of remote Chinese antiquity. In the meantime, a good number of scholars represented by Yu Xingwu 于省吾 (1896-1984), Jiang Shaoyuan 江绍源 (1898-1963), Wen Yiduo 闻一多 (1899-1946), and Gao Heng 高亨 (1900-86) launched research on the text and commentaries of the *Zhou yi* per se. Different from the former scholars who venerated the basic text of the *Zhou yi* as a sacred canon, they believed there was neither any subtle and profound philosophy nor any moral edification inherent to it. In their opinions, the hexagram and line statements are nothing but notes from divination, and thus they mainly devoted themselves to the demonstration of what they alleged the real meanings of the text as oracular utterances to be, hence the overall discarding of the traditional image-numerological and meaning-principle approaches. Though today it seems that there are many places needing scrutiny or rediscussion regarding their studies, and even that there are many mistakes in their conclusions, their approach was revolutionary then; it broke down the fences of traditional approaches and established a new paradigm for the study of the basic text of the *Zhou yi*. The above-mentioned approaches were not only the most distinctive characteristics of the earlier half of the 20th century's *Yi* studies, but also the brightest spot of the studies of the basic text in the whole 20th century's *Yi* research. All these predecessors' writings on the *Yi* available to us are collected in these *Collected Articles*. Additionally, a note worth raising here is that, in these predecessors' probings, most scholars concluded that the Ten Wings of the Commentaries were completed in the mid-Warring States period (475-221 B.C.E.). Just as Mr. Wu Huaiqi 吴怀祺 asserts on this issue: "There are various points of view on the date of completion of the Commentaries and unanimity has not been reached on the time of completion of the sequence of the Ten Wings, yet the main body of the Commentaries was surely completed in the Warring States period."[dcclxxi] Most scholars accept this point of view. In the past, I myself also held that the main chapters of the "Ten Wings" were completed in the mid-Warring States period. Yet, along with my deepening understanding of the Mawangdui 马王堆 silk manuscript of the *Yi zhuan*, I find that the point of view cannot endure. This will be discussed in other paragraphs of the preface.

The most distinctive feature of the *Zhou yi* compared to other Confucian Classics lies in its image-numerological system. The term "image-number" might provisionally be said to have first appeared in the *Zuo zhuan* 左传 (Zuo's Commentaries on the *Spring and Autumn Annals*) record of the 15th year of Duke Xi 僖公 (645 B.C.E.) of the state of Lu: "Duke Hui 惠公 of the state of Jin sighed after he was captured and taken to the state of Qin 秦: 'If my father the previous Duke had followed the counsel of Shi su's 史苏 prognostication, I should not have been trapped like this.' Minister Han Jian 韩简 who was also captured by the Qin army reasoned: 'Signs on the drilled and scorched tortoise shells exhibit the images, whereas divination by yarrow stalks demonstrates numbers. There are images on tortoise shells upon its birth and the images will expand and split, which can lead to numbers. It is your father's breaching of morality but not the numbers or fate that accounted for your failure.

What has it got to do with Shi su's divination?'"[dcclxxii] Du Yu 杜预 (222-285) annotated this record in this way: "It means that tortoises show the oracle by images, yarrow stalks by numbers. Images and numbers are thus produced, hence the oracles."[dcclxxiii] The *Zuo zhuan zheng yi* 左传正义 (*Correct Meaning of Zuo's Commentary on the Spring and Autumn Annals*) elaborates: "While divining, the tortoise shells demonstrate signs and thus reveal oracles with the images of metal, wood, water, fire, and earth. The hexagrams are obtained by the division of yarrow stalks which reveal oracles by the numbers."[dcclxxiv] As the *Book of Changes* was originally an oracular book, the original meaning of image-number ought to have been derived from divination. It is said in the *Xici zhuan* 系辞传 (*Commentary on the Appended Phrases*): "The holy sages instituted the trigrams and hexagrams, observed the images contained in them, and then appended the statements, in order to indicate good fortune and misfortune."[dcclxxv] It was along with this course of study that the philosophical connotations or meanings and principles of the *Zhou Changes* were brought forth. Wei Litong 魏荔彤 (1670-?) asserts in his *Da yi tong jie* 大易通解 (*A Thorough Interpretation of the Great Changes*): "The meanings and principles or philosophical connotations of the *Zhou yi* originated from its images and numbers. Before the statements were appended, the *Changes* possessed no words, when the meanings and principles were the conceptual body with image-number as its function; since the statements have been appended, images and numbers turned out to be the body, whereas the meanings and principles were exposed by the statements and play the role of function."[dcclxxvi] This view is the best interpretation for the following part in the *Xici zhuan* 系辞传 (*Commentary on the Appended Phrases*):

> The Master said: Writing cannot express words completely. Words cannot express thoughts completely.
> Are we then unable to see the thoughts of the holy sages?
> The Master said: The holy sages set up the images in order to express their thoughts completely; they devised the hexagrams in order to express the true and false completely. Then they appended the statements and so could express their words completely.[dcclxxvii]

So, in the basic text of the *Zhou yi*, the meanings and principles are derived from its images and numbers, and the breadth and depth of content in terms of the meanings and principles were greatly expanded by the "Ten Wings" traditionally credited to Confucius. It is on account of this that the study of the *Changes* in past dynasties never got beyond these two approaches.

As we mentioned previously, the study of the *Zhou Changes* in the 20th century had overridden the division into image-numerology and meaning-principle schools. But this does not mean that the study of these two traditional approaches may be discarded, as any branch of scholarship has to root and develop from its traditions; traditional image and numerology-oriented study of the *Changes* also developed in the past century. So far as the study of images and numbers in the 20th century is concerned, there were both creations of new domains and deepened studies of the traditional approach. In the earlier period of the past century, the great masters who were genuinely well versed in the study of the *Changes* include: Shang Binghe 尚秉和 (1870-1950) who authored *Jiao shi yi gu* 焦氏易诂 (Exegesis of Jiao's *Changes*) and *Jiao shi yi lin zhu* 焦氏易林注 (Annotations to *Jiao's Forest of Changes*); Xu Ang 徐昂 who composed *Jing shi yi zhuan jian* 京氏易传笺 (Notes to *Jing's Commentary on the Changes*) and *Zhou yi Yu shi xue* 周易虞氏学 (The Learning of the *Zhou Changes* Based on [the Interpretations of] Yu Fan]; and Li Yizhuo 李翊灼 who wrote *Zhou yi Yu shi yi jian ding* 周易虞氏易笺订 (Notes from Reading *Yu's Commentary on the Zhou Changes*). All of these works can be regarded as magnum opuses of the study of the Han Yi tradition succeeding the philological school masters of the Qing dynasty. Additionally, there was a great master of the *Changes* whose name is Ma Yifu 马一浮 (1883-1967), who integrated *Changes* scholarship, Daoism, Buddhism, and Confucianism into one entity, taking both image-numerology and meaning-principle into consideration. His masterpieces on the *Changes* include "Edification by the *Changes*" (*Yi jiao* 易教) and "Exposition of the Implications of the Images" (*Guan xiang zhi yan* 观象厄言), which are collected in *Ma Yifu ji* 马一浮集 (Collected Works of Ma Yifu) (vol. 1). Since these works belong to monographs or some chapter or chapters in various books, they will not be included in the *Collected Articles*. Yet, we should always remember these masters' contributions to the study of the *Changes*. Besides this, in the 1950s, Shen Diemin 沈瓞民 (1878-1969) discriminated and analyzed in detail the source and formation of image-numerological formulae. Mr. Qu Wanli's 屈万里 (1907-1979) *Xian qin han wei yi li shu ping* 先秦汉魏易例述评 (Accounts of and Comments on the Formulae of the *Changes* from the pre-Qin [before 221 B.C.E.] to Wei [220-265] Dynasties) is highly valuable in distinguishing the formulae of the late Zhou dynasty from those of the Han tradition. After the foundation of the People's Republic of China (1949), the study of the *Changes* was at a low ebb for a long period of time, and the study of image-numerology in mainland China ground to a halt. It was not until the middle of the 1980s that traditional image-numerology was positively affirmed in my *Zhou yi gai lun* 周易概论 (An Introduction to the *Zhou Changes*). In 1984, Mr. Xiao Jiefu 萧萐父 (1924-2008) planned, prepared, and organized the first national academic conference on the *Zhou yi*. In 1987, I planned, prepared, and organized the first international academic conference on the *Zhou Changes* in mainland China, in which over 200 scholars from six countries and regions participated—an exceptionally grand occasion. It was through extensive broadcasting of the conference by mass media that the study of the *Changes* was brought to a new phase of prosperity in mainland China. Then, in 1988, we prepared and constructed the *Zhouyi* Research Center in Shandong University to devote ourselves to the study of image-numerology. In the same year, we sponsored the academic journal *Zhouyi yanjiu* 周易研究 (Studies of *Zhou yi*), the only journal of *Yi* studies allowed to be published in mainland China. Over the past two decades, it was with the help of this journal that scholars could access and appreciate the variety of articles available and submit their own papers to the journal, extensively pushing forward the study of the *Changes*. Since its foundation, the *Zhouyi* Research Center at Shandong University has published three volumes of *Xiang shu yi xue yan jiu* 象数易学研究 (Studies of Image-numerology of the *Changes*), having also published a series of articles related to image-numerology. Moreover, many books concerning image-numerology came out. Through the efforts of the faculty of the center and other insightful scholars, the study of traditional image-numerology has recovered and has improved in breadth and depth. In the meantime, influenced by Western natural science, the study of the *Changes* from the angle of science and technology became a new topic in the 20th century's *Yi* studies. Studies on the relationship between the *Changes* and natural science are mainly intended to decipher and elucidate the image-numerology of the *Changes* from modern theories and concepts of science. For instance, the study of the relationship between Leibniz's binary system and the Former-heaven diagram can well exemplify this approach. Therefore, study of the relationship between the *Changes* and natural science belongs to a new image-numerological mode that emerged under the influence of ideas in modern science. In other words, the mode is but a mutation of traditional image-numerology of the *Changes* in modern society. Not only does it involve the relationship between the image-numerological mode and ancient Chinese science and technologies, but it also relates to the issue of taking theories of modern science to interpret image-numerology of the *Zhou Changes*. Before the foundation of People's Republic of China (1949), Hang Xinzhai 杭辛斋 (1869-1924), Shen Zhongtao 沈仲涛, Xue Xueqian 薛学潜, Ding Chaowu 丁超五 (1884-1967), and Liu Zihua 刘子华 (1899-1992) had made innovative explorations of the correlation between the *Changes* and natural science. Since the 1980s, along with "traditional Chinese culture fever" and "*Zhouyi* fever," study of the scientific value of the *Changes* has been proliferating vigorously. But most of these studies lapsed into eisegesis and thus quickly hauled down their colors in defeat. By the 1990s, more and more scholars began to rethink this topic and held that it was significant for us to probe the influence of the *Zhouyi* upon ancient Chinese science and technology, especially upon Chinese astronomy, whereas the connection between image-numerology of the *Changes* and modern science should be circumspectly considered.

Along with the rise of the modern discipline of Chinese philosophy, the study of traditional meanings and principles accordingly turned into the study of the "philosophy of the *Changes*." This research set out sporadically from the beginning of the 20th century, and by the 1960s, scholars began to examine the thought of the text and commentaries through the vision of Marxist dialectical materialism, which led to debates on whether the thought reflected in the *Yi jing* is attributable to materialism or idealism. Additionally, the methodology in studying the *Zhou Changes* was also discussed. Many scholars—including Feng Youlan 冯友兰 (1895-1990), Ren Jiyu 任继愈 (1916-2009), Li Jingchun 李景春

(1904-79), Wang Ming 王明, Fang Li 方鼒, Li Jingchi 李镜池 (1902-75), and Shen Diemin 沈瓞民 (1878-1969)—took part in these discussions. But most of the studies with this special background broke away from the historical vein of *Changes* scholarship. Because these studies labeled the contents of the *Zhou Changes* and characterized the documents as materialist or idealist, the essence and splendor of the philosophy of the *Changes* were not brought to light. But during this period, an excellent, highly philosophical work on the *Changes*—Xiong Shili's 熊十力 (1885-1968) *Qian kun yan* 乾坤衍 (Elaboration on Qian [☰] and Kun [☷])—came out. Though some points of view in the book need further discussion, the insight into the Confucian internal cultivation and external statecraft elucidated in the book is generally acceptable. Along with the spring breeze of the opening to the outside world in the 1980s, the study of the *Changes* ensnared by the segregation of materialism from idealism in the past gradually achieved amelioration, and the study of the philosophy of the *Changes* began to run deep, which was mainly manifested in the significant exploration of two aspects. One aspect was the philosophical retrospective on the origin of the *Yi jing*—its oracular function. The other was related to discussions on the value orientation and cosmic consciousness conceived in the text and commentaries of the *Zhou Changes*. As for the former aspect, Swiss analytical psychologist C. G. Jung proposed "synchronicity" to explicate the reason that divinations by the *Yi jing* can enable us to have foresight, while Chung-ying Cheng 成中英 accounted for the rationality of divination by the *Yi jing* with the experience accumulated before the *Yj jing* had been composed. For the other aspect, in the 1930s, Su Yuanlei 苏渊雷 (1908-95) and Xiong Shili 熊十力 (1885-1968) successively elucidated the quality of inexhaustible creativity conceived in the *Zhou Changes*. Then, the eminent poetlike philosopher Thome H. Fang 方东美 (1899-1977) also constructed his metaphysics with the quality of inexhaustible creativity of the great *Changes* as its core. Since 1990, attention to ecology and bioethics has been rising in mainland China, hence there are more and more studies on the bio-philosophy of the *Changes* and the ecological philosophy conceived in the *Yi jing*. These studies concerning the philosophy of the *Changes*, so to speak, have completely overstepped the field of vision of the course of ancient meanings and principles, and could be regarded as a new development of the philosophy of the *Changes* under contemporary consciousness—of course, many of these studies lack sufficient depth, and some studies concerning East-West comparison still remain superficial. Particularly important, the counterpart of the sentence of *Sheng zhi wei yi* 生生之谓易 (literally, producing and reproducing or inexhaustible creativity is called the Change) in the received version of *Zhou Changes* was *Sheng zhi wei yi* 生之谓易 (producing or creativity is called the Change) in the Mawangdui silk manuscript of the *Zhou yi*, their philosophical connotations being much different.

The study of the scholarship on the *Changes* is also related to the philosophy of the *Changes*. Many contents in the previously mentioned image-numerology and meaning-principle studies belong to the study of the history of *Changes* scholarship, which will not be repeated here. Yet, it is noteworthy that, on account of different divisions of branches of learning, scholars engaged in *Changes* scholarship are mainly those engaged in philosophy studies in mainland China, whereas in Taiwan, *Yi jing* scholars are mainly those occupied with the study of Chinese literature. This phenomenon brought the study of the history of *Changes* scholarship in mainland China under a philosophical vision. This on one hand deepened our cognition of the thought of traditional *Changes* scholarship and its development, but on the other hand also shrouded many noteworthy fields of *Changes* scholarship in the guise of Classics studies. We contend that, from the Han (206 B.C.E.-220 C.E.) through Qing (1644-1911) dynasties, the *Zhou Changes* was always venerated as the first of the Five Confucian Classics; therefore, the study of the history of *Changes* scholarship must be conducted under the perspective of Classical studies and must be put in the context of the academic temperament of traditional Classical studies and their development. Otherwise, we can neither explore the spiritual and cultural implications of the *Changes* nor shed light on the functions of *Changes* scholarship in the development of culture. We should not confine the study of the *Changes* to just analyzing conceptual implications and the development of the *Changes* scholarship; as Zhu Xi 朱熹 (1130-1200) asserts, "There are images in the *Changes*. If we make use of them, we can find their systemic analogical connections, and if we extend them, we can enlarge their field of successful application. They are not allegories only. But the Han (206 B.C.E.-220 C.E.) scholars tried to explore their concreteness and lapsed into stagnation, whereas Wang Bi 王弼 (226-249) and his

Characteristics of the *Yi* Studies in the 20th Century: A Preface to the *Collected Quintessential Articles of the Yi Studies of the Past Century and Decade* (1900-2009)

followers attempted to expand their functions but were accused of frivolousness and lack of foundations."[dcclxxviii] I believe that the study of the history of *Changes* scholarship as Classics studies is sure to be able to deepen and carry forward the overall study of the entire Confucian Classics. In this sense, it reminds me of what at the outset of the preface was mentioned—namely that, on account of the influence from Western academia, there appeared many new domains and subjects in the study of the *Changes* in the 1940s, forming some Occidentalized paradigm. But a cycle of Jia zi 甲子 (i.e., 60 years) later, along with China's comprehensive prosperity, demands to return to tradition are arising, and in a sense the Occidental mode of thought and disciplinary structure has begun to become a kind of hindrance to the study of traditional academia. Is this a vivid embodiment of the rule of changes that the extreme Bo [䷖, Peeling, 23] will surely give rise to Fu [䷗, Returning, 24] and extreme Pi 否 ䷋ (Stagnation, 12) will certainly lead to Tai 泰 (Peace or Fluency, 11) in the *Zhou Changes*?

Second, another "great event" in the 20th century's *Yi jing* study was the excavation of a great deal of literature concerning the *Changes*. The documents related to the *Changes* unearthed in the past century mainly include the following five kinds: one is the silk manuscript of the *Zhou yi* excavated at Mawangdui 马王堆, Changsha 长沙 City, Hunan 湖南 Province in 1973, including the basic text of the 64 hexagrams and six chapters of commentaries of *Er san zi wen* 二三子问 (Several Disciples Asked), *Xi ci* 系辞 (Appended Statements), *Yi zhi yi* 易之义 (The Properties of the *Changes*), *Yao* 要 (The Essentials), *Miu he* 缪和, and *Zhao li* 昭力; one is the Han 汉 bamboo-slip manuscript of the *Zhou yi* excavated at Shuanggudui 双古堆, Fuyang 阜阳 City, Anhui 安徽 Province in 1977; another is the Warring States period (475-221 B.C.E.) bamboo-slip manuscript of the "record of divination" unearthed at Tianxingguan 天星观, Jiangling 江陵 City, Hubei 湖北 Province in 1978; yet another is the Qin 秦 (221-206 B.C.E.) bamboo-slip manuscript of *Gui zang* 归藏 excavated at Wangjiatai 王家台, Jiangling 江陵 City, Hubei Province in 1993; the last one is the Warring States period Chu 楚 bamboo-slip manuscript of *Zhou yi* purchased by the Shanghai Museum from Hong Kong.

From the end of the 1970s to the outset of the 1980s, study of the numerical trigrams, tetragrams, and hexagrams (*shuzi gua* 数字卦)

became the hot spot in *Changes* scholarship. Studies of three-number trigrams and six-number hexagrams originated from the strange characters on bones and bronze objects, as well as earthen wares. In 1956, Li Xueqin 李学勤 for the first time correlated these strange characters to divinatory numbers. In 1978, in an academic symposium held in Changchun 长春, Jilin 吉林 Province, Zhang Zhenglang 张政烺 (1912-2005) applied the milfoil-stalk method of divination mentioned in the *Xici* 系辞 (Commentary on the Appended Phrases) to the deciphering of the numerical symbols on what was then the latest unearthed bones at Zhouyuan 周原 and verified that they ought to be divinatory numbers. Later, many scholars took part in the research and discussions related to numerical hexagrams. So far, some approve of and some still disagree with this assertion. But it is undeniable that numerical hexagrams have become an important issue that cannot be ignored in the *Changes* scholarship. After the text of the Mawangdui silk manuscript of the *Zhou yi* was published in 1984, the study of the silk manuscript of *Zhou yi* became a new hot spot. Zhang Zhenglang 张政烺 (1912-2005), Rao Zongyi 饶宗颐, Yu Haoliang 于豪亮, Han Zhongmin 韩仲民, Li Xueqin 李学勤, Zhang Liwen 张立文, and Liu Dajun 刘大钧 successively published a good number of related articles. But the silk manuscript of the *Yi zhuan* (Commentaries on the *Changes*) was not published until the mid-1990s. Once it had been promulgated, it occasioned an upsurge of studies, hence a good number of achievements related to its dating, academic attributes, exegesis, image-numerology, and the situations of the *Yi* studies in the earlier period, and so on. The deeper the studies go, the more academia acknowledges that the silk manuscript of the "Commentaries" can not only solve many problems pending in the academic history but also greatly help the studies on the earlier period *Changes* scholarship to run deep, exposing the abundant and broad cultural and philosophical connotations of the earlier scholarship on the *Changes*. This irrefutably demonstrated the academic significance and value of the studies of the silk manuscript of *Yi zhuan*. In my opinion, the highest value of the silk manuscript's text and commentaries of the *Zhou yi* lies in that it provides an intact literature for the study of the Western Han (206 B.C.E.-25C.E.) New-text Confucian Classics, which had lost transmission more than a millennium before. This manuscript and the Chu bamboo-slip manuscript of *Zhou yi* can confirm each other and enable us to see the Han dynasty New-text *Zhou yi* the way it was, and the pre-Qin Old-text *Zhou yi* the way it was, having greatly enlarged our vision in studying the Confucian Classics. Therefore, I call these archaeological documents a "world-shaking event" in *Changes* scholarship. For instance, the silk manuscript of the *Yi zhuan* (Commentaries on the *Changes*) can play a very important role for us in exploring the relationship between Confucius and the *Zhou yi* and the completion of the received version of the *Yi zhuan*.

The relationship between the *Changes* and Confucius has been a very important issue in the history of Confucian Classics studies. Scholars used to cite from Confucius' utterance that "*Jia wo shu nian, wushi yi xue yi, keyi wu da guo yi* 加我数年, 五十以学《易》, 可以无大过矣 (literally, Give me a few more years, even if I began to study the *Changes* from the age of 50, I would not make big mistakes)" from the *Analects* (7: 17) as testimony to demonstrate that Confucius studied the *Changes*. But many scholars apply the Lu 鲁 version *Analects* and repunctuate the utterance as "*Jia wo shu nian, wushi yi xue, yi keyi wu da guo yi* 加我数年, 五十以学, 亦可以无大过矣 (literally, Give me a few more years, even if I had began learning knowledge from the age of fifty, I also would not make big mistakes)" to deny Confucius's having studied the *Changes*. Former scholars such as Ouyang Xiu 欧阳修 (1007-73), Zhao Rumei 赵汝楳, Yao Jiheng 姚际恒, and Cui Shu 崔述 (1739-1816) all doubted whether Confucius had composed the "Ten Wings" or some part of them in the received version of the *Zhou Changes*. Along with the upsurge of doubting their antiquity, some overly suspicious scholars take this as testimony denying Confucius's involvement in the *Zhou yi*. It can be seen that whether Confucius composed the *Yi zhuan* or not was a disputable issue. But the excavation of the silk manuscript *Yi zhuan*, within which there is a chapter called *Yao* 要 (The Essentials) recording the discussions on the *Changes* between Confucius and his disciples in detail, has surely manifested the close relationship between Confucius and the *Changes*. The particularly important thing is that the chapter *Yao* recorded Confucius's attitude to the divinatory attributes of the *Changes* and his concerns about the book. Though the chapter *Yao* was lost and unavailable to former scholars, in this chapter, Confucius expresses his keynote for *Changes* studies, which has exerted extremely great influence upon later scholars' approaches to the *Changes*. As it says in the Chapter *Yao*:

The Master said: "As for the *Changes*, I do indeed put its prayers and divinations last, only observing its virtue and propriety. Being mysteriously assisted and reaching the numbers, and understanding the numbers to reach virtue, is to have humanness (?) and to put it into motion properly. If the commendations do not lead to the number, then one merely acts as a magician; if the number does not lead to virtue, then one merely acts as a scribe. The divinations of scribes and magicians tend toward it but are not yet there, delight in it but are not correct. Perhaps it will be because of the *Changes* that sires of later generations will doubt me. I seek its virtue and nothing more. I am on the same road as the scribes and magicians but end up differently. The gentleman seeks blessings through the conduct of virtue; that is why he sacrifices, but little; he seeks auspiciousness through the righteousness of his humaneness; that is why he divines, but rarely. Do not the divinations of priests and magicians come last!"[dcclxxix]

In this paragraph, Confucius sets forth the issue of the positions of divination and virtue. Obviously, he contends that virtue and rectitude are superior to divinations and formulates a methodology for the study of the *Changes* in asserting that, "being mysteriously assisted and reaching the numbers, and understanding the numbers to reach virtue, is to have humanness (?) and to put it into motion properly." "Being mysteriously assisted and reaching the numbers" refers to the idea that (the holy sage) "was mysteriously assisted by the gods [*shenming* 神明, literally, 'the numinous and the bright'] and so initiated the use of yarrow stalks. He made Heaven three and Earth two and so provided the numbers with a basis"[dcclxxx] mentioned in the beginning of the *Shuogua* 说卦 (Discussion of the Trigrams, one of the "Ten Wings"). "Understanding the number to reach virtue" holds the same meaning as the following: The holy sage "observed the changes between *yin* and *yang* and so established the trigrams. As the trigrams are begun and are dispersed through the movement of the hard and soft lines, he initiated the use of such lines. He was in complete accord with the Dao and with Virtue, and the principles involved conform to righteousness. He explored principles to the utmost and dealt thoroughly with human nature, and

Characteristics of the *Yi* Studies in the 20th Century: A Preface to the *Collected Quintessential Articles of the Yi Studies of the Past Century and Decade* (1900-2009)

in doing so arrived at the workings of fate."[dcclxxxi] With a comprehensive survey of the Chapter *Yao*, we can find that the new methodology Confucius specifies is congruent with the sayings in the part of *Shuo gua* mentioned above. Then Confucius worries: "Perhaps it will be because of the *Changes* that sires of later generations will doubt me." But what is the doubtful point? Confucius's attitude to the *Changes*, especially to the divinations of the *Changes*, is different from that of the magicians and scribes, in that his purpose with the *Changes* is "to observe its virtue and propriety." Put in another way, Confucius thought virtues were the more important things. He contends that "the gentleman seeks blessings through the conduct of virtue; that is why he sacrifices, but little; he seeks auspiciousness through the righteousness of his humaneness; that is why he divines, but rarely." This attitude is consistent with the attitude mentioned in the *Analects* that Confucius "reveres the Spirits and keeps them at a distance." (6:22) The emphasis on Dao (Way) and virtue in *Shuogua* 说卦 (Discussion of the Trigrams) and *Wenyan* 文言 (Commentary on the Words of the Text), and the advocacy of virtue in *Tuan* 彖 (Commentary on the Judgments), *Xiang* 象 (Commentary on the Images), and *Xici* 系辞 (Commentary on the Appended Phrases), are specific embodiments of Confucius's concept of the core value of the *Changes* and the transference and renovation from the magicians and oracular historians' divination to observing virtue. Regarding this new purport in the study of the *Changes*, Confucius also felt uneasy and was afraid to be criticized by later generations, which is manifested in his anxiety: "Perhaps it will be because of the *Changes* that sires of later generations will doubt me."

But the method in interpreting the *Changes* by combining divination and virtue was not initiated by Confucius at all, in that there were antecedents. In "the Ninth Year of Duke Xiang" (564 B.C.E.) in the *Zuo zhuan* 左传 (Zuo's Commentaries on the *Spring and Autumn Annals*), Mu Jiang 穆姜 interpreted Hexagram Sui [☱☳, Following, 17] like this: "As it says in the *Zhou Changes* that 'Sui consists of *yuan* 元, *heng* 亨, *li* 利, and *zhen* 贞 and there will be no blame,' where *yuan* is the leader of men; *heng* is the coincidence of beauty; *li* is coalescence with righteousness; [and] *zhen* is the very trunk of human affairs. (The noble man) embodying benevolence is sufficient to be a leader of men; the beautiful virtue in him is sufficient to make men live in accordance with propriety; he engenders fitness in people sufficient to keep them in harmony with righteousness, and his constancy is firm enough to serve as the trunk for human affairs.[dcclxxxii] He who does not tarnish these four virtues will follow the tendency and get out of the place without any blame. But as a woman I took part in a sinister plot, and being in an inferior female position, I have no benevolence; this cannot match the quality of *yuan*. I disturbed the governance of the state, which cannot be called *heng*; my bad deeds do harm to myself, which cannot be called *li*; I discarded my noble position and became promiscuous, which cannot match the quality of *zhen*. Those who have these four virtues can follow without blame, but I possess none of them: how can I be freed from this place! I have done so many evil things, shouldn't I be blamed?"[dcclxxxiii] The comments here on the divination from the angle of virtue are congruent with Confucius's purport on the *Changes* as elucidated in the Chapter *Yao* 要 in the silk manuscript of the *Zhou yi*. Moreover, the four virtues explicated by Mu Jiang are fundamentally the same as what the *Wenyan* 文言 (Commentary on the Words of the Text) elucidates, demonstrating that Mu Jiang's explanation was highly valued by Confucius. The priority of virtue can also be seen in the statements of the basic text of the *Zhou Changes*, as the third line statement of hexagram Heng [☷, Duration, 32] tells us, "This one does not persevere in maintaining his virtue, so he might have to bear the shame of it, for the constancy would be debased,"[dcclxxxiv] and the fifth line of hexagram Ji ji [☷, Ferrying Complete, 63] is affiliated with it in that "the neighbor in the east [hinting at the Shang dynasty which was losing virtue] slaughters an ox, but this falls short of the simple *yue* sacrifice of the neighbor [implying the smaller state of Zhou which was accumulating virtue and finally replaced the Shang dynasty and established the Zhou dynasty], which really provides that one with blessings."[dcclxxxv] These statements are also manifestations of the emphasis of virtues.

But the words genuinely and systematically explicating virtues should be the "Ten Wings" credited to Confucius. These words passed down to the Han dynasty (206 B.C.E.-220 C.E.), under the name of Confucius, turned out to be an authoritative interpretation of the basic text of the *Zhou Changes*. Thus far, the study of the *Changes* had fundamentally separated itself from divination, and the basic text of the *Changes* was interpreted by man's conduct.

Characteristics of the *Yi* Studies in the 20th Century: A Preface to the *Collected Quintessential Articles of the Yi Studies of the Past Century and Decade* (1900-2009)

Although Confucius attempted to pursue the virtues conceived in the *Zhou yi*, he still paid attention to divination, by which the numbers can be obtained, and by those numbers virtue can be viewed. And in spite of the fact that the destination of Confucius was different from that of magicians and official diviners, the road they tread is the same. Therefore, both the received version of the "Ten Wings" and the silk manuscript of the commentaries preserved affirmations of divination, among which the clearest expression was recorded in Chapter *Yao* (The Essentials) of the silk manuscript as follows: "When the Master aged he delighted in the *Changes*; when at home it was at his mat, and when traveling it was in his pack. [...] Zigong 子贡 doubted: 'Does the Master also believe in milfoil divination?' The Master responded: 'I am right in only seventy out of one hundred prognostications. Even with the prognostications of Liangshan of Zhou one necessarily follows them most of the time and no more.'"[dcclxxxvi] Many discussions on divination in the *Xi ci* 系辞 (Commentary on the Appended Phrases), *Shuogua* 说卦 (Discussion of the Trigrams), and *Xiang* 象 (Commentary on the Images) might be traced back to this record about Confucius's attention to divination.

But later-generation Confucians still worried that people might doubt Confucius on account of his application of divination and thus softly separated divination from the essence of the *Zhou yi*. For example, in the "Treatise on Literature and Art" (*Yiwen zhi* 艺文志) of the *Han shu* (History of the Western Han Dynasty [206 B.C.E.-9 C.E.]), the books interpreting the text and commentaries of the *Zhou Changes* were put in the first place of the first category of Confucian Classics, whereas the contents related to divination were put in categories of milfoil stalks and tortoise shells (*Shi gui* 筮龟) or miscellaneous divinations (*Za zhan* 杂占), which were arranged under the categories of calendar and the five agents, the role of divination being much reduced. This kind of division was continued from the Han (206 B.C.E.-220 C.E.) through the Qing (1616-1912) dynasties, one after another. Importantly, only Zhu Xi 朱熹 (1130-1200) discerned what others had not discovered and exposed the original divinatory feature of the *Zhou Changes* in his *Zhouyi ben yi* 周易本义 (The Original Meaning of the *Zhou Changes*). Yet, because the separation of the *Zhou yi* from divination had formed a habitual tendency, Zhu Xi's effort did not make the *Zhou Changes* return to its original image-numerological sense.

The image-numerology we mention today is not the image-numerology previously referred to in the *Zuo zhuan* 左传 (Zuo's Commentary on the *Spring and Autumn Annals*) and the *Shuogua* 说卦 (Discussion of the Trigrams). For the meanings and principles of the *Zhou yi*, as mentioned above, along with the elevation of Confucius's position, the "Ten Wings" turned out to be an integral part of the *Zhou yi*. By extant documents, it can be seen that, at least before the end of the Eastern Han dynasty (25-220), scholars had interpreted the "Ten Wings" by imagery. In their opinion, the words of the "Ten Wings" also resulted from "observing images." This hermeneutics was really bound to raise suspicion.

By comparing some characters in the silk manuscript with those in the received version of the *Zhou yi*, it can be seen that the silk manuscript was copied in or after the reign of Gaozhu 高祖 (the first emperor of the Western Han) (r. 206-195 B.C.E.) and before the reign of Emperor Wen (r. 179-157 B.C.E.). And by contrast, many testimonies demonstrate that the received version of *Xici* 系辞 (Commentary on the Appended Phrases) was reformulated upon the silk manuscript of the *Xici*. In light of this, I have pointed out that *Xici*, *Tuan* 彖, and *Xiang* 象 might have been completed very much earlier, comparatively, but the words of these wings ought to have been formulated when Emperor Wu 武帝 (r. 140-87 B.C.E.) enacted the order to establish the Five Classics Erudites (in 136 B.C.E.). At least the received version of *Xici* should have had its form finalized during this period. Additionally, there is another piece of material that could attest to this assertion. It says in the "Author's Postscript" in the *Shi ji* (Historical Records) written by Sima Qian 司马迁 (145 B.C.E.- 90 B.C.E.):

> *Tai shi gong* 太史公 (literally, the Official Historian, the title of the author, i.e., Sima Qian) says: "our forefather had these words: when five hundred years had passed since the death of Duke Zhou, Confucius was born; it has been five hundred years since Confucius's death to now: he who can succeed the sage's time, rectify the *Yi zhuan* 易传, carry forward the connotations

of the *Chun qiu* 春秋 (Spring and Autumn Annals), and base himself upon the original meanings of the *Shi* 诗 (Classic of Poetry), *Shu* 书 (Classic of History), *Li* 礼 (Classic of Rites), and *Yue* 乐 (Classic of Music), will be this man! Will be this man! I will not decline to shoulder this responsibility."[dcclxxxvii]

Here the reference of "rectifying the *Yi zhuan* (Commentaries on the *Changes*) demonstrates that *Yi zhuan* at that time was not perfect and needed Sima Qian's 司马迁 (145-90 B.C.E.) efforts to rectify or integrate the related materials. Meanwhile, Sima Qian mentioned that "the *Changes* was related to heaven-earth, *yin-yang*, and five-agents, so its strong point is explication of changes."[dcclxxxviii] This manifests that there ought to have been "five-agents" in the *Yi zhuan* Sima Qian had seen, which is consistent with the silk manuscript of the *Yi zhuan*, but there is no mention of "five-agents" in the received version of *Yi zhuan*. Additionally, there were many reference materials in the literature of the Han dynasty allegedly cited from *Yi zhuan* but unavailable in the received version of the *Yi zhuan*. This demonstrates that, before the finalization of the received version of the *Yi zhuan*, there were many versions of *Yi zhuan* being disseminated. After Emperor Wu established the Five Classics Erudites, the *Changes* turned out to be a kind of official learning by which people could receive scholarly honor or official rank. To unify the standard, the variety of *Yi zhuan* being transmitted was integrated into one complete version, which was officially determined. This might be the cause of Sima Qian's mentioning "rectifying (or integrating) the *Yi zhuan*."[dcclxxxix] The rather recently finalized received version of the *Yi zhuan* (at least the received version of *Xici*)—under the circumstances of those times of an atmosphere of venerating the Classics and the Dao (Way)—was credited to Confucius, one of the three sages, and thus was elevated to the same level as the text derived from the observation of images. It can be seen that, in the Eastern Han dynasty (25-220), the annotations to the *Changes*, at least to the *Yi zhuan*, had slipped away from the right track.

The above-mentioned is my view on the relationship between Confucius and the *Changes* and the completion time of the final revision of the *Yi zhuan*, which is capable of mutual proof based on both the excavated and received literature. In the 1920s, Mr. Wang Guowei 王国

维 (1877-1927) said: "It is fortunate for us to live today when the unearthed materials in addition to received materials are available to us. The former can be based to supplement and rectify the latter, and attest to some facts of the ancient books. It is not until today that we can satisfy the method of double evidence."[dccxc] So, the study of the excavated documents is quite significant. Along with the deepening of the study, research on bamboo slips and silk manuscript of the *Changes* so far has become the commanding height and new hot spot in *Changes* scholarship, and new achievements constantly come out, which may lead to rewriting the history of the Confucian Classics studies.

As previously mentioned regarding the transference of the core values of the *Changes* from magicians and scribes' emphasis on divination to the stress on virtues, because later-generation Confucians worried that people might suspect Confucius's favor toward divination, divination was stealthily separated from the meanings of the *Classic of Changes*. The Tang dynasty (618-907) scholar Li Dingzuo's 李鼎祚 *Zhou yi ji jie* 周易集解 (Collected Explanations of the *Zhou Changes*) preserved abundant materials of the Han (206 B.C.E.-220 C.E.) image-numerological tradition, in which the annotations of Eastern Han (25-220) experts, and especially Ma Rong 马融 (79-166), Xun Shuang 荀爽 (128-190), and Yu Fan 虞翻 (164-233), were kept comparatively intact. The Han tradition image-numerology based on these annotations absolutely differs from the original image-numerology. But people had formed the habit of defining the Han *Yi* tradition as the image-numerology of the *Changes*, so we still classify the collected articles by this custom and attribute divination studies to the category of *Shu* 术数 (The Arts of Calculation) as previous Confucians did. But the contents of the earlier *Shu* 术数 and image-numerology were similar to the *Fang shu* 方术 (Occult-oriented Arts) in the Han dynasty, which does include divination. Even in the Han dynasty (206 B.C.E.-220 C.E.), many Confucian elite literati were well versed in prognostic art, such as: Xiahou Shichang 夏侯始昌 thoroughly understanding the Five Classics and teaching the *History* and Qi 齐 tradition of *Poetry*; Jing Fang 京房 (77-37 B.C.E.) majoring in the *Changes*; Yi Feng 翼奉 majoring in the Qi tradition of *Poetry*; and Li Xun 李寻 majoring in the *Classic of History*. In the beginning of the Han dynasty, Tian He 田何 taught both the "contemporary meanings" and "ancient meanings" of the *Changes*. The former was related to "observing of virtues," which drastically improved the fusion of the *Zhou yi* and Confucianism, and made the interpretations transcend the original meanings of the *Changes*. The latter might be so-called "magicians and official diviners' divinations." The contents relating to the *Changes* in the *Shu shu* 术数 (Arts of Calculation) and *Fang shu* 方术 (Occult-oriented Arts), and those concerning prognostications by anomalies in Meng Xi's 孟喜 and Jing Fang's 京房 *Changes*, as well as the *Yi wei* 易纬 (Apocrypha of the *Changes*), also might be traced back to the "ancient meanings" of the *Changes* taught by Tian He 田何. A great portion of the *Yi wei* 易纬 involves *gua-qi* 卦气 theory (correlating the seasonal points to the trigrams and hexagrams) as credited to Meng Xi 孟喜 and Jing Fang 京房. So, the phenomenon that some eminent experts at *Shu shu* 术数 and *Fang shu* 方术 were also well versed in the *Changes* might have originated from this fusion.

Later people were afraid that the *Shu shu* 术数 "might be made up by those small men who painstakingly desire to discern the Dao (Way) of heaven and tend to diminish the great into the small, and draw the far-reaching back to what is close, hence destroying the Dao (Way) and making its understanding difficult."[dccxci] The "Treatise on Literature and Art" (*Yiwen zhi* 艺文志) of the *Han shu* 汉书 (History of the Western Han Dynasty) further explained why the *Shu shu* 术数 gradually gave rise to confusions, as in the section of Five-Agents: "The Five Agents refer to five regular forms and vital forces, which originated from the theory of the cycle of the five virtues. By extreme analogy, it is adaptable to all aspects in detail by which the *Shu shu* 术数 magicians foretell fortune or misfortune, and thus circulates in the world, gradually causing confusions."[dccxcii] Therefore, since the Han dynasty, the *Shu shu* 术数 brought forth confusion and disintegrated the Dao (Way). By the Qing dynasty (1644-1912), the editors of the *Si ku quan shu* 四库全书 (Complete Collection of the Four Treasuries) classified the catalogue of *Shu shu* 术数 into six items, including numerology (*shuxue* 数学), phenologiomancy (*zhanhou* 占候), geomancy (*xiangzhai xiangmu* 相宅相墓), auguromancy (*zhanbu* 占卜), physiognomy, and *Yin-yang* and Five-Agents. Today, the *Shu shu* 术数 is generally divided into three aspects. One is concerned with longevity, including the prolonging of life, herbal medicine, *Qi gong* 气功, alchemical refinery, sexual skills, diet, skills of abstinence from eating cereals, and so on; one is about prognostication, including divination by tortoise shells, divination by the *Changes*, divination by other books, hemerology (*zeji* 择吉), divination by three kinds of divinatory boards (*san shi* 三式), oniromancy (*zhanmeng* 占梦), auguromancy (*cezi shu* 测字术), geomancy (*kanyu* 堪舆), astrology (*zhanxing shu* 占星术), meteorology (*zhanhou* 占候), physiognomy (*xiangren shu* 相人术), the art of fate calculation (*suanming shu* 算命术), and so on; one is miscellaneous divination, including sorcery, necromancy, conjuring, witchcraft, etc. Yet, in a narrow sense, *Shu shu* 术数 mainly refers to the former two categories.

If we classify ancient people's studies of the *Changes* into two types, of (1) *Shu shu*-oriented *Changes* and (2) Classic-oriented *Changes*, then the former in the cultural development was the origin of both types. Therefore, though today the latter belongs to the study under the discipline of Chinese philosophy and the former is confined to folklore, neither can ignore the primal studies of the *Shu shu*-oriented *Changes*. Interestingly, since the 20th century, the study of the *Zhou Changes* has continued following the historical choice of the past two millennia, so the Classic-oriented *Changes* scholarship and philosophical *Changes* scholarship became the orthodoxy in academic circles, spawning a great volume of articles. In contrast, though the study of *Shu shu* gradually recovered and thus there have been more and more works concerning divination, Feng shui 风水 (literally, Wind & Water, also rendered as geomancy), physiognomy, *Qi meng* 奇门, *Liu ren* 六壬, and *Ming li* 命理 (literally, principle for fate, a.k.a. art of eight-character and Chinese astrology), and so on, by and large, many of them still lapse into "diminishing the great into the small and drawing the far-reaching back to what is close,"[dccxciii] and few of them have genuinely probed into the origin and quintessence of *Shu shu* 术数.

After the general survey of the 20th century's study of the *Changes*, we should particularly point out that, since 1949, *Changes* scholarship in Taiwan as an organic component of the *Yi* studies of China turned out to be unusually conspicuous, which can be represented by works of the experts on the *Changes* such as Gao Ming 高明, Qu Wanli 屈万里 (1907-79), Li Hanshan 李汉三, Hu Zifeng 胡自逢, Cheng Shiquan 程石泉

(1909-2005), Huang Qingxuan 黄庆萱, Gao Huaimin 高怀民, Dai Lianzhang 戴琏璋, Xu Qinting 徐芹庭, and those New-Confucians such as Thome Fang 方东美 (1899-1977), Tang Junyi 唐君毅 (1909-78), and Mou Zongsan 牟宗三 (1909-95). Additionally, the journals of *Zhong hua yi xue* 中华易学 (*Changes* Studies of China) sponsored by Chen Lifu 陈立夫 (1898-2001) and Li Kaixuan 黎凯旋, as well as *Yi xue yan ju* 易学研究 (Studies of *Changes* Scholarship) sponsored by Zhang Tingrong 张廷荣, and their discourses have been making not a trivial contribution to the popularity and enhancement of *Yi* studies in Taiwan.

The 20th century has become history. The study of history relates to the issue of "documents." But "documents" only are not enough; it also needs healthy "consciousness of philology." Especially after having experienced the vacuum of thought of the Cultural Revolution (1966-76), people hold little "consciousness of philology" and know almost nothing of it. Most of the articles from the 1970s to the 1980s, under the influence of the Cultural Revolution, are implicated with "leftist" ideology, and with almost no references, but they state one's personal views with certainty. Yet, little did they know that, as early as the end of the Qing dynasty (1616-1912) and the beginning of the Republic of China, some related achievements had far surpassed their academic level. Since the 1990s, along with rapid economic development, the pace of modern life has become faster and faster, and the whole society is suffused with blundering wind eager for quick success and instant benefits. Consequently, many researchers cannot wholeheartedly focus on research, and particularly due to the connection of promotion of professional title with the amount of published articles, a great quantity of articles has been spawned. Most of these "highly yielded" writings are mechanically pieced together from similar achievements published in previous years, contributing no novel ideas at all. This phenomenon was excusable in the 1970s and 1980s, in that then there was "no consciousness of philology." By the 1990s, though, these secondhand documents were flooding in, and even now are still spreading. This kind of "pseudoconsciousness of philology" is more worrying. On this account, we have devoted lots of resources and manpower to the compilation of the *Bai nian yi xue jing hua ji cheng* 百年易学精华集成 (Collected Quintessential Articles of the *Yi* Studies of the Past Century and Decade [1900-2009]) in order first to make a retrospective and summary of the *Yi* studies of the past century and decade, and to make an adequate preparation for the next step—the composition of the history of the *Yi* studies of the 20th century—and then to provide references to the 20th-century *Changes* scholarship for further studies, and collectively exhibit the excellent achievements of each subject and the level of research so as to remove the negative effects of the pseudo consciousness of philology and push *Changes* scholarship forward rather than mark time or retreat. Though we strive to make the *Collected Articles* as essential as possible, we cannot guarantee that we could absolutely prevent every pseudo philological article from being selected. In light of this, we need the readers' forgiveness.

There are generally two modes for the compilation of historical materials and literature: One is in the order of chronicle; the other is by categories. On these grounds, our integral notion for the selection of the articles is: first of all, making a macroscopic table of contents to collect as many articles as possible, which can reflect features of different periods, then putting the excellent articles belonging to the same subject together, and finally arranging them, under different categories, in light of their problematic qualities and the chronological order of writing in order to expose the contextual affiliations of different issues under different categories. Because in practical manipulation there were differences between the ease and difficulties in collecting the articles, on the whole, we attempt to optimize the collection through the classification of "Preliminary Compilation" and "Continued Compilation." The one that includes work coming out in publication is the "Preliminary Compilation," which is further classified into eight columns: 1) Studies of the Text and Commentaries of the *Zhou yi*; 2) Studies of Excavated Literature; 3) Studies of Image-numerology; 4) Studies of the Philosophy of the *Changes*; 5) Studies of the History of *Changes* Scholarship; 6) *Zhou yi* and Chinese Culture; 7) *Zhou yi* and Natural Science; and 8) *Zhou yi* and *Shu shu* 术数 (The Arts of Calculation). Though this kind of process of selecting and editing articles greatly amplified the amount of work, it also greatly enhances the academic content and value, and provides more convenience for users.

The collection of the past century's articles is a work to carry forward our cause and forge into the future. In the past century, *Changes* scholarship realized a turn from the Classical research paradigm into a modern research paradigm, bringing forth many significant and valuable achievements, and a decade has passed in the 21st century. It is now the time to summarize and reflect upon *Changes* scholarship of the past century and decade. But this summary and reflection must be based upon a sufficient grasp of the materials, and upon an in-depth and accurate understanding of the development, characteristics, and achievements of the past century's *Yi* studies. It is our hope that this collection will provide help toward this summary and reflection so as to improve the completion of outstanding achievements concerning the 20th century's *Yi* studies and provide references and inspiration for future studies of the *Changes*.

At last, we make a simple review for the course of the compilation of the collection. At the end of the past century, Professor Ni Ce 倪策, an eminent Sinologist of Cornell University, who established friendship with our center many years ago, passed away. Before his death, he donated the replicated articles concerning the *Changes* and the materials clipped from newspapers and journals over his whole life to our center. The time span of these materials encompasses nearly 90 years from 1900 to 1988. Particularly, the original materials taken from the newspapers and journals from the 1920s to the 1940s, which themselves have value as relics of a previous cultural period and reflect the style and feature of the *Yi* studies of their time, have turned out to be a rare treasure on account of their short-time release and small circulation. Now, when the collection is to go to press, we refer to these materials to honor his memory.

As the only research institute of the *Changes* under the Ministry of Education of China, the Center for Zhouyi and Ancient Chinese Philosophy of Shandong University is supposed to make an overall review and summary for the 20th century's studies of the *Changes*. So, the center made a decision to organize manpower and resources in 2004 in order to make an overall and systematic search, collection of, and sorting out of all of the articles in Chinese published since 1900. I assumed the post of chief-editor, and my colleague Li Xinping 黎馨平 was concretely responsible for the organizing of manpower and at first selecting the articles published in the journal of *Zhouyi yan jiu* 周易研究 (Studies of Zhouyi) and those collected in our center's library. In January 2005, we began to collect and select overseas articles. Professor Lai Guisan 赖贵三 from Taiwan's Normal University was in charge of the collection of overseas materials. There were over 20 scholars and graduate students who joined in this work. The participants mainly include Li Qiuli 李秋立, Han Huiying 韩慧英, Gao Yuangui 高源贵, Guo Yongzhen 郭永振, Zhang Kebin 张克宾, Gao Yuan 高原, Chen Yanjie 陈彦杰, Zhu Rui 朱瑞, Ma Qianqian 马倩倩, Gu Jiming 谷继明, Hu Shiying 胡士颖, Wang Tianzong 王天宗, Yang Xuexiang 杨学祥, and Lü Xiangguo 吕相国. This project took us five years and was completed in the end of 2009. To guarantee continuity and integrity, articles and documents from 1900 to 2009 were also collected. During this process, we collected about 13,100 items for a table of contents, and over 9,700 articles were available, of which 6,500 articles were reviewed and 1,500 articles were selected. In selecting the achievements of the past century and decade as the contents in the Preliminary Compilation, our editors absolutely did not take into account whether the viewpoint is in congruity with our own or not as the criterion for acceptance or rejection but took as an important standard whether an article can represent ingenious achievements reflecting a time of great change, or whether it inherits the tradition along with the author's particular insights or not. Owing to the intention to keep the original features and horizons of the time, for the articles of the earlier period or unique papers, we tried our best to collect all of them, no matter whether their points of view are insightful enough or not. Therefore, the large-sized collection consisting of over 20 million Chinese characters embodies this kind of spirit:

> Neither one nor inconsistent, different paths lead to the same destination;
> Both clarified and annotated, the variety of views is gathered together.

This is a couplet written by me, and I would like to contribute it to the publication of the collection. This reminds me of an event that occurred more than 20 years ago: In the winter of 1989, Mr. Shi Wei 施维 scheduled the organization of a large-scale and comprehensive collection of the previous Confucians' works of the *Changes* from the Han dynasty (206 B.C.E.-220 C.E.) up to then, and asked me to be in charge of the compilation of a large-sized contribution—*yi xue ji cheng* 易学集成 (Collected Works of *Changes* Scholarship). After that, he kept writing to me, and I responded constantly to perfect the table of contents. Though at last this work was not accomplished, I still replied in such a way: "Those since antiquity who wanted to accomplish great causes never lacked specific plans in their hearts, but it is not advisable having accomplished schedules in one's heart. Without a long-term schedule, it will be difficult for one to end well; with a too calculated schedule, it will be difficult for one to start well. [...] Let alone how few overly calculated schemes there are in the world. Therefore, owing to the originality of Qian [☰, symbolizing heaven], the beginning of the myriad things emerges. Where there is a good beginning, there will be a great accomplishment." Our deeds of today just meet the historical opportunity that could enable us to accomplish this milestone cultural project. Is it a kind of destiny? In the unseen world, we just responded to our fate [i.e., sense of mission] with schedules but without excessively calculated schemas, and with organized manpower and material resources to plunge into this project. Additionally, we specially invite Mr. Shi Wei, as the initiator in charge of the designing, editing, and publication of the book, to realize our aspiration established 20 years ago. More coincidentally, next year is the 110th anniversary of our Shandong University, and as the time span of the articles collected from 1900 to 2009 also equals to 110, we will dedicate this collection to the anniversary. It is also a kind of destiny!

I sincerely extend my thanks to Mr. Lian Zhan 连战, and professors Rao Zongyi 饶宗颐, Tang Yijie 汤一介, and Li Xueqin 李学勤 for their inscriptions for the *Collected Quintessential Articles*.

> With a smile on the clouds we see the peach blossoms
> When 30 years have passed we have just arrived at home
> From now on along with the spring breeze and rain
> We will follow the running water to the ends of the earth.

It took us five years to complete this collection by 2009, when 30 years have just passed since I was transferred to work at Shandong University. This poem composed by Huang Shangu 黄山谷 (1045-1105), a Confucian, vividly reveals my present feelings, hence its citation as the end of the preface.

January 2010 at my study room called *Yunqian shuzhai* 运乾书斋

Endnotes

i   Li Xueqin 李学勤 (ed.), *Chunqiu zuo zhuan zhengyi* 春秋左传正义 (Correct Meaning of *Zuo's Commentary on the Spring and Autumn Annals*). Beijing: Beijing University. Press, 1999, 269.

ii   Ibid., 870-1.

iii   Ibid., 1254.

iv   Li Xueqin 李学勤 (ed.), *Zhou li zhushu* 周礼注疏 (The *Zhou Rituals* with Zheng Xuan's Commentary and Jia Gongyan's Subcommentary). Beijing: Beijing University Press, 1999, 637.

v   Lin Zhongjun 林忠军, *Zhouyi zhenshi xue chanwei* 周易郑氏学阐微 (A Subtle Elucidation of Zheng Xuan's Scholarship on the *Changes*). Shanghai: Shanghai guji Press, 2005, 439.

vi   Ibid., 439.

vii   Richard John Lynn, *The Classic of Changes: A New Translation of the I Ching as Interpreted by Wang Bi*. New York: Columbia University Press, 1994, 89, slightly modified.

viii   Wang Xianshen 王先慎, *Hanfei zi jijie* 韩非子集解 (Collected Explanations of the *Hanfei zi*), in the *Zhuzi jicheng* 诸子集成 (Collected Works of the Famous Philosophers), vol. 5. Beijing: Zhonghua shuju, 1954, 109.

ix   Lu Deming 陆德明, *Jingdian shiwen* 经典释文 (Exegetical Texts of the Classics). Shanghai: Shanghai guji chubanshe, 2013, 73.

x   Liu Yujian 刘玉建, *Zhouyi zhengyi daodu* 周易正义导读 (A Guide Book to the *Correct Meaning of the Zhou Changes*). Jinan: Qilu shushe Press, 2005, 92.

xi   Lin Zhongjun 林忠军, *Yi wei daodu* 易纬导读 (A Guide Book to the *Apocrypha of the Changes*). Jinan: Qilu shushe Press, 2002, 124.

xii   Xu Shen 许慎 (c.58-c.147), *Shuowen jiezi* 说文解字 (Explanation of Simple and Composite Characters). Beijing: Zhonghua shuju, 1963, 198.

xiii   Lu Deming 陆德明, *Jingdian shiwen* 经典释文 (Exegetical Texts of the Classics). Shanghai: Shanghai guji chubanshe, 2013, 73.

xiv   Richard John Lynn, *The Classic of Changes: A New Translation of the I Ching as Interpreted by Wang Bi*. New York: Columbia University Press, 1994, 80, slightly modified.

xv   Ibid., 40.

xvi   Ibid., 66.

xvii   Ibid., 77.

xviii	Li Xueqin 李学勤 (ed.), *Zhou li zhushu* 周礼注疏 (The *Zhou Rituals* with Zheng Xuan's Commentary and Jia Gongyan's Subcommentary). Beijing: Beijing University Press, 1999, 637.
xix	Ibid., 637.
xx	Ibid., 637.
xxi	Wang Xianqian 王先谦, *Zhuang zi jijie* 庄子集解 (Collected Explanations of the *Zhuang zi*), in the *Zhuzi jicheng* 诸子集成 (Collected Works of the Famous Philosophers), vol. 3. Beijing: Zhonghua shuju, 1954, 216.
xxii	Li Xueqin 李学勤 (ed.), *Shangshu zhengyi* 尚书正义 (Correct Meaning of the *Classic of History*). Beijing: Beijing University Press, 1999, 314.
xxiii	Li Xueqin 李学勤 (ed.), *Zhou li zhushu* 周礼注疏 (The *Zhou Rituals* with Zheng Xuan's Commentary and Jia Gongyan's Subcommentary). Beijing: Beijing University Press, 1999, 637.
xxiv	Richard John Lynn, *The Classic of Changes: A New Translation of the I Ching as Interpreted by Wang Bi*. New York: Columbia University Press, 1994, 80, 77, slightly modified.
xxv	Liu An 刘安 et al., *Huainanzi* 淮南子 (Masters in the State of Huainan), in the *Zhuzi jicheng* 诸子集成 (Collected Works of the Famous Philosophers), vol. 7. Beijing: Zhonghua shuju, 1954, 374.
xxvi	Richard John Lynn, *The Classic of Changes: A New Translation of the I Ching as Interpreted by Wang Bi*. New York: Columbia University Press, 1994, 61, slightly modified.
xxvii	Fang Xuanling 房玄龄, *Jin shu* 晋书 (History of the Jin Dynasty [265-420]). Beijing: Zhonghua shuju, 1999, 948.
xxviii	Ban Gu 班固, *Han shu* 汉书 (History of the Western Han Dynasty [206 B.C.E.-9 C.E.]). Beijing: Zhonghua shuju, 1962, 1704.
xxix	Lin Zhongjun 林忠军, *Yi wei daodu* 易纬导读 (A Guide Book to the *Apocrypha of the Changes*). Jinan: Qilu shushe Press, 2002, 83.
xxx	Liu Yujian 刘玉建, *Zhouyi zhengyi daodu* 周易正义导读 (A Guide Book to the *Correct Meaning of the Zhou Changes*). Jinan: Qilu shushe Press, 2005, 94.
xxxi	Ban Gu 班固, *Han shu* 汉书 (History of the Western Han Dynasty [206 B.C.E.-9 C.E.]). Beijing: Zhonghua shuju, 1962, 3602.
xxxii	Fan Ye 范晔, **Hou han shu** 后汉书 (History of the Eastern Han Dynasty [25-220]). Beijing: Zhonghua shuju, 1965, 2052-2053.
xxxiii	Liu Yujian 刘玉建, *Zhouyi zhengyi daodu* 周易正义导读 (A Guide Book to the *Correct Meaning of the Zhou Changes*). Jinan: Qilu shushe Press, 2005, 443.
xxxiv	Richard John Lynn, *The Classic of Changes: A New Translation of the I Ching as Interpreted by Wang Bi*. New York: Columbia University Press, 1994, 146, slightly modified
xxxv	Ibid., 150, slightly modified.
xxxvi	Ibid., 140, slightly modified.
xxxvii	Ban Gu 班固, *Han shu* 汉书 (History of the Western Han Dynasty [206 B.C.E.-9 C.E.]). Beijing: Zhonghua shuju, 1962, 1703.
xxxviii	Ibid., 1704.
xxxix	Chen Shou 陈寿, *Sanguo zhi* 三国志 (History of the Three Kingdoms [220-280]). Beijing: Zhonghua shuju, 1959, 136.

xl. See the *tongzhitang jingjie be* 通志堂经解 version of the *Gu Zhou yi* 古周易 (Ancient *Zhou yi*). *Shaoshi wenjian hou lu* 邵氏闻见后录 also referred to it.

xli. Ban Gu 班固, *Han shu* 汉书 (History of the Western Han Dynasty [206 B.C.E.-9 C.E.]). Beijing: Zhonghua shuju, 1962, 1704.

xlii. Lin Zhongjun 林忠军, *Yi wei daodu* 易纬导读 (A Guide Book to the *Apocrypha of the Changes*). Jinan: Qilu shushe Press, 2002, 138-9.

xliii. Liu Xiang 刘向, *Zhanguo ce* 战国策 (Strategies of the Warring States). Jinan: Qilu shushe Press, 2005, 124-125.

xliv. Richard John Lynn, *The Classic of Changes: A New Translation of the I Ching as Interpreted by Wang Bi*. New York: Columbia University Press, 1994, 81.

xlv. Ban Gu 班固, *Han shu* 汉书 (History of the Western Han Dynasty [206 B.C.E.-9 C.E.]). Beijing: Zhonghua shuju, 1962, 1258.

xlvi. Liu An 刘安 et al., *Huainanzi* 淮南子 (Masters of Huainan), in the *Zhuzi jicheng* 诸子集成 (Collected Works of the Famous Philosophers), vol. 7. Beijing: Zhonghua shuju, 1954, 157.

xlvii. Ban Gu 班固, *Han shu* 汉书 (History of the Western Han Dynasty [206 B.C.E.-9 C.E.]). Beijing: Zhonghua shuju, 1962, 2717.

xlviii. Ibid., 2858. The "Explanation of the Classic" (*Jingjie* 经解) of the *Liji* 礼记 (Record of Ritual) and the "Establishment of Foundations" (*Jianben* 建本) of the *Shuoyuan* 说苑 (Garden of Sayings) also cited these phrases, except for one or two different characters.

xlix. Xu Shen 许慎 (c.58-c.147), *Shuowen jiezi* 说文解字 (Explanation of Simple and Composite Characters). Beijing: Zhonghua shuju, 1963, 72.

l. Liu Xiang 刘向 (author) and Xiang Zonglu 向宗鲁 (collator), *Shuo yuan jiaozheng* 说苑校证 (A Collated Version of the *Garden of Sayings*). Beijing: Zhonghua shuju, 2009, 241.

li. Richard John Lynn, *The Classic of Changes: A New Translation of the I Ching as Interpreted by Wang Bi*. New York: Columbia University Press, 1994, 360.

lii. Huan Kuan 桓宽, *Yantie lun* 盐铁论 (Discussions over Salt and Iron), in the *Zhuzi jicheng* 诸子集成 (Collected Works of the Famous Philosophers), vol. 7. Beijing: Zhonghua shuju, 1954, 27.

liii. Huang Shouqi 黄寿祺 and Zhang Shanwen 张善文 (ed.), *Zhou yi yanjiu lunwenji* 周易研究论文集 (第一辑) (Collected Papers Related to *Zhou yi* Studies) (I). Beijing: Beijing Normal University Press, 1987, 286-287.

liv. Li Jingchi 李镜池, *Zhou yi tanyuan* 周易探源 (An Investigation into the Origins of the *Zhou Changes*). Beijing: Zhonghua shuju, 1978, 301.

lv. Ibid., 310.

lvi. Ibid., 311-319.

lvii. Huang Shouqi 黄寿祺 and Zhang Shanwen 张善文 (ed.), *Zhou yi yanjiu lunwenji* 周易研究论文集 (第一辑) (Collected Papers Related to *Zhou yi* Studies) (I). Beijing: Beijing Normal University Press, 1987, 416-417.

lviii. Richard John Lynn, *The Classic of Changes: A New Translation of the I Ching as Interpreted by Wang Bi*. New York: Columbia University Press, 1994, 67, slightly modified.

lix. Wang Xianqian 王先谦, *Zhuang zi jijie* 庄子集解 (Collected Explanations of the *Zhuang zi*), in the *Zhuzi jicheng* 诸子集成 (Collected Works of the Famous Philosophers), vol. 3. Beijing: Zhonghua shuju, 1954, 223.

lx	Richard John Lynn, *The Classic of Changes: A New Translation of the I Ching as Interpreted by Wang Bi*. New York: Columbia University Press, 1994, 47.
lxi	Huang Shouqi 黄寿祺 and Zhang Shanwen 张善文 (ed.), *Zhou yi yanjiu lunwenji* 周易研究论文集 (第一辑) (Collected Papers Related to *Zhou yi* Studies) (I). Beijing: Beijing Normal University Press, 1987, 416.
lxii	Wang Xianqian 王先谦, *Zhuang zi jijie* 庄子集解 (Collected Explanations of the *Zhuang zi*), in the *Zhuzi jicheng* 诸子集成 (Collected Works of the Famous Philosophers, vol. 3. Beijing: Zhonghua shuju, vol. 3, 1954, 83.
lxiii	Ibid., 83.
lxiv	Ibid., 83.
lxv	Ibid., 83.
lxvi	Richard John Lynn, *The Classic of Changes: A New Translation of the I Ching as Interpreted by Wang Bi*. New York: Columbia University Press, 1994, 120-121, modified.
lxvii	Wang Xianqian 王先谦, *Zhuang zi jijie* 庄子集解 (Collected Explanations of the *Zhuang zi*), in the *Zhuzi jicheng* 诸子集成 (Collected Works of the Famous Philosophers, vol. 3. Beijing: Zhonghua shuju, vol. 3, 1954, 82.
lxviii	Ibid., 84.
lxix	Ibid., 64.
lxx	Ibid., 206.
lxxi	Richard John Lynn, *The Classic of Changes: A New Translation of the I Ching as Interpreted by Wang Bi*. New York: Columbia University Press, 1994, 137.
lxxii	Wang Xianqian 王先谦, *Zhuang zi jijie* 庄子集解 (Collected Explanations of the *Zhuang zi*), in the *Zhuzi jicheng* 诸子集成 (Collected Works of the Famous Philosophers, vol. 3. Beijing: Zhonghua shuju, vol. 3, 1954, 104.
lxxiii	Richard John Lynn, *The Classic of Changes: A New Translation of the I Ching as Interpreted by Wang Bi*. New York: Columbia University Press, 1994, 488, slightly modified.
lxxiv	Ibid., 280.
lxxv	Ibid., 388.
lxxvi	Ibid., 86-87.
lxxvii	Lou Yulie 楼宇烈 et al., *Xun zi xinzhu* 荀子新注 (New Annotations to the *Xun zi*). Beijing: Zhonghua shuju, 2018, 543.
lxxviii	Richard John Lynn, *The Classic of Changes: A New Translation of the I Ching as Interpreted by Wang Bi*. New York: Columbia University Press, 1994, 329, modified.
lxxix	Ibid., 83.
lxxx	Lou Yulie 楼宇烈 et al., *Xun zi xinzhu* 荀子新注 (New Annotations to the *Xun zi*). Beijing: Zhonghua shuju, 2018, 104.
lxxxi	Richard John Lynn, *The Classic of Changes: A New Translation of the I Ching as Interpreted by Wang Bi*. New York: Columbia University Press, 1994, 78, slightly modified.
lxxxii	Lou Yulie 楼宇烈 et al., *Xun zi xinzhu* 荀子新注 (New Annotations to the *Xun zi*). Beijing: Zhonghua shuju, 2018, 209.
lxxxiii	Richard John Lynn, *The Classic of Changes: A New Translation of the I Ching as Interpreted by Wang Bi*. New York: Columbia University Press, 1994, 81.

lxxxiv	Lou Yulie 楼宇烈 et al., *Xun zi xinzhu* 荀子新注 (New Annotations to the *Xun zi*). Beijing: Zhonghua shuju, 2018, 170.
lxxxv	Richard John Lynn, *The Classic of Changes: A New Translation of the I Ching as Interpreted by Wang Bi*. New York: Columbia University Press, 1994, 83-84.
lxxxvi	Lou Yulie 楼宇烈 et al., *Xun zi xinzhu* 荀子新注 (New Annotations to the *Xun zi*). Beijing: Zhonghua shuju, 2018, 122.
lxxxvii	Richard John Lynn, *The Classic of Changes: A New Translation of the I Ching as Interpreted by Wang Bi*. New York: Columbia University Press, 1994, 59.
lxxxviii	Lou Yulie 楼宇烈 et al., *Xun zi xinzhu* 荀子新注 (New Annotations to the *Xun zi*). Beijing: Zhonghua shuju, 2018, 6.
lxxxix	Ibid., 566.
xc	Richard John Lynn, *The Classic of Changes: A New Translation of the I Ching as Interpreted by Wang Bi*. New York: Columbia University Press, 1994, 137.
xci	Lou Yulie 楼宇烈 et al., *Xun zi xinzhu* 荀子新注 (New Annotations to the *Xun zi*). Beijing: Zhonghua shuju, 2018, 42.
xcii	Richard John Lynn, *The Classic of Changes: A New Translation of the I Ching as Interpreted by Wang Bi*. New York: Columbia University Press, 1994, 133.
xciii	Ibid., 129, slightly modified.
xciv	Ibid., 130-131.
xcv	Ibid., 452, modified.
xcvi	Ibid., 452.
xcvii	Ibid., 280, slightly modified.
xcviii	Ibid., 280, slightly modified.
xcix	Ibid., 144.
c	Ibid., 143.
ci	Ibid., 502.
cii	Ibid., 501, slightly modified.
ciii	Ibid., 351.
civ	Ibid., 357-358, slightly modified.
cv	Ibid., 357, slightly modified.
cvi	Ibid., 120.
cvii	Ibid., 92.
cviii	Ibid., 159, modified.
cix	Ibid., 165.
cx	Fang Xuanling 房玄龄 et al., *Jin shu* 晋书 (History of the Jin Dynasty [265-420]). Beijing: Zhonghua shuju, 1999, 948.
cxi	Richard John Lynn, *The Classic of Changes: A New Translation of the I Ching as Interpreted by Wang Bi*. New York: Columbia University Press, 1994, 119-120.
cxii	Ibid., 519.
cxiii	Ibid., 539.
cxiv	Ibid., 329.
cxv	Ibid., 297.
cxvi	Liu Yujian 刘玉建, *Zhou yi zhengyi daodu* 周易正义导读 (A Guide Book to the Correct Meaning of the Zhou Changes). Jinan: Qilu shushe Press, 2005, 441.
cxvii	Gao Heng 高亨, *Zhou yi dazhuan jinzhu* 周易大传今注 (Modern Annotations to the *Great Commentaries on the Zhou Changes*). Jinan: Qilu shushe Press, 1998, 4.

cxviii	Richard John Lynn, *The Classic of Changes: A New Translation of the I Ching as Interpreted by Wang Bi*. New York: Columbia University Press, 1994, 467.
cxix	Cui Shu 崔述, *Cui Dongbi yishu* 崔东壁遗书 (Posthumous Papers of Cui Dongbi [i.e., Cui Shu]). Shanghai: Shanghai guji chubanshe, 1983, 311.
cxx	Richard John Lynn, *The Classic of Changes: A New Translation of the I Ching as Interpreted by Wang Bi*. New York: Columbia University Press, 1994, 461.
cxxi	Ibid., 287.
cxxii	Ibid., 289.
cxxiii	Ibid., 397.
cxxiv	Ibid., 376.
cxxv	Ibid., 318.
cxxvi	Ibid. 305, slightly modified.
cxxvii	Ibid., 546, slightly modified.
cxxviii	Ibid., 330.
cxxix	Ibid., 300.
cxxx	Ibid. 86, slightly modified.
cxxxi	Ibid., 66, slightly modified.
cxxxii	Hou Wailu 侯外庐, *Zhongguo sixiangshi* 中国思想通史 (A General History of Chinese Thought), vol.1. Shanghai: Shenghuo, duoshu, xinzhi sanlian shudian, 1947, 288.
cxxxiii	Lou Yulie 楼宇烈 et al., *Xun zi xinzhu* 荀子新注 (New Annotations to the *Xun zi*). Beijing: Zhonghua shuju, 2018, 84.
cxxxiv	Richard John Lynn, *The Classic of Changes: A New Translation of the I Ching as Interpreted by Wang Bi*. New York: Columbia University Press, 1994, 78, slightly modified.
cxxxv	Ibid., 63.
cxxxvi	Ibid., 133.
cxxxvii	Ibid., 136.
cxxxviii	Ibid., 130, slightly modified.
cxxxix	Ibid., 149, slightly modified.
cxl	Ibid., 133, modified.
cxli	Ibid., 133.
cxlii	Ibid., 148.
cxliii	Ibid., 149, slightly modified.
cxliv	Ibid., 170.
cxlv	Ibid., 170-1.
cxlvi	Ibid., 179.
cxlvii	Ibid., 207.
cxlviii	Ibid., 289.
cxlix	Ibid., 399-400.
cl	Ibid., 408.
cli	Ibid., 487-491.
clii	Li Xueqin 李学勤 (ed.), *Chunqiu zuo zhuan zhengyi* 春秋左传正义 (Correct Meaning of *Zuo's Commentary on the Spring and autumn Annals*). Beijing: Beijing University Press, 1999, 755.
cliii	Sima Qian 司马迁, *Shiji* 史记 (Historical Records). Beijing: Zhonghua shuju, 1959, 1259.

cliv	Richard John Lynn, *The Classic of Changes: A New Translation of the I Ching as Interpreted by Wang Bi*. New York: Columbia University Press, 1994, 280.
clv	Ibid., 388.
clvi	Ibid., 286.
clvii	Ibid., 273, modified.
clviii	Ibid., 165.
clix	Ibid., 411, slightly modified.
clx	Ibid., 159.
clxi	Ibid., 171.
clxii	Ibid., 216.
clxiii	Ibid., 130.
clxiv	Ibid., 251, modified.
clxv	Guo Moruo 郭沫若, *Shi pipan shu* 十批判书 (A Book of Ten Critical Chapters). Beijing: Kexue chubanshe, 1956, 133-134.
clxvi	Richard John Lynn, *The Classic of Changes: A New Translation of the I Ching as Interpreted by Wang Bi*. New York: Columbia University Press, 1994, 133.
clxvii	Ibid., 135.
clxviii	Ibid., 132.
clxix	Ibid., 312.
clxx	Ibid., 84.
clxxi	Ibid., 133.
clxxii	Ibid., 52.
clxxiii	Ibid., 87.
clxxiv	Ibid., 138.
clxxv	Ibid., 56.
clxxvi	Ibid., 66.
clxxvii	Lou Yulie 楼宇烈 et al., *Xun zi xinzhu* 荀子新注 (New Annotations to the *Xun zi*). Beijing: Zhonghua shuju, 2018, 84.
clxxviii	Guo Moruo 郭沫若, *Shi pipan shu* 十批判书 (A Book of Ten Critical Chapters). Beijing: Kexue chubanshe, 1956, 132.
clxxix	Richard John Lynn, *The Classic of Changes: A New Translation of the I Ching as Interpreted by Wang Bi*. New York: Columbia University Press, 1994, 31.
clxxx	Ibid., 219.
clxxxi	Ibid., 220.
clxxxii	Ibid., 224, slightly modified.
clxxxiii	Ibid., 132, slightly modified.
clxxxiv	Ibid., 145, slightly modified.
clxxxv	Ibid., 201, slightly modified.
clxxxvi	Ibid., 206, slightly modified.
clxxxvii	Ibid., 267.
clxxxviii	Ibid., 274.
clxxxix	Ibid., 281, slightly modified.
cxc	Ibid., 313, slightly modified.
cxci	Ibid., 319, slightly modified.
cxcii	Ibid., 325.
cxciii	Ibid., 330.
cxciv	Ibid., 341.

cxcv	Ibid., 346.
cxcvi	Ibid., 406.
cxcvii	Ibid., 430.
cxcviii	Ibid., 439, slightly modified.
cxcix	Ibid., 453.
cc	Ibid., 468.
cci	Ibid., 539.
ccii	Ibid., 547.
cciii	Ibid., 138.
cciv	Ibid., 188, slightly modified.
ccv	Ibid., 226.
ccvi	Ibid., 271.
ccvii	Ibid., 303.
ccviii	Ibid., 315, modified.
ccix	Ibid., 333.
ccx	Ibid., modified.
ccxi	Ibid., 384.
ccxii	Ibid., 414.
ccxiii	Ibid., 456.
ccxiv	Ibid., 498.
ccxv	Ibid., 527.
ccxvi	Ibid., 542.
ccxvii	Ibid., 549-550.
ccxviii	Ibid., 80.
ccxix	Ibid., 50.
ccxx	Ibid., 67.
ccxxi	Ibid., 75.
ccxxii	Ibid., 49, modified.
ccxxiii	Ibid., 56-57, 68.
ccxxiv	Huang Zongxi's 黄宗羲 (author) and Zheng Wangeng 郑万耕 (punctuator), *Yixue xiangshu lun* 易学象数论 (Discussion of Image-numerology in the *Changes* Scholarship). Beijing: Zhonghua shuju, 2010, 117.
ccxxv	Please see Richard John Lynn, *The Classic of Changes: A New Translation of the I Ching as Interpreted by Wang Bi*. New York: Columbia University Press, 1994, 122-124, from "Qian [Pure Yang] means strength" to the end of the Wing.
ccxxvi	Richard Rutt, *The Book of Changes (Zhouyi)*. Richmond, Surry: Cuzon, 1996, 176, modified.
ccxxvii	Ibid., 192, modified.
ccxxviii	Ibid., 199, modified.
ccxxix	Richard John Lynn, *The Classic of Changes: A New Translation of the I Ching as Interpreted by Wang Bi*. New York: Columbia University Press, 1994, 92.
ccxxx	Ibid., 120.
ccxxxi	Ibid., 539, slightly modified.
ccxxxii	Ibid., 78, modified.
ccxxxiii	Ibid., 88, slightly modified.
ccxxxiv	Ibid., 243.

ccxxxv	Zhang Wenzhi 张文智, *Zhou yi jiie daodu* 周易集解导读 (A Guide Book to the Collected Explanations of the Zhou yi). Jinan: Qilu shushe Press, 2005, 174-5.
ccxxxvi	Richard John Lynn, *The Classic of Changes: A New Translation of the I Ching as Interpreted by Wang Bi*. New York: Columbia University Press, 1994, 252.
ccxxxvii	Zhang Wenzhi 张文智, *Zhou yi jiie daodu* 周易集解导读 (A Guide Book to the Collected Explanations of the Zhou yi). Jinan: Qilu shushe Press, 2005, 179.
ccxxxviii	Richard John Lynn, *The Classic of Changes: A New Translation of the I Ching as Interpreted by Wang Bi*. New York: Columbia University Press, 1994, 231, modified.
ccxxxix	Zhang Wenzhi 张文智, *Zhou yi jiie daodu* 周易集解导读 (A Guide Book to the Collected Explanations of the Zhou yi). Jinan: Qilu shushe Press, 2005, 166.
ccxl	Richard John Lynn, *The Classic of Changes: A New Translation of the I Ching as Interpreted by Wang Bi*. New York: Columbia University Press, 1994, 203, modified.
ccxli	Ibid., 154., modified.
ccxlii	Zhang Wenzhi 张文智, *Zhou yi jiie daodu* 周易集解导读 (A Guide Book to the Collected Explanations of the Zhou yi). Jinan: Qilu shushe Press, 2005, 120.
ccxliii	Richard John Lynn, *The Classic of Changes: A New Translation of the I Ching as Interpreted by Wang Bi*. New York: Columbia University Press, 1994, 232, modified.
ccxliv	Zhang Wenzhi 张文智, *Zhou yi jiie daodu* 周易集解导读 (A Guide Book to the Collected Explanations of the Zhou yi). Jinan: Qilu shushe Press, 2005, 167.
ccxlv	Ibid., 121.
ccxlvi	Ibid., 141.
ccxlvii	Ibid., 217.
ccxlviii	Richard John Lynn, *The Classic of Changes: A New Translation of the I Ching as Interpreted by Wang Bi*. New York: Columbia University Press, 1994, 383, modified.
ccxlix	Lin Zhongjun 林忠军, *Yi wei daodu* 易纬导读 (A Guide Book to the *Apocrypha of the Changes*). Jinan: Qilu shushe Press, 2002, 82.
ccl	Richard John Lynn, *The Classic of Changes: A New Translation of the I Ching as Interpreted by Wang Bi*. New York: Columbia University Press, 1994, 255, modified.
ccli	Zhang Wenzhi 张文智, *Zhou yi jiie daodu* 周易集解导读 (A Guide Book to the Collected Explanations of the Zhou yi). Jinan: Qilu shushe Press, 2005, 181.
cclii	Richard John Lynn, *The Classic of Changes: A New Translation of the I Ching as Interpreted by Wang Bi*. New York: Columbia University Press, 1994, 224.
ccliii	Zhang Wenzhi 张文智, *Zhou yi jiie daodu* 周易集解导读 (A Guide Book to the Collected Explanations of the Zhou yi). Jinan: Qilu shushe Press, 2005, 162.
ccliv	Ibid., 246.
cclv	Ibid., 125.
cclvi	Ibid., 189.
cclvii	Ibid., 171.
cclviii	Ibid., 181.
cclix	Richard John Lynn, *The Classic of Changes: A New Translation of the I Ching as Interpreted by Wang Bi*. New York: Columbia University Press, 1994, 263, modified.

cclx	Zhang Wenzhi 张文智, *Zhou yi jiie daodu* 周易集解导读 (A Guide Book to the Collected Explanations of the Zhou yi). Jinan: Qilu shushe Press, 2005, 181.
cclxi	Richard John Lynn, *The Classic of Changes: A New Translation of the I Ching as Interpreted by Wang Bi*. New York: Columbia University Press, 1994, 121-122, slightly modified.
cclxii	Ibid., 154, modified.
cclxiii	Ibid, 236.
cclxiv	Richard Rutt, *The Book of Changes (Zhouyi)*. Richmond, Surry: Cuzon, 1996, 176, modified.
cclxv	Richard John Lynn, *The Classic of Changes: A New Translation of the I Ching as Interpreted by Wang Bi*. New York: Columbia University Press, 1994, 91-92, slightly modified.
cclxvi	Ibid., 120, modified.
cclxvii	Ibid., 338.
cclxviii	Lin Zhongjun 林忠军, *Zhou yi zhenshi xue chanwei* 周易郑氏学阐微 (A Subtle Elucidation of Zheng Xuan's Scholarship on the *Changes*). Shanghai: Shanghai guji Press, 2005, 306.
cclxix	Richard John Lynn, *The Classic of Changes: A New Translation of the I Ching as Interpreted by Wang Bi*. New York: Columbia University Press, 1994, 305.
cclxx	Zhang Wenzhi 张文智, *Zhou yi jiie daodu* 周易集解导读 (A Guide Book to the Collected Explanations of the Zhou yi). Jinan: Qilu shushe Press, 2005, 208.
cclxxi	Ibid., 420.
cclxxii	Ibid., 420.
cclxxiii	Ibid., 191.
cclxxiv	Ibid., 225.
cclxxv	Lin Zhongjun 林忠军, *Zhou yi zhenshi xue chanwei* 周易郑氏学阐微 (A Subtle Elucidation of Zheng Xuan's Scholarship on the *Changes*). Shanghai: Shanghai guji Press, 2005, 287.
cclxxvi	Richard John Lynn, *The Classic of Changes: A New Translation of the I Ching as Interpreted by Wang Bi*. New York: Columbia University Press, 1994, 305-6, slightly modified.
cclxxvii	Ibid., 159.
cclxxviii	Zhang Wenzhi 张文智, *Zhou yi jiie daodu* 周易集解导读 (A Guide Book to the Collected Explanations of the Zhou yi). Jinan: Qilu shushe Press, 2005, 124.
cclxxix	Richard John Lynn, *The Classic of Changes: A New Translation of the I Ching as Interpreted by Wang Bi*. New York: Columbia University Press, 1994, 209, slightly modified.
cclxxx	Ibid., 509.
cclxxxi	Ibid., 406.
cclxxxii	Ibid., 346, modified.
cclxxxiii	Ibid., 153, modified.
cclxxxiv	Ibid., 163, modified.
cclxxxv	Ibid., 206.
cclxxxvi	Ibid., 215.
cclxxxvii	Ibid., 193.
cclxxxviii	Ibid., 203-4.
cclxxxix	Ibid., 391.

ccxc	Ibid., 398-9.
ccxci	Ibid., 540.
ccxcii	Ibid., 548.
ccxciii	Ibid., 254, slightly modified.
ccxciv	Ibid., 119, slightly modified.
ccxcv	Ibid., 49, modified.
ccxcvi	Ibid., 49.
ccxcvii	Ibid., 62, modified.
ccxcviii	Ibid., 65, modified.
ccxcix	Ibid., 67, modified.
ccc	Ibid., 75, modified.
ccci	Ibid., 89.
cccii	Ibid., 152, slightly modified. These remarks hint that hexagram Zhun [䷂] is changed from hexagram Kan [䷜] when the bottom line and the second line of the latter exchange positions to signify the intercourse of the hard and the soft [noted by the translator].
ccciii	Ibid., 387. This means that hexagram Sun 损 [䷨] is changed from hexagram Tai 泰 [䷊] when line 3 and line 6 of the latter exchange positions [noted by the translator].
ccciv	Ibid., 396. This signifies that hexagram Yi 益 [䷩] is changed from hexagram Pi 否 [䷋] when line 4 and line 1 of the latter exchange positions [noted by the translator].
cccv	Ibid., 229, slightly modified. This means that hexagram Qian 谦 [䷎] is transformed from hexagram Bo 剥 [䷖] when line 6 and line 3 of the latter exchange positions [noted by the translator].
cccvi	Ibid., 249, modified. This means that hexagram Gu 蛊 [䷑] is transformed from hexagram Tai 泰 [䷊] when line 1 and line 6 of the latter exchange positions [noted by the translator].
cccvii	Ibid., 280, modified. This means that hexagram Bo 剥 [䷖] is derived from hexagram Guan 观 [䷓] when the fifth *yang* line of the latter is changed into its opposite *yin* line [noted by the translator].
cccviii	Ibid., 285, modified. This means that hexagram Fu 复 [䷗] results from the upside-down placement of hexagram Bo 剥 [䷖] [noted by the translator].
cccix	Ibid., 293, slightly modified. This signifies that hexagram Wuwang 无妄 [䷘] is derived from hexagram Da zhuang 大壮 [䷡] by changing the positions of the original upper and lower hexagrams [noted by the translator].
cccx	Ibid., 329, slightly modified.
cccxi	Ibid., 335, slightly modified.
cccxii	Ibid., 368.
cccxiii	Ibid., 424, modified.
cccxiv	Ibid., 512, slightly modified.
cccxv	Ibid., 272, slightly modified. This means that hexagram Bi [䷇] is transformed from hexagram Tai [䷊], with the latter's second and top lines' positions being exchanged [noted by the translator].
cccxvi	Ibid., 152.
cccxvii	See Zhang Wenzhi 张文智, *Zhou yi jijie daodu* 周易集解导读 (A Guidebook to the Collected Explanations of the Zhou Changes). Jinan: Qilu shushe Press, 2005, 118.

cccxviii	Ibid., 71.
cccxix	Richard John Lynn, *The Classic of Changes: A New Translation of the I Ching as Interpreted by Wang Bi*. New York: Columbia University Press, 1994, 159, slightly modified.
cccxx	See Zhang Wenzhi张文智, *Zhou yi jijie daodu* 周易集解导读 (A Guidebook to the *Collected Explanations of the Zhou Changes*). Jinan: Qilu shushe Press, 2005, 253 and 254. This means that if the second and fourth lines of hexagram Qian [☰] move to the second line and fourth line positions of hexagram Kun [☷], respectively, hexagram Jie [䷻] will be produced [noted by the translator].
cccxxi	Ibid., 320.
cccxxii	Ibid., 130.
cccxxiii	Ibid., 236.
cccxxiv	Ibid., 257.
cccxxv	Ibid., 139.
cccxxvi	Ibid., 208.
cccxxvii	Ibid., 336.
cccxxviii	Ibid., 336.
cccxxix	Ibid., 339.
cccxxx	Ibid., 118.
cccxxxi	Ibid., 122.
cccxxxii	See Xiao Hanming萧汉明, *Zhou yi benyi daodu* 周易本义导读 (A Guide Book to the *Original Meaning of the Zhou Changes*). Jinan: Qilu shushe Press, 2003, 72-78.
cccxxxiii	Ibid., 103.
cccxxxiv	Richard John Lynn, *The Classic of Changes: A New Translation of the I Ching as Interpreted by Wang Bi*. New York: Columbia University Press, 1994, 89.
cccxxxv	Ibid., 193.
cccxxxvi	Ibid., 203.
cccxxxvii	Ibid., 325.
cccxxxviii	Ibid., 509, slightly modified.
cccxxxix	Ibid., 255, modified.
cccxl	Ibid., 162, modified.
cccxli	Ibid., 391.
cccxlii	Ibid., 392.
cccxliii	Ibid., 468.
cccxliv	Ibid., 166.
cccxlv	Ibid., 548, slightly modified.
cccxlvi	Ibid., 205.
cccxlvii	Ibid., 211.
cccxlviii	Ibid., 130-131, modified.
cccxlix	Ibid., 219.
cccl	Ibid., 80, slightly modified.
cccli	See Zhang Wenzhi张文智, *Zhou yi jijie daodu* 周易集解导读 (A Guidebook to the *Collected Explanations of the Zhou Changes*). Jinan: Qilu shushe Press, 2005, 396.
ccclii	Richard John Lynn, *The Classic of Changes: A New Translation of the I Ching as Interpreted by Wang Bi*. New York: Columbia University Press, 1994, 65, slightly modified.

ccclii	See Zhang Wenzhi 张文智, *Zhou yi jijie daodu* 周易集解导读 (A Guidebook to the *Collected Explanations of the Zhou Changes*). Jinan: Qilu shushe Press, 2005, 118.
cccliv	Ibid., 297.
ccclv	Lin Zhongjun 林忠军, *Yi wei daodu* 易纬导读 (A Guidebook to the *Apocrypha of the Changes*). Jinan: Jinan: Qilu shushe Press, 2002, 81.
ccclvi	See Zhang Wenzhi 张文智, *Zhou yi jijie daodu* 周易集解导读 (A Guidebook to the *Collected Explanations of the Zhou Changes*). Jinan: Qilu shushe Press, 2005, 198.
ccclvii	Ibid., 270.
ccclviii	Ibid., 179.
ccclix	Richard John Lynn, *The Classic of Changes: A New Translation of the I Ching as Interpreted by Wang Bi*. New York: Columbia University Press, 1994, 329, slightly modified.
ccclx	Ibid., 132, slightly modified.
ccclxi	Ibid., 132, slightly modified.
ccclxii	Ibid., 149-150, slightly modified.
ccclxiii	Lin Zhongjun 林忠军, *Yi wei daodu* 易纬导读 (A Guidebook to the *Apocrypha of the Changes*). Jinan: Jinan: Qilu shushe Press, 2002, 78.
ccclxiv	Li Xueqin 李学勤 (ed.), *Chunqiu zuozhuan zhengyi* 春秋左传正义 (Correct Meaning of Zuo's Commentary on the Spring and Autumn Annals). Beijing: Beijing University Press, 1999, 1720.
ccclxv	Xu Shen 许慎 (c.58-c.147), *Shuowen jiezi* 说文解字 (Explanation of Simple and Composite Characters). Beijing: Zhonghua shuju, 1963, 69.
ccclxvi	Ibid., 96.
ccclxvii	Richard John Lynn, *The Classic of Changes: A New Translation of the I Ching as Interpreted by Wang Bi*. New York: Columbia University Press, 1994, 60-61, slightly modified.
ccclxviii	Ibid., 60, slightly modified.
ccclxix	Ibid., 61-62, slightly modified.
ccclxx	Ban Gu 班固, *Han shu* 汉书 (History of the Western Han Dynasty [206 B.C.E.-9 C.E.]). Beijing: Zhonghua shuju, 1962, 983.
ccclxxi	See Liu Yujian 刘玉建, *Zhou yi zhengyi daodu* 周易正义导读 (A Guidebook to the *Correct Meaning of the Zhou Changes*). Jinan: Qilu shushe Press, 2005, 384.
ccclxxii	Ibid., 384.
ccclxxiii	Richard John Lynn, *The Classic of Changes: A New Translation of the I Ching as Interpreted by Wang Bi*. New York: Columbia University Press, 1994, 132.
ccclxxiv	See Liu Yujian 刘玉建, *Zhou yi zhengyi daodu* 周易正义导读 (A Guidebook to the *Correct Meaning of the Zhou Changes*). Jinan: Qilu shushe Press, 2005, 384-5.
ccclxxv	Ibid., 385.
ccclxxvi	See Zhang Wenzhi 张文智, *Zhou yi jijie daodu* 周易集解导读 (A Guidebook to the *Collected Explanations of the Zhou Changes*). Jinan: Qilu shushe Press, 2005, 369.
ccclxxvii	See Xiao Hanming 萧汉明, *Zhou yi benyi daodu* 周易本义导读 (A Guidebook to the *Original Meaning of the Zhou Changes*). Jinan: Qilu shushe Press, 2003, 238.
ccclxxviii	Richard John Lynn, *The Classic of Changes: A New Translation of the I Ching as Interpreted by Wang Bi*. New York: Columbia University Press, 1994, 63.
ccclxxix	Ibid., 60.
ccclxxx	Ban Gu 班固, *Han shu* 汉书 (History of the Western Han Dynasty [206 B.C.E.-9 C.E.]). Beijing: Zhonghua shuju, 1962, 4170.

ccclxxxi	See Zhang Wenzhi张文智, *Zhou yi jijie daodu* 周易集解导读 (A Guidebook to the *Collected Explanations of the Zhou Changes*). Jinan: Qilu shushe Press, 2005, 373.
ccclxxxii	Richard John Lynn, *The Classic of Changes: A New Translation of the I Ching as Interpreted by Wang Bi*. New York: Columbia University Press, 1994, 61.
ccclxxxiii	Ibid., 61-62, slightly modified.
ccclxxxiv	Zhu Xi 朱熹, *Yixue qimeng* 易学启蒙 (Introduction to the Study of the *Changes*), in *Zhu zi quanshu* (Collected Works of Zhu Xi), vol. 1. Shanghai: Shanghai guji chubanshe and Hefei: Anhui jiaoyu chubanshe, 2002, 253-254.
ccclxxxv	Richard J. Smith, *Fathoming the Cosmos and Ordering the World: The Yijing (I-Ching, or Classic of Changes and Its Evolution in China*. Charlottesville: University of Virginia Press, 2008, 230-1, slightly modified.
ccclxxxvi	Ibid., 29, modified.
ccclxxxvii	Li Xueqin 李学勤 (ed.), *Chunqiu zuozhuan zhengyi* 春秋左传正义 (Correct Meaning of the *Zuo's Commentary on the Spring and Autumn Annals*). Beijing: Peking University Press, 1999, 614.
ccclxxxviii	Ibid., 1503-1509.
ccclxxxix	Liu Guangben 刘光本, *Zhou yi gushi kao tongjie* 周易古筮考通解 (A Thorough Interpretation of Shang Binghe's *Textual Research on Divinations by the Zhou Changes in Ancient Times*). Taiyuan: Shanxi guji chubanshe, 1994, 9-10.
cccxc	Ouyang Xiu 欧阳修, *Ouyang xiu quanji* 欧阳修全集 (*Collected Works o Ouyang Xiu*). Beijing: Zhonghua shuju, 2001, 207.
cccxci	Ren Farong 任法融, *Zhou yi cantongqi shiyi* 周易参同契释义 (An Explanation of the Meaning of the *Token for the Agreement of the Three According to the Zhou Changes*). Beijing: Dongfang chubanshe, 2012, 49.
cccxcii	Liu Guangben 刘光本, *Zhou yi gushi kao tongjie* 周易古筮考通解 (A Thorough Interpretation of Shang Binghe's *Textual Research on Divinations by the Zhou Changes in Ancient Times*). Taiyuan: Shanxi guji chubanshe, 1994, 11.
cccxciii	Richard J. Smith, *Fathoming the Cosmos and Ordering the World: The Yijing (I-Ching, or Classic of Changes and Its Evolution in China*. Charlottesville: University of Virginia Press, 2008, 230-1, slightly modified.
cccxciv	Li Xueqin 李学勤 (ed.), *Chunqiu zuozhuan zhengyi* 春秋左传正义 (Correct Meaning of the *Zuo's Commentary on the Spring and Autumn Annals*). Beijing: Peking University Press, 1999, 426-427.
cccxcv	Ibid., 1011-1013.
cccxcvi	Ibid., 305-306.
cccxcvii	Ibid., 267-273.
cccxcviii	Xu Yuangao 徐元诰, *Guyu jijie* 国语集解 (Collected Explanations of the *Sayings of the States*)(Amendment). Beijing: Zhonghua shuju, 2002, 340-342.
cccxcix	Li Xueqin 李学勤 (ed.), *Chunqiu zuozhuan zhengyi* 春秋左传正义 (Correct Meaning of the *Zuo's Commentary on the Spring and Autumn Annals*). Beijing: Peking University Press, 1999, 869-871.
cd	Xu Yuangao 徐元诰, *Guyu jijie* 国语集解 (Collected Explanations of the *Sayings of the States*)(Amendment). Beijing: Zhonghua shuju, 2002, 343-345.
cdi	Li Xueqin 李学勤 (ed.), *Chunqiu zuozhuan zhengyi* 春秋左传正义 (Correct Meaning of the *Zuo's Commentary on the Spring and Autumn Annals*). Beijing: Peking University Press, 1999, 373-374.
cdii	Ibid., 776-780.

cdiii	Richard J. Smith, *Fathoming the Cosmos and Ordering the World: The Yijing (I-Ching, or Classic of Changes) and Its Evolution in China*. Charlottesville: University of Virginia Press, 2008, 230.
cdiv	Ibid., 230.
cdv	Ibid., 230.
cdvi	Ibid., 230, slightly modified.
cdvii	Ibid., 230-1.
cdviii	Richard John Lynn, *The Classic of Changes: A New Translation of the I Ching as Interpreted by Wang Bi*. New York: Columbia University Press, 1994, 243.
cdix	Richard J. Smith, *Fathoming the Cosmos and Ordering the World: The Yijing (I-Ching, or Classic of Changes and Its Evolution in China*. Charlottesville: University of Virginia Press, 2008, 231, slightly modified.
cdx	Li Xueqin 李学勤 (ed.), *Chunqiu zuozhuan zhengyi* 春秋左传正义 (Correct Meaning of the *Zuo's Commentary on the Spring and Autumn Annals*). Beijing: Peking University Press, 1999, 871.
cdxi	Richard John Lynn, *The Classic of Changes: A New Translation of the I Ching as Interpreted by Wang Bi*. New York: Columbia University Press, 1994, 455, slightly modified.
cdxii	Wang Chong 王充, *Lun Heng* 论衡 (Discourses Weighed in the Balance), in *Zhuzi jicheng* 诸子集成 (Collected Works of the Famous Philosophers), vol. 7. Beijing: Zhonghua shuju, 1954, 237.
cdxiii	Richard John Lynn, *The Classic of Changes: A New Translation of the I Ching as Interpreted by Wang Bi*. New York: Columbia University Press, 1994, 431, modified.
cdxiv	Liu Guangben 刘光本, *Zhou yi gushi kao tongjie* 周易古筮考通解 (A Thorough Interpretation of Shang Binghe's *Textual Research on Divinations by the Zhou Changes in Ancient Times*). Taiyuan: Shanxi guji chubanshe, 1994, 166.
cdxv	Ibid., 166.
cdxvi	Ibid., 59.
cdxvii	Ibid., 215.
cdxviii	Ibid., 151.
cdxix	Li Xueqin 李学勤 (ed.), *Chunqiu zuozhuan zhengyi* 春秋左传正义 (Correct Meaning of the *Zuo's Commentary on the Spring and Autumn Annals*). Beijing: Peking University Press, 1999, 1172.
cdxx	Ibid., 269.
cdxxi	Ban Gu 班固, *Han shu* 汉书 (History of the Western Han Dynasty [206 B.C.E.-9 C.E.]). Beijing: Zhonghua shuju, 1962, 1723.
cdxxii	Ibid., 3583.
cdxxiii	Sima Qian 司马迁, *Shiji* 史记 (Historical Records). Beijing: Zhonghua shuju, 1959, 1937.
cdxxiv	Ouyang Xiu 欧阳修, *Ouyang Xiu Quanji* 欧阳修全集 (Collected Works of Ouyang Xiu). Beijing: Zhonghua shuju, 2001, 220.
cdxxv	Ibid., 220.
cdxxvi	Richard John Lynn, *The Classic of Changes: A New Translation of the I Ching as Interpreted by Wang Bi*. New York: Columbia University Press, 1994, 66, modified.
cdxxvii	Ibid., 77.
cdxxviii	Ibid., 119.

cdxxix	Ouyang Xiu 欧阳修, *Ouyang Xiu Quanji* 欧阳修全集 (Collected Works of Ouyang Xiu). Beijing: Zhonghua shuju, 2001, 221.
cdxxx	Ban Gu 班固, *Han shu* 汉书 (History of the Western Han Dynasty [206 B.C.E.-9 C.E.]). Beijing: Zhonghua shuju, 1962, 3589.
cdxxxi	Please see *The Analects of Confucius* (7:16).
cdxxxii	Richard John Lynn, *The Classic of Changes: A New Translation of the I Ching as Interpreted by Wang Bi*. New York: Columbia University Press, 1994, 338.
cdxxxiii	Sima Qian 司马迁, *Shiji* 史记 (Historical Records). Beijing: Zhonghua shuju, 1959, 1947.
cdxxxiv	Ban Gu 班固, *Han shu* 汉书 (History of the Western Han Dynasty [206 B.C.E.-9 C.E.]). Beijing: Zhonghua shuju, 1962, 1968.
cdxxxv	Ibid, 3599.
cdxxxvi	Richard John Lynn, *The Classic of Changes: A New Translation of the I Ching as Interpreted by Wang Bi*. New York: Columbia University Press, 1994, 425.
cdxxxvii	Zhu Zhen 朱震, *Hanshang yizhuan* 汉上易传 (Zhu Zhen's Commentary on the *Changes*). Beijing: Jiuzhou Press, 2012, 157.
cdxxxviii	Wei Zheng 魏征 (et al), *Sui shu* 隋书 (History of the Sui Dynasty [581-618]). Beijing: Zhounghua shuju, 1973, 913.
cdxxxix	Richard John Lynn, *The Classic of Changes: A New Translation of the I Ching as Interpreted by Wang Bi*. New York: Columbia University Press, 1994, 306, slightly modified.
cdxl	Ibid., 214, slightly modified.
cdxli	Zhang Wenzhi张文智, *Zhou yi jijie daodu* 周易集解导读 (A Guidebook to the Collected Explanations of the Zhou Changes). Jinan: Qilu shushe Press, 2005, 157.
cdxlii	Ibid., 202.
cdxliii	Richard John Lynn, *The Classic of Changes: A New Translation of the I Ching as Interpreted by Wang Bi*. New York: Columbia University Press, 1994,48, slightly modified.
cdxliv	Lu Deming 陆德明, *Jingdian shiwen* 经典释文 (Exegetical Texts of the Classics). Shanghai: Shanghai guji chubanshe, 2013, 121.
cdxlv	Ban Gu 班固, *Han shu* 汉书 (History of the Western Han Dynasty [206 B.C.E.-9 C.E.]). Beijing: Zhonghua shuju, 1962, 3602.
cdxlvi	Wei Zheng 魏征 (et al), *Sui shu* 隋书 (History of the Sui Dynasty [581-618]). Beijing: Zhounghua shuju, 1973, 912.
cdxlvii	Richard John Lynn, *The Classic of Changes: A New Translation of the I Ching as Interpreted by Wang Bi*. New York: Columbia University Press, 1994,209.
cdxlviii	Lin Zhongjun 林忠军, *Zhou yi zhenshi xue chanwei* 周易郑氏学阐微 (A Subtle Elucidation of Zheng Xuan's Scholarship on the *Changes*). Shanghai: Shanghai guji Press, 2005, 256.
cdxlix	Richard John Lynn, *The Classic of Changes: A New Translation of the I Ching as Interpreted by Wang Bi*. New York: Columbia University Press, 1994, 322.
cdl	Lin Zhongjun 林忠军, *Zhou yi zhenshi xue chanwei* 周易郑氏学阐微 (A Subtle Elucidation of Zheng Xuan's Scholarship on the *Changes*). Shanghai: Shanghai guji Press, 2005, 296.
cdli	Richard John Lynn, *The Classic of Changes: A New Translation of the I Ching as Interpreted by Wang Bi*. New York: Columbia University Press, 1994, 359.

cdlii	Lin Zhongjun 林忠军, *Zhou yi zhenshi xue chanwei* 周易郑氏学阐微 (A Subtle Elucidation of Zheng Xuan's Scholarship on the *Changes*). Shanghai: Shanghai guji Press, 2005, 314.
cdliii	Richard John Lynn, *The Classic of Changes: A New Translation of the I Ching as Interpreted by Wang Bi*. New York: Columbia University Press, 1994, 321, modified.
cdliv	Lin Zhongjun 林忠军, *Zhou yi zhenshi xue chanwei* 周易郑氏学阐微 (A Subtle Elucidation of Zheng Xuan's Scholarship on the *Changes*). Shanghai: Shanghai guji Press, 2005, 294.
cdlv	Richard John Lynn, *The Classic of Changes: A New Translation of the I Ching as Interpreted by Wang Bi*. New York: Columbia University Press, 1994, 430.
cdlvi	Lin Zhongjun 林忠军, *Zhou yi zhenshi xue chanwei* 周易郑氏学阐微 (A Subtle Elucidation of Zheng Xuan's Scholarship on the *Changes*). Shanghai: Shanghai guji Press, 2005, 333-4.
cdlvii	Richard John Lynn, *The Classic of Changes: A New Translation of the I Ching as Interpreted by Wang Bi*. New York: Columbia University Press, 1994, 185, modified.
cdlviii	Lin Zhongjun 林忠军, *Zhou yi zhenshi xue chanwei* 周易郑氏学阐微 (A Subtle Elucidation of Zheng Xuan's Scholarship on the *Changes*). Shanghai: Shanghai guji Press, 2005, 249.
cdlix	Ban Gu 班固, *Han shu* 汉书 (History of the Western Han Dynasty [206 B.C.E.-9 C.E.]). Beijing: Zhonghua shuju, 1962, 961.
cdlx	Ibid., 958-960.
cdlxi	Lu Deming 陆德明, *Jingdian shiwen* 经典释文 (Exegetical Texts of the Classics). Shanghai: Shanghai guji chubanshe, 2013, 92.
cdlxii	Lin Zhongjun 林忠军, *Zhou yi zhenshi xue chanwei* 周易郑氏学阐微 (A Subtle Elucidation of Zheng Xuan's Scholarship on the *Changes*). Shanghai: Shanghai guji Press, 2005, 359.
cdlxiii	Lu Deming 陆德明, *Jingdian shiwen* 经典释文 (Exegetical Texts of the Classics). Shanghai: Shanghai guji chubanshe, 2013, 100.
cdlxiv	Ibid., 60.
cdlxv	See Liu Yujian 刘玉建, *Zhou yi zhengyi daodu* 周易正义导读 (A Guidebook to the Correct Meaning of the Zhou Changes). Jinan: Qilu Shushe Press, 2005, 384.
cdlxvi	Ban Gu 班固, *Han shu* 汉书 (History of the Western Han Dynasty [206 B.C.E.-9 C.E.]). Beijing: Zhonghua shuju, 1962, 3602.
cdlxvii	Lin Zhongjun 林忠军, *Yiwei daodu* 易纬导读 (A Guidebook to the *Apocrypha of the Changes*). Jinan: Qilu shushe Press, 2002, 77.
cdlxviii	Xueqin 李学勤 (ed.), *Liji zhengyi* 礼记正义 (Correct Meaning of the *Record of Ritual*). Beijing: Peking University Press, 1999,460.
cdlxix	Richard John Lynn, *The Classic of Changes: A New Translation of the I Ching as Interpreted by Wang Bi*. New York: Columbia University Press, 1994, 51, modified.
cdlxx	Ibid., 77.
cdlxxi	Ibid., 66.
cdlxxii	Ibid., 92.
cdlxxiii	Ibid., 274.
cdlxxiv	Ibid., 120.
cdlxxv	Ibid., 47.

cdlxxvi Ibid., 132.

cdlxxvii Zhang Wenzhi 张文智, *Zhou yi jijie daodu* 周易集解导读 (A Guide Book to the *Collected Explanations of the Zhou Changes*). Jinan: Qilu shushe Press, 2005, 92.

cdlxxviii Richard John Lynn, *The Classic of Changes: A New Translation of the I Ching as Interpreted by Wang Bi*. New York: Columbia University Press, 1994, 205.

cdlxxix Zhang Wenzhi 张文智, *Zhou yi jijie daodu* 周易集解导读 (A Guide Book to the *Collected Explanations of the Zhou Changes*). Jinan: Qilu shushe Press, 2005, 151.

cdlxxx Richard John Lynn, *The Classic of Changes: A New Translation of the I Ching as Interpreted by Wang Bi*. New York: Columbia University Press, 1994, 336.

cdlxxxi Zhang Wenzhi 张文智, *Zhou yi jijie daodu* 周易集解导读 (A Guide Book to the *Collected Explanations of the Zhou Changes*). Jinan: Qilu shushe Press, 2005, 227. Translator's Note: It means that in his view hexagram Heng [☳☴] is transformed from hexagram Tai [☷☰] through the exchange of positions of line 4 and line 1 of the latter.

cdlxxxii Richard John Lynn, *The Classic of Changes: A New Translation of the I Ching as Interpreted by Wang Bi*. New York: Columbia University Press, 1994, 345.

cdlxxxiii Zhang Wenzhi 张文智, *Zhou yi jijie daodu* 周易集解导读 (A Guide Book to the *Collected Explanations of the Zhou Changes*). Jinan: Qilu shushe Press, 2005, 233.

cdlxxxiv Richard John Lynn, *The Classic of Changes: A New Translation of the I Ching as Interpreted by Wang Bi*. New York: Columbia University Press, 1994, 144.

cdlxxxv Zhang Wenzhi 张文智, *Zhou yi jijie daodu* 周易集解导读 (A Guide Book to the *Collected Explanations of the Zhou Changes*). Jinan: Qilu shushe Press, 2005, 144.

cdlxxxvi Richard John Lynn, *The Classic of Changes: A New Translation of the I Ching as Interpreted by Wang Bi*. New York: Columbia University Press, 1994, 51.

cdlxxxvii Zhang Wenzhi 张文智, *Zhou yi jijie daodu* 周易集解导读 (A Guide Book to the *Collected Explanations of the Zhou Changes*). Jinan: Qilu shushe Press, 2005, 356.

cdlxxxviii Richard John Lynn, *The Classic of Changes: A New Translation of the I Ching as Interpreted by Wang Bi*. New York: Columbia University Press, 1994, 143, modified.

cdlxxxix Zhang Wenzhi 张文智, *Zhou yi jijie daodu* 周易集解导读 (A Guide Book to the *Collected Explanations of the Zhou Changes*). Jinan: Qilu shushe Press, 2005, 108.

cdxc Richard John Lynn, *The Classic of Changes: A New Translation of the I Ching as Interpreted by Wang Bi*. New York: Columbia University Press, 1994, 137.

cdxci Zhang Wenzhi 张文智, *Zhou yi jijie daodu* 周易集解导读 (A Guide Book to the *Collected Explanations of the Zhou Changes*). Jinan: Qilu shushe Press, 2005, 99.

cdxcii Richard John Lynn, *The Classic of Changes: A New Translation of the I Ching as Interpreted by Wang Bi*. New York: Columbia University Press, 1994, 138, slightly modified.

cdxciii Zhang Wenzhi 张文智, *Zhou yi jijie daodu* 周易集解导读 (A Guide Book to the *Collected Explanations of the Zhou Changes*). Jinan: Qilu shushe Press, 2005, 105.

cdxciv Richard John Lynn, *The Classic of Changes: A New Translation of the I Ching as Interpreted by Wang Bi*. New York: Columbia University Press, 1994, 381.

cdxcv Zhang Wenzhi 张文智, *Zhou yi jijie daodu* 周易集解导读 (A Guide Book to the *Collected Explanations of the Zhou Changes*). Jinan: Qilu shushe Press, 2005, 254.

cdxcvi Richard John Lynn, *The Classic of Changes: A New Translation of the I Ching as Interpreted by Wang Bi*. New York: Columbia University Press, 1994, 208, slightly modified.

cdxcvii	Chen Shou 陈寿, *Sanguo zhi* 三国志 (History of the Three Kingdoms). Beijing: Zhonghua shuju, 1959, 1321.
cdxcviii	This is from Yu's annotation to the Judgment of hexagram Kan [☵, Sink Hole, 29]; see Zhang Wenzhi 张文智, *Zhou yi jijie daodu* 周易集解导读 (A Guide Book to the *Collected Explanations of the Zhou Changes*). Jinan: Qilu shushe Press, 2005, 215.
cdxcix	Richard John Lynn, *The Classic of Changes: A New Translation of the I Ching as Interpreted by Wang Bi*. New York: Columbia University Press, 1994, 66.
d	Zhang Wenzhi 张文智, *Zhou yi jijie daodu* 周易集解导读 (A Guide Book to the *Collected Explanations of the Zhou Changes*). Jinan: Qilu shushe Press, 2005, 381-2.
di	Richard John Lynn, *The Classic of Changes: A New Translation of the I Ching as Interpreted by Wang Bi*. New York: Columbia University Press, 1994, 526, slightly modified.
dii	See Zhang Huiyan's 张惠言 (1761-1802) *Yiyi bie lu* 易义别录 (Separate Record of the Meanings of the *Changes*), *juan* 1.
diii	Richard John Lynn, *The Classic of Changes: A New Translation of the I Ching as Interpreted by Wang Bi*. New York: Columbia University Press, 1994, 249, modified.
div	Ibid., 280.
dv	Ban Gu 班固, *Han shu* 汉书 (History of the Western Han Dynasty [206 B.C.E.-9 C.E.]). Beijing: Zhonghua shuju, 1962, 3160.
dvi	Please see Lin Zhongjun 林忠军, *Yiwei daodu* 易纬导读 (A Guidebook to the *Apocrypha of the Changes*). Jinan: Qilu shushe Press, 2002, 140-183.
dvii	Richard John Lynn, *The Classic of Changes: A New Translation of the I Ching as Interpreted by Wang Bi*. New York: Columbia University Press, 1994, 66.
dviii	Ibid., 445, slightly modified.
dix	Ibid., 121-122, slightly modified.
dx	Ibid., 286, slightly modified.
dxi	Ban Gu 班固, *Han shu* 汉书 (History of the Western Han Dynasty [206 B.C.E.-9 C.E.]). Beijing: Zhonghua shuju, 1962, 3390.
dxii	Ibid., 3390.
dxiii	Richard John Lynn, *The Classic of Changes: A New Translation of the I Ching as Interpreted by Wang Bi*. New York: Columbia University Press, 1994, 61.
dxiv	Li Xueqin 李学勤 (ed.), *Liji zhengyi* 礼记正义 (Correct Meaning of the *Book of Rites*). Beijing: Peking University Press, 1999, 544.
dxv	Li Xueqin 李学勤 (ed.), *Chunqiu zuozhuan zhengyi* 春秋左传正义 (Correct Meaning of Zuo's Commentary on the *Spring and Autumn Annals*). Beijing: Peking University Press, 1999, 1172.
dxvi	Ibid., 305.
dxvii	Ibid., 306.
dxviii	Ban Gu 班固, *Han shu* 汉书 (History of the Western Han Dynasty [206 B.C.E.-9 C.E.]). Beijing: Zhonghua shuju, 1962, 3597-3598.
dxix	Ibid., 3620.
dxx	Fan Ye 范晔, *Houhan shu* 后汉书 (History of the Eastern Han Dynasty [25-220]). Beijing: Zhonghua shuju, 1965, 1213.

dxxi	Pi Xirui 皮锡瑞, *Jingxue lishi* 经学历史 (A History of Confucian Classics Studies). Beijing: Zhonghua shuju, 2008, 137.
dxxii	Richard John Lynn, *The Classic of Changes: A New Translation of the I Ching as Interpreted by Wang Bi*. New York: Columbia University Press, 1994, 31.
dxxiii	Ibid., 31.
dxxiv	Ibid., 32, slightly modified.
dxxv	Ibid., 32, slightly modified.
dxxvi	Ibid, 32.
dxxvii	Ibid., 32.
dxxviii	Ibid., 32.
dxxix	Ibid., 32.
dxxx	Ibid., 94-95.
dxxxi	Ibid., 133.
dxxxii	Ibid., 136, slightly modified.
dxxxiii	Ban Gu 班固, *Han shu* 汉书 (History of the Western Han Dynasty [206 B.C.E.-9 C.E.]). Beijing: Zhonghua shuju, 1962, 3597-3598.
dxxxiv	Zhao Shixiu 赵师秀, *Qingyuan zhai shiji* 清苑斋诗集 (Collection of Zhao Shixiu's Poems), in the *Yongjia si ling shiji* 永嘉四灵诗集 (Collection of the Four Talents' Poems from Yongjia County, Zhejiang Province). Hangzhou: Zhejiang guji chubanshe, 1985, 270.
dxxxv	Wei Zheng 魏征 (et al), *Sui shu* 隋书 (History of the Sui Dynasty [581-618]). Beijing: Zhounghua shuju, 1973, 911.
dxxxvi	Richard John Lynn, *The Classic of Changes: A New Translation of the I Ching as Interpreted by Wang Bi*. New York: Columbia University Press, 1994, 285.
dxxxvii	Ibid., 286.
dxxxviii	See Liu Yujian 刘玉建, *Zhou yi zhengyi daodu* 周易正义导读 (A Guide Book to the *Correct Meaning of the Zhou Changes*). Jinan: Qilu shushe Press, 2005, 213.
dxxxix	Richard John Lynn, *The Classic of Changes: A New Translation of the I Ching as Interpreted by Wang Bi*. New York: Columbia University Press, 1994, 208.
dxl	Ibid., 208, slightly modified.
dxli	Ibid., 129.
dxlii	Ibid., 129, slightly modified.
dxliii	Wei Zheng 魏征 (et al), *Sui shu* 隋书 (History of the Sui Dynasty [581-618]). Beijing: Zhounghua shuju, 1973, 913.
dxliv	Ibid., 913.
dxlv	See Liu Yujian 刘玉建, *Zhouyi zhengyi daodu* 周易正义导读 (A Guide Book to the *Correct Meaning of the Zhou Changes*). Jinan: Qilu shushe Press, 2005, 93.
dxlvi	Ibid., 94.
dxlvii	Ibid., 94.
dxlviii	Ibid., 92.
dxlix	Ibid., 89.
dl	Ibid., 89.
dli	Ibid., 89.
dlii	Richard John Lynn, *The Classic of Changes: A New Translation of the I Ching as Interpreted by Wang Bi*. New York: Columbia University Press, 1994, 67.
dliii	Ibid., 67.

dliv See Liu Yujian 刘玉建, *Zhou yi zhengyi daodu* 周易正义导读 (A Guide Book to the *Correct Meaning of the Zhou Changes*). Jinan: Qilu shushe Press, 2005, 89.

dlv Ibid., 89.

dlvi Richard John Lynn, *The Classic of Changes: A New Translation of the I Ching as Interpreted by Wang Bi*. New York: Columbia University Press, 1994, 80, modified.

dlvii See Liu Yujian 刘玉建, *Zhou yi zhengyi daodu* 周易正义导读 (A Guide Book to the *Correct Meaning of the Zhou Changes*). Jinan: Qilu shushe Press, 2005, 89.

dlviii Ibid., 53, slightly modified.

dlix Ibid., 129.

dlx Ibid., 89.

dlxi See Liu Yujian 刘玉建, *Zhou yi zhengyi daodu* 周易正义导读 (A Guide Book to the *Correct Meaning of the Zhou Changes*). Jinan: Qilu shushe Press, 2005, 97.

dlxii Richard John Lynn, *The Classic of Changes: A New Translation of the I Ching as Interpreted by Wang Bi*. New York: Columbia University Press, 1994, 32.

dlxiii Ibid., 134.

dlxiv Ibid., 147.

dlxv See Liu Yujian 刘玉建, *Zhou yi zhengyi daodu* 周易正义导读 (A Guide Book to the *Correct Meaning of the Zhou Changes*). Jinan: Qilu shushe Press, 2005, 126.

dlxvi Richard John Lynn, *The Classic of Changes: A New Translation of the I Ching as Interpreted by Wang Bi*. New York: Columbia University Press, 1994, 248, modified.

dlxvii Ibid., 249.

dlxviii Ibid. 504.

dlxix Ibid. 505, slightly modified.

dlxx See Liu Yujian 刘玉建, *Zhou yi zhengyi daodu* 周易正义导读 (A Guide Book to the *Correct Meaning of the Zhou Changes*). Jinan: Qilu shushe Press, 2005, 194.

dlxxi Richard John Lynn, *The Classic of Changes: A New Translation of the I Ching as Interpreted by Wang Bi*. New York: Columbia University Press, 1994, 121.

dlxxii Ibid., 399.

dlxxiii Zhang Wenzhi 张文智, *Zhou yi jijie daodu* 周易集解导读 (A Guide Book to the *Collected Explanations of the Zhou Changes*). Jinan: Qilu shushe Press, 2005, 84.

dlxxiv Richard John Lynn, *The Classic of Changes: A New Translation of the I Ching as Interpreted by Wang Bi*. New York: Columbia University Press, 1994, 66, slightly modified.

dlxxv Li Xueqin 李学勤 (ed.), *Shangshu zhengyi* 春秋左传正义 (Correct Meaning of the *Classic of History*). Beijing: Peking University Press, 1999, 503.

dlxxvi See Zhang Wenzhi 张文智, *Zhou yi jijie daodu* 周易集解导读 (A Guide Book to the *Collected Explanations of the Zhou Changes*) (Jinan: Qilu shushe Press, 2005, 383) or Liu Yujian 刘玉建, *Zhou yi zhengyi daodu* 周易正义导读 (A Guide Book to the *Correct Meaning of the Zhou Changes*) (Jinan: Qilu shushe Press, 2005, 396).

dlxxvii Richard John Lynn, *The Classic of Changes: A New Translation of the I Ching as Interpreted by Wang Bi*. New York: Columbia University Press, 1994, 60.

dlxxviii Ban Gu 班固, *Han shu* 汉书 (History of the Western Han Dynasty [206 B.C.E.-9 C.E.]). Beijing: Zhonghua shuju, 1962, 985.

dlxxix Lin Zhongjun 林忠军, *Yi wei daodu* 易纬导读 (A Guide Book to the *Apocrypha of the Changes*). Jinan: Qilu shushe Press, 2002, 126.

dlxxx Lin Zhongjun 林忠军, *Zhou yi zhenshi xue chanwei* 周易郑氏学阐微 (A Subtle Elucidation of Zheng Xuan's Scholarship on the *Changes*). Shanghai: Shanghai guji Press, 2005, 383-4.

dlxxxi Zhang Wenzhi 张文智, *Zhou yi jijie daodu* 周易集解导读 (A Guide Book to the *Collected Explanations of the Zhou Changes*). Jinan: Qilu shushe Press, 2005, 371.

dlxxxii Xiao Hanming 萧汉明, *Zhou yi benyi daodu* 周易本义导读 (A Guide Book to the *Original Meaning of the Zhou Changes*). Jinan: Qilu shushe Press, 2003, 68.

dlxxxiii Lin Zhongjun 林忠军, *Yi wei daodu* 易纬导读 (A Guide Book to the *Apocrypha of the Changes*). Jinan: Qilu shushe Press, 2002, 94.

dlxxxiv Ibid., 94.

dlxxxv Ibid., 94.

dlxxxvi Please see Liu Baozhen 刘保贞, *Yitu mingbian daodu* 易图明辨导读 (A Guidebook to the *Clarifying Critique of the Illustrations Associated with the Changes*). Jinan: Qilu shushe Press, 2004,124.

dlxxxvii For the detailing of these controversies, please see Huang Zhongxi 黄宗羲 (author) and Zheng Wangeng's 郑万耕 (punctuator) *Yixue xiangshu lun* 易学象数论 (Discussion of Images and Numbers in *Changes* Scholarship) (Beijing: Zhonghua shuju, 2010, 16-7) or the brief introduction to Liu Mu's *Yishu gouyin tu* 易数钩隐图 (Investigation into the Hidden: Illustrations of *Changes* Numerology) in Yongrong 永瑢 et al., *Siku quanshu zongmu* 四库全书总目 (General Catalogue of the Complete Collection of the Four Treasuries)(Beijing: Zhonghua shuju, 1965, 5).

dlxxxviii Xiao Hanming 萧汉明, *Zhou yi benyi daodu* 周易本义导读 (A Guide Book to the *Original Meaning of the Zhou Changes*). Jinan: Qilu shushe Press, 2003, 78.

dlxxxix See Richard John Lynn, *The Classic of Changes: A New Translation of the I Ching as Interpreted by Wang Bi*. New York: Columbia University Press, 1994, 121.

dxc Ibid., 124, slightly modified.

dxci Ibid., 56, modified.

dxcii Zhang Wenzhi 张文智, *Zhou yi jijie daodu* 周易集解导读 (A Guide Book to the *Collected Explanations of the Zhou Changes*). Jinan: Qilu shushe Press, 2005, 361.

dxciii Richard John Lynn, *The Classic of Changes: A New Translation of the I Ching as Interpreted by Wang Bi*. New York: Columbia University Press, 1994, 150.

dxciv Zhang Wenzhi 张文智, *Zhou yi jijie daodu* 周易集解导读 (A Guide Book to the *Collected Explanations of the Zhou Changes*). Jinan: Qilu shushe Press, 2005, 117.

dxcv John S. Major, Sarah A. Queen, Andrew Seth Meyer, and Harold D. Roth (trans. and eds.), *The Huainanzi*. New York: Columbia University Press, 2010, 569.

dxcvi Richard John Lynn, *The Classic of Changes: A New Translation of the I Ching as Interpreted by Wang Bi*. New York: Columbia University Press, 1994, 129, modified.

dxcvii Zhang Wenzhi 张文智, *Zhou yi jijie daodu* 周易集解导读 (A Guide Book to the *Collected Explanations of the Zhou Changes*). Jinan: Qilu shushe Press, 2005, 91.

dxcviii Ibid., 158.

dxcix Ibid., 159.

dc Li Xueqin 李学勤 (ed.), *Chunqiu zuozhuan zhengyi* 春秋左传正义 (Correct Meaning of the *Zuo's Commentary on the Spring and Autumn Annals*). Beijing: Beijing University Press, 1999, 310.

dci	Richard John Lynn, *The Classic of Changes: A New Translation of the I Ching as Interpreted by Wang Bi*. New York: Columbia University Press, 1994, 123.
dcii	Zhang Wenzhi 张文智, *Zhou yi jijie daodu* 周易集解导读 (A Guide Book to the Collected Explanations of the Zhou Changes). Jinan: Qilu shushe Press, 2005, 158.
dciii	Ibid., 159.
dciv	Team for Cultural Relics of Anhui Province, Museum of Fuyang Prefecture, Bureau of Culture of Fuyang County, "A Brief Report on the Excavation of the Western Han Marquis Ruyin's Tomb at Shuanggudui of Fuyang County" (*Fuyang shuanggudui xihan ruyinhou mu fajue jianbao* 阜阳双古堆西汉汝阴侯墓发掘简报), in *Wenwu* 文物 (Cultural Relics), no.8 (1978), 18-9.
dcv	Liu Xu 刘昫 et al., *Jiu Tang shu* 旧唐书 (Old Book of the Tang [618-907]). Beijing: Zhonghua shuju, 1998, 626.
dcvi	Hou Wailu 侯外庐, Qiu Hansheng 邱汉生, and Zhang Qizhi 张岂之 (ed.), *Songming lixue shi (shang)* 宋明理学史(上) (A History of the Song-Ming [960-1644] Neo-Confucianism) (I). Beijing: Renming chubanshe, 1984, 9.
dcvii	Ibid., 10.
dcviii	Richard John Lynn, *The Classic of Changes: A New Translation of the I Ching as Interpreted by Wang Bi*. New York: Columbia University Press, 1994, 132.
dcix	Liang Weixian 梁韦弦, *Cheng shi yizhuan daodu* 程氏易传导读 (A Guidebook to Cheng Yi's Commentary on the Changes). Jinan: Qilu shushe Press, 2003, 51.
dcx	Richard John Lynn, *The Classic of Changes: A New Translation of the I Ching as Interpreted by Wang Bi*. New York: Columbia University Press, 1994, 47, slightly modified.
dcxi	Cheng Hao 程颢 and Cheng Yi 程颐, *Er Cheng ji* 二程集 (Collected Works of Cheng's Brothers). Beijing: Zhonghua shuju, 2004, 1027.
dcxii	Richard John Lynn, *The Classic of Changes: A New Translation of the I Ching as Interpreted by Wang Bi*. New York: Columbia University Press, 1994, 51.
dcxiii	Cheng Hao 程颢 and Cheng Yi 程颐, *Er Cheng ji* 二程集 (Collected Works of Cheng's Brothers). Beijing: Zhonghua shuju, 2004, 1028.
dcxiv	Lu Deming 陆德明, *Jingdian shiwen* 经典释文 (Exegetical Texts of the Classics). Shanghai: Shanghai guji chubanshe, 2013, 122.
dcxv	Ibid., 1028.
dcxvi	Richard John Lynn, *The Classic of Changes: A New Translation of the I Ching as Interpreted by Wang Bi*. New York: Columbia University Press, 1994, 54.
dcxvii	Cheng Hao 程颢 and Cheng Yi 程颐, *Er Cheng yi shu* 二程遗书 (Analects of Cheng's Brothers). Shanghai: Shanghai guji chubanshe, 2000, 277.
dcxviii	Richard John Lynn, *The Classic of Changes: A New Translation of the I Ching as Interpreted by Wang Bi*. New York: Columbia University Press, 1994, 62.
dcxix	Cheng Hao 程颢 and Cheng Yi 程颐, *Er Cheng yi shu* 二程遗书 (Analects of Cheng's Brothers). Shanghai: Shanghai guji chubanshe, 2000, 103.
dcxx	Richard John Lynn, *The Classic of Changes: A New Translation of the I Ching as Interpreted by Wang Bi*. New York: Columbia University Press, 1994, 63.
dcxxi	Cheng Hao 程颢 and Cheng Yi 程颐, *Er Cheng yi shu* 二程遗书 (Analects of Cheng's Brothers). Shanghai: Shanghai guji chubanshe, 2000, 94.
dcxxii	Richard John Lynn, *The Classic of Changes: A New Translation of the I Ching as Interpreted by Wang Bi*. New York: Columbia University Press, 1994, 418.
dcxxiii	Ibid., 418, slightly modified.

dcxxiv	Liang Weixian 梁韦弦, *Cheng shi yizhuan daodu* 程氏易传导读 (A Guidebook to *Cheng Yi's Commentary on the Changes*). Jinan: Qilu shushe Press, 2003, 267.
dcxxv	Cheng Hao 程颢 and Cheng Yi 程颐, *Er Cheng yi shu* 二程遗书 (Analects of Cheng's Brothers). Shanghai: Shanghai guji chubanshe, 2000, 213.
dcxxvi	Ibid., 225.
dcxxvii	See Liu Yujian 刘玉建, *Zhouyi zhengyi daodu* 周易正义导读 (A Guide Book to the *Correct Meaning of the Zhou Changes*). Jinan: Qilu shushe Press, 2005, 89.
dcxxviii	Richard John Lynn, *The Classic of Changes: A New Translation of the I Ching as Interpreted by Wang Bi*. New York: Columbia University Press, 1994, 274.
dcxxix	Ibid., 152, slightly modified.
dcxxx	Ibid., 153, slightly modified.
dcxxxi	Ibid., 170, slightly modified.
dcxxxii	Ibid., 171, slightly modified.
dcxxxiii	Ibid., 191, slightly modified.
dcxxxiv	Ibid., 223, slightly modified.
dcxxxv	Ibid., 286, modified.
dcxxxvi	Ibid., 280, modified.
dcxxxvii	Ibid., 396. [It means that hexagram Yi ䷩ was derived from the exchange of the positions of line 1 and line 4 of hexagram Pi ䷋, indicating that one *yang* line of the upper trigram of Qian ☰ of the latter was diminished and transformed into trigram Xun ☴ while the lower trigram Kun ☷ of the latter was increased with the *yang* line diminished from the upper trigram and turned to be trigram Zhen ☳.]
dcxxxviii	Ibid., 389, slightly modified.
dcxxxix	Ibid., 385. [It means that hexagram Sun ䷨ was derived from the exchange of the positions of line 3 and line 6 of hexagram Tai ䷊, the diminution of a *yang* line from the lower trigram Qian ☰ and the increase of the *yang* line in the upper trigram Kun ☷ of the latter.]
dcxl	Ibid., 404, slightly modified.
dcxli	Ibid., 411, slightly modified.
dcxlii	Ibid., 438, slightly modified.
dcxliii	Ibid., 452.
dcxliv	Ibid., 266.
dcxlv	Liang Weixian 梁韦弦, *Cheng shi yizhuan daodu* 程氏易传导读 (A Guidebook to *Cheng Yi's Commentary on the Changes*). Jinan: Qilu shushe Press, 2003, 154.
dcxlvi	Ibid., 154.
dcxlvii	Ibid., 154.
dcxlviii	Richard John Lynn, *The Classic of Changes: A New Translation of the I Ching as Interpreted by Wang Bi*. New York: Columbia University Press, 1994, 66.
dcxlix	Liang Weixian 梁韦弦, *Cheng shi yizhuan daodu* 程氏易传导读 (A Guidebook to *Cheng Yi's Commentary on the Changes*). Jinan: Qilu shushe Press, 2003, 154.
dcl	Wang Yinglin 王应麟, *Kunxue jiwen* 困学纪闻 (Notes and Knowledge from Learning in Difficulty). Shanghai: Shanghai gujie Press, 2008, 87.
dcli	Richard John Lynn, *The Classic of Changes: A New Translation of the I Ching as Interpreted by Wang Bi*. New York: Columbia University Press, 1994, 63.
dclii	Cheng Hao 程颢 and Cheng Yi 程颐, *Er Cheng yi shu* 二程遗书 (Analects of Cheng's Brothers). Shanghai: Shanghai guji chubanshe, 2000, 200.

dcliii	Ibid., 207.
dcliv	Richard John Lynn, *The Classic of Changes: A New Translation of the I Ching as Interpreted by Wang Bi*. New York: Columbia University Press, 1994, 120, modified.
dclv	Li Jingde 黎靖德 (ed.), *Zhuzhi yulei* 朱子语类 (A Compilation of the Classified Questions and Answers between Zhu Xi's Disciples and Zhu Xi). Beijiing: Zhounghua shuju, 1986, 1922.
dclvi	Zhang Wenzhi 张文智, *Zhouyi jijie daodu* 周易集解导读 (A Guide Book to the Collected Explanations of the Zhou Changes). Jinan: Qilu shushe Press, 2005, 88.
dclvii	Xiao Hanming 萧汉明, *Zhouyi benyi daodu* 周易本义导读 (A Guide Book of the Original Meaning of the Zhou Changes). Jinan: Qilu shushe Press, 2003, 80.
dclviii	Richard John Lynn, *The Classic of Changes: A New Translation of the I Ching as Interpreted by Wang Bi*. New York: Columbia University Press, 1994, 129.
dclix	Xiao Hanming 萧汉明, *Zhouyi benyi daodu* 周易本义导读 (A Guide Book of the Original Meaning of the Zhou Changes). Jinan: Qilu shushe Press, 2003, 167.
dclx	Ibid., 167.
dclxi	Richard John Lynn, *The Classic of Changes: A New Translation of the I Ching as Interpreted by Wang Bi*. New York: Columbia University Press, 1994, 460-1.
dclxii	Xiao Hanming 萧汉明, *Zhouyi benyi daodu* 周易本义导读 (A Guide Book of the Original Meaning of the Zhou Changes). Jinan: Qilu shushe Press, 2003, 187, [and in this way, the meaning of the whole sentence will come to be: "(The ability to control the ladle and) the fragrant wine shows that this one may thereby be entrusted with the maintenance of the ancestral temple."].
dclxiii	Ibid., 224.
dclxiv	Richard John Lynn, *The Classic of Changes: A New Translation of the I Ching as Interpreted by Wang Bi*. New York: Columbia University Press, 1994, 524.
dclxv	Xiao Hanming 萧汉明, *Zhouyi benyi daodu* 周易本义导读 (A Guide Book of the Original Meaning of the Zhou Changes). Jinan: Qilu shushe Press, 2003, 224.
dclxvi	Ibid., 153.
dclxvii	Ibid., 217.
dclxviii	Richard John Lynn, *The Classic of Changes: A New Translation of the I Ching as Interpreted by Wang Bi*. New York: Columbia University Press, 1994, 360.
dclxix	Xiao Hanming 萧汉明, *Zhouyi benyi daodu* 周易本义导读 (A Guide Book of the Original Meaning of the Zhou Changes). Jinan: Qilu shushe Press, 2003, 127.
dclxx	Liang Weixian 梁韦弦, *Cheng shi yizhuan daodu* 程氏易传导读 (A Guidebook to Cheng Yi's Commentary on the Changes). Jinan: Qilu shushe Press, 2003, 223.
dclxxi	Richard John Lynn, *The Classic of Changes: A New Translation of the I Ching as Interpreted by Wang Bi*. New York: Columbia University Press, 1994, 432.
dclxxii	Xiao Hanming 萧汉明, *Zhouyi benyi daodu* 周易本义导读 (A Guide Book of the Original Meaning of the Zhou Changes). Jinan: Qilu shushe Press, 2003, 141.
dclxxiii	Ibid., 162.
dclxxiv	Ibid., 226.
dclxxv	Ibid., 80.
dclxxvi	Ibid., 80.
dclxxvii	Ibid., 81.
dclxxviii	Ibid., 80.

dclxxix	Richard John Lynn, *The Classic of Changes: A New Translation of the I Ching as Interpreted by Wang Bi*. New York: Columbia University Press, 1994, 65, slightly modified.
dclxxx	Ibid., 65-6, slightly modified.
dclxxxi	Ibid., 75.
dclxxxii	Huang Zhongxi 黄宗羲 (author) and Zheng Wangeng 郑万耕 (punctuator), *Yixue xiangshu lun* 易学象数论 (Discussion of Images and Numbers in *Changes* Scholarship). Beijing: Zhonghua shuju Press, 2010, 27.
dclxxxiii	Richard John Lynn, *The Classic of Changes: A New Translation of the I Ching as Interpreted by Wang Bi*. New York: Columbia University Press, 1994, 51.
dclxxxiv	Cheng Hao 程颢 and Cheng Yi 程颐, *Er Cheng ji* 二程集 (Collected Works of Cheng's Brothers). Beijing: Zhonghua shuju, 2004, 1028.
dclxxxv	Zhang Zai 张载, *Zhang Zai ji* 张载集 (Collected Works of Zhang Zai). Beijing: Zhonghua shuju, 1978, 181.
dclxxxvi	Ibid., 182.
dclxxxvii	Ibid., 204.
dclxxxviii	Ibid., 204.
dclxxxix	Richard John Lynn, *The Classic of Changes: A New Translation of the I Ching as Interpreted by Wang Bi*. New York: Columbia University Press, 1994, 51, modified.
dcxc	Liu Yujian 刘玉建, *Zhouyi zhengyi daodu* 周易正义导读 (A Guide Book to the Correct Meaning of the Zhou Changes). Jinan: Qilu shushe Press, 2005, 371.
dcxci	Ibid., 371.
dcxcii	Zhang Zai 张载, *Zhang Zai ji* 张载集 (Collected Works of Zhang Zai). Beijing: Zhonghua shuju, 1978, 182.
dcxciii	Liu Yujian 刘玉建, *Zhouyi zhengyi daodu* 周易正义导读 (A Guide Book to the Correct Meaning of the Zhou Changes). Jinan: Qilu shushe Press, 2005, 373-374.
dcxciv	Ibid., 373-374.
dcxcv	Zhang Zai 张载, *Zhang Zai ji* 张载集 (Collected Works of Zhang Zai). Beijing: Zhonghua shuju, 1978, 182.
dcxcvi	Ibid., 185.
dcxcvii	Richard John Lynn, *The Classic of Changes: A New Translation of the I Ching as Interpreted by Wang Bi*. New York: Columbia University Press, 1994, 134.
dcxcviii	Ibid., 148.
dcxcix	Ibid., 168.
dcc	Ibid., 231.
dcci	Yongrong 永瑢 et al., *Siku quanshu zongmu* 四库全书总目 (General Catalogue of the *Complete Collection of the Four Treasuries*). Beijing: Zhonghua shuju, 1965, 24.
dccii	Xiao Hanming 萧汉明, *Zhouyi benyi daodu* 周易本义导读 (A Guide Book to the Original Meaning of the Zhou Changes). Jinan: Qilu shushe Press, 2003, 78.
dcciii	Richard J. Smith, *Fathoming the Cosmos and Ordering the World: The Yijing (I-Ching, or Classic of Changes and Its Evolution in China*. Charlottesville: University of Virginia Press, 2008, 162.
dcciv	Ibid., 241.
dccv	Ibid., 249, modified.
dccvi	Ibid., 162.

Endnotes

dccvii Yongrong 永瑢 et al., *Siku quanshu zongmu* 四库全书总目 (General Catalogue of the *Complete Collection of the Four Treasuries*). Beijing: Zhonghua shuju, 1965, 30.

dccviii Ibid., 30.

dccix Pi Xirui 皮锡瑞, *Jingxue lishi* 经学历史 (A History of Confucian Classics Studies). Beijing: Zhonghua shuju, 2008, 289.

dccx Ibid., 299.

dccxi Yongrong 永瑢 et al., *Siku quanshu zongmu* 四库全书总目 (General Catalogue of the *Complete Collection of the Four Treasuries*). Beijing: Zhonghua shuju, 1965, 35.

dccxii Ibid., 35.

dccxiii Ibid., 35.

dccxiv Fu Heng 傅恒 et al. (ed.), *Zhou yi shu yi* 周易述义 (Narration of the Meaning of the *Zhou Changes*), in Ji Yun 纪昀 et al. (ed.), *Siku quanshu* 四库全书 (Imperial Edition of the Complete Collection of the Four Treasuries), vol. 38, 565.

dccxv Richard John Lynn, *The Classic of Changes: A New Translation of the I Ching as Interpreted by Wang Bi*. New York: Columbia University Press, 1994, 152.

dccxvi Ibid., 122.

dccxvii According to the "Discussion of the Trigrams" (*Shuogua* 说卦), Kun [☷] "is the multitude of things themselves." See Ibid., 123.

dccxviii According to the "Discussion of the Trigrams" (*Shuogua* 说卦), The inner trigram Zhen [☳] is "the Eldest Son" [see Ibid., 123], whereas the fifth line statement of hexagram Shi [䷆, The Army, 7] is "the eldest son *takes command* of the Army" (see Ibid., 180, slightly modified).

dccxix The bottom line statement of hexagram Zhun [䷂, Birth Thrones, 3] is, "It is fitting to establish a *chief*."

dccxx In hexagram Zhun [䷂, Birth Thrones, 3], both the bottom line and the fifth line are *yang* lines, so they have the same nature [and the fifth line corresponds to an *established* ruler].

dccxxi Fu Heng 傅恒 et al. (ed.), *Zhou yi shu yi* 周易述义 (Narration of the Meaning of the *Zhou Changes*), in Ji Yun 纪昀 et al. (ed.), *Siku quanshu* 四库全书 (Imperial Edition of the Complete Collection of the Four Treasuries), vol. 38, 572.

dccxxii Zhang Huiyan 张惠言, *Zhou yi Yushi yi* 周易虞氏易 (The Meaning of the *Zhou Changes* Based on [the Interpretations of] Yu Fan), in Liu Dajun 刘大钧 and Lin Zhongjun 林忠军 (eds.), vol. 10 of the *Ruzang jinghua bian* 儒藏精华编 (Collection of Quintessential Confucian Works). Beijing: Beijing University Press, 2010, 9.

dccxxiii Yongrong 永瑢 et al., *Siku quanshu zongmu* 四库全书总目 (General Catalogue of the *Complete Collection of the Four Treasuries*). Beijing: Zhonghua shuju, 1965, 1.

dccxxiv Ibid., 1.

dccxxv Ibid., 20.

dccxxvi Richard John Lynn, *The Classic of Changes: A New Translation of the I Ching as Interpreted by Wang Bi*. New York: Columbia University Press, 1994, 60, slightly modified.

dccxxvii Ibid., 445.

dccxxviii Ibid., 518.

dccxxix	Yongrong 永瑢 et al., *Siku quanshu zongmu* 四库全书总目 (General Catalogue of the Complete Collection of the Four Treasuries). Beijing: Zhonghua shuju, 1965, 21.
dccxxx	Ibid., 23.
dccxxxi	Ibid., 28.
dccxxxii	Richard John Lynn, *The Classic of Changes: A New Translation of the I Ching as Interpreted by Wang Bi*. New York: Columbia University Press, 1994, 80, slightly modified.
dccxxxiii	Yongrong 永瑢 et al., *Siku quanshu zongmu* 四库全书总目 (General Catalogue of the Complete Collection of the Four Treasuries). Beijing: Zhonghua shuju, 1965, 43.
dccxxxiv	Ibid., 43-44.
dccxxxv	Ibid., 44.
dccxxxvi	Ibid., 6.
dccxxxvii	Ibid., 18.
dccxxxviii	Ibid., 23.
dccxxxix	Ibid., 49.
dccxl	Ibid., 49.
dccxli	Richard John Lynn, *The Classic of Changes: A New Translation of the I Ching as Interpreted by Wang Bi*. New York: Columbia University Press, 1994, 77, slightly modified.
dccxlii	Yongrong 永瑢 et al., *Siku quanshu zongmu* 四库全书总目 (General Catalogue of the Complete Collection of the Four Treasuries). Beijing: Zhonghua shuju, 1965, 49.
dccxliii	Ibid., 80
dccxliv	Ibid., 56-7.
dccxlv	Ibid., 77.
dccxlvi	This essay was originally published in Liu Dajun刘大钧, *Najia shifa* 纳甲筮法 (Thee-Coin Method of Divination) (Jinan: Qilu shushe Press, 1995), and then was collected in Liu Dajun 刘大钧, *Hong yi ji* 弘易集 (Collection of the Speeches and Prefaces to Promote Scholarship on the *Changes*) (Shanghai: Shanghai Library and Shanghai kexue jishu wenxian chubanshe, 2013, 100-101).
dccxlvii	Richard John Lynn, *The Classic of Changes: A New Translation of the I Ching as Interpreted by Wang Bi*. New York: Columbia University Press, 1994, 274.
dccxlviii	For the detailing of his views, please see his *Essay on Man*.
dccxlix	Richard John Lynn, *The Classic of Changes: A New Translation of the I Ching as Interpreted by Wang Bi*. New York: Columbia University Press, 1994, 77, slightly modified.
dccl	This essay was originally published in Liu Dajun刘大钧, *Najia shifa* 纳甲筮法 (Thee-Coin Method of Divination) (Jinan: Qilu shushe Press, 1995), and was then collected in Liu Dajun 刘大钧, *Hong yi ji* 弘易集 (Collection of the Speeches and Prefaces to Promote Scholarship on the *Changes*) (Shanghai: Shanghai Library and Shanghai kexue jishu wenxian chubanshe, 2013, 102-103).
dccli	Ban Gu 班固, *Han shu* 汉书 (History of the Western Han Dynasty [206 B.C.E.-9 C.E.]). Beijing: Zhonghua shuju, 1962, 1704.
dcclii	Ibid., 1771.
dccliii	Ibid., 1773.

dccliv	Ibid., 1766.
dcclv	Ibid., 1769.
dcclvi	Please see the "Congratulatory Letter from the Famous Scholar Feng Youlan", in Liu Dajun 刘大钧 (ed.), *Da yi jiecheng* 大易集成 (Proceedings of the 1st International Symposium on the *Book of Changes*), the 2nd edition. Shanghai: Shanghai Library and Shanghai kexue jishu wenxian chubanshe, 2017, 3.
dcclvii	See *Zhouyi yanjiu* 周易研究 (Studies of Zhouyi), 1992 (2), 2.
dcclviii	Ban Gu 班固, *Han shu* 汉书 (History of the Western Han Dynasty [206 .B.C.E-9 C.E.]). Beijing: Zhonghua shuju, 1962, 1704.
dcclix	Sima Qian 司马迁, *Shi ji* 史记 (Historical Records). Beijing: Zhonghua shuju, 1959, 1937.
dcclx	Ban Gu 班固, *Han shu* 汉书 (History of the Western Han Dynasty [206 B.C.E.-9 C.E.]). Beijing: Zhonghua shuju, 1962, 3589.
dcclxi	Guo Qiyong 郭奇勇, *Jian bo xue yu zhongguo sixiang shi yanjiu* 简帛学与中国思想史研究 (Unearthed Bamboo-slip and Silk Manuscripts and the History of Chinese Ideologoy), in the *Guangming Daily*, July 31, 2001.
dcclxii	Anold J. Tonybee and Daisaku Ikeda (authors), Feng Feng 冯峰, Jun Xueyan 隽雪艳, and Sun Bin 孙彬 (trans.), *Xuanze shengming: Tangenbi yu Chitian Dazuo duihualu* 选择生命——汤因比与池田大作对谈录 (Choose Life: A Dialogue between Daisaku Ikeda and Anold J. Toynbee). Beijing: The Commercial Press, 2017, 475.
dcclxiii	Richard John Lynn, *The Classic of Changes: A New Translation of the I Ching as Interpreted by Wang Bi*. New York: Columbia University Press, 1994, 143, modified.
dcclxiv	Ban Gu 班固, *Han shu* 汉书 (History of the Western Han Dynasty [206 B.C.E.-9 C.E.]). Beijing: Zhonghua shuju, 1962, 1704.
dcclxv	Yongrong 永瑢 et al., *Siku quanshu zongmu* 四库全书总目 (General Catalogue of the *Complete Collection of the Four Treasuries*). Beijing: Zhonghua shuju, 1965, 1.
dcclxvi	Hu Yuan 胡瑗, *Zhou yi kouyi* 周易口义 (Oral Meanings of the *Zhou Changes*). Changchun: Jilin Publishing Company, Ltd., 2005, 6-7.
dcclxvii	Liu Junzhu 刘君祖, *Yi jing yu xiandai shenghuo* 易经与现代生活 (*Yi jing* and Contemporary Life). Shanghai: Shanghai sanlian shudian, 2009, 96.
dcclxviii	Ibid., 119.
dcclxix	This article was originally published in Chinese in *Zhouyi yanjiu* 周易研究 (Studies of Zhou yi), no.1 (2010): 3-12, and then was collected in Liu Dajun 刘大钧, *Hong yi ji* 弘易集 (Collection of the Speeches and Prefaces to Promote Scholarship on the *Changes*), Shanghai: Shanghai Library and Shanghai kexue jishu wenxian chubanshe, 2013, 193-207.
dcclxx	Feng Youlan 冯友兰, "Preface" to his *Zhongguo zhexue shi xinbian* 中国哲学史新编 (A New Compilation of the History of Chinese Philosophy), vol. 1. Beijing: Remin Press, 1982, 12.
dcclxxi	Wu Huaiqi 吴怀祺, "*Zhou yi yanjiu bashi nian* 周易研究八十年" (80 Years of the Studies of the *Zhou Changes*), in *Zhouyi yanjiu* 周易研究 (Studies of the Zhou yi), no.2 (1989), 96.

dcclxxii	Li Xueqin 李学勤 (ed.), *Chunqiu zuozhuan zhengyi* 春秋左传正义 (Correct Meaning of the *Zuo's Commentary on the Spring and Autumn Annals*). Beijing: Peking University Press, 1999, 382.
dcclxxiii	Ibid., 382.
dcclxxiv	Ibid., 382.
dcclxxv	Richard Wilhelm (tr., rendered into English by Cary Baynes), *The I Ching or Book of Changes*, 3rd ed. Princeton: Princeton University Press, 1967, 287, modified.
dcclxxvi	Wei Litong 魏荔彤, "Introductory Remarks" (*Juan shou* 卷首), in the *Da yi tongjie* 大易通解 (A Thorough Interpretation of the Great *Changes*), vol.1, the *Wen yuan ge* version of the *Siku quanshu* (Complete Collection of the Four Treasuries). Shanghai: Shangwu yinshuguan, 1935, 1.
dcclxxvii	Richard Wilhelm (tr., rendered into English by Cary Baynes), *The I Ching or Book of Changes*, 3rd ed. Princeton: Princeton University Press, 1967, 322, slightly modified.
dcclxxviii	Zhu Xi朱熹, *Hui'an ji yi xiang shuo* 晦庵集·易象说 ("On the Images of the *Changes*" in the *Collected Works of Zhu Xi*), vol. 67, the *Wen yuan ge* 文渊阁 version of the *Si ku quan shu*四库全书 (Complete Collection of the Four Treasuries).
dcclxxix	Edward L. Shaughnessy, *I Ching: The Classic of Changes*. New York: Ballantine Books, 1996, 241, modified.
dcclxxx	Richard John Lynn, *The Classic of Changes: A New Translation of the I Ching as Interpreted by Wang Bi*. New York: Columbia University Press, 1994, 119, slightly modified.
dcclxxxi	Ibid., 119-120, slightly modified.
dcclxxxii	Ibid., 130, slightly modified.
dcclxxxiii	Li Xueqin 李学勤 (ed.), *Chunqiu zuozhuan zhengyi* 春秋左传正义 (Correct Meaning of the *Zuo's Commentary on the Spring and Autumn Annals*). Beijing: Peking University Press, 1999, 870-871.
dcclxxxiv	Richard John Lynn, *The Classic of Changes: A New Translation of the I Ching as Interpreted by Wang Bi*. New York: Columbia University Press, 1994, 338.
dcclxxxv	Ibid., 541, slightly modified.
dcclxxxvi	Edward L. Shaughnessy, *I Ching: The Classic of Changes*. New York: Ballantine Books, 1996, 239-241, slightly modified.
dcclxxxvii	Sima Qian 司马迁, *Shi ji* 史记 (Historical Records). Beijing: Zhonghua shuju, 1959, 3296.
dcclxxxviii	Ibid., 3297.
dcclxxxix	Ibid., 3296.
dccxc	Wang Guowei 王国维, *Gushi xinzheng* 古史新证 (New Evidence about Ancient [Chinese] History). Beijing: Qinghua University Press, 1994, 2-3.
dccxci	Ban Gu 班固, *Han shu* 汉书 (History of the Western Han Dynasty [206 B.C.E.-9 C.E.]). Beijing: Zhonghua shuju, 1962, 1767.
dccxcii	Ibid., 1769.
dccxciii	Ibid., 1767.

List of Proper Nouns

Baihu tong yi 白虎通义 (Comprehensive Discussions at the White Tiger Hall)
Bai nian yi xue jing hua ji cheng 百年易学精华集成 (Collected Quintessential Articles of the *Yi* Studies of the Past Century and Decade [1900-2009])
Ban Gu 班固 (32-92)
Bao Xi 包牺, a.k.a. Fu Xi 伏羲 (c. mid- or late Neolithic Age, the domesticator of animals and progenitor of Chinese civilization)
Bei qi 北齐 (the Northern Qi, 550-577)
Boliao 伯廖 (a prince of the State of Zheng in the Springs and Autumns period [770-476 BCE])
bushi 卜筮 (Divination)

Cai Mo 蔡墨 (an official historian of the State of Jin in the Springs and Autumns period [770-476 BCE])
Cai Yuanding 蔡元定 (1135-98)
cehou pai 测候派 (school of meteorological observation)
cezi shu 测字术 (auguromancy)
Chen 陈 (557-589)
Chen Chengzi 陈成子 [i.e. Chen Heng 陈恒]
Cheng Shiquan 程石泉 (1909-2005)
Cheng shi Yizhuan 程氏易传 (Cheng Yi's [1033-1107] Commentary on the *Changes*)
Chen Guan 陈瓘 (1057-1124, whose courtesy name was Liaozhai 了斋)
Cheng Yi 程颐 (1033-1107)
Chengzhai Yizhuan 诚斋易传 (Chengzhai's Commentary on the *Changes*)
Chen Huanzi 陈桓子 (a.k.a. Tian Wuyu 田无宇)
Chen Lifu 陈立夫 (1898-2001)
Chen Tuan 陈抟 (871-989)
Chen Wan 陈完 [a.k.a. Jingzhong 敬仲]
Chong'er 重耳 (671-628 BCE)
chu hou 初候 (initial phenology)
Chui Shu 崔述 (1739-1816)
chunfen 春分 (Vernal Equinox, 4th lunar term)

Chunyu Jun 淳于俊 (fl. 256)
chushu 处暑 (Limit of Heat, 14th solar term)
Ciming 慈明 (courtesy name of Xun Shuang 荀爽 [128-190])
Cui Dongbi yishu 崔东壁遗书 (Posthumous Papers of Cui Dongbi [i.e., Cui Shu崔述])
Cui Jing 崔憬 (a Tang [618-907] scholar)
Cui Liangzuo 崔良佐 (fl. 732)
Cui Shu 崔述 (1740-1816)
Cui Wuzi 崔武子 [a.k.a. Cui Zhu 崔杼, d. 546 BCE]

dabu 大卜 (Grand Official Diviners)
dahan 大寒 (Great Cold, 24th solar term)
Dai Zhen 戴震 (1724-77)
Da lüe 大略 (Great Strategies)
dashu 大暑 (Great Heat, 12th solar term)
Da xiang 大象 (Commentary on the Great Images)
Da xue 大学 (Great Learning)
daxue 大雪 (Great Snow, 21st solar term)
Dayan xuantu 大衍玄图 (Mysterious Charts for the Grand Expansion [Divinatory Method by Milfoil Stalks])
Da yi jishuo 大易辑说 (Collected Discussions of the Great *Changes*)
Da yi tong jie 大易通解 (A Thorough Interpretation of the Great *Changes*)
Ding Chaowu 丁超五 (1884-1967)
Ding Kuan 丁宽 (a famous disciple of Tian He 田何 [fl. c. 200 BCE, the progenitor of the teaching of the *Changes* after the foundation of the Han dynasty (206 B.C.E.-220 C.E.)])
Dongfang Shuo zhuan 东方朔传 (Biography of Dongfang Shuo)
Donggu Yi yizhuan 东谷易翼传 (Appended Commentaries to Donggu's *Changes*)
Dong Kai 董楷 (fl. 1265-74)
Dong Yu 董遇 (a scholar of the late Three Kingdoms period [220-280])
Dong Zhenqing 董真卿 (fl. ca. 1330)
dongzhi 冬至 (Winter Solstice, 22nd solar term)
Du Yi juyao 读易举要 (Essentials of Reading the *Changes*)
Du Yu 杜预 (222-285)

Er san zi wen 二三子问 (Several Disciples Asked)

Fang shu 方术 (Occult-oriented Arts)
Fei's Fenye 费氏分野 (Field Allocation Taught by Fei Zhi)
Fei shier zi 非十二子 (Criticizing the Twelve Masters)
Fei's Yilin 费氏易林 (Forest of *Changes* by Fei Zhi)
Feixiang 非相 (Criticizing Physiognomy)
Fei Zhi 费直 (the progenitor of the Ancient Text tradition of the *Changes* in the Western Han dynasty)

List of Proper Nouns

Fengchuan Yishuo 丰川易说 (Discussion of the *Changes* by Fengchuan)
Feng shui 风水 (lit., Wind & Water, also rendered as "geomancy")
Feng Youlan 冯友兰 (1895-1990)
Fuheng 傅恒 (c. 1720-70)
Fusi 辅嗣 (courtesy name of Wang Bi [226-249])
Fu Xi 伏羲, a.k.a. Bao Xi 包牺 (c. mid- or late Neolithic Age, the domesticator of animals and progenitor of Chinese civilization)

Gan Bao 干宝 (d. 336)
Gaoguixiang gong zhuan 高贵乡公传 (Biography of Duke Gaoguixiang)
Gao Heng 高亨 (1900-86)
Gongsun Lu 公孙禄 (a Western Han [206 BCE-8 CE] scholar)
Gongyang zhuan 公羊传 (Gongyang's Commentary on the *Springs and Autumns Annals*)
Guan xiang zhi yan 观象卮言 (Exposition of the Implications of the Images)
Guicang 归藏 (Return to the Hidden)
Gu Jiegang 顾颉刚 (1893-1980)
Guliang zhuan 谷梁传 (Guliang's Commentary on the *Springs and Autumns Annals*)
Gu ming 顾命 (Deathbed Testament)
Guo Moruo 郭沫若 (1892-1978)
Gu shi bian 古史辨 (Debates on Ancient History)
Guo yu 国语 (Sayings of the States)
Guo Zhongshu 郭忠恕 (d. 977)
Guyi yinxun 古易音训 (Pronunciation and Exegesis of the Ancient *Changes*)
guyu 谷雨 (Grain Rain, 6th lunar term)
Gu zhou yi dinggu 古周易订诂 (Rectification and Phonetic and Semantic Exegesis of the Ancient *Zhou Changes*)

Hanfeizi 韩非子 (Master Hanfei [c. 280-233 BCE])
Hang Xinzhai 杭辛斋 (1869-1924)
Han jian 汗简 [a collection of ancient Chinese characters]
hanlu 寒露 (Cold Dew, 17th solar term)
Hanshan Yizhuan 汉上易传 (Commentary on the *Changes* by Zhu Zhen [1072-1138])
Han shu 汉书 (History of the Western Han Dynasty [206 BCE-9 CE])
Han Xuan 韩宣 [d. 514 BCE]
Han Ying 韩婴 (a famous early Western Han [206 BCE-9 CE] scholar)
He Kai 何楷 (1594-1645)
he tu 河图 (Yellow River Chart)
He Yan 何晏 (d. 249)
Hongfan 洪范 (Great Plan)
Hou Guo 侯果 [a scholar in the early Tang dynasty]
Houhan shu 后汉书 (History of the Eastern Han Dynasty [25-220])

Hou Wailu 侯外庐 (1903-1987)
Huainan zi 淮南子 [written by the intellectuals surrounding Liu An 刘安 (179-122 BCE), then the king of the state of Huainan]
Huang Daozhou 黄道周 (1585-1646)
Huang di 黄帝 [Yellow Emperor, 2717-2599 BCE, a legendary sage ruler]
Huang di neijing 黄帝内经 (Yellow Emperor's Canon of Internal Medicine)
Huangji jingshi 皇极经世 (Supreme Principles That Rule the World)
Huang Shangu 黄山谷 (1045-1105)
Huang Ze 黄泽 (1259-1346)
Huang Zongxi 黄宗羲 (1610-95)
Huang Zongyan 黄宗炎 (1616-86)
Hu Bingwen 胡炳文 (1250-1333)
Hu Guang 胡广 (1370-1418)
Huian 晦庵 (a courtesy name of Zhu Xi 朱熹 [1130-1200])
Hui Dong 惠栋 (1697-1758)
Hui Shi 惠施 (390-318 BCE)
Hu Wei 胡渭 (1633-1714)
Hu Xianglin 胡祥麟 (d. 1823)
Hu Yan 狐偃 (c. 715-629 BCE)
Hu Yigui 胡一桂 (1260-1346)
Hu Yuan 胡瑗 (993-1059)

Jia Gongyan 贾公彦 (a famous Tang [618-907] scholar)
Jiang Shaoyuan 江绍源 (1898-1963)
Jiao shi yi gu 焦氏易诂 (Exegesis of Jiao's *Changes*)
Jiao shi yi lin zhu 焦氏易林注 (Annotations to Jiao's *Forest of Changes*)
Jiaosi zhi 郊祀志 (Outskirts Sacrifice Treatise)
Jiao Xun 焦循 (1763-1820)
Jie 桀 [the last emperor of the Xia dynasty (c. 2100-c. 1600 BCE), a notorious tyrant]
Jielao 解老 (Interpreting *Lao zi*)
Jing bu 经部 (the classical category)
Jingdian shiwen 经典释文 (Exegetical Texts of the Classics)
Jing Fang 京房 (77-37 BCE)
Jing Fang Yizhuan 京房易传 (Jing Fang's Commentary on the *Changes*)
Jingji zhi 经籍志 (Treatise on Classics and Literature)
Jingshi Duan Jia 京氏段(殷)嘉 (Jing Fang's and Yin Jia's Scholarship on the *Changes*)
Jing shi yi zhuan jian 京氏易传笺 (Notes to Jing's Commentary on the *Changes*)
Jingxue tonglun 经学通论 (A Comprehensive Discussion of Classical Studies)
jingzhe 惊蛰 (the Waking of Insects, 3rd solar term)
Jin hou 晋侯 (Marquis Jin [i.e., Duke Wen of Jin 晋文公, 671-628 BCE])
Jin Ligong 晋厉公 (Duke Li of Jin, d. 573 BCE)
Jin shu 晋书 (History of the Jin Dynasty [265-420])
Jin Wengong 晋文公 (Duke Wen of Jin, 671-628 BCE)

List of Proper Nouns

Jin yu 晋语 (Sayings of the State of Jin)
Jilan tu 稽览图 (Consultations Charts)
Jiujia yi 九家易 (The Nine Schools' *Changes*)
Jiujing ziyang 九经字样 (The Pictograms of the Characters in the Nine Classics)
Jiu Tangshu 旧唐书 (Old Book of Tang [618-907])
Ji Xiaolan 纪晓岚 (1724-1805)
Ji Yun 纪昀 (1724-1805)

Kangxi 康熙 (r. 1662-1722)
kanyu 堪舆 (geomancy)
Kong Anguo 孔安国 (156-74 BCE)
Kong Chengzi 孔成子 [a minister of the State of Wei in the Springs and Autumns period (770-476 BCE)]
Kong Yingda 孔颖达 (574-648)
Kongzi shijia 孔子世家 (Household of Confucius)

Lai Zhide 来知德 (1525-1604)
Lao zi 老子 (c. 571-471 BCE)
Lao zi zhu 老子注 (Commentaries on the *Lao zi*)
Lao zi weizhi lüeli 老子微指略例 (General Remarks on the Purports of the *Lao zi*)
Liaozhai Yishuo 了斋易说 (Liaozai's Discussion of the *Changes*)
lichun 立春 (Beginning of Spring, 1st solar term)
Liang 梁 (502-557)
Liangqiu He 梁丘贺 (fl. c. 60 BCE)
Lianshan 连山 (Linked Mountains)
lidong 立冬 (Beginning of Winter, 19th solar term)
Lieshan shi 列山氏 (Lord Lieshan)
Li Guang 李光 (1078-1159)
Li Guangdi 李光地 (1642-1718)
Li ji 礼记 (Record of Ritual)
Li Jingchi 李镜池 (1902-75)
Li Jingchun 李景春 (1904-79)
Lingshu jing 灵枢经 (Canon of Miraculous Pivot)
Lin Guangshi 林光世 (a. k. a. Shuicun 水村 [lit., watery village], fl. 1259)
liqiu 立秋 (Beginning of Autumn, 13th solar term)
Li Rui 李锐 (1768-1817)
lishu 历书 (Calendrical Book)
Liu An 刘安 (179-122, king of the State of Huainan 淮南)
Liu Biao 刘表 (142-208)
Liu Huan 刘瓛 (434-89)
Liu Jingsheng 刘景升 (142-208)
liuri qifen 六日七分 (six days and seven divisions)
Liu Xiang 刘向 (77-6 BCE)

Liu Xin 刘歆 (50 BCE-23 CE)
Liu Xin zhuan 刘歆传 (Biography of Liu Xin [50 BCE-23 CE])
Liu Zihua 刘子华 (1899-1992)
lixia 立夏 (Beginning of Summer, 7th lunar term)
Liyi zhi 礼仪志 (Treatise on the Rites and Rituals)
Lü 履 [☱, Treading, 10]
Lü 旅 [☶, The Wanderer, 56]
Lu chunqiu 鲁春秋 (Springs and Autumns Annals of the State of Lu, i.e., the History of the State of Lu)
Lu Deming 陆德明 (c. 550-630)
Lu Ji 陆绩 (187-219)
Lu Jiuyuan 陆九渊 (1139-1193)
lüli zhi 律历志 (Treatise on Pitch Pipes and Calendar)
Lun heng 论衡 (Discourses Weighed in the Balance)
Lun Yi dazhuan de zhuzuo niandai yu zhexue sixiang 论易大传的著作年代及哲学思想 (On the Dating and Philosophical Ideas of the "Great Commentaries on the *Changes*")
luo shu 洛书 (Luo River Diagram)
Lu Xiangshan 陆象山 (1139-93)
Lü Zhuqian 吕祖谦 (1137-81)

Ma Guohan 马国翰 (1794-1857)
mangzhong 芒种 (Grain in Ear, 9th solar term)
Mao Qiling 毛奇龄 (1623-1716)
Maoshi 毛诗 (Mao edition of the *Classic of Poetry*)
Ma Rong 马融 (79-166)
Ma Yifu 马一浮 (1883-1967)
Ma Yifu ji 马一浮集 (Collected Works of Ma Yifu)
Meihua yi shu 梅花易数 (Plum-blossom Numerology of *Changes*)
Mengshi Jing Fang 孟氏京房 (Jing Fang's *Changes* Based on Meng Xi's *Yi* Learning)
Meng Xi 孟喜 (fl. c. 50 BCE)
Meng zi 孟子, Mencius (c. 372-c. 289 BCE)
Ming 明 (1368-1644)
Ming jia 名家 (School of Logicians)
Ming li 命理 (lit., principle for fate, a. k. a. art of eight-character and Chinese astrology)
ming shi 明筮 (Clarifying Milfoil-stalk Divination)
Mingxiang 明象 (Clarifying the Images)
Miucheng xun 缪称训 (Profound Percepts)
Mo hou 末候 (final phenology)
Mo Zongsan 牟宗三 (1909-95)

Najia shifa 纳甲筮法 (Three-Coin Method of Divination)

Najia shifa jiangzuo 纳甲筮法讲座 (Lectures on the *Najia* Divination Method)
Northern Qi 北齐 (550-577)

Ouyang Xiu 欧阳修 (1007-1072)

Pi Xirui 皮锡瑞 (1850-1908)

Qi 齐 (a state in the Zhou dynasty [1046-256 BCE])
Qi 齐 (479-502)
Qian kun yan 乾坤衍 (Elaboration on Qian [☰] and Kun [☷])
Qian kun zao du 乾坤凿度 (Opening Up the Regularities of the [Hexagrams] Qian [☰] and Kun [☷])
Qianlong 乾隆 (r. 1735-95)
Qian Mu 钱穆 (1895-1990)
Qian zao du 乾凿度 (Opening Up the Regularities of the [Hexagram] Qian [☰])
Qi Xuanwang jian Yan Chu 齐宣王见颜斶 (King Xuan of Qi Interviews Yan Chu)
Qin 秦 (221-206 BCE)
Qin bo 秦伯 (Count Qin [i.e., Duke Mu of Qin 秦穆公, d. 621 BCE])
Qing 清 (1616-1912)
qingming 清明 (Pure Brightness, 5th lunar term)
Qingshi gao 清史稿 (Draft of History of the Qing Dynasty [1616-1912])
Qin Mugong 秦穆公 (Duke Mu of Qin, d. 621 BCE)
qiufen 秋分 (Autumnal Equinox, 16th solar term)
Qiu Hansheng 邱汉生 (1912-92)
Qiyang 岐阳 [the birthplace of the Zhou dynasty]
Quan xue 劝学 (Encouraging Study)
Quanyan xun 诠言训 (Sayings Explained)
Qu Wanli 屈万里 (1907-1979)

Renjian xun 人间训 (Treatise on Human Nature)
Ren Jiyu 任继愈 (1916-2009)
renshi 人事 (human affairs)
Ruan Yuan 阮元 (1764-1849)
Rujia ba pai de pipan 儒家八派的批判 (Critique of the Eight Confucian Schools)
Rulin zhuan 儒林传 (Biographies of the Confucians)
Ru xiao 儒效 (Effects of Confucians)

Sanguo zhi 三国志 (History of the Three Kingdoms [220-280])
San yi beiyi 三易备遗 (Memorandum for the Three Kinds of *Changes*)
Shang 商 (c. 1600-1046 BCE)
Shang Binghe 尚秉和 (1870-1950)
Shang shu 尚书 (Classic of History)
Shao Yong 邵雍 (1011-77)
Shen Diemin 沈瓞民 (1878-1969)

Sheng Nong 神农 (c. late Neolithic Age, the inventor of Chinese agriculture, medicine and pharmacy)
Shi pipan shu 十批判书 (A Book of Ten Critical Chapters)
Shi Chou 施雠 (fl. c. 50 BCE)
shi fa 筮法 (Method of Divination)
Shifa mantan 筮法漫谈 (Causerie about Methods of Divination)
Shi gui 筮龟 (milfoil stalks & tortoise shells)
Shigui lei 蓍龟类 (Catalogue of [Divination by] Tortoise Shells and Milfoil Stalks)
Shiji 史记 (Historical Records)
Shipu 世谱 (Genealogy of Past Dynasties)
Shiyi 十翼 (Ten Wings)
Shi yi 筮仪 (Etiquette for Milfoil-stalk Divination)
shuangjiang 霜降 (Frost's Descent, 18th solar term)
Shu Cai 蜀才 (a scholar in the early Tang dynasty [618-907])
Shuicun Yi jing 水村易镜 (Mirror of the *Changes* by Shuicun)
Shun 舜 [c. 2250-c. 2150, a legendry sage ruler in ancient Chinese who succeeded to the throne after Lord Yao 尧]
Shunzhi 顺治 (r. 1644-61)
Shuogua 说卦 ("Explaining the Trigrams" or "Discussion of the Trigrams")
Shuogua zhuan 说卦传 ("Explaining the Trigrams" or "Discussion of the Trigrams")
Shuowen jiezi 说文解字 (Explanation of Simple and Composite Characters)
Shuoyuan 说苑 (Garden of Sayings)
Shushu lei 术数类 (The Arts of Calculation)
Shu Xi zhuah 束晳传 (Biography of Shu Xi)
shuxue 数学 (numerology)
shuzi gua 数字卦 (numerical trigrams, tetragrams, or hexagrams)
Sikong Jizi 司空季子 (657-570 BCE)
Siku quanshu 四库全书 (Complete Collection of the Four Treasuries)
Siku quanshu zongmu 四库全书总目 (General Catalogue of the *Complete Collection of the Four Treasuries*)
Siku quanshu zongmu tiyao 四库全书总目提要 (Annotated General Catalogue of the *Complete Collection of the Four Treasuries*)
Sima Qian 司马迁 (145-90 BCE)
Sima Qian zhuan 司马迁传 (Biography of Sima Qian [145-90 BCE])
Si-Meng xuepai 思孟学派 (Si-Meng [i.e., Zi si 子思 (483-402 BCE)] and Mencius [372-289 BCE] Confucian School)
Si zhu mingli 四柱命理 (Four-pillar Theory about One's Destiny, a.k.a. Chinese Astrology)
Song 宋 (960-1279)
Song Zhong 宋衷 (a scholar of the late Three Kingdoms period [220-280])
suanming shu 算命术 (art of fate calculation)
Sui shu 隋书 (History of the Sui Dynasty [581-618])
Sun Quan 孙权 (182-252)
Su Yuanlei 苏渊雷 (1908-1995)

Taiji tu 太极图 (Diagram of the Supreme Ultimate)
Taiji tu shuo 太极图说 (An Explanation of the "Diagram of the Supreme Ultimate")
Taishigong zixu 太史公自序 (Author's Postscript)
tai yi 太一 (Great One)
Tang 唐 (618-907)
Tang Junyi 唐君毅 (1909-1978)
Tang shu 唐书 (History of the Tang Dynasty [618-907])
Tang taizong 唐太宗 (Emperor Taizong of Tang [r. 627-49])
Tian He 田何 (fl. c. 200 BCE, the progenitor of the teaching of the *Changes* after the foundation of the Han dynasty [206 BCE-220 CE])
Tian Wangsun 田王孙 (an Erudite of the *Classic of Changes* during the reign of Emperor Xuan [r. 74-49 BCE])
Tian xia 天下 (Under Heaven)
Tian yun 天运 (Motions of Heaven)
Tuan 彖 (Commentary on the Judgments)
Tuan zhuan 彖传 (Commentary on the Judgments)
tu shu 图书 (chart or diagram)
Tushu bianhuo 图书辨惑 (Straightening Out the Confusing Points Related to the *He tu* [Yellow River Chart] and the *Luo shu* [Luo River Diagram])
Tu shuo 图说 (Discussion of the Charts)
Tushu yuantuan bian 图书原舛编 (Real Original Sources for the *He tu* and the *Luo shu*)
tushu zhi xue 图书之学 (*he tu* and *luo shu*-based learning)

Wang Bi 王弼 (226-249)
Wang Chong 王充 (27-c. 97)
Wang Fuzhi 王夫之 (1619-92)
Wang Guowei 王国维 (1877-1927)
Wang Shenzi 王申子 (fl. 1313)
Wang Su 王肃 (195-256)
Wang Xinjing's 王心敬 (a. k. a. Fengchuan 丰川, 1656-1738)
Wang Yi 王廙 (276-322)
Wang Yinglin 王应麟 (1223-96)
Wanming jing 万名经 (Canon of the Ten Thousand Names)
Wei 魏 (220-265)
Wei Boyang 魏伯阳 (a famous Eastern Han Daoist priest traditionally viewed as the progenitor of Alchemical Daoism)
Wei Liaoweng 魏了翁 (1178-1237)
Wei Litong 魏荔彤 (1670-?)
Wei Si 魏斯 [a.k.a. Marquis Wen of Wei 魏文侯] (472-396 BCE)
Weixiang wang 魏襄王 (King Xiang of Wei, r. 318-296 BCE)
Wei Xianzi 魏献子 (d. 509 BCE, a great official of the State of Zheng in the Springs and Autumns period [770-476 BCE])
Wei Zhao 韦昭 (204-273)

Wen hou 文侯 (Marquis Wen [805-746 BCE])
Wen wang 文王 (King Wen [1152-1056 BCE])
Wen wang liushisi gua guabian tu 文王六十四卦卦变图 (Chart for the System of Hexagram Changes of King Wen's Sixty-four Hexagrams)
Wenyan 文言 (Commentary on the Words of the Text)
Wenyan zhuan 文言传 (Commentary on the Words of the Text)
Wen Yiduo 闻一多 (1899-1946)
Wujing daquan 五经大全 (Great Comprehensive [Compilation of] the Five Classics)
Wujing zhengyi 五经正义 (Correct Meaning of the Five Classics)
Wushun 武顺 (Complying with the Dao (Way) in Military Affaires)
Wu wang 武王 (King Wu [c.1087-1043 BCE])
wuxing 五行 (five-agent)
Wuxing zhi 五行志 (Five Agents Treatise)

Xia 夏 (c. 2100-c. 1600 BCE)
Xiahou Zhao 夏侯灶 (d. 165)
Xiang 象 (Commentary on the Images)
xiangren shu 相人术 (physiognomy)
Xiang shu yi xue yan jiu 象数易学研究 (Studies of Image-numerology of the Changes)
Xiang Xiu 向秀 (c. 227-272)
xiangzhai xiangmu 相宅相墓 (geomancy)
Xiang zhuan 象传 (Commentary on the Images)
Xian qin han wei yi li shu ping 先秦汉魏易例述评 (Accounts of and Comments on the Formulae of the Changes from the Pre-Qin [before 221 BCE] to Wei [220-265] Dynasties)
xiaohan 小寒 (Lesser Cold, 23rd solar term)
xiaoman 小满 (Grain Full, 8th solar term)
Xiao Jiefu 萧箑父 (1924-2008)
xiaoshu 小暑 (Slight Heat, 11th solar term)
Xiaoxiang 小象 (Commentary on the Small Images)
xiaoxue 小雪 (Light Snow, 20th solar term)
xiazhi 夏至 (Summer Solstice, 10th solar term)
Xici 系辞 ("Commentary on the Appended Phrases" or "Great Treatise")
Xici zhuan 系辞传 ("Commentary on the Appended Phrases" or "Great Treatise")
Xiong Shili 熊十力 (1885-1968)
Xue Rengui 薛仁贵 (614-683)
Xugua 序卦 (Orderly Sequence of the Hexagrams)
Xugua zhuan 序卦传 (Orderly Sequence of the Hexagrams)
Xulu 序录 (Prefatory Notes)
Xun Shuang 荀爽 (128-190)
Xun zi 荀子 (c. 313-238 BCE)
Xu Shen 许慎 (c. 58-147)

Yan Shigu 颜师古 (581-645)
Yang Wanli 杨万里 (1127-1206, a. k. a. Chengzhai 诚斋)
Yang Xiong 扬雄 (53 BCE-18 CE)
Yantie lun 盐铁论 (Discussions over Salt and Iron) [written in 81 BCE]
Yao 尧 [c. 2300-c. 2200 BCE, a legendary sage ruler in ancient China]
Yao 要 (The Essentials)
Yao Xin 姚信 (a Three Kingdoms period [220-280] scholar)
Yichuan 伊川 (courtesy name of Cheng Yi 程颐 [1033-1107])
Yi dazhuan 易大传 (Great Commentaries on the *Changes*)
Yi Hanxue 易汉学 (Han Scholarship on the *Changes*)
Yi hanxue kao 易汉学考 (Textual Research on [Hui Dong's] *Han Scholarship on the Changes*)
Yi hanxue shicheng biao 易汉学师承表 (Table of the Lineages and Affiliations of the Scholars Mentioned in [Hui Dong's] *Han Scholarship on the Changes*)
Yihua 易话 (Remarks on the *Changes*)
Yi jiao 易教 (Edification by the *Changes*)
Yi jing 易经 (Classic of Changes)
Yi jing yu xiandai shenghuo 《易经》与现代生活 (The *Yi jing* and Contemporary Life)
Yi lei 易类 (Catalogue Attributed to the *Changes*)
Yilin 易林 (Forest of the *Changes*)
Yi lun 易论 (Discussion on the *Changes*)
Yin 殷 (c.1600-1046 BCE)
yin yang shuo 阴阳说 (Discussions of *yin* and *yang*)
Yishu gouyin tu 易数钩隐图 (Investigation into the Hidden: Illustrations of *Changes* Numerology)
Yi shuo 易说 (An Explanation of the *Changes*)
Yi tongzi wen 易童子问 (Questions from a Youth about the *Changes*)
Yitu lüe 易图略 (An Outline of the Diagrams of the *Changes*)
Yitu Mingbian 易图明辨 (A Clarifying Critique of the Illustrations Associated with the *Changes*)
Yitu tiaobian 易图条辨 (Detailed Discrimination of the Illustrations Associated with the *Changes*)
Yi wang xiang 易忘象 (Forgetting the Images of the *Changes*)
Yi wei 易纬 (Apocrypha of the *Changes*)
Yiwei lüeyi 易纬略义 ([A Brief Introduction to] the Meaning of the Apocrypha of the *Changes*)
Yi weiyan 易微言 (Subtlety of the *Changes*)
Yiwen zhi 艺文志 ("Treatise on Art and Literature" or "Art and Literature Treatise")
Yixian 矣鲜 (courtesy name of Lai Zhide 来知德 [1525-1604])
yi xiang 逸象 (lost images)
Yi xiang 易象 (lit., Images of the *Changes*)
Yixiang zheng 易象正 (Rectification of the Images of the *Changes*)

Yi xue ji cheng 易学集成 (Collected Works of *Changes* Scholarship)
Yixue lanshang 易学滥觞 (Origin of *Changes* Studies)
Yixue qimeng 易学启蒙 (Introduction to the Study of the *Changes*)
Yixue xiangshu lun 易学象数论 (Discussion of Images and Numbers in *Changes* Scholarship)
Yi xue yan ju 易学研究 (Studies of *Changes* Scholarship)
Yiyi bielu 易义别录 (Supplement to the Meaning of the *Changes*)
Yi zan 易赞 (Praising the *Changes*)
Yi zhangju 易章句 (Sentence by Sentence Interpretation of the *Changes*)
Yi zhi yi 易之义 (The Properties of the *Changes*)
Yi zhoushu 逸周书 (Lost Book of Zhou)
Yi zhuan 易传 (Commentaries on the *Changes*)
Yuan 元 (1271-1368)
Yuanhui 元晦 (a courtesy name of Zhu Xi 朱熹 [1130-1200])
Yue ling 月令 (Monthly Ordinances)
Yu Fan 虞翻 (164-233)
Yuhan shan fang ji yishu 玉函山房辑佚书 (Collection of Lost Texts from the Treasury Chamber 'Jade Slipcase')
Yushi xiaoxi 虞氏消息 (Waxing and Waning [of the Hexagrams] Based on [the Interpretations of] Yu Fan)
Yushi yi xiaoxi tuoshuo 虞氏易消息图说 (An Explanation of the Diagram of Waxing and Waning Conceived in Yu Fan's *Changes* Scholarship)
Yushi yibian biao 虞氏易变表 (Table of Interchangeability [of the Hexagrams] Based on [the Interpretations of] Yu Fan)
Yushi yihou 虞氏易候 (Meteorology of the *Changes* Based on [the Interpretations of] Yu Fan)
Yushi yili 虞氏易礼 (Rituals of the *Changes* Based on [the Interpretations of] Yu Fan)
Yushi yishi 虞氏易事 (Events of the *Changes* Based on [the Interpretations of] Yu Fan)
Yushi Yixue huibian 虞氏易学汇编 (A Compilation of Yu Fan's Scholarship on the *Changes*)
Yushi yiyan 虞氏易言 (Words of the *Changes* Based on [the Interpretations of] Yu Fan)
yushui 雨水 (Rainwater, 2nd solar term)
Yu Wan 俞琰 (1258-1314)
Yu Xingwu 于省吾 (1896-1984)
Yu Yue 俞樾 (1821-1907)

Zagua 杂卦 (Hexagrams in Irregular Order)
Zaiyi Menshi Jing Fang 灾异孟氏京房 (Analysis of Omens and Anomalies by Jing Fang's and Meng Xi's Theories)
Zaiyou 在宥 (Footloose)
Za zhan 杂占 (miscellaneous divinations)

zeji 择吉 (hemerology)
Zengbu Zhou yi Zheng zhu 增补周易郑注 (Supplement to Zheng Xuan's Commentary on the *Changes*)
Zeng Zhao 曾钊 (1793-1854)
Zeng zi 曾子 (505-435 BCE) [a renowned disciple of Confucius]
Zhai Zixuan 翟子玄 (an early Tang [618-907] scholar)
zhanbu 占卜 (auguromancy)
Zhang Cizhong 张次仲 (1589-1676)
Zhang Dainian 张岱年 (1909-2004)
Zhang Huiyan 张惠言 (1761-1802)
Zhang Taiyan 章太炎 (1869-1936)
Zhanguo ce 战国策 (Strategies of the Warring States)
Zhang Zai 张载 (1020-78)
Zhang Zhao 张昭 (156-236)
Zhang Zhenglang 张政烺 (1912-2005)
zhanhou 占候 ("phenologiomancy" or "meteorology")
zhanmeng 占梦 (oniromancy)
zhanxing shu 占星术 (astrology)
Zhao Meng 赵孟 (chief minister of the State of Jin in the Springs and Autumns period [770-476 BCE])
Zhao Shixiu 赵师秀 (1170-1219)
Zheng Gangzhong 郑刚中 (1088-1154)
Zheng Ruxie 郑汝谐 (a. k. a. Donggu 东谷, 1126-1205)
Zhengshi yaochen bu 郑氏爻辰补 (Supplement to Zheng Xuan's *Yaochen* Theory)
Zhengshu 正叔 (courtesy name of Cheng Yi 程颐 [1033-1107])
Zheng Xuan 郑玄 (127-200)
zhong hou 中候 (middle phenology)
Zhong hua yi xue 中华易学 (*Changes* Studies of China)
Zhonghui 仲晦 (a courtesy name of Zhu Xi 朱熹 [1130-1200])
Zhongni 仲尼 (i.e., Confucius)
Zhongxiang 仲翔 (courtesy name of Yufan 虞翻 [164-233])
Zhongni dizi liezhuan 仲尼弟子列传 (Biographies of Confucius's Disciples)
Zhongguo sixiangshi 中国思想史 (A History of Chinese Thought)
Zhong yong 中庸 (Doctrine of the Mean)
Zhou 周 (1046-256 BCE)
Zhou Dunyi 周敦颐 (1017-73)
Zhou li 周礼 (Zhou Rituals)
Zhou li dabu 周礼·大卜 ("Grand Official Diviners" in the *Zhou Rituals*)
Zhou yi 周易 (the *Book of Changes*, the *Classic of Changes*, or the *Zhou Changes*)
Zhou yi baishu 周易稗疏 (A Detailed Commentary on the *Zhou Changes*)
Zhou yi benyi 周易本义 (Original Meaning of the *Zhou Changes*)
Zhou yi benyi fulu zuanshu 周易本义附录纂疏 (Appended Sub-commentaries to [Zhu Xi's] *Original Meaning of the Zhou Changes*)

Zhou yi benyi tongshi 周易本义通释 (A Thorough Explanation of [Zhu Xi's] *Original Meaning of the Zhou Changes*)

Zhou yi bushu 周易补疏 (Supplemented Sub-commentaries on the *Zhou Changes*)

Zhou yi cantongqi 周易参同契 (Token for the Agreement of the Three According to the *Zhou Changes*)

Zhou yi Cheng-Zhu zhuan yi zhezhong 周易程朱传义折中 (Synthesis of [Cheng Yi's] Commentary and [Zhu Xi's] *Original Meaning of the Zhou Changes*)

Zhou yi daquan 周易大全 (Great Comprehensive [Compilation of] the *Zhou Changes*)

Zhou yi dazhuan 周易大传 (Great Commentaries on the *Zhou Changes*)

Zhou yi dazhuan jinzhu 周易大传今注 (Modern Annotations to the *Great Commentaries on the Zhou Changes*)

Zhou yi fenye 周易分野 (Distinction of the *Zhou Changes*)

Zhou yi gai lun 周易概论 (An Introduction to the *Zhou Changes*)

Zhou yi guabian juyao 周易卦变举要 (Essentials of Hexagram Transformations of the *Zhou Changes*)

Zhou yi guatu shuo 周易卦图说 (Illustrations of the Hexagrams and Trigrams of the *Zhou Changes*)

Zhou yi gushi kao tongjie 周易古筮考通解 (A Thorough Interpretation of the *Textual Research of Ancient Divinatory Cases by the Zhou Changes*)

Zhou yi huitong 周易会通 (A Comprehensive Compilation on the *Zhou Changes*)

Zhou yi huti xiangshu 周易互体详述 (A Detailed Description of the *Huti* [Overlapping Trigrams] Approach to the *Zhou Changes*)

Zhou yi huti zheng 周易互体徵 (Evidence for the *Huti* [Overlapping Trigrams] Approach to the *Zhou Changes*)

Zhou yi kuiyu 周易窥余 (Discerning the Remnant Discussions on the *Zhou Changes*)

Zhou yi jiaokan ji 周易校勘记 (Notes from Emendating the *Zhou Changes*)

Zhou yi jijie 周易集解 (Collected Explanations of the *Zhou yi*)

Zhou yi jiie daodu 周易集解导读 (A Guide Book to the *Collected Explanations of the Zhou yi*)

Zhou yi jishuo 周易集说 (Collected Discussions on the *Zhou Changes*)

Zhou yi jiwen 周易辑闻 (An Unofficial History of the *Zhou Changes*)

Zhou yi jizhu 周易集注 (Collected Commentaries on the *Zhou Changes*)

Zhou yi juzheng 周易举正 (An Illustration of the Correct Meanings of the *Zhou Changes*)

Zhou yi lüeli 周易略例 (General Remarks on the *Zhou Changes*)

Zhou yi nan Wang Fusi yi 周易难王辅嗣义 (Questioning and Reproaching Wang Bi for His Meanings of the *Zhou Changes*)

Zhou yi qiankun san xiang 周易乾坤三象 (Three Images of Hexagrams Qian [☰] and Kun [☷] of the *Zhou Changes*)

Zhou yi qiyuan 周易起元 (Exploring the Origin of the *Zhou Changes*)

Zhou yi shu 周易述 (Description of the *Zhou Changes*)

Zhou yi shuyi 周易述义 (Narration of the Meaning of the *Zhou Changes*)

Zhou yi tanyuan 周易探源 (An Investigation into the Origins of the *Zhou Changes*)

Zhou yi tushuo 周易图说 (Discussion of the Illustrations Related to the *Zhou Changes*)

Zhou yi wanci kunxue ji 周易玩辞困学记 (Notes about the Phrases of the *Zhou Changes* from Learning in Difficulty)

Zhou yi wuxiang shiyi 周易物象释疑 (Clearing up Doubts About the Images of Objects in the *Zhou Changes*)

Zhou yi xiang lun 周易象论 (Discussions on the Images of the *Zhou Changes*)

Zhou yi xintu 周易新图 (New Charts for the *Zhou Changes*)

Zhou yi xinzhuan shu 周易新传疏 (A Sub-commentary on the New Commentaries [i.e., Wang Bi's Commentaries] on the *Zhou Changes*)

Zhou yi xinzhu benyi 周易新注本义 (Original Meaning of the New Commentaries on the *Zhou Changes*)

Zhou yi Xunshi jiujia 周易荀氏九家 (Nine Masters' [Interpretations Collected] of the *Zhou Changes* from Xun's Family)

Zhou yi Xunshi jiujia yi 周易荀氏九家易 (The Meaning of the *Zhou Changes* Based on [the Interpretations of] the Nine Scholars from Xun's Family)

Zhouyi yanjiu 周易研究 (Studies of Zhouyi)

Zhou yi yaobian yiyun 周易爻变义蕴 (Meaning and Essence of the Line Transformations in the *Zhou Changes*)

Zhou yi yaochen shen Zheng yi 周易爻辰申郑义 (An Extension of the Meaning of Zheng Xuan's *Yaochen* Theory)

Zhou yi yaoyi 周易要义 (Essential Meaning of the *Zhou Changes*)

Zhou yi yinyi 周易音义 (Pronunciation and Meaning in the *Zhou Changes*)

Zhou yi Yushi lüeli 周易虞氏略例 (General Remarks on the *Zhou Changes* Based on [the Interpretations of] Yu Fan)

Zhou yi Yushi xue 周易虞氏学 (The Learning of the *Zhou Changes* Based on [the Interpretations of] Yu Fan)

Zhou yi Yushi yi 周易虞氏易 (The Meaning of the *Zhou Changes* Based on [the Interpretations of] Yu Fan)

Zhou yi Yushi yi jian 周易虞氏易笺 (Notes on the Meaning of the *Zhou Changes* Based on [the Interpretations of] Yu Fan)

Zhou yi Yushi yi jian ding 周易虞氏易笺订 (Notes from Reading Yu's Commentary on the *Zhou Changes*)

Zhou yi Zheng Kangcheng yaochen tu 周易郑康成爻辰图 (*Zhou Changes*-based Diagram of *yaocheng* Invented by Zheng Xuan)

Zhou yi Zheng Kangcheng zhu 周易郑康成注 (Zheng Xuan's Commentary on the *Changes*)

Zhou yi Zhengshi zhu 周易郑氏注 (Zheng Xuan's Annotations to the *Zhou Changes*)

Zhou yi zhengyi 周易正义 (Correct Meaning of the *Zhou Changes*)

Zhou yi zhengyi Juanshou 周易正义卷首 (the "Prologue" to the *Correct Meaning of the Zhou yi*)

Zhou yi Zhengzhu houding 周易郑注后定 (A Determined Version of Zheng Xuan's Commentary on the *Zhou Changes*)
Zhou yi zhezhong 周易折中 (A Balanced Compendium on the *Zhou Changes*)
Zhou yi zhi zhizuo shidai 周易之制作时代 (Dating of the *Zhou Changes*)
Zhou yi zhu 周易注 ("Annotations to the *Zhou Changes*" or 'Commentaries on the *Zhou Changes*")
Zhou yi zhuan yi fulu 周易传义附录 (Appended Discussions to [Cheng Yi's] Commentary and [Zhu Xi's] Original Meaning of the *Zhou Changes*)
Zhuang zi 庄子 (369-286 BCE)
Zhuang zi neipian 庄子内篇 ("Internal Chapters" of *Zhuang zi*)
Zhuang zi waipian 庄子外篇 ("External Chapters" of *Zhuang zi*)
Zhuan Sun 颛孙
Zhufu Yan 主父偃
Zhujia Yixue bielu 诸家易学别录 (Supplement to the Variety of Scholars' Study of the *Changes*)
Zhushu jinian 竹书纪年 (Bamboo Annals)
Zhusi kao xin lu 洙泗考信录 (Textual Research on Confucius's Life Story)
Zhu Xi 朱熹 (1130-1200)
Zhu Yuansheng 朱元升 (d. 1273)
Zhu Zhen 朱震 (1072-1138, a. k. a. Mr. Hanshang 汉上)
Zi Gong 子贡 (520-446 BCE)
Zi si 子思 (483-402 BCE)
Zi Xia 子夏 (507 BCE-?) [one of the seventy-two famous disciples of Confucius]
Zundao pian 遵道篇 (Reverence for Dao [Way])
Zuo zhuan 左传 (Zuo's Commentary on the *Springs and Autumns Annals*)

Glossary

ba 八 (eight)
bagong 八宫 (eight palaces)
bagua zhi xiang 八卦之象 (eight-trigram images)
baihu 白虎 (white tiger)
bailu 白露 (White Dew, 15th solar term)
baixing 百姓 (common people)
banxia sheng 半夏生 (Pinellia ternate grows)
bi 比 (adjacent, neighboring)
bi 辟 (sovereign)
bian 变 (conversion)
bian 弁 (lit., a kind of man's cap used in ancient times)
bian 遍 (universality)
bian dong buju, zhouliu liuxu 变动不居，周流六虚 (Change and action in the world never stand still but keep flowing all through the six positions)
bianli 遍理 (universal principle)
bian yi 变易 (change)
bianzhan 变占 (prognostication by changing line(s))
bing 丙 (the 3rd heavenly stem)
bise er cheng dong 闭塞成冬 (people shut doors in winter)
bu 卜 (tortoise-shell divination)
buyi 不易 (no change)
buzheng 不正 (incorrect position)

caomu huang luo 草木黄落 (grass and trees wither)
caomu mengdong 草木萌动 (grasses and trees bud)
chang 鬯 (fragrant wine)
cha yi haoli, miu yi qianli 差以毫釐,谬以千里 (If at the beginning you are off by a hair, in the end you will miss it by miles)
chen 辰 (the 3rd lunar month)
cheng 诚 (sincerity)
cheng 承 (yielding)

cheng 乘 (mounting)
chengshu 成数 (completion numbers)
chenwei 谶纬 (prophetic-apocryphal texts)
chong 虫 (insect)
chou 丑 (the 12th lunar month)
chuzhong 处中 (being located at the middle)
cuogua 错卦 (interchanging hexagrams)

dafu 大夫 (grand masters)
Da lüe 大略 (Great Strategies)
dao 道 (Way)
daode 道德 (way and virtue)
daren 大人 (great man)
da yan 大衍 (great expansion)
dayu shixing 大雨时行 (it often rains cats and dogs)
de tai zhi ba 得泰之八 (obtaining the eight of Tai [, Peace, 11])
dewei 得位 (matching its position)
dexing 德行 (moral conduct)
dezheng 得正 (gaining a correct position)
dezhong 得中 (gaining the middle or centrality)
ding 丁 (the 4th heavenly stem)
dingning 丁宁 (urging again and again)
di shi dong 地始冻 (ground begins to freeze)
Diyi guimei 帝乙归妹 (The sovereign Yi had his younger sister married)
dongjing 东井 [lit., Eastern Well, i.e., Gemini]
dong jing 动静 (movements and stillness)
dou 斗 (Dipper)
dushi 笃实 (the sincere and substantial)

er 二 (two)
er pian 二篇 (lit., two chapters)
er yong wu yaowei, zhouliu xing liuxu 二用无爻位，周流行六虚 (Although the "Using of Nine" and the "Using of Six" do not have concrete line position, they circulate in the six positions of the hexagram")

fandui gua 反对卦 (inverted hexagrams)
fandui zhi xiang 反对之象 (inverted images)
fangwei zhi xiang 方位之象 (directional images)
feifu 飞伏 (manifest-latent)
fou 缶 (earthenware)
fu 覆 (inversion)
fu 孚 (trust, sincerity)
Fuxi bagua cixu 伏羲八卦次序 (Fuxi's Sequence of the Eight Trigrams)

Glossary

Fuxi bagua fangwei 伏羲八卦方位 (Fuxi's Positioning of the Eight Trigrams)
Fuxi liushi si gua cixu 伏羲六十四卦次序 (Fuxi's Sequence of the Sixty-four Hexagrams)
Fuxi liushi si gua fangwei 伏羲六十四卦方位 (Fuxi's Positioning of the Sixty-four Hexagrams)

ganying 感应 (stimulus and response)
gao 膏 (fat)
geng 庚 (the 7th heavenly stem)
gong 公 (duke)
gouchen 勾陈 (Ursae Minoris)
gu 蛊 (poison)
guabian 卦变 (hexagram changes)
guabian tu 卦变图 (Table of Hexagram Changes)
guale fa 挂扐法 (dangling-and-clamping-stalk method)
gua-qi 卦气 (a theory correlating trigrams and hexagrams with the seasonal points)
gui 簋 (food bowl)
gui 癸 (the 10th heavenly stem)
gui shen 鬼神 (ghosts and spirits)
guoshe fa 过揲法 (counting-off-stalk method)
guzhi yi leiting 鼓之以雷霆" (It [the Dao] arouses things with claps of thunder and thunderbolt)

hai 亥 (the 10th lunar month)
hanchan ming 寒蝉鸣 (cicadas cry)
he 和 (harmony)
heng 亨 (prevalence)
hong cang bu jian 虹藏不见 (rainbows hide and disappear)
hong shi jian 虹始见 (rainbows begin to appear)
hongyan bei 鸿雁北 (Anser cygnoides come from south)
hou 侯 (marquis)
houtian 后天 (posterior to heaven, Later Heaven)
Houtian bagua fangwei 后天八卦方位 (Eight Trigrams' Positions of the Later Heaven)
hui 悔 (remorse)
huiwang 悔亡 (regret vanishes)
hundun 浑沌 (chaos)
huti 互体 ("overlapping" or "nuclear")
huti zhi xiang 互体之象 ("overlapping images" or "nuclear trigrams")
huxiang 互象 (overlapping images)

ji 己 (the 6th heavenly stem)
jia 甲 (the 1st heavenly stem)
jiang 降 (falling)
jiang 将 (senior general)
ji ru 鸡乳 (chickens begin to hatch)
Jiugong bafeng 九宫八风 (Nine Palaces and Eight Winds)
jiyu baoshang 系于苞桑 (tying it to a healthy, flourishing mulberry)
ju 据 (basing)
juan 卷 (lit., scrolls, i.e., chapters)
juexue 绝学 (ultimate study)
jun 君 (sovereign)
juzhong 居中 (residing in the middle)

kang long 亢龙 (A dragon that overreaches)

laoyang 老阳 (old *yang*)
laoyin 老阴 (old *yin*)
lei nai fasheng 雷乃发声 (thunder rumbles)
li 礼 (etiquettes)
li 理 (principle)
li 利 (benefits)
li 吏 (official)
lianhu 连互 (consecutive overlapping)
lishu 历书 (Calendrical Book)
liuhua zhi xiang 六画之象 (six-line images)
liuqin 六亲 (six-relative)
liu shen 六神 (six spirits) [equated with the six lines of a hexagram according to certain rules]
lixue 理学 (Neo-Confucianism, lit., Learning of Principle)
louguo ming 蝼蝈鸣 (mole crickets sing)

mao 卯 (the 2nd lunar month)
mijiao jie 麋角解 (moose shed their horns)
mengqi 蒙气 (atmospheric haze)
mingjiu fu qi yi 鸣鸠拂其羽 (cuckoos flap)
ming shi 明筮 (Clarifying Milfoil-stalk Divination)

najia 纳甲 (attaching the heavenly stems and earthly branches into the hexagrams)

pangtong 旁通 (lateral linkage)
pangtong gua 旁通卦 (laterally linked hexagrams)

qing 卿 (lower minister)
qinglong 青龙 (Green Dragon)
qiuyin jie 蚯蚓结 (earthworms curl up)
que shichao 鹊始巢 (magpies begin to build nests)

ren 壬 (the 9th heavenly stem)
rizhong 日中 ("midday" or "the sun at zenith")
rizhong ze zhe 日中则昃 (as soon as the sun reaches the meridian it declines)

sangong 三公 (three dukes)
san shi 三式 (divination by three kinds of divinatory boards)
santong 三统 (lit., Three Concordances) [a kind of calendar used since late Western Han]
Santong li 三统历 (Three-concord Calendar)
shan e 善恶 (good and evil)
shangxia jing 上下经 (upper and lower scriptures)
shangxia xiang yi 上下象易 (exchange of positions of the upper and lower trigrams)
shaoxiang 扫象 (sweeping away images)
shaoyang 少阳 (young *yang*)
shaoyin 少阴 (young *yin*)
shen 申 (the 7th lunar month)
shengjiang 升降 (rising and falling)
shengshu 生数 (producing numbers)
shi 筮 (milfoil-stalk divination)
shi dian 始电 (lightning flashes)
shi'er qinchen 十二禽辰 (twelve animals)
shiwei 失位 (losing a correct position)
shiyao 世爻 (generational line)
shiying 世应 (generation-response)
shizhong 时中 ("timeliness and the Mean" or "timely centrality")
shu bu po zhu 疏不破注 (sub-commentary ought not to go beyond the commentary)
shuiquan dong 水泉动 (spring water in movement)
shui shi bing 水始冰 (water begins to freeze)
si 巳 (the 4th lunar month)
sihua lianhu 四画连互 (four-line consecutive overlapping)

taibu 太卜 (grand official diviners)
Taiji 太极 (lit., Supreme Ultimate)
taishi 太史 (Official Historians)
taiyi 太一 (Great One)
Taiyi jiugong zhanpan 太乙九宫占盘 (Divinatory Board of the Great One with Nine Palaces)
taiyin 太阴 (Senior Yin)
tao shi hua 桃始华 (peaches begin to bloom)
tengshe 螣蛇 (winged snake, i.e., Andromedae)
tianchu 天厨 [lit., heavenly kitchen, i.e., Draco]
Tian dao 天道 (Dao [Way] of Heaven)
tianming 天命 (mandate of heaven)
tianyi 天一 (Heavenly One)
tianzi 天子 (Son of Heaven)

wangdao 王道 (kingly way)
wanglai 往来 (going and coming)
wei 未 (the 6th lunar month)
weitian zhi ming, wumu buyi 维天之命，于穆不已 (the way of Heaven is perfect and endless)
wenhua 文化 (literally, pattern and transformation, generally translated as *culture*)
Wenwang bagua cixu 文王八卦次序 (King Wen's Sequence of the Eight Trigrams)
Wenwang bagua fangwei 文王八卦方位 (King Wen's Positioning of the Eight Trigrams)
wu 午 (the 5th lunar month) [the 7th earthly branch, equated with south]
wu 戊 (the 5th heavenly stem)
wu 无 (non-existence, no being, or non-actuality)
wuhua lianhu 五画连互 (five-line consecutive overlapping)
wujing boshi 五经博士 (Erudites of the Five Confucian Classics)

xiangxing zhi xiang 像形之象 (pictographic images)
xiantian 先天 (prior to heaven, Former Heaven)
Xiantian bagua fangwei 先天八卦方位 (Eight Trigrams' Positions of the Former Heaven)
Xiantian tu 先天图 (Chart of the Former Heaven Sequence)
xiao xi 消息 (waning and waxing)
xin 辛 (the 8th heavenly stem)
xingming 性命 (nature and fate)
xu 虚 (void)
xu 戌 (the 9th lunar month)
xuanniao zhi 玄鸟至 (swallows come from the south)
xuanwu 玄武 (black tortoise)
Xuanyuan 轩辕 (i.e., Yellow Emperor, a legendary sage ruler in ancient China)

yan beixiang 雁北乡 (wild geese begin to migrate toward north)
yaochen 爻辰 (lit., line-month, correlating the earthly branches, which correspond to the twelve pitch pipes and twelve lunar months, with the hexagrams)
yaowei zhi xiang 爻位之象 (line-position images)
yi 乙 (the 2nd heavenly stem)
yi 易 ("easiness" or "change")
yin 寅 (the 1st lunar month)
ying 应 (response)
yingyao 应爻 (response line)

Yi yi dao yin yang 易以道阴阳 (the *Yi* [Changes] is that which discourses upon *yin* 阴 and *yang* 阳)
yong jiu 用九 (lit., "the Using of Nine")
yong liu 用六 (lit., "the Using of Six")
you 酉 (the 8th lunar month)
you hun 游魂 (Wandering Soul)
yuanshi 元士 (gentlemen beginning their official careers)

zhan shi 占筮 (milfoil-stalk divination)
zhao yao 招摇 [i.e., Big Dipper]
zhechong shizhen 蛰虫始振 (dormant insects begin to come out of hibernation)
zheng 正 (rectitude, correct, uprightness, rectify)
zhengshi 正时 (rectifying the time)
zhengzhong 正中 (rectitude and middle)
zhi gou 雉雊 (pheasants begin to chirp)
zhong 中 ("centrality," also rendered "the Mean," "middle," "mid," "center," and so on)
zhongdao 中道 (Dao [Way] of the Mean)
zhongqi 中气 (middle *Qi* [material force])
zhong zheng 中正 ("centrality and rectitude", "the Mean and rectitude" or "the Mean and uprightness)
zhuhou 诸侯 (feudal lords)
zi 子 (the 11th lunar month) [the 1st earthly branch, corresponding to north]
zonggua 综卦 (inverse hexagrams)
zongmiao 宗庙 (ancestral temple)
zhuque 朱雀 (rosefinch)

Professor Liu Dajun

As the President of Chinese Learned Society of *Zhou yi* and the Director of the Center for Zhouyi & Ancient Chinese Philosophy at Shandong University, Professor Liu Dajun 刘大钧 is also a Counselor for the Counselors Office of the State Council of China and the editor-in-chief of the academic journal of *Zhouyi Studies* (*Zhouyi yanjiu* 周易研究). Now he is the author of over a dozen books.

He organized the first international conference on the *Zhou yi* to be held in mainland China in 1987, which lifted off the "*Zhou yi* Fever" in mainland China. Hence Professor Liu became a household name and legendary figure across the country. Professor Chung-ying Cheng frequently praises him, saying that Professor Liu had established many milestones in the history of the *Zhou yi* studies.

Zhang Wenzhi

An associate professor and deputy director at the Center for Zhouyi & Ancient Chinese Philosophy of Shandong University, Zhang Weizhi now is also the director of the Editorial Board of *Zhouyi Studies* (English Version). The author of four books related to the *Zhou yi* (Book of Changes), he received his B. A. in English Language and Literature in 1990, and received his PhD in Chinese philosophy in 2010. Focusing on the studies of image-numerology of the *Zhou yi*, he was selected and invited to be a 2007-08 academic year visiting scholar at Harvard-Yenching Institute and a 2012-13 visiting fellow in Erlangen-Nuremberg University, Germany.